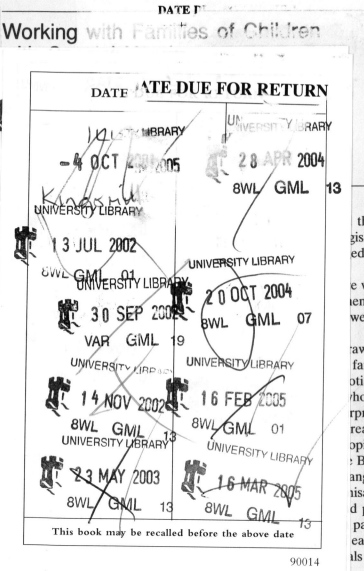

...9

the parents
...gislation and
...ed failure to

...e will always
...embers and
...well as coop-

...aws on case
...family work
...otiating part-
...hole family;
...rprofessional
...reader reach
...oping model.
...e British situ-
...anges in the
...isation. The
...d practice to
...partnerships
...each chapter
...als and those

Naomi Dale was Director of the KIDS Family Centre, Camden. She is currently a consultant clinical psychologist in the Neurodisability Service of Great Ormond Street Hospital for Children, based at the Wolfson Centre. An expert in family work, she is also involved in professional training and research into partnership support services.

Working with Families of Children with Special Needs

Partnership and Practice

Naomi Dale

London and New York

1000895712

First published 1996
by Routledge
11 New Fetter Lane, London EC4P 4EE

Simultaneously published in the USA and Canada
by Routledge
29 West 35th Street, New York, NY 10001

Typeset in Times by Florencetype Ltd, Stoodleigh, Devon

Printed and bound in Great Britain by Clays Ltd, St. Ives PLC

British Library Cataloguing in Publication Data
A catalogue record for this book is available from the British Library

Library of Congress Cataloguing in Publication Data
A catalogue record for this book has been requested

ISBN 0-415-11410-1 (hbk)
ISBN 0-415-11411-X (pbk)

In memory of Lilly Glucksmann,
colleague and friend

Contents

Figures and tables

FIGURES

TABLES

Preface

A book has a history and a context. This book can be traced back to a long period of learning at the KIDS Family Centre, Camden, London, of effective ways of working in partnership with families of children with special needs, when working there as the clinical psychologist and Centre Director during the 1980s. The context was the growing disillusionment in the mid to late 1980s of the rhetoric of 'partnership' practice, following the failure of the 1981 Education Act to inject partnership into the professional–parent relationships in education (House of Commons Select Committee Report, 1987). Through my experience at the KIDS Family Centre and later when running regular training courses on partnership practice for multi-disciplinary professionals, I became increasingly convinced that one of the problems of implementing partnership practice was that it was premised on an assumption or illusion of 'cooperation' between the professional and the parent or family. This did not reflect the real-life encounters of many professionals and parents when trying to collaborate together and nor could it generate a realistic conceptual framework for practice that would gauge when partnership work was feasible or untenable. Without this, professionals have had little way of knowing (when they were facing difficulties and differences of opinion in their relating with a parent) whether they could still continue with partnership practice or whether they should abandon the attempt.

As part of and within a movement of thinking about possible conceptual frameworks for partnership practice, a Negotiating Model for partnership work has been developed for this book. The model presents an explanatory framework for making sense of present-day partnership relationships and it also promotes a form of partnership practice. It is not intended as a critique of other partnership models and it has evolved from predecessors (see models by Cunningham and Davis, 1985, Appleton and Minchom, 1991). But it offers an alternative framework by looking at partnership work from a different angle. In the model presented in this book, dissent and disagreement as well as negotiation and cooperation are focused on. This permits a framework and methods of practice for

working with the everyday differences of opinion that are frequently
encountered between professionals and parents. But there is another
objective. By attempting to establish under what conditions dissent
becomes a 'conflict' and the parent and professional are no longer able
to work together, I have tried to chart the realistic possibilities for partnership practice within present-day organisational and family contexts and
also to map the limits to partnership work in the current and possibly
future circumstances. Within a period of organisational change and
upheaval, it has become an imperative to find out what we need to hold
on to or to alter if partnership practice is going to become or remain a
viable form of professional practice and relationship. I admit my bias; my
experiences at the KIDS Family Centre convinced me of the singular
benefit for parents and staff of working in partnership. But the conditions
of the Centre were unusual and the experiences were at a particular
conjuncture of history and context. Whether this book can hold onto and
move forward the special insights and experiences of this period remain
to be seen.

This book is a combination of theory and ideas for practice, so that it
can provide a framework for thinking and practice on working with families of children with special needs and partnership methods. It is not a
comprehensive survey of the extensive research literature, but draws on
a selection of relevant articles and studies. Further, it cannot attempt to
cover the breadth of developmental and social psychology, sociology,
anthropology, organisational theory, and philosophy that converge on this
subject. Many of the chapters combine theory/research and practice guidelines, to show how one grows out of the other and to make the
connections. I hope it will be useful to practising professionals from a
wide range of disciplinary backgrounds, who are working with children
with disabilities and special needs and their families, though my background as a clinical psychologist must clearly affect the perspective and
approach. Professional development exercises are included at the end of
each chapter to help to relate the readings to individual practice and work
settings. The scope of the book may also be of interest to researchers and
service planners who are considering related issues and intervention
approaches for families of children with special needs. But the ultimate
judges of the effectiveness of this approach must be the many parents,
children and families who are at the receiving end of professional services.
They, in the end, are the intended beneficiaries.

The terms 'special needs' or 'disability' are used broadly to refer to
children with learning difficulties and/or physical disabilities. Although the
main focus has been on children with long-term special needs (i.e. where
there is a 'restriction or lack of ability to perform normal activities, which
has resulted from the impairment of a structure or function of the body
or mind' (OPCS, 1989)) and who are likely to need long-term support

and assistance in education, the book may have relevance for working with families with a chronically ill child or more short-term developmental needs. The case examples used in this book are authentic and are taken from my working experience or from experiences shared by colleagues and course participants of the Tavistock Clinic training course. Names and identifying features have been changed to protect the families' and professional workers' confidentiality.

To help readers find their way round the book, each chapter begins with a short section outlining its content and ends with a summary of the principal issues discussed. To suit the varying interests and time availability of busy professionals, chapters can be read separately or in succession, though to grasp the book's theoretical orientation fully may require reading through the different subject topics to see how different levels of perspective and organisation interconnect. It is, however, strongly advised that the reader begins with Chapter 1 before reading further. In this chapter, various existing and potential forms of professional–parent relationships are discussed within the context of changing parental and professional roles in society. The Negotiating Model, which is used as the main conceptual framework underpinning the partnership practice explored in the remainder of the book, is presented in this chapter.

Acknowledgements

This book would not have been possible without the generosity and trust of many families of children with special needs who let me into their lives and were willing to share their experiences with me during my years at the KIDS Family Centre, Camden; I am deeply indebted to them for their openness. I also wish to acknowledge the staff of the Centre, from whom I learnt so much about professional practice and partnership work. The research work at the Centre was aided by a grant from the King Edward Hospital Trust Fund and the contribution of the late Lilly Glucksmann, who brought empathy and insight into her role as interviewer.

I owe my interest in partnership practice to Elizabeth and John Newson of the Child Development Research Unit, University of Nottingham, who started my thinking on the subject during my period in their department. In recent years, two colleagues have joined me in developing the Working in Partnership with Families of Children with Special Needs course at the Tavistock Clinic: Doris Leibowitz and Liz Kennedy have provided invaluable guidance and encouragement. Liz Kennedy has been very influential in extending my ideas and has designed some of the exercises included in this book. Successive waves of course participants have shared experiences and ideas and helped shape the approach used in this book. Thank you, too, to colleagues and friends who have stimulated and challenged me and made incisive comments on sections of this book; in particular, Jennifer Clegg, Cliff Cunningham, Hilton Davis, Madeleine Ismach, Helen McConachie, Michael Safier and Vijaya Venkatesan. Ruth Dale read through the whole manuscript and made useful critical comments.

On the home front, my parents Ruth and David Dale have given me unremitting support and help. I wish to thank, Mala and the late Maurice Tribich for their generous assistance. Finally, my deepest gratitude to my husband Jeffrey Tribich for his enduring support and encouragement and to Miriam and Samuel for their forbearance and good humour.

Chapter 1

Conceptual frameworks for partnership work

A parent sits at home awaiting a new health visitor. She contemplates the arrival with trepidation. 'What will she be like? Will we get on? . . . How will she react to my daughter? . . . Will she be of any help? . . . ' She looks across at her young daughter playing on the floor, and recalls some of the many demands and difficulties of cystic fibrosis over the last few years. Then she thinks of the future and is overwhelmed with a sudden surge of anxiety. A long road of uncertainties and worries lies ahead. The door bell rings.

A health visitor drives up to the house of a family she is visiting for the first time. She knows from the case notes that the family has a 3-year-old girl with cystic fibrosis. She feels a certain apprehension: 'I haven't had any experience of cystic fibrosis. . . . Will I appear ignorant? . . . I've heard this mother gets anxious and upset . . . Will she be very needy? . . . Do I have enough time to help her?' Her thoughts stray to the many other competing demands of her large caseload, and she gets out of her car feeling stressed and inadequate. She walks to the front door and rings the bell.

A professional and parent come together for the first time. They bring their own worries and concerns, their own priorities and responsibilities. Somehow these have to be woven together into a relationship that works for both parties. Collaboration on the same project or issue is frequently referred to as a '*partnership*'. But how useful is the term 'partnership'? What does it tell us about their relationship?

We start by examining the scope and limits of the term 'partnership' in its broadest sense, as the first step in building a case for a particular definition and conceptual model of partnership: the Negotiating Model of partnership.

RELATIONSHIPS AND PARTNERSHIPS

The *Concise Oxford Dictionary* defines a partner as a '*sharer* (with person, in or of thing)'. Resources, responsibilities, expertise, abilities, joint

activities and power may all be shared. Risks and rewards may be apportioned. Through sharing, a goal may be reached, risks and decisions
may be taken together. The route to reaching a shared objective may
be easily negotiated or may arouse argument and dissent. Since the converse of sharing is 'not sharing', an association where there is little shared
decision-making or activity is unlikely to constitute a *partnership*.

Partnerships can vary structurally. Some entail occasional meetings;
others require recurrent meetings and extended time. They may evolve
through informal encounters or formal arrangements with legally defined
and ethical obligations, such as in business partnerships and professional–client relationships. Two or more persons may be involved.

The form and degree of cooperation can vary. In some partnerships,
the partners work as separately as possible, only coming together to
regulate the minimum shared activity necessary to prevent the partnership collapsing. In others, the partners take little or no action without
consulting each other: full negotiation is needed before anything is implemented.

Each partnership has an internal power balance which will predispose
the members towards a more egalitarian or more unequal relationship.
One partner may take a senior role and the other a junior. One partner
may have greater authority to make decisions than the other, or have
greater control over resources and more resources at their disposal than
the other.

The partners in a relationship may hold similar or differing interests,
that is, the concerns that are seen as of greatest benefit or advantage to
themselves or the party they represent. Cooperation may be more achievable between partners who share similar interests. When interests diverge,
a relationship may tend to shift into conflict and eventually disintegrate.

Partnerships also differ in terms of gains and losses. In some partnerships, when one person gains the other loses. (According to games theory,
a zero sum 'game' is one where, at the end of the game, the total wins
equal the total losses.) If both partners have need of the same set of finite
resources, the acquisition by one partner of the majority of the resources
must limit the other to a smaller share. In other relationships, if one person
gains, the other person stands to gain, or conversely, if one loses, the
other stands to lose (a non-zero sum 'game').

We can see from the above that the term 'partnership' does not tell us
a great deal about the extent of cooperation and reciprocity between two
or more partners, except to suggest that there *is* some form of mutual
cooperation and influence. The point to be made here is that, unless
defined very specifically for the parent–professional relationship, the term
can be used loosely to imply cooperation without telling us much about
the extent of shared decision-making, the degree of consensus or disagreement, the power differences, and gains and losses between the partners.

Apart from being uninformative, it may mislead by obscuring important differences between types of parent–professional relationships, which affect the possibilities for collaboration.

The case is persuasive for a more specific definition, but as we embark on our search we immediately face a first obstacle. It is extremely difficult to categorise professional–parent relationships into 'types', because each relationship is unique. Every parent and family situation has its own idiosyncrasies, and each professional has unique characteristics and ways of working and relating. The concern is not to lose the individuality and creativity of these relationships in a mechanistic and reductionist definition. Nevertheless, some common features can be identified across parent–professional relationships, which derive from the *role relationship* itself. The parent–professional relationship is a formal one, with each partner taking up a specified social role in relation to the other. The roles of 'parent' and 'professional' impose certain rights and duties on the incumbents of each position, to do with how that role position is constructed in society. Each position carries a set of associated norms, obligations and expected behaviours, and, as a result, each partner has expectations of how they or the other should behave together. For example, a patient expects and knows roughly how to behave with their doctor and vice versa. Consequently, there are relatively predictable patterns of behaviour and communication which are normally (or ideally) shown between parents and professionals, even though there will be individual idiosyncrasies within each relationship.

It is to these common patterns in parent–professional relationships that we turn our attention. But before looking at these, I would like to outline a few thoughts on conceptual frameworks.

Using conceptual frameworks

Descriptive and explanatory frameworks for describing role behaviours and role relationships can be referred to as conceptual frameworks or 'models'. These intellectual frameworks are useful for distinguishing between different 'types' of role relationships, although in doing this, they may simplify the complexity of a relationship. Because they simplify and extract from what is going on in real life by focusing on normative role behaviour and ignoring the individuality of each person and relationship, they must be considered as 'idealised' and not a full picture of the reality. For example, a relationship may shift between different types of role behaviour on different occasions. But their value is in providing and explaining a pattern and permitting prediction from complex dynamics and interactions.

More specifically, 'partnership' models (discussed later in the chapter) provide hypothetical frameworks of how a partnership should or could work. They set out some minimum necessary prerequisites for partnership relationships, and thereby also define outer limits beyond which a partnership cannot operate. They can be used to guide and inform professional training and practice and their merits can be tested through direct practice and evaluation.

As we move forward now towards examining different parent–professional relationships it may be valuable to examine separately the 'role partners'. *Who* is 'the parent', 'the professional' and 'the child'? What are their contemporary roles? What contextual factors affect their role possibilities? How might these factors contribute to or determine the structure of the relationship and role behaviours with each other?

THE ROLE PARTNERS

The professional

The notion of the 'professional' role is controversial since some argue for a restricted usage of the term to refer to 'full professionals' in the traditional sense (e.g. doctors, lawyers, architects, university lecturers) and others argue for a wider application to 'people workers' (e.g. nurses, social workers, teachers; see Bennett and Hokenstad, 1973). The latter differ in their training, the nature of their acquired knowledge base, and their role and function from the so-called traditional professional (see further in Bennett and Hokenstad). But increasingly within the childcare field, the term 'professional' is applied to all trained, qualified persons with a responsibility for the welfare of children, and used to distinguish qualified from unqualified lay persons, such as voluntary workers, untrained childminders, or parents. It includes paediatricians, social workers, therapists, health visitors, teachers, qualified nursery staff, and others.

The professional, as implied in this book, holds a specialised body of knowledge and skills and has undertaken a period of training (often prolonged) to acquire them. This expertise distinguishes and distances the professional from the lay person and also from members of other professions. Those with a particular qualification may hold an exclusive right to practise the profession, and are permitted to control their own body of knowledge. They are responsible for delivering their specific expertise and knowledge through their professional practice. A profession may be marked by its own professional culture and code of ethics developed by its members, including a service ethic in relation to clients (Greenwood, 1966). Depending on their disciplinary role, they may have legally enshrined powers and requirements to carry out certain duties and make certain decisions.

Although professionals traditionally tended to be self-employed, today they may be employed by and/or represent powerful interest bodies, such as an education authority, health authority or local government council. Although professionals are generally personally and professionally committed to working on behalf of their client, they may be pulled between competing pressures from their client and employer. The concept of 'client' has been subjected to contradictory demands; many professionals still regard the child (and/or family) as their client, but the employing authority (as 'purchaser' in a purchaser/provider organisational structure in health and education) may view itself as the dominant 'client' (see p. 297).

The parent

According to the Children Act 1989, the parent is, in their parental role, a lay person with 'parental responsibility' for the care and upbringing of children born to them (or adopted by them, or given 'parental responsibility' by the State to look after the child in a temporary capacity). The child will generally be living with them, and the parent has full legal responsibility for the child's care and upbringing from birth until legally defined adulthood (16 years of age). It is expected by society that the parent provides adequate forms of 'good enough parenting', and the State has the power to intervene through statute if a parent fails to meet minimum standards.

As we will see below, parents in their parental role (although not necessarily in their other occupational or socio-economic roles) occupy a lower social status than professionals. Although frequent rhetoric has been made of the immense importance of parenting, minimum practical recognition has been given to the validity and usefulness of their expertise and experiences. The unpaid and unlimited hours of parenting contrast with the professional's role, where there is remuneration for specific hours of employment.

Power and authority

Where the parent and professional stand in relation to each other, in terms of power and authority, affects the kind of relationship they can sustain, and clearly has great significance for the possibilities of partnership explored in this book. Power conveys influence (and sometimes authority) to exert change in a particular direction or to preserve the status quo. Thus, whoever has greater sources of powers is in 'the driving-seat' of control in the relationship.

Any analysis of their relative statuses will need to take heed of different kinds of *power*. A useful classification of different sources of power has been provided by Charles Handy (1985), drawing on and modifying the original classification by John French and Bertram Raven (1959). Handy suggests five main sources of 'social' power, which are expressed through different forms of influence over the other person:

- *physical power*
- *resource power*
- *position power*   } kinds of power.
- *expert power*
- *personal power*

Applying this classification to professionals, it is quickly evident that professionals enjoy a relatively high status and have or are perceived as having considerable power. Their prescribed position and role legitimises their *position power* and gives them the right to dispense their disciplinary duties and obligations. They also have *resource power*, derived from control of resources (such as service allocation, budget control) and *expert power* derived from having greater or more authoritative knowledge and expertise than the parent. Expert power may be exerted through possessing information which is not available to the parent. Individual professionals may use informal *personal power* gained from sheer force of personality (often referred to as *charisma*). In the event of non-compliance or challenge from the parent, the professional may also draw on back-up forms of power to maintain the authority of their position, such as through using resource power to withhold services. In exceptional circumstances, *physical power* of the State can be invoked to support the professional's position (e.g. the police and social services intervening to remove a child when the professional alleges child abuse by a parent).

Taking all this into account, professionals have, not surprisingly, been perceived as having considerable power, and have been generally treated with deferential respect and high regard by their clients and society at large. The client, in the reciprocal position of being the target of the professional's power, must be prepared to follow the professional's instructions or advice and be persuaded by the professional's superior knowledge and ability.

But how professionals are viewed, and what powers they really hold is not static, as shown by recent changes in professional position. In the 1980s and 1990s, a political and populist movement has challenged the traditional autonomy, privilege and 'vested interests' of a range of professionals, as part of a political/social process of shifting power from professionals to lay people or to central government (see further on pp. 296–7). As a result, some professionals have far less control and autonomy over resource allocation and professional enterprise than hitherto.

Notwithstanding this, parents individually or collectively still wield considerably less power than the professional, although the picture is complex and changing. They generally lack *resource power*, unless they are on a management committee managing a service (such as parent school governors in a grant-maintained school) or have sufficient funds to purchase their own services privately. They lack *expert power*, although this is beginning to change with greater authority given to parental knowledge and decision-making (e.g. under the 1993 Education Act). Until very recently, parents of children with special needs have had little formally prescribed *position power*, but this is changing under legislation granting them new rights as parents (such as the 1981 and 1993 Education Acts and 1989 Children Act in the UK). Without other forms of power, some parents are left only with informal *personal power* at their disposal, obtaining their preferences through strength of personality and assertiveness. This can be harnessed to challenge the professional either overtly or covertly. A refusal to comply with professional advice, a refusal to join in or an opting out of a service may in effect be a challenge of the professional's position and expert powers. Using their personal power, parents may be aggressive (bullying, hostile, threatening), critical or demanding. Occasionally, a parent resorts to coercing professionals, using the threat of *physical power* (physical assault) against the professional.

Weighing all this up, it appears that professionals mainly occupy a higher position than the parent. Although the power balance is changing, in general the parent is not on a 'level playing field' with the professional and this has considerable significance for the possibilities of their relationship. Unless parents have some equivalent power sources to professionals, parents are limited to either using their own informal power or drawing on a kind of *pseudo-power*, that is, power dispensed by the professional and depending on their largesse. But at an interpersonal level, the personal power can shift from the professional to the parent or back again, depending on who is being more assertive during their actual encounter.

If parents do, however, use their new potential power in law to challenge professionals and local authorities in the courts, a growth of a more litigious relationship between parents and authorities may be witnessed in future years (see further Chapters 2 and 11).

The child

Since most discussion and practice of partnership work has until recently focused on the parent and the professional, neither the child with special needs nor other children in the family have been regarded as potential role partners in a partnership relationship. Parents or professionals have had legal responsibility for making decisions on behalf of the child until adulthood, and children have lacked powers to intervene in these decisions.

With recent legislation (the Children Act, 1989) and recognition of child rights (government ratification of United Nations Convention Rights of the Child in 1991; the European Convention of Human Rights), however, the child is beginning to be considered as a person to be respected in their own right and not as a 'property' of their parents (see further Chapter 11). Partnership work of the future will need to be viewed progressively as a system of relationships between the professional, the parent and the child, with the child as a participating person in their own right.

THE HISTORICAL BACKGROUND OF THE PARTNERSHIP MOVEMENT

Before proceeding to explore how the partners might come together to form a partnership, it is useful to look at the recent historical background of parent–professional relationships and the development of 'parental involvement', as these form the precedents of present and future practice. We need to examine 'where we have come from', what factors are ushering in change, and what kind of change may be possible within current contexts.

For many years parents of children with special needs were left largely unsupported and received little help from professionals (Mittler and Mittler, 1983). The focus was predominantly on the child and the dominant training model and practice of the *professional as expert* (see following) tended to work against establishing cooperative relationships with parents.

The professional as expert

This is the traditional way of working with children with special needs, and is particularly evident in traditional doctor–patient (medical) relationships. In this approach, the professional uses their position and expert powers (see p. 6) to make judgements and to take control of what needs doing. Whether the parent is involved or not is secondary, and the parental function is mainly limited to providing information (when requested by the professional) and complying with professional advice and treatment. The parent may be informed of professional decisions, but is not brought into the decision-making process. The views, feelings and wishes of the parent are not necessarily consulted. In this kind of relationship, the child is positioned as the passive 'client' or 'patient' and the parent has a very limited role (see Figure 1.1).

Until relatively recently, the professional 'as expert' could provide a remedial service for the child or place the child in a special school without consulting the parent. Professional reports could be written and case conferences could be convened without parental involvement and access. Parents were expected to defer to professional judgement.

Not surprisingly in a relationship that remained relatively unchallenged in structure for over twenty years, there were apparent advantages for both the parent and professional. But as the brief critique in Appendix 1.1 shows, there were also disadvantages for both parties. And consequently, from the early 1970s onwards, this exclusion of parents from professional intervention has been subjected to rigorous challenge. In addition changes in the physician–patient relationship, as it becomes more impersonal, specialised and short-term as a result of professionalisation, bureaucratisation and popular mobility, have been associated with the evident decline in confidence in and respect for physicians since 1950 onwards (Betz and O'Connell, 1983).

Arguments in favour of greater parental involvement have come from parents, professionals, local authorities, and governmental committees and reports (see details in Appendix 1.2). Although the proposals are diverse, complex and at times contradictory (Pugh and De'Ath, 1989), the combined case is highly persuasive (see the seminal text of the period, Mittler and McConachie, 1983). It is these apparent positive benefits for children, parents and professionals from increasing parental involvement which provide the main rationale for shifting away from the traditional parent–professional relationship to one of greater collaboration and partnership.

The tradition of the professional as expert continues, nonetheless, to command an influence, with the one-way delivery of professional expertise still dominating the interactions of some professionals with parents.

The transplant relationship

We move on to the second principal role relationship between parents and professionals, the *transplant relationship* (the term was originally coined by Dorothy Jeffree, cited in Mittler and Mittler, 1983). From the early 1970s onwards, researchers and practitioners looked towards explicitly involving parents. They perceived parents as an untapped resource for helping in the therapy of the child and the home as a potentially important learning setting. In the transplant way of working, professionals share or transplant their skills and expertise to parents, to help them become more competent, confident and skilled. Parents are assisted to become actively involved and to *participate* in the role of 'co-teachers' or 'co-educators'. Variations of this form of relationship have become firmly established through widespread development of parent education behavioural workshops and the classic Portage home learning programmes (see further in Chapter 8).

Both the parent and the professionals' roles differ from the traditional expert–client relationship (see previously). The parent is now seen as a resource with particular competences which can be utilised (see Figure 1.1) and is expected to be an involved participant. The professional takes on the functions of *instructor* and *consultant* to the parent, as well as being

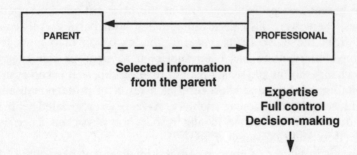

**Selected information
from the parent**

**Expertise
Full control
Decision-making**

(i) The expert model

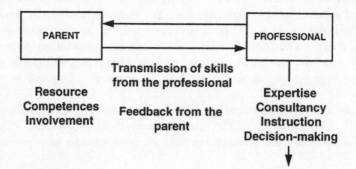

**Transmission of skills
from the professional**

**Resource
Competences
Involvement**

**Feedback from the
parent**

**Expertise
Consultancy
Instruction
Decision-making**

(ii) The transplant model

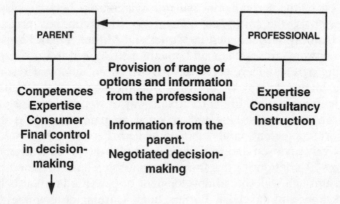

**Provision of range of
options and information
from the professional**

**Competences
Expertise
Consumer
Final control
in decision-
making**

**Information from the
parent.
Negotiated decision-
making**

**Expertise
Consultancy
Instruction**

(iii) The consumer model

Source: Cunningham and Davis, 1985

Figure 1.1 Models of parent–professional relationships

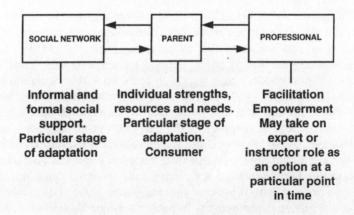

Actively promote parent's control and power

Be sensitive to unique adaptational style of each
family and social network

(iv) The empowerment model

Source: Appleton and Minchom, 1991

Figure 1.1 continued

the expert, to guide the parent's activity with the child. A two-way dialogue is initiated, where the professional transmits skills to the parent and the parent gives feedback on the intervention.

Nevertheless, the professional preserves similar powers (position and expert, see p. 6) to that of the expert model and retains final control in decision-making. The professional designs the teaching programme and generally tells the parent how and what to teach.

Again, there are advantages and disadvantages of this relationship for each party, and a brief critique of the transplant relationship is presented in Appendix 1.1.

TOWARDS A PARTNERSHIP RELATIONSHIP

Because the power of authority continues to rest primarily with the professional in the *transplant* form of relationship (see previously), it has been argued that this way of working is not a full *partnership* relationship (e.g. Cunningham and Davis, 1985). The 1980s have been marked by the widespread discussion and endorsement of the concept of *partnership*, which is the third form of parent–professional relationship. The DES Warnock Report (1978), the Children Act 1989 (DoH, 1991a) and the Education Act 1993 (DoE, 1994) all emphasise the desirability of professionals achieving a *partnership* relationship with parents.

But as argued earlier in this chapter, the term 'partnership' is vague and potentially misleading unless defined more specifically. Thus, various writers and practitioners have sought to come up with a definition on *partnership* for working with parents (see Appendix 1.3 for definitions). Differing definitions and interpretations of the concept have often been developed to suit the purposes of the particular group of people involved (Wolfendale, 1983). What emerges is a considerable overlap and consensus between the definitions, but also differences in emphasis and focus. It is worth noting here that there is no universally accepted definition or statement on what might represent the minimum basic requirements of a parent–professional partnership. Whether a single definition is desirable is a moot point. Furthermore, the possibilities of partnership are not finite, but (as shown later in the book) develop and change within changing social-political and organisational conditions.

As discussed previously, conceptual models of partnership are to some extent hypothetical in that they are proposing a relatively new form of relationship between parents and professionals. Yet all three models described below have grown out of actual practice of partnership in a variety of different settings. Throughout the book, the strength of the Negotiating Model to provide workable directions for overcoming some of the challenges of working in partnership is considered, but its full value can only be established through further practice and evaluative research.

Much of the current debate on how professionals work with families revolves around the issue of power. *What are the sources of power for parents? Who is the expert and has the valued knowledge? Who is authorised to act? Who has the right to make the final decision if there is a lack of agreement between the professional and the parent?* The following models are all distinguished by their specific and diverse responses to these questions, although they have many overlapping features in common.

The parent as consumer   Rogerian

The Consumer Model developed by Cunningham and Davis (1985) is one of the first conceptual frameworks for *partnership* work (see Figure 1.1). The authors argued that parents should be given new rights, with some shift of power from the professional to the parent. The parent would be given new resource power, with some control over access to resources, and be considered as a *consumer* who has the right to select appropriate services and intervention for their child. The parent should also be given expert power; for the first time, the parent is credited as having an expertise (the knowledge of their own child and family) that is distinct and separate from the professional's expertise. Parents will draw on their own knowledge of their personal circumstances when deciding what they need and want for their child.

Because the parent would now be able to share in resource power and allocation with the professional, the professional's influence would become more one of exchange, negotiation and bargaining. Their function would be to guide the parent in reaching effective and appropriate decisions. They would still take up a combination of role positions and behaviours as the 'expert', 'instructor' and 'consultant' to the parent, and the model does not minimise the importance of professional instruction and expertise. But additionally, the professional provides the parent with a range of options and information, to help the parent be informed, to evaluate alternatives, and to make realistic and effective decisions. This is possible only if the professional has learnt a considerable amount about the parent and family, through listening and understanding the parents' views, aims, expectations, current situation and resources.

Although often done informally in the past, the parent would now have the overt right to opt out of or not take up services. This means that the parent could now challenge the professional's position or expert power without being sanctioned by the professional, and hence this contributes to a weakening of the professional's traditional sources of power.

Decision-making should proceed through a process of two-way dialogue and negotiation. 'Negotiation within the context of a mutually respecting relationship is the foundation. By negotiation we mean a process by which the professional and parent attempt to reach mutually acceptable agreements' (Cunningham and Davis, 1985: 13).

A brief critique of the *consumer* relationship is presented in Appendix 1.1. Particular note should be taken of the criticism of the term 'consumer', bearing in mind the current widespread practice of referring to service users (and their carers) as consumers.

The Empowerment Model

This is a second model of *partnership* put forward by Peter Appleton and Philip Minchom (1991). Two strands of thinking and practice converge in this model: the consumer model described previously and the social network/systems model (described further in Chapter 6), to create an emergent model of *empowerment*. It combines the right of the parent as a consumer to choose to engage with the service at a level which suits them personally with a recognition on the professional side that the family is a system and social network. Each family is made up of interlocking social relationships, within the family itself and also with wider social groups (extended family, friends, work colleagues, cultural groups). The network and system will have an important impact on how individual family members cope with the child with special needs and what strengths members can draw on (see Figure 1.1).

Because of varying strengths between families, each family (and set of parents) will have a unique adaptational style and differing needs, and the professional would need to take this into account in intervention with the family and in what could be expected from them at any particular moment in time. The professional will also need to consider what kind of help the parent may need in order to take up a position as a *partner*, i.e. how they would need to be *empowered*. The professional would be required actively to promote the parent's sense of control over decisions affecting their child and be sensitive to parents' rights to get involved in professional services to an extent that they choose.

The authors argue that from this emergent perspective it is possible to re-appraise the *expert* and *transplant* models positively and to recognise that some parents and children will indeed benefit from a service delivered in an expert or transplant style. However, the Empowerment Model would put these forward as options for the family/professional system at a particular point in time.

A brief critique of the empowerment relationship is presented in Appendix 1.1.

The Negotiating Model

As the critiques of the previous two partnership models show (see Appendix 1.1), both have considerable strengths in what they offer conceptually, as well as some limitations. In response to this, the third model of partnership draws on the two previous models, but also offers an alternative and additional framework.

This model is the main conceptual framework underlying the rest of the book, and the rationale for its development and its theoretical basis are described in Appendix 1.3. It is called the *Negotiating Model* because it focuses on negotiation as a key transaction for partnership work. It offers a framework for exploring a partnership practice that can embody or respond to the constraints and reality of actual power relations and positions of the parent and professional within present or future societal contexts.

The definition of partnership which I have developed for the Negotiating Model is of 'a working relationship where the partners use negotiation and joint decision-making and resolve differences of opinion and disagreement, in order to reach some kind of shared perspective or jointly agreed decision on issues of mutual concern'. (Please note that the term 'perspective' is used broadly to refer to the cognitive/emotional viewpoint of the person, i.e. how they construe a situation, and their feelings about it. It includes perceptions, feelings, concepts, values and beliefs.)

The model strives to address how diverse and even discrepant viewpoints can be brought together and reconciled to allow joint activity and decision-making, whilst recognising that dissent may be a major factor in the parent–professional relationship.

The model has a number of key elements, which are described briefly below (see also Figure 1.2).

Key elements of the model

Its premise is that the parent and professional have separate and potentially highly valuable contributions to offer to children with special needs and other family members, so each may require the contribution of the other. But they come to the joint encounter with separate and often different perspectives (or ways of viewing or construing their situations) because they belong to social roles which have differing functions, responsibilities, power positions and possibly interests and operate within different social/organisational structures (see Figure 1.2). Their different positioning within society leads to varying and multiple perspectives of the same situation.

When the professional has a responsibility to provide a service to the child and family, they must strive to bridge the gap between the various perspectives. This requires learning about the parent's perspective through considerable listening, inquiry and openness. The professional working in partnership may adopt a variety of role positions and behaviours (such as the 'expert', 'instructor', 'consultant' or 'facilitator'), but the positioning options are to be negotiated with the parent.

Crucially, decision-making proceeds through a two-way dialogue and negotiation whereby each partner brings in their own perspective to assist in the decision-making. The transaction of negotiation lends itself to two-way effects, and one influence of change for both the parent and professional is likely to be through the negotiation process. Negotiation can lead to two different outcomes: a shared understanding and *consensus* or a lack of shared understanding and *dissent*. But dissent is not necessarily incompatible with a partnership relationship.

The feedback loop in Figure 1.2 suggests that transactions in a partnership relationship may be a cyclical process which shifts back and forth between agreement and disagreement, shared understandings and differences of viewpoint. Differences of opinion may arise for a variety of reasons, such as differences in understanding and priorities. All will need to be worked with constructively where possible, using negotiation and disagreement resolution strategies. Notwithstanding this, when the parent and professional are in extreme disagreement or conflict, the partnership may be temporarily or permanently inoperative.

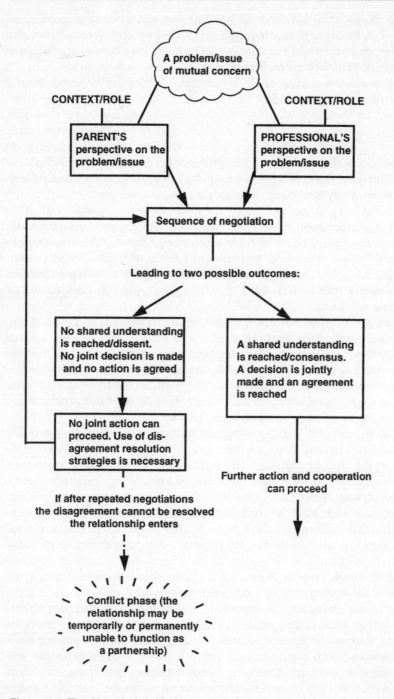

Figure 1.2 The Negotiating Model

The Negotiating Model proposes that how the parent and professional view a situation or problem together, what options they have for dealing with it, and whether their differences are resolvable will be affected or determined by their roles, their power positions, and the social, economic and organisational contexts in which they function. The possibilities or constraints of partnership relationships cannot necessarily be understood without an analysis of the personalities involved, an analysis of their roles and their power positioning, and an analysis of the wider systems, structures and policies: such as family network, community or ethnic group membership, social and political policy, and organisational structure. This argues for the importance and centrality of a multiple-level analysis (see further in Appendix 1.3).

The professional still retains position, expert and resource powers (see p. 6), but these powers are weaker than in the traditional expert model because the parent can now enter into the professional's decision-making without being sanctioned. How much the parent *shares* in position, expert and resource powers depends to some extent on the goodwill and knowledge of the individual professional and also on how much power the professional has to distribute them, and, fundamentally, on whether the parent has independent rights in law to participate and take some control.

Because of differences between role positions and perspectives, working together may not always be harmonious or straightforward. Mutual trust and openness may not be easily acquired or even possible. The model aims to clarify what distinguishes disagreement from conflict, i.e. what degree of dissent can be accommodated within a partnership relationship and what precipitates its breakdown or outer limit of functioning. This is discussed further in the following section.

The limits of partnership

Knowledge of the outer limits of partnership is important for a number of reasons. It can help develop a realistic understanding of what is possible to aim for with a family within current societal or organisational constraints. It may help illuminate which role, power, organisational or other factors might require changing in order to permit greater consensus and cooperation between the parent and professional. It can help signify the limit of responsibility of the professional.

If certain elements are crucial to a negotiating partnership, then it follows that the absence or infrequency of these elements may prevent a partnership from being set up or continuing. Within the framework of the Negotiating Model, a partnership may be inoperative under the four conditions listed below. Conflict may develop as a result of the individual's personality, or may be determined by the situation, or probably often as a combination of both. Although none of these conditions is absolute and each may be resolved constructively in the individual relationship, the likelihood of a temporary or long-term breakdown of a partnership is greatly increased in the following circumstances.

1. Either the parent or professional is unwilling or unable to meet each other and enter into a collaborative relationship. Personal circumstances on either side may reduce the likelihood of cooperation. Chronic stress and burnout may contribute to potentially strained and explosive relationships or encounters that become adversarial (Seligman and Darling, 1989). Family members may be under considerable stress in coping with their situation, professionals may be anxious and stressed because of the demanding work with families and stressful work environments.

2. Either the parent or the professional makes *all* the decisions, and there is no willingness or ability to make decisions jointly (i.e. to negotiate and resolve problems together) (McConkey, 1986).

   Structural inequalities and/or a refusal to share power may prevent them meeting on a sufficiently equal footing to engage in negotiated decision-making and action. If one partner has, for example, much greater resource power (see p. 6) and is unwilling to share it with the less powerful partner, the latter partner is unable to exert any control over resource allocation. Lack of resource power on the professional's side can also lead to conflict, if the professional has less resource power than the parent wants (e.g. a shrinking wheelchair budget).

3. If interests, viewpoints, priorities and values become too opposing, the parent and professional may enter into a conflictual relationship and their two positions may become antagonistic. This includes when the parent and professional *continue to disagree*, even after different strategies to resolve the disagreement and negotiations have been tried, or when the parent takes up a formal complaint (as in appeal cases and other litigation).

4. In circumstances where the initial contract (see p. 42) sets limiting parameters to the negotiating relationship (e.g. in child protection cases, where a parent is required to fulfil basic minimum parenting responsibilities), there is repeated failure to keep within the parameters (e.g. the parent fails to meet the basic minimum requirements). See further Chapter 11.

In this chapter we have looked at the importance of reaching a clearly specified definition on partnership. By exploring traditional and newer forms of parent–professional relationships, the changing power relationships and ways of relating between parents and professionals in the recent past and present have been charted. A Negotiating Model has been introduced as a framework for exploring how partnership can or might proceed within present-day and changing society. Key features of this model are

its focus on perspectives and role positions within societal and organisational contexts, the process of negotiation and dissent, and the constraining
limits to partnership work. This model will be drawn on throughout the
book in thinking about a variety of purposes between the professional
and the parent/family. A potential value of this model is that it can help
highlight what kind of partnership work is feasible within present-day
society, and what changes may be necessary to secure certain partnership
possibilities or what structures and processes may need preserving.

In Chapter 2, the introductory meeting between a professional and a
parent/family and the preliminaries to setting up a partnership relationship are considered.

PROFESSIONAL DEVELOPMENT EXERCISES

EXERCISE 1.1 HOW I EXPERIENCE DIFFERENT RELATIONSHIPS

1. Consider your relationship with
    i)   your GP,
    ii) your spouse, or boy/girlfriend, or close intimate friend,
    iii) an admired, more experienced colleague you wish to impress.

2. Then on a separate sheet of paper, write down six statements of
    how you feel in relationship to your GP.

3. Do the same for the other two relationships.

4. Compare your responses and draw out any summary points about
    your different kinds of relationships.

5. Draw out insights gained from looking at your own experience to
    identify what may be important for the parent in relationship to
    you as a professional. Write down your ideas.

EXERCISE 1.2 HOW I CHARACTERISE MY WORK WITH PARENTS

1. Use a separate sheet of paper to complete in writing your responses to the following statements.

   i)   My job description states that my work with children and families should:

   ii) I see my job with parents as involving:

   iii) Compared with my work with children with disabilities/special needs, my work with parents is:

   iv) I think I work with parents:

Then read Chapter 1 and consider your responses with reference to each conceptual framework of parent–professional relationships. Which model most closely approximates your current style of working with parents and families?

Which model most closely approximates the work of your agency?

APPENDICES

APPENDIX 1.1 CRITIQUE OF DIFFERENT FORMS OF PARENT–PROFESSIONAL RELATIONSHIPS

Chapter 1 describes a variety of different forms of parent–professional relationships. As the following critique shows, there are arguments in favour as well as criticisms of each of the different kinds of relationship.

The professional as expert

Arguments in favour

The professional uses their position and expert powers (see p. 6) for skilled competent intervention towards the child with special needs, and the responsibility for intervention is taken off the parents' shoulders. This may be especially appropriate if parents do not have time, inclination, capability or expertise to give similar assistance themselves. Moreover, parents in emotional shock and psychological turmoil may not be able to take up the position of *partner*, at least temporarily, and the professional may have to take over responsibility for a limited time.

Criticisms

It has been described as authoritarianism bound up with the industrialised and bureaucratised state and society (Illich, 1975). Without shared power and responsibility between the parent and professional, the child and parents are placed in a subordinate, powerless position. This may reduce control over their own lives, and may contribute to reduced personal efficacy and dependency (ibid.). It can also have a negative impact on the parent–child and family relationships (see too DHSS Court Report, 1976). The apparently powerful image of the professional inflates unrealistic parental expectations about what the professional can achieve (such as a possibly fictitious view that the professional is in control of resource allocation and funding). Without opportunity to negotiate, the client may sometimes resort to deriding the professional's intervention as the only means of exerting personal power (e.g. 'I've tried all their advice – none of it works . . .'). A narrow focus on the child excludes wider aspects of the child's 'world', including parents, siblings, and other family members, who may all have a crucial role to play in the effectiveness of an intervention and the wellbeing of the child and family (see Chapter 6). Lack of involvement of the parents can lead to a *mismatch* between parental and professional goals (Cunningham and Davis, 1985, Marteau *et al.*, 1987);

the expert's prescriptions may be inappropriate to the family's needs, values and lifestyle.

The transplant relationship

Arguments in favour

Professionals have to adapt their methods of practice to incorporate working with parents. This requires acquiring skills in transmitting their expertise, communicating with and involving parents. Through their involvement with professionals, parents become more involved, capable, knowledgeable and assertive (see Chapter 8).

Criticisms

It assumes that all parents are motivated (and able) to use professional expertise to help their own child. It ignores differences between families in parenting style, family relationships, resources, values and culture. For example, some parents may not feel comfortable in the role of 'teacher' to their child (Turnbull and Turnbull, 1982). Many interventions have focused on mothers and ignored the possible adverse effect of this on fathers and the family system (see Chapter 6). Arguments have been put forward that this is not a full *partnership* relationship (e.g. Cunningham and Davis, 1985). The professional retains control of the main decisions, and the parent may become dependent on this external expertise and less confident in their own abilities. The power of authority remains with the professional.

The parent as consumer

Arguments in favour

A working model of partnership is presented, which has been tested and shown to work effectively in various service settings (e.g. Davis and Rushton, 1991). Partnership is central to the relationship and depends on joint cooperation and *negotiation*; each partner is recognised as having equivalent expert powers. A critical aim is to give parents a greater sense of control (e.g. overcoming the feeling that they always have to fight for everything). The model has been seen as having extensive, radical implications for service planning and delivery, because services would need to be highly flexible to be able to provide the individually tailored help (Appleton and Minchom, 1991). The importance of the parental viewpoint gives parents a crucial role to play in the planning and management of services (Pugh and De'Ath, 1989), which would confer on those involved a new position power.

Criticisms

In contrast to the conventional professional-led assessment of child and family needs, this model assumes that parents (acting as 'consumers') can adequately represent their own and their child's needs. The viability of this has been questioned, because parents vary manifestly in their capability of assessing needs (Appleton and Minchom, 1991). Some may not be in a position to assess their child's needs, some may have difficulty reasoning rationally at a particular moment in time, and some may have needs that conflict with those of their child. A minority of parents neglect and abuse their child and cannot be permitted to represent their child's needs.

The concept of the parent as a 'consumer' who shares resource power may not be realistic in an economic context of reduced and limited service resources and financial constraints on budgets. A 'consumer' implies a 'purchaser of goods or services' (as against a 'producer' or supplier of services). The power of the *consumer* depends on the purchasing power and resources of the parent to obtain or 'buy' the service, and, in a market relationship, the power to select and choose services from a range of options. If service provision availability is limited and few options are open to an individual family, it is unlikely that the parent (or necessarily the professional) has much 'consumer' or resource power.

This model bears comparison with parent-centred counselling, which aims to facilitate the client to make effective decisions and solve their personal problems. As a working method, it may be more appropriate for enabling and facilitating the parent's *own* problem-solving than for joint enterprises where the professional has a responsibility to incorporate their own viewpoint into the final decision-making (such as reaching a diagnosis, developing a remedial/educational service, providing a health care service).

The empowerment relationship

Arguments in favour

This model emphasises the diversity between parents in their psychological and social resources, and recognises that these differences will affect a parent's ability to take up a position as a partner. Because of the greater disadvantages of some parents, an enabling relationship from the professional (a form of client empowerment) is advocated.

Criticisms

The model focuses on one form of empowerment, but other forms may be needed to alter the relative imbalance of power and control between the parent and professional (see p. 7). Some form of 'citizen empowerment' may be required for parents to act as partners, such as increased legal rights.

APPENDIX 1.2 THE CASE FOR PARENTAL INVOLVEMENT

The following arguments have been proposed for the involvement of parents in professional activity.

1. *The professional needs parental cooperation to do their own job effectively* (DES Plowden Report, 1967, DHSS Court Report, 1976, DES Warnock Report, 1978). Health care, remedial therapy, and education depend on active parental involvement and support if they are to benefit the child sufficiently. This includes involvement and cooperation with the child's professionals. The parent also has a unique and special knowledge and understanding about the child, which can be harnessed to make a significant contribution to that child's health and development.

2. *Parents are a potential resource for helping their child with special needs.* Gains picked up through a learning programme can be consolidated at home, and the home itself offers important opportunities for learning. Parents are able to pick up skills in behavioural and structured teaching techniques and use them successfully for teaching their child, and their teaching involvement can complement the professional's (see Chapter 8). Some parents are very keen to capitalise on new teaching methods with their child and to take a positive role in furthering their child's learning (see p. 200).

   Part of the relatively new enthusiasm for involving parents may derive from the growing shortage of skilled staff and drying up of public funds (Mittler and Mittler, 1983). But the idea of using parents (primarily mothers) depends on the contentious assumption of public agencies that mothers are available during working hours to meet professionals (see further discussion in New and David, 1985). This takes little account of mothers who work part or full-time and are unable to make day-time appointments. The expectation that mothers can provide an alternative labour supply highlights one of the potential contradictions of the parental involvement movement. In a period of changing work patterns for mothers and diminishing resources and increasing pressures on family life, it may be paradoxical to expect mothers to want or to be able to become more involved with professionals.

3. *Parents need support and guidance to help them carry out their parenting of a disabled child* (Younghusband et al., 1970, DHSS Court Report, 1976, Hannam, 1975, Glendenning, 1983, Ayer and Alaszewski, 1984). Many parents, even if they have other children, feel

at a considerable loss in knowing how to rear a child with special needs and need practical advice and assistance. Instead of focusing on the child alone, it has been demonstrated to be more beneficial to the child to help the parents directly so that they become more able to care for their child effectively (Davis and Rushton, 1991).

4. *Unless professionals work alongside parents supportively, their actions can have a disabling impact on the parent* (see DHSS Court Report, 1976, DES Warnock Report, 1978). For example, parents may feel undermined in their confidence to care for their child by professional criticisms. Insensitive interactions by professionals have been shown to have a direct bearing on parents' emotional recovery from the initial trauma of diagnosis (Quine and Rutter, 1994; and see Chapter 3). This contrasts with assistance that builds on the parents' self-esteem, confidence and dignity and helps the parents' adaptation to disability and care of their child (Brimblecombe and Russell, 1988).

5. *The family has a key role in the child's life* (Children Act, 1989). A central theme in the Children Act (and also the DES Warnock Report, 1978, and the 1993 Education Act) is the importance of partnership with parents and (where the child has sufficient understanding) with the child. In the Children Act, the concept of partnership is based on the belief that the family home is the natural and most appropriate place for the majority of children. Because families are already caring for children, supporting them to do so is in the best interests of the child and is viewed as the best allocation of resources from the local authority.

6. *Children are individuals with their own needs, wishes and feelings* (DES Warnock Report, 1978, Children Act, 1989, Education Act, 1993) and the family has a unique and special knowledge of their child (see above).

7. *Families provide continuity for children throughout their childhood* (Children Act, 1989).

8. *The child's needs cannot be separated from the family process and functioning*, from a systemic point of view. The child is in relationship with all other family members, and relationships within the family have an interactive effect with each other (see Chapter 6).

9. *Parents want to be more involved in activities and decisions on their child's education and childcare.* There has been a widespread demand to be more actively involved in those decisions and activities involving their child's education that were traditionally controlled by professionals, as part of a movement towards more client/consumer power (reflected in the 'charter' movement of the 1980s and 1990s in the UK and similar movements in the USA and worldwide). Changing expectations in parents have been expressed through the parental power movement of the 1970s and 1980s. How far individual parents want to

be involved in activities with professionals appears variable (see Pugh and De'Ath, 1989; and see Chapters 8 and 10), but studies suggest that sizeable proportions of parents want to be more closely involved in and participate in decision-making around their child's education (Smith, 1980, Tizard *et al.*, 1981).

APPENDIX 1.3 DEFINITIONS OF PARTNERSHIP

A selection of available definitions and interpretations of the concept of partnership is shown here.

1. 'a relationship in which the professional serves the parents, by making appropriate expertise available to them for their consideration ... (that is) one of *complementary expertise*, since the expert knowledge of parents on themselves, their aims, their situation generally and their children, complements what the professional has to offer including specialist knowledge, and the skills to communicate it' (Davis, 1985, p. 19).
2. '*equivalent expertise*. Partner characteristics include
   - parents are active and central in decision-making and its implementation,
   - parents perceived as having equal strengths and equivalent expertise,
   - parents are able to contribute to as well as receive services,
   - parents share responsibility, thus they and professionals are mutually accountable' (Wolfendale, 1983).
3. 'Partnership involves a *full sharing of knowledge, skills and experiences* ... partnership can take many forms, but it must by definition be on *a basis of equality*, in which each side has areas of knowledge and skill that it contributes to the joint task of working with the child' (Mittler and Mittler, 1983, pp. 10 and 11).
4. 'a working relationship that is characterised by a *shared sense of purpose, mutual respect and the willingness to negotiate*. This implies a sharing of information, responsibility, skills, decision-making and accountability' (Pugh and De'Ath, 1989, p. 68).
5. 'full partnership: parents have the *right to select and decide*, they are considered experts. In particular, they can choose the professionals they want to work with. Partnership is a political question, it is about *sharing power*' (Lane, 1988).
6. 'a dialogue between parents and helpers working in partnership. ... Professionals have their own distinctive knowledge and skills to contribute to parents' understanding of how best to help their handicapped child, but these form a part, not the whole, of what is needed. Parents can be effective partners only if professionals take notice of what they say and of how they express their needs and treat their

contribution as intrinsically important. Even where parents are unable to contribute a great deal themselves, at any rate to start with, their child's welfare will depend upon the extent to which they understand and can apply the measures recommended by professionals and can help to monitor their effects' (DES Warnock Report, 1978, para. 9.6).

7. 'partnership and consultation with parents and children on the basis of careful joint planning and agreement is the guiding principle for the provision of services whether within the family home or where children are provided with accommodation under voluntary arrangements. Such arrangements are intended to assist the parent and enhance, not undermine, the parent's authority and control. This approach should also be developed when a child is in care, provided that it does not jeopardise his welfare' (DoH, 1991a, Vol. 6, 6.4).

APPENDIX 1.4 DEVELOPING THE NEGOTIATING MODEL

I find working in partnership is all very well with those parents who support what you're trying to do ... but what about the difficult ones? ... those who won't join in or can't see what you're getting at ... or do things with their child you don't agree with ... ? (physiotherapist attending the Tavistock training course on *Working in Partnership*).

When working as a clinical psychologist and manager at the KIDS Family Centre for families of children with special needs (see description in Chapter 10), my colleagues in the team and I were faced with the challenge of developing a workable partnership practice in an anti-discriminatory approach. Parents and families using the Centre differed greatly in class, ethnicity, family circumstances, and child needs. Some worked comfortably with the professional's way of viewing their child and the various service interventions of the Centre; with others, a big chasm separated the parents' and professionals' worlds. A crucial question became how could joint decision-making and collaboration proceed with those parents who started at an apparent disadvantage of viewing the joint situation/their child differently from the professional?

There was going to be no easy answer to this question, but a method of practice was developed at the Centre which in time demonstrated that the staff could work cooperatively and effectively with parents from a wide variety of backgrounds. In addition to a particular organisational, team and service structure, management and set of policies designed and developed to facilitate partnership work (see Chapter 10), two other elements seemed necessary for success. Firstly, a willingness in attitude and a commitment to partnership work and power sharing in the staff, and secondly, a conceptual framework and methodology of practice that could encompass the *diversity* and discrepancies between parents and between parents and professionals.

Although parent-centred counselling methods were a valuable means of helping parents resolve their own problems and were frequently adopted by the staff (see *Consumer Model*, p. 13), there were circumstances when the staff members had a responsibility or judged it appropriate to transmit their own perspective to the parent. They might want to share their professional expertise and knowledge, they might have their advice sought, they might be delivering a remedial service to the child. They could be called upon to consult on a child's special needs with a nursery or school. To develop a conceptual framework that could accommodate the professional's perspective and expertise, partnership work was viewed as a coming together of professional and parental powers and responsibilities. To avoid implying an abdication of professional responsibility, control was seen as shifting between the parent and professional in some dynamic tension. The parent preserved control through consent and negotiation, but the professional was also maintaining control through carrying out professional obligations and responsibilities and participating in the negotiation.

To achieve a more egalitarian practice that did not discriminate against the parents' rights to be involved and consulted, the staff members had to advance through collaboration and negotiated decision-making with all parent users of the Centre. The parents' and professionals' viewpoints had to be brought together through negotiation without the staff members sanctioning those parents who disagreed with them or perceived the situation differently. The staff had to be willing to work constructively with parental dissent; over time, dissent became perceived as an integral part of partnership work. Many of the components of the Negotiating Model and the associated practice were explored through ongoing professional practice and development at the KIDS Family Centre.

But the final catalyst for development of the model came from running a training course in partnership practice for multi-disciplinary professionals at the Tavistock Centre. The initial period of designing the course content was beset with various problems. I found no conceptual model giving enough detail of the negotiation process and how it might work in practice to guide the design of the training material. Moreover, no other partnership models in the field of special education needs incorporated in detail the issue of 'disagreement' or dissent; yet practitioners coming onto the course frequently wanted ideas and methods for handling differences of opinion and conflict with parents.

During regular proceedings of the course, the sharing of experiences by groups of professionals from a wide variety of disciplinary and agency backgrounds revealed an often inseparable connection between the way they worked individually with parents and families and the organisational context in which they worked. A role analysis, a power analysis and an analysis of the organisational context were often necessary to make sense of what was happening in the individual parent–professional relationship. This stimulated a need for a training model and method that could respond to the confines and possibilities of partnership work in varied organisational settings. All these factors gave the impetus for designing the Negotiating Model; past and present colleagues and trainees have contributed to the development of the model.

No single conceptual model can easily encompass all the issues (and levels) needed to be taken into account when putting partnership into practice. Partnership is a multi-level concept and process, involving socio-legal, ideological, organisational and ethical aspects as well as personal and interpersonal dimensions. The model developed in this book comes within the intellectual tradition known as social constructionism, which originated with Mead (1934) and Vygotsky (Wertsch, 1985) and has more recently incorporated concepts of post-structuralism and post-modernism (see Shotter and Gergen, 1989). Instead of seeing human behaviour as located within the individual, social constructionism sees human behaviour as a product of the human community and seeks to understand the relationship between the individual and society. It argues for the necessity of multiple perspectives at different levels of social organisation in order to understand theoretically the exchange and the connections between the individual and their social environment, and that without these multiple levels of analysis vital information is missing for making sense of human experience and behaviour. For recent applications of social constructionism to explain processes of therapy, people with learning disabilities and child development see McNamee and Gergen, 1992, Clegg, 1993, and Newmann and Holzman, 1993.

As will be demonstrated throughout this book, what is possible for the individual parent and professional in partnership practice frequently cannot be understood without looking for multiple explanations at the personal, interpersonal, organisational and power/ideological levels and the connections between these levels. It is suggested in the Negotiating Model that partnership practice functions on five different levels:

1. the personal (the inner psychological functioning, the personal perspective),
2. the interpersonal (transactions and communications between the partners),
3. the organisational (family structure and process, organisational team structure and process),
4. the positional (role and power positions),
5. the ideological (beliefs, ideology).

The final two levels must incorporate local and central governmental policies and legislation. These five levels are not hierarchically ordered, but are conceived as collateral (in that the personal will be imbued with the ideological, the interpersonal with the positional, etc.). The division into these various levels has been influenced by Doise (1986), who used four levels (the intrapersonal, the interpersonal and situational, the positional, and the ideological) to develop a theory of knowledge for understanding the relationship of the individual to society; he viewed true understanding as being revealed in the linkages or 'articulations' between the different levels.

What can be achieved in partnership practice may depend ultimately on each level of functioning. For example, the personal make-up of the parent and professional will affect the kind of relationship they build together. The employing agency or organisational context of the professional will affect the options open to the professional (and the parent). Wider contexts of governmental policies and legislation will influence or determine the possibilities available to the partners. Changes at one level may be impeded by resistance at another level. Nevertheless, any shift or modification towards partnership practice at one level may have important repercussions for functioning at the other levels, so a change process could begin at any level. The Negotiating Model attempts to integrate elements of the different levels, whilst focusing predominantly on how they come together at the *interpersonal* level.

Although the Negotiating Model may be seen as a predominantly *cognitive* approach on the intrapersonal and interpersonal level, in that it focuses on what the parent and family members and professional are 'thinking' about (how they 'construe' their situation, their beliefs, their understandings), it is not always valid or useful to separate thoughts from emotions. All feelings have a 'thinking' corollary, and many thoughts arouse emotions. As suggested by some of the Professional Development exercises in this book, professional development for partnership practice may require an exploration of one's personal beliefs, views and feelings, since all of these may impinge on and influence the parent–professional relationship.

The Negotiating Model in practice

The following real-life case example shows negotiation in practice. The process of interaction and communication fits neatly into the elements of the Negotiating Model described on p. 14. Names have been changed to protect confidentiality.

Martha is the mother of a 3-year-old daughter, Katrina, with severe cerebral palsy involving all four limbs. She had been receiving home visits from a physiotherapist, Nicky, from a local child development team over the last year on a three-weekly basis. The visits had been going well, and Martha and Nicky had built up a mutually respectful and cohesive relationship together. Martha appreciated the regular guidance and support she received from Nicky.

Then a new problem surfaced. Martha informed Nicky that she wanted Katrina to go to a Conductive Education group which had just been set up locally. She was very keen to try it out, because she had heard of success stories of children who had gone to the Peto Institute in Hungary. In the course of discussion, Nicky and Martha's two different perspectives became very apparent. Neither viewed the situation in the same way.

Nicky was very concerned about the Conductive Education group, and said that she felt it was inappropriate for Katrina. She added that it could not work alongside her own physiotherapy input, as the two systems of intervention were incompatible with each other (for example, on positioning the child). Martha, on the other hand, felt that she should try any kind of therapy that might possibly help overcome Katrina's problems. They strived to reach a shared decision, but neither could agree to the same option of action.

They then sought some resolution of their difference of opinions. They went on talking and listening to each other's viewpoint, and then compared them. Because they had a strong, trusting relationship, Martha felt able to share her viewpoint with Nicky without feeling that Nicky would discount or denigrate it. She was, however, very anxious that Nicky might withdraw her service from the family.

Martha saw her own interests in 'being a good mother' and this involved getting as much help for Katrina as possible. Nicky had different interests: she felt that she ought to perform to her best professional competence, which meant using her professional judgement effectively for the child. From her viewpoint, her input to Katrina would be undermined by an alternative system of therapy which would be confusing for the parent and child and also demand physical movements which contradicted those she was encouraging in Katrina. She was also under pressure from her employer, her local unit manager. The health authority unit was committed to helping the maximum number of children with the limited service provision available. If a child like Katrina could receive alternative assistance elsewhere, then the unit manager would want Nicky to release Katrina's place and offer it to another priority child.

Nevertheless, Nicky was committed to considering the parent's needs and concerns as well as the child's as she believed in working in partnership with parents. Further discussion and negotiation showed that Martha did not feel willing to let go of her desire to try out the new group.

To try and resolve their disagreement, at least for the time being, Nicky reassured Martha that they shared some common ground: they were both committed to helping Katrina's physical development. She then proposed a compromise action (which would temporarily balance the parent's interests, her own as a professional, and the unit manager's interests). She suggested that she continue to visit Martha on a three-weekly basis over the next four months, as long as Martha put the effort into carrying out her physiotherapy advice in the intervening weeks (she expressed her concerns that her advice on positioning would contradict that of the Conductive Education group). Meanwhile, Martha and Katrina would start attending the Conductive Education group for the next few months to see how they found it. Then in four months' time, they would jointly review Katrina's progress, and decide on what options to pursue next.

Martha was satisfied with this proposal and each party proceeded with the arrangement as decided between them.

Postscript. At the review meeting four months later, it was still not possible to get a consensus between Martha's and Nicky's viewpoints. Martha was enjoying meeting other parents at the Conductive Education group and finding it helpful for her and Katrina, but she also relied on the physiotherapy advice and support from Nicky. Nicky was dissatisfied with this situation, but she felt it was important to continue to assist the family as this was Martha's expressed wish. Her unit manager was, however, anxious to release more physiotherapy sessions for priority children on the waiting list. A further compromise was decided on. Martha would continue to attend the Conductive Education group with Katrina. Nicky would continue to visit Martha with physiotherapy advice, but at less frequent intervals of once a month.

Six months later, Martha spontaneously stopped attending the Conductive Education group when Katrina entered full-time school. She continued to maintain a cooperative relationship with Nicky, who assisted the transition of Katrina into school. Nicky acted as the key worker coordinating the physiotherapy input at school and at home.

Chapter 2

Beginnings

A relationship starts with a beginning, when each partner comes together for the first time. Within a partnership approach, the main aim of an introductory meeting would be to meet in such a way that facilitates the possibility of building a partnership. The way the introduction is conducted and the role the professional demonstrates may set the pattern for later encounters. This chapter draws on the Negotiating Model described in Chapter 1 to give practical ideas for introducing a partnership. Methods of establishing role responsibilities and contributions are examined. The more problematic issue of dealing with a failure to carry out a role responsibility is also discussed.

We start by looking at what might be realistically achieved in the first or early meetings.

INTRODUCTIONS

Initial aims

An introduction is both a one-off encounter which sets out to achieve various aims, and also a process of familiarisation. The aims (and how the first meeting progresses) will be dictated partly by how the professional perceives their own role and also the kind of relationship they wish to set up with the family (Appleton and Minchom, 1991). But whether these are fulfilled or not will depend too on the reactions of the parent and also the transactions that unfold between them. Although a variety of different aims might be pursued in the early meetings, some basic ones are particularly appropriate for beginning a partnership, as listed below.

'Joining' the family

This first one suggests a genuine and sincere attempt to meet a family on their own terms.

The parent and professional may hold preconceived notions even before they meet. For the parent, prior experience or notions gained from others, the media, etc., lead to certain ideas of what a 'health visitor' or a 'doctor' is like. The 'psychologist' may be viewed as a 'shrink'; the 'social worker' 'might take my child away'. In turn, casenotes, discussions with colleagues and notions of 'this kind of family' convey ideas on the parents and family to the professional. Then the two parties meet and first impressions are formed, which either buttress or challenge these previous notions. A professional may come across as friendly, warm, accessible or cold, distant and patronising. A parent may appear friendly, open and welcoming, or hostile, suspicious and unreceptive; relaxed and outgoing, or nervous and withdrawn. They are both likely to notice each other's social class and skin colour and possibly ethnic membership, which, if similar, can add an instant bond of familiarity or, if different, create a gulf of separation and strangeness. Subsequently, these initial impressions are consolidated further or altered as they get to know each other better.

Getting to know a family on its own terms is facilitated by meeting in a relaxed, informal manner, in a place that is conducive to the family and least disruptive of their daily routines. Ideally, it would be at a time when all significant members of the family could be present, and a clear message is given that their caregiving role is valued (ibid.) (see further about working with the whole family in Chapter 6). To indicate that one is receptive to the family's own views, it would be advisable to respond to their initial concerns rather than to impose one's professional agenda (Appleton and Minchom, 1991). For example, if the parents expressed concern about their child's motor delay, then it might be more appropriate for a physiotherapist to make the first visit than a health visitor or social worker.

This process of 'joining' may be pursued in a single meeting, or a series of meetings to dispel initial suspicion by the family and to develop familiarity and mutual understanding. A key element is that the professional gradually becomes perceived as trustworthy, competent, concerned and sincere.

Finding out parental expectations and feelings

The second aim is to establish the parent's expectations and feelings about the referral to the professional. The referral can be viewed as a kind of *punctuation*, that is, something which shifts or changes the preceding flow of events and interactions in the family or between the family and its professional network. To gain a better idea of where it fits into the family's life, one will want to learn about the events leading up to it and feelings about the referral. Of interest would be

- Whether the family, a professional or someone else had made the referral, and why?
- What events or change led to the referral?
- What do the parents feel about the referral?
- What are they expecting from this meeting with the professional?
- What are they looking for?

The following examples reveal the importance of this inquiry by showing what can go wrong if the initial expectations and feelings are not identified or responded to appropriately.

1. A social worker visited a family at home to discuss leisure activities for the young person with special needs. The family were completely unreceptive, having expected to talk about their appalling housing difficulties.
2. A second family resented being referred to the occupational therapy department because they felt already overloaded with hospital appointments; they were unenthusiastic about joining the occupational therapist's play programme.
3. A third family were referred to a voluntary agency when contact between them and their statutory services broke down. The referring professionals in the statutory network were hoping that the voluntary agency would provide a substitute service. This initial expectation was not made clear to either the voluntary agency or the family; in the first meeting, both parties felt uncomfortable and confused about what to expect from each other or what to offer.

Learning about the family's concerns and needs

The third aim of learning about the family's general concerns and needs is connected with the previous one. Open-ended questions by the professional like 'How can I help?' or 'Can I be of any help?' invite the parent or family member to take control in the dialogue and express their concerns and needs and what they are looking for. This is facilitated by careful questioning and listening (see Chapters 4 and 7).

Nevertheless, this communication is not always straightforward. How the parent perceives the professional and their role as 'patient' or 'client', and how the professional interacts verbally or non-verbally with the parent may lead to inhibition and silence on the parent's side. This has been demonstrated vividly in doctor–patient encounters, where at least half of a patient sample showed minimal participation in the consultation (Tuckett *et al.*, 1982; Robinson, 1989). Lacking knowledge about the family background and culture, the professional may misinterpret what is said about the family's concerns and needs or impose inappropriate assumptions (a particular risk with families of ethnic minorities, as Robina

Shah argues in her 1992 study of Asian families with children with disabilities).

This exploratory phase may require considerable time. In some family situations, the initial presenting problem is not the most significant problem for the family, or the family has difficulty identifying what it is looking for. Rather than move towards a specific 'contract' prematurely (see later), an extended exploratory period may be productive.

Sharing professional information or advice

A fourth objective may be to provide professional information or advice, to help the parent become more informed and in response to parental inquiries. This permits a parent to make an informed choice on whether to take up a service offer. But, as said previously, communication difficulties may hinder the initial meetings, especially if the parent and professional lack a common base of knowledge and values. This issue is discussed further in Chapter 4.

Negotiating options

This fifth aim would be paramount because it starts the process of negotiation of the partnership relationship, according to the Negotiating Model. One preliminary form of negotiation might be to select service options or the particular service offered by the new professional. To help the parent evaluate various options, the professional may wish to introduce their own perspective of what could be helpful and beneficial for the child and family. Through negotiation, mutual agreement may be reached on whether a parent will take up or reject a particular service option, and both parties can now move forward cooperatively (or separate, if appropriate).

But the possibility of differences of opinion and dissent in the early meetings is also assumed by the Negotiating Model. A parent might be reluctant to take up the option which the professional believes would benefit the child with special needs. A professional with few service options to offer may fail to meet a parent's initial expectations. Differing interests may also skew the initial negotiations. For example, one professional actively persuaded a hesitant parent to join a service because the service contract with the local authority depended on the maximum number of eligible children using the service (to the parent's chagrin at not being offered the service she had initially requested).

The fragility of their relationship at this stage may make it difficult to accommodate dissent and to 'contain' negative feelings. Dissatisfied and unresolved, their encounter may break down, with the parties separating prematurely. A further risk is of the parent conceding to the professional's authority and persuasiveness and complying, whether this accords with their own wish or not. Neither outcome would necessarily be in the longer-term interest of the parent, child or professional. Recognising the legitimacy of dissent and strategies for resolving differences of opinion may be required (see Chapter 4).

Control over the introduction process

A final aim would be to help the parent feel in control of the process of introduction as a beginning of sharing control in the partnership. Many structural factors will tip the power balance in the professional's favour (see Chapter 1). In addition, the parent may be psychologically vulnerable, further reducing their control of the encounter. Following the diagnosis of their child's disability, a parent in a state of acute shock and psychological turmoil may be unable to take in external information, make decisions or negotiate. Active measures would be needed to prevent the parent becoming helpless and powerless (this is expanded on in Chapter 3).

Having looked at initial aims, we now turn to a further set of negotiations.

MOVING FORWARD TOGETHER

If moving forward together, more negotiations would be required to decide on what is to be delivered and expected from each other. These negotiations might precede or follow the decision to take up a service.

Coordinating the parent and professional roles

Working together depends on synchronising the parent and professional roles so that their contributions within the relationship are mutually compatible and enhancing. But their role differences are likely to lead to different contributions and responsibilities (see too Darling, 1983 and Cunningham and Davis, 1985) and different knowledge bases and skills, commitments and investment (see Table 2.1).

Attempts to bring these differing perspectives and contributions together can lead to frustration and dissatisfaction on both sides, as well as misunderstanding and lack of respect (Darling, 1983). Unless they can be coordinated satisfactorily, it is unlikely that it will be mutually satisfying or productive to work together. One useful method of bringing the two roles together initially is to identify a *common purpose* or *shared concern*, or *mutual interest* through which each partner seeks to gain from the collaboration. This might be, for example,

Table 2.1 Different and complementary roles

Parent's role	Professional's role
To carry out duties, obligations, rights, responsibilities in position of a parent	To carry out obligations, duties, responsibilities, rights in position of a professional, depending on discipline, job position and employing agency
Direct experience of having a child with special needs	Experience of a wide range of children with special needs and their families
Holistic perspective on one's child in many roles, e.g. sibling, grandchild, pupil	Often specific interest in one area of the child (speech, movement, health) and view of the child in one role (client, patient, or pupil)
Intimate knowledge of own family members and relationships, culture, values, aspirations, resources, needs, support network	Learnt academic knowledge in particular aspects of special needs (medical, educational, etc.) and in family processes and psychological functioning. Knowledge of the service system (e.g. referral methods)
May have direct access to particular services	May have direct access to services May manage services, control resource allocation and funding
Total lifelong commitment to whole child with special needs	Temporary commitment to aspects of child
Legal guardian and parental responsibility for child until adulthood	Short-term professional responsibility
Concern for individual child	Balancing concern for individual child with the wider group of children
High emotional involvement	Lower emotional involvement
High attachment	More detached concern
Interests vary: e.g. to gain the greatest advantage for one's child, to meet the needs of parent or other members of the family, to balance economic and parenting responsibilities	Interests vary: e.g. to gain the greatest advantage for the individual child, to serve the needs of employing authority

Source: adapted from Katz, 1984 and Cameron and Sturge-Moore, 1990; it draws on the work of Elizabeth and John Newson (1976)

- a shared concern in a child's medical condition and health improvement,
- a mutual commitment to achieving the same developmental goal for the child,
- separate legal responsibilities and rights to participate in the same formal education assessment process,
- a shared interest as the user and provider in the management of the service,
- a shared need to resolve a problem concerning respite in provision for the family.

Having identified some common purpose together, the parent and professional are better equipped to explore how their two roles might work to complement each other.

Contributions and responsibilities

The process of clarifying each partner's contributions and responsibilities follows on from this. In the framework of a negotiating partnership, what each is to offer is explicitly negotiated rather than assumed. But the parent can do this fully only if adequate information has been provided. For instance, if a parent were to negotiate their level of involvement in a home teaching programme, they might need to know something about the possible consequences for the child of varying levels of parental teaching before reaching a decision. Some of the challenges for the professional in helping the parent to be adequately informed and for the parent in reaching an informed consent are discussed further in Chapter 8 (p. 173).

The formality of this clarification process is time-consuming and possibly disconcerting to the parent. It also requires a degree of explicitness of professional objectives that the professional may not be accustomed to giving to the parent (and child), thinking that certain objectives, such as 'improving parenting skills' or 'building the parent's confidence' or 'changing dysfunctional patterns in the family' should not be discussed with the family.

Notwithstanding these difficulties, the mutual responsibilities and contributions should be established as soon as the professional has achieved a 'joining' of the family (see earlier) because early clarification can avoid later misunderstanding and disappointment. Both parties stand to gain from it. There is a greater likelihood of 'matching' between their expectations and goals (c.f. p. 21); the parent is more likely to feel in control of what is offered subsequently and feel greater satisfaction; and the parent is more likely to deliver their contribution because of agreement at the outset. A series of studies of doctor–patient communication show

Table 2.2 Checklist of parent and professional responsibilities

The box can be filled in by ticking or grading, as appropriate.

Area of responsibility	Parent	Professional	Other
Practical care at night			
Practical and emotional care:			
morning			
afternoon			
early evening			
Provision of respite care			
Daytime routines			
Setting behaviour boundaries and discipline			
Play and stimulation			
Outings and leisure activities			
Education and learning			
Physiotherapy			
Occupational therapy			
Speech therapy			
Diagnosis and assessment of special needs			
Provision of information on special needs			
Provision of information on benefits, services, resources			
Choice of nursery and school			
Provision of nursery and school			
Provision of special resources			
Provision of medical and paramedical care			
Health care			
Self-development of parent/parenting skills			
Provision of counselling			
Family support/well being of siblings and family members			
Looking at child's needs within the family			
Overcoming marital problems			
Overcoming family relationship problems			
Organising the child/family's service network			
Planning for			
short-term			
long-term needs and life-style			
of child/person with special needs			
Dealing with financial/housing problems			
Other			

more positive outcomes of consultations (e.g. greater patient satisfaction and adherence to treatment) if there is a 'match' between doctors' and patients' views (Eisenthal and Lazare, 1979, Tuckett *et al.*, 1985).

This negotiation is not necessarily a one-off exercise because responsibilities may alter over time with a particular parent and family. Expectations may also alter, and may need to be explored again at later dates. Turn to Appendix 2.1 for a sample introduction which includes a basic negotiation of expectations, contributions and responsibilities.

The checklist in Table 2.2 shows a list of possible responsibilities and contributions of parents and professionals. Which ones will be important for a particular relationship will depend on the individual circumstances of the partners and the purpose of their collaboration. As a practical measure, one could use a checklist like this to identify and agree on separate and overlapping responsibilities with a parent. It could usefully form the basis for a discussion on what help might be needed by a parent to carry out their responsibilities. A further value is that the limits of the professional's responsibilities and sphere of effectiveness may become more evident to the parent (and the professional).

Facing the possibility of failure?

A difficult issue to introduce early on (or later) is the implication(s) of possible failure of role responsibility. This topic is often avoided when starting off a new relationship with a parent and family, because of fear of jeopardising the relationship and being viewed as 'custodians' rather than partners. Nevertheless, an avoidance of this issue gives a quasi-egalitarian appearance to the relationship which is not founded on a substantive equality of role positions and powers. Any childcare professional is required in law to intervene in cases of child abuse and neglect, whether the parent consents to this or not. In exceptional circumstances, childcare professionals can draw on their back-up power (the physical power of police, courts, see p. 6); even if not used, the presence of this potential power source can exert a coercive influence over parents.

Even with the risk of stifling the growth of a future partnership, it is probably better to be honest with the parent. By explicitly setting out the limits of the relationship, future conflict could be avoided. Any statutory intervention on behalf of the child is likely to undermine the parent's trust and their future partnership together if the parent had not been forewarned of the possibility. In light of this, it might be a more realistic base for partnership work to openly acknowledge and work with this real imbalance in structural power than to gloss over it.

At the KIDS Family Centre, an introductory leaflet was distributed to all new service users which spelled out the possibility of statutory intervention, without parental consent, if the staff had significant concerns about the child's care and welfare (see Chapter 10). Further consideration on the issue of failure of parental or professional responsibility is given in Appendix 2.2.

Making a contract

Talking through and negotiating responsibilities and contributions can be likened to a bargaining *exchange* process, e.g. What I will be able to do if you do X *or* If I do X what I can expect from you. It should lead to an agreement along the lines of

● What I can offer. . . .
● What you can expect from me. . . .
● What you will offer. . . .
● What I can expect from you. . . .

and this forms the basis for a *contract*. Statements of the If you do X, I will do Y, can be useful in setting some limiting parameters. Although a contract in this circumstance is not formal or legally binding, it does set out mutual expectations and intended behaviours. Depending on the family and situation, it may be useful to put this in writing, with each party retaining their own copy (although for others, this may be too formal and unnecessary). It is often appropriate to repeat this process with the family at later dates.

Although establishing a contractual relationship (Cunningham and Davis, 1985), making a contract can be at different levels of specificity. It may be appropriate to have a more open-ended contract of 'family counselling' for a limited time period in some family situations where space and time is needed for exploring complex or unresolved issues and concerns (and before opting to select a specific service or pursue a specific behavioural or treatment objective).

With the risk of litigation burgeoning as a result of parents' increased legal powers (see Appendix 2.2 and Chapter 11), it is advisable to ensure adequate time to establish mutually accepted responsibilities and expected contributions from early on in the relationship. Having agreed on an initial contract, the parent and professional are more likely to proceed cooperatively and the likelihood of later adversarial conflict should be greatly reduced.

RELATIONSHIP-BUILDING

Having completed an introduction and arranged to meet again, the process of relationship-building is started. Partnership methods can be appropriately applied to one-off encounters, and many of the features of a negotiating partnership discussed in this book are as important in a single meeting as in a longer-term relationship.

Notwithstanding its value for one-off encounters, partnership work is perhaps best advanced in a longer-term relationship. Familiarity, trust, respect and understanding are all fostered within conditions of adequate time and repeated meetings. Time and considerable perseverance will be needed to learn about a parent and their family system and culture, to understand a parent's perspective, to share one's professional under-standings, and to negotiate decisions.

Likewise, a parent may need time and multiple meetings to accept a professional as a partner. Barriers of class, gender and ethnicity will need surmounting. New or enhanced social/communication skills and ways of relating may be required for participating with professionals, including negotiation and decision-making skills. Time will be needed to hear the professional's view of the child and their circumstances, and to gain some understanding of the professional's expertise. All these demands suggest that partnership work cannot be hurried, and this has significant implica-tions for professional time and staff resourcing and for parental time and family resources.

As we will see at other points later in the book, the quality of the rela-tionship achieved will in many ways determine the success of the negotiations and the ability to resolve decisions.

One final point on relationship-building is that a relationship is a dynamic process and an entity. It is built and sustained through the mutu-ally influencing contributions of each partner, and grows out of their combined contributions. On this account, one cannot adequately under-stand or grasp a parent–professional relationship by looking at each person's contribution separately. Their relationship is built from and reflects their continual interaction and mutually influencing current and past encounters. Within their present interactions are sown the seeds of possible future encounters. But from the present will emerge the new and the unexpected.

In this chapter, we have explored how the process of introduction by a professional may set the stage for future partnership relating. Attention has been paid to the various aims to pursue in the early meetings, to the negotiation of service options, to the clarification of role responsibilities and contributions, and to the attainment of an agreement or 'contract'. The difficult issue of failed responsibility was also approached, with emphasis given to the importance of being honest from the beginning about the limits of the relationship. In the next chapter, we shall focus on the psychological reactions and perspective of the parent.

PROFESSIONAL DEVELOPMENT EXERCISE

EXERCISE 2.1 INTRODUCING YOURSELF

You are meeting a parent for the first time. How do you introduce yourself and what you are planning to do?

1. Spend five minutes thinking about your own work practice and your usual ways of introducing yourself. Write down on a separate sheet of paper a sample introduction by yourself.

2. Then write your responses to the following questions:
   i) Is your sample representative of your usual way of introducing yourself? If not, why do your introductions vary – what contributes to differences in your introductions?
   ii) What do you experience and feel when you introduce yourself to a parent and family? And how does this affect your introduction?
   iii) Assuming you're setting out to build a partnership with parents and families, is there anything you would like to alter to improve your manner of introduction?
   iv) What constraints (personal or organisational), if any, prevent you currently implementing your 'ideal' introduction?
   v) Now read the sample introduction in Appendix 2.1 and compare it with your own sample. Reconsider your responses to questions 2 (3) and (4). Have you changed them in any way, and why?

APPENDICES

APPENDIX 2.1 SAMPLE INTRODUCTION

This is a sample of an introduction (the names have been changed to protect confidentiality).

Helen, an occupational therapist, introduced herself during her first home visit to parents Jack and Sarah. Their daughter, Carla, aged 18 months, has been diagnosed as autistic. Abbreviated extracts from their one-hour introductory visit are given below.

(*Helen*)   I'm Helen, an occupational therapist or OT; do you know anything about occupational therapy? (*she explains here*) My role is to help children do appropriate activities. I help children with special needs in their everyday activities like feeding, dressing, bathing, so that they become more independent and also help their learning and development through play. Does this sound what you might be looking for? Can I be of any help?

(*Sarah*)   We want to know how we can play with Carla. We've tried playing with her, but it's difficult to find anything to get through to her. She cries a lot and throws her toys around or spends ages fiddling around, bits of string or pieces she finds on the floor. It's very hard knowing how to please her . . . and how to get her learning.

(*Helen*)   (*after a long discussion with Jack and Sarah about Carla and her early history*) I'd be able to visit you at home and give ideas on how to play with Carla. You know . . . finding things that could interest her and give you more fun together, also activities that could help her learn and develop. The other service I can offer is at the CDC (Child Development Centre); do you remember looking in on the room with parents and children playing? Once a fortnight there's a playgroup for parents and children with special needs. Two occupational therapists (myself and Jan) help the mums with learning activities. There's also time for tea and a chat with the other mums (and a few dads come too). What do you feel about either of these services? Carla could join both if you want. Quite a few parents and children find it helpful to use both services at the same time.

(*Jack to Sarah*)   What do you think? I think home visits would be great, be a real support for you, and I could be here sometimes too.

(*Sarah*)   Well, we were saying, before you came, that we'd really like someone to show us how to help Carla at home. I think home visits would be very helpful . . . also just knowing that I could talk to someone regularly about Carla. (*Sarah expressed here an interest in attending the play group at a later date, but difficulty with her present working arrangements.*) But what would home visits involve – would they take up a lot of time? I work every morning so I'm only free in the afternoons . . . the child minder could help, but I'd like to be at the visits.

(*Helen*)   I think I could arrange something . . . (*she looks in her diary*). I'd need to discuss this first with the rest of the Child Development Team, but it looks like I could offer a time on Tuesday afternoons, probably late afternoon, if this suited you both. Shall I tell you more about the service? . . . As an occupational therapist, I will have ideas of play activities that might work well with Carla, but you know Carla much better than I do, and what kind of things will fit in best in your home. So you joining in and sharing your own ideas will be very useful. Also, when I'm not here you could go on doing the activity with Carla between my visits . . . that way she'll pick up the activity much quicker and you'll be able to tell me on my next visit how she's been getting on. It means that we would be together for about an hour each visit. I could visit once a fortnight. When I visit we'd try out various activities, and then decide together on one or two that you can continue to use with Carla during the period until my next visit . . . (*further details on the service were given here*). How does this sound to you? How do you feel about joining in and carrying on with the play activity in between my visits? Would you like this kind of involvement or would you like some other kind of help instead?

(*Sarah*)   It sounds like it could be very helpful . . . anything to help Carla.

APPENDIX 2.2 CONSIDERING FAILURE OF RESPONSIBILITY

Some of the issues raised in this chapter are discussed further here.

A failure to carry out defined responsibilities is not always followed by a breakdown in collaboration. On both sides, there may be constraining circumstances which prevent the carrying out of duties. Financial, housing, marital problems or competing childcare demands may, for example, hinder a parent meeting all the physical and care needs of the child with special needs (e.g. Dunst and Leet, 1987). Likewise, a professional may not be in control of financial budgets which determine whether they can deliver the kind of service that they promised the parent. But in a relationship where there is mutual trust, honesty and goodwill, allowances may be made by one to the other for changing contributions or failed responsibilities. A professional may help a parent overcome current difficulties and constraints which are getting in the way of fully caring for the child, or at least may offer accepting understanding and support. The professional may reduce or alter their expectations of the parent.

There is, however, likely to be a floor level of *minimum responsibility* or 'minimal expectations' (Cunningham and Davis, 1985), below which it may be difficult or impossible for parents and professionals to work together collaboratively (see Chapter 1). If a parent fails to satisfy the minimum expectations of adequate protection and care of their child, within the concept of 'good enough parenting' held in our society, the professional is bound to draw on statutory powers to intervene on behalf of the child. This may severely test the possibility of future collaboration. Nevertheless, even in this extreme situation, the Children Act and all associated regulations and guidance still point the way towards continued parental participation and partnership wherever possible (see further Chapter 11).

When it comes to failure of 'professional responsibility', parents have had, until recently, few powers at their disposal and few avenues to challenge professional practice (such as incompetence, negligence, failure to provide a service, disrespectful behaviour and lack of consultation of the parent). Parents could turn to the Ombudsman, the officer responsible for investigating complaints of public services. But although the Ombudsman could reprimand a local Council and demand a formal apology to the user, their power is restricted because their word is not law and binding. Complaints against individual professionals could also be taken to professional associations responsible for self-regulating the professions (such as the General Medical Council); though concerns have been voiced of a possible bias towards protecting the profession rather than the public interest in regard to some regulating councils (BBC Radio 4, *File on 4*, 28 June, 1994). Under the Citizen's Charter, service users are being encouraged to complain to the provider, but complaints may lead to sanctioning and removal of the service in some instances (e.g. Association of Community Health Councils, 1994).

This situation is beginning to change with the introduction of legislation giving parents new rights and new possibilities in law. Under the 1993 Education Act and 1989 Children Act, parents can appeal against local authority decisions on special education and childcare (see further Chapter 11). Cases of extreme incompetence and personal damages can be fought through the courts at great cost, and the late 1980s and 1990s have witnessed a growth of private litigation cases. A number of landmark cases are testing breach of statutory duty by local authorities, charging the authorities with causing personal damages and seeking financial redress (e.g. victims of abuse versus Leicestershire County Council, 1994, Keating versus Bromley Council, 1994). The courts will be increasingly required to take responsibility for resolving the growing litigious conflicts between users and public service providers.

Chapter 3

The parent's perspective

Parents rarely expect their child's disabling condition or life-threatening illness. The confirmation or diagnosis, whether at birth or later, often creates an immense crisis of changed expectations and hopes, and parents may experience intense reactions during the early days. In this chapter, we will be looking at some of the ways in which professionals can help parents through this initial traumatic period and beyond. Various psychological theories and frameworks will be introduced as a basis for informing and guiding practice.

The moment a parent comes into contact with a professional, a transaction begins. One principal issue explored in this chapter is the impact of the parent's responses, beliefs and behaviours on the professional, and in reverse, the influence of the professional's beliefs and behaviours on the parent's adjustment to having a child with special needs. As a starting point, parental and professional beliefs about disability will be examined.

BELIEFS ABOUT DISABILITY

A disabling condition in the child unites the parent with the professional, and their various beliefs and views on the disability are likely to colour their reactions to each other (and to the child). These beliefs and attitudes will be closely bound up with the way in which disability is viewed by the wider society (or the minority ethnic group to which the parent belongs).

The available beliefs and 'models' for socially interpreting the nature of disability are multiple and changing rapidly (see Wolfensberger, 1975, Ryan and Thomas, 1981). Nineteenth-century views of poor racial heredity and social inadequacy as causes of 'sub-normality' still appear to exert some influence, as do more traditional religious and moral beliefs (Ryan and Thomas, 1981). But the overriding viewpoint in modern Western industrial capitalist societies has been, until very recently, of disability as a *separate and marginal condition*, with disabled people perceived as less capable and less valuable than non-disabled people. Disabled children were institutionalised in the past, and older disabled people have frequently been segregated from the rest of the population. From the 1960s onwards, an alternative 'model' has been championed of disabled people as a deprived and stigmatised minority group. The roots of this prejudice have been argued as lying in, amongst other factors, the predominance of medical ideas in the care of disabled people and the management of disability as a pathology; a general lack of contact with disabled people and the popular fear of the unknown, and the idealised images of 'normality' in the media and literature.

These prejudices are beginning to be overcome with the advent of more positive images of disability in the media, more assertive campaigning for equal rights by disabled people themselves (see p. 117), and 'normalisation' principles pursued by some service providers (Wolfensberger, 1972). There is a major shift in many Western societies away from a medical 'model' of interpretation of disability to an educational model linked to a human rights sociological approach.

Within this complexity of available beliefs and 'models', parents may adopt different and changing responses to their child's disability. Many react to the initial 'news' with what has been until recently the dominant societal response to disability, which is generally rejecting and negative. In the search for meaning for their situation, some parents may resort to traditional beliefs and see their child as the consequence of a misdeed or misfortune of their own or as a blessing in disguise from God, sent to test their faith and fortitude (Ryan and Thomas, 1981). Other beliefs and 'models' may become more significant at a later stage in their child's life-cycle, such as the human rights belief in the value of their child and the right of their child to a fair share of resources and a full place in society.

All this implies that the professional must avoid assuming the same common beliefs and attitudes in all parents, or that an individual parent's views are unchanging. A parent may hold different kinds of beliefs at the same time, and these beliefs may alter in response to different events and demands facing the child with special needs and the family. Parents of ethnic minority groups will be as individual and heterogeneous in their beliefs as parents of the majority culture; they may hold a variety of religious and cultural ethnic beliefs, Western medical and educational 'models', and combinations of both (see Robina Shah's study of Asian families, 1992, and p. 64).

The professional, in turn, draws on their previously established notions of disability when giving the 'diagnosis' or breaking the news to parents. These vary too, because of variation in personal beliefs (see social influences previously) and also the uncertainty in the nature of professional knowledge itself (Marteau, 1989). This is contrary to the widespread

assumption that professionals are 'neutral' carriers of 'standard' empirically based knowledge. Their attitudes and beliefs may affect how they
respond to the child and the parents; negative views on disability may be
applied to both. For example, a paediatrician who viewed a child's physical disabling condition as a 'medical failure' conveyed his sense of failure
and hopelessness to a couple receiving a diagnosis. When the parents
refused to accept such a pessimistic outlook, the paediatrician regarded
them as 'denying the handicap'.

It is important to be aware of the influence of beliefs, because how the
individual professional views the child with special needs has been found
to be linked to parents' evaluation of their helpfulness or lack of help
(Byrne *et al.*, 1988).The most frequent criticism of paediatricians, cardiac
specialists, audiologists and general practitioners, who were found to be
unhelpful in this study, was of their pessimistic views and negative attitudes. Exercise 3.1 gives an opportunity to explore your own beliefs and
attitudes and to consider how they might influence your intervention with
a child with special needs and the child's parents.

We move on to look at parental responses, and how they come together
with professional responses, in one of the most difficult encounters they
are likely to face together: the giving or receiving of news of disability
and special needs.

GIVING THE NEWS OF DISABILITY

Breaking the news about disability or a life-threatening illness is one of
the most stressful tasks for medical professionals. Anticipating the interview may evoke feelings of anxiety, distress, inadequacy or defensiveness,
with worries about how best to communicate the news, what to say about
the child's prognosis, and how to handle the parents during their first
shock. A doctor may feel implicated, if the disabling condition developed
during the perinatal period (such as during birth asphyxia). Not surprisingly, some professionals use personal defence strategies (such as avoiding
breaking the news and getting another colleague to do it, giving the news
abruptly, or communicating in ways that do not give the true picture) to
reduce their stress and anxiety levels.

It is often the first meeting with the parents, particularly if the disclosure comes straight after the birth. The professionals may know nothing
about the parents and have no information or previous contact to draw
on, yet they have to impart news that will have a lifelong implication for
the family concerned. Because of their unfamiliarity with the family they
may have little knowledge about the practical implications of the disability
for them.

'The bearer of bad news is always despised ...'

In the meeting when the diagnosis is given, particularly if it is unexpected, the parents may not instantaneously take in the severity of the diagnosis until phrases like 'brain damage', 'handicap', 'autistic', 'Down's syndrome', 'spastic' start to hammer the message home. Immediately the parents start realising the extent and severity of their child's condition they may react with intense shock and distress. In later recall, some phrases may stand out and others may be forgotten, some comments may be distorted or altered in their minds (Ley, 1979). For some parents, the memory of how they are told is remembered with acute vividness, immediacy and clarity months and years after the diagnosis, as if they are reliving the events as they happened (Cunningham, 1984).

The news may be so difficult to take in that some parents will refuse to accept it for a while and may reject the person conveying the news. Intense and sometimes irrational responses stemming from personal grief are common during the diagnostic and post-diagnostic period (Kennedy, 1970, Emde and Brown, 1978). There has been a tendency for professionals, particularly in the medical profession, to perceive these reactions as exclusively to do with the parents' personal *psychological* adjustments to the news.

Although often a highly difficult and painful process of personal adjustment for parents, there is growing evidence that *the way in which parents are told the news* affects how they adjust to the situation and their treatment of the child (Pugh and Russell, 1977, Svarstad and Lipton, 1977, Cunningham *et al.*, 1984). Apart from apparently unusual cases where parents reject and/or do not benefit from any professional help, however sensitively and carefully offered, many parents and families seem to respond positively to humane, skilled intervention.

It is extremely important to recognise this, because the manner in which the news is broken to parents continues to arouse great dissatisfaction and anger in parents. Most surveys (including recent studies) document high levels of dissatisfaction; this has been shown for parents of children with Down's syndrome (e.g. Carr, 1970, Drillien and Wilkinson, 1964, Berg *et al.*, 1969), spina bifida (Hare *et al.*, 1966) and severe learning disabilities (Quine and Pahl, 1986). Parents complain about delays and evasions in the telling, being given false assurances, being told in an abrupt and uncaring way, having the negative consequences of the child's condition emphasised, each parent being told separately, being left to break the news to the other parent, being told in a public place, and not being given access to a private place afterwards.

But research findings are now available to suggest that parental dissatisfaction is not inevitable. In a landmark study, Cunningham *et al.* (1984) interviewed 62 sets of parents with Down's syndrome babies, identified at birth. Of these sets, 58 per cent expressed some form of dissatisfaction with the timing or manner of telling. A 'model procedure' (see further Appendix 3.1) was then instituted in one health authority. In contrast to previous practice, all the parents (100 per cent) who were informed using this new procedure registered satisfaction. Moreover, they showed *positive attitudes towards their child, themselves and their ongoing professional services and help* six months later.

This contrasts vividly with the study's control group of parents who were told the news using the standard procedures of other health authorities. Levels of dissatisfaction remained high, and only 20 per cent expressed satisfaction. Six months later, parents expressed anger and less positive attitudes towards their child, themselves and their ongoing professional help. The authors concluded that the manner in which the news was given appeared to have a long-term impact on parental attitudes and acceptance of their child.

In a further study, Quine and Rutter (1994) interviewed 166 mothers of children with severe learning disabilities around the time of the first diagnosis. They were asked to rate the doctor's affective behaviour and their understanding and memory of the information they received. Measures were also included on the child's age when the diagnosis was made and how satisfied they were with the way in which they were told the diagnosis. Similar to other studies, 58 per cent of parents reported dissatisfaction with the communication. Satisfaction was found to be much higher if the person communicating the diagnostic information was perceived as having a sympathetic manner, being direct and approachable, showing understanding of the mother's concern, and being a good communicator (and these findings fit in with the social psychological model developed by Korsch et al. (1968) which focuses on the importance of affect and social interaction for parental satisfaction in a paediatric context).

Developing quality practice

There is no perfect or single way of disclosing the news of disability/special needs to parents. Even with careful and sensitive intervention, there will be times when professional intervention fails with a particular family and it is realistic to accept the limitations of one's own practice and assistance. Nevertheless, a well-established body of literature from researchers, practitioners and parents confirms the kind of assistance that is most helpful to parents and embodies what parents want. (See Appendix 3.1 for a set of guidelines derived from this literature.) It has been recommended that all maternity units and primary-care teams should have guidelines on procedures to be followed in the event of the birth of a disabled baby (Independent Development Council for People with Mental Handicap,

1982), and Appendix 3.1 could form the basis for setting a code of quality. Notwithstanding this recommendation, many of these guidelines cannot be operationalised without supporting organisational structures, procedures and policies (see further Chapter 12). You might find it useful at this stage to perform Exercise 3.2, which gives an opportunity to consider how well your agency is prepared for and equipped to give diagnoses or assessment verdicts of disability/special needs.

The communication challenge

We talked briefly in Chapter 2 about the challenge for the professional in transmitting their information and expertise to the parent. A main communication task during the diagnostic period is to communicate information about the child's condition and special needs to the parent in terms that can be understood and remembered (Ley, 1989) and which will enable the parent to start adjusting to the reality of the child's condition. This includes specialised knowledge on the causes of the child's condition, its characteristics, and some of its potential consequences and future prognosis. Adequate information probably reduces the stress and anxiety of uncertainty and 'meaninglessness' (see references to Seligman and Darling, later in chapter). But many parents (74 per cent in Quine and Rutter's study, 1994) claim to have received insufficient information at the time of diagnosis; this fits in with the widespread dissatisfaction of patients generally in the lack of information received from hospital or general practitioners (see review by Ley, 1989).

Information is needed that can be understood and remembered (ibid.); but the content and process of communication requires careful consideration to achieve this. Many factors may reduce the parent's understanding of the professional's messages, such as differences in their understandings, their 'models' and conceptions of disability, causality and prognosis, and unfamiliarity of the medical vocabulary (Boyle, 1970). These can lead to errors in the parent's understanding (Ley, 1989). The following example shows how an apparently 'clear' message of diagnosis was interpreted in an unexpected way, as a result of a parent's pre-existing belief system.

A young woman was extremely shocked to learn that she had a baby with Down's syndrome. She continued to show total disbelief that this was possible weeks after the diagnosis was given. The paediatrician was puzzled that she was continuing to show such disbelief, until he found out that she believed that Down's syndrome babies could be born only to older mothers and never to younger mothers like herself. The paediatrician provided her with new information on the prevalence and causes of Down's syndrome. This information helped her to change her belief system on Down's syndrome, and, following this, she began to adapt to the diagnosis.

Effective communication depends not only on the successful transmission of the information, but also on a discerning awareness of the parent's understandings and other factors which may affect the communication process. In addition to the more cognitive aspects of information transmission, the affective style of the person communicating, i.e. a sympathetic approach, sensitivity and approachability, is likely to be as equal in importance (see Quine and Rutter, 1994). Chapter 4 gives guidelines on communicating professional expertise (see p 80).

A final point to consider here is that the communication of the child's diagnostic condition should not be seen as a discrete or short-term exercise. Some parents achieve a full understanding of what the professional is trying to communicate only through *direct experience and learning from their own child and situation*; this may take months, if not years in some cases. A father of a 16-year-old daughter with severe learning difficulties said 'It's only now that I realise what I should have realised right at the beginning ...' (Shared Concern film by SOPHIE/King's Fund). The professionals who may not have been involved in the initial disclosure, but who are involved with the family at a later date, may need to continue the learning process of the parent in ways that are responsive to the parent's own pace of understanding and development.

Starting negotiation

In the previous chapter, we began discussing the difficulty for a parent in shock to take control in any dialogue and activity with professionals. To assist greater parental control, it is advisable to negotiate sensitively and carefully whenever possible. This includes informing about and explaining the intervention or assistance, seeking consent before proceeding, and where possible, offering options to be selected. Questions to facilitate negotiation and greater control might include

Would you prefer to meet your health visitor at home or in hospital?

Is there anybody else you want to talk to at the moment?

Do you feel ready to meet the Portage worker and hear about the Portage service?

We would like to transfer Timothy to another specialist unit at the Donville Hospital. I'd like to tell you more about this, and then find out if you are willing for us to go ahead ...

The early period of negotiation should be viewed as part of the process of support and counselling that may be required during and after the diagnosis. The parent's own requests and needs should be responded to as fully as possible, and counselling assistance may help the parent to express their needs and concerns. Interventions should as far as possible keep to the parent's pace unless the child's condition demands immediate response (as in life-saving or urgent medical treatment). Any successful negotiation depends on insight into and understanding of what a parent is perceiving and feeling. But apart from time constraints and competing job demands (such as a clinic with a crowded waiting room) which can limit the professional's opportunity to learn about the parent (or willingness or ability to take on the parent's concerns, the professional may lack an understanding of the psychological reactions shown by the parent and how best to respond to these. A variety of conceptual frameworks is presented in the following section to help inform practice.

MAKING SENSE OF PARENTS' REACTIONS

Various psychological models have been put forward to describe and explain parents' reactions to the initial news or 'diagnosis'. None can fully encompass and explain the total range and intensity of reactions which parents may be experiencing, but all have generated useful ideas and guidance for practice. Because each model permits some prediction of what a parent might go through, the professional can be more prepared to respond in appropriate and beneficial ways. The models can be divided roughly between those that are *personal* (i.e. that view parental adjustment as mainly a problem within the parent or individual) and those that are *interpersonal* (i.e. that see adjustment as having a social dimension). Clearly, where one locates the source and process of adjustment has considerable implications for professional intervention.

As will be shown, some of the models can be usefully combined together to give a 'multiple-level' perspective (see Appendix 1.3). Nevertheless, the models all have their limitations and these should be given due consideration before being applied (see the *In perspective* sections following). Because research is still inconclusive about the superiority of any of the models (compared with the others) and each may give a useful, but partial perspective, the professional would be advised to use an eclectic approach (drawing on different models to make sense of varying reactions between and within parents). Use of the models to inform thinking should not be a substitute for active listening and learning from each parent individually; untested assumptions can block listening. Broader issues on the scope and limitation of conceptual frameworks have been discussed in Chapter 1, page 3.

The Stage Model

This model proposes that parents pass through a series of emotional stages before they accept a diagnosis of disability in their child. Many studies have referred to a sequence of stages (see review in Blacher, 1984a). The sequence of stages bears many similarities to that experienced by the bereaved in their reactions to death and dying.

Drotar *et al.* (1975) describe the following stages:

1. *shock*. Most parents' initial reaction is overwhelming shock, because they had anticipated a normal baby.
2. *denial*. Parents try to escape from the reality by disbelieving the diagnosis.
3. *sadness, anger, anxiety*. A common reaction is intense sadness and grieving, which accompanies or follows denial. Strong anger may also be expressed.
4. *adaptation*. Eventually the intense feelings subside and parents are able to care for their child.
5. *reorganisation*. Positive, long-term acceptance is finally developed.

Feelings of grief and mourning

During the early *traumatic* period, parents are likely to have a grief reaction or psychic crisis. During this period, which usually lasts from a few days following the disclosure to about twelve weeks (Cunningham and Sloper, 1977a), parents will go through a number of different stages or phases. See Table 3.1.

In perspective: the Stage Model

This *personal* model focuses on the emotional adjustments following diagnosis and predicts that parents will show an increased level of psychological distress in the early period (this has been borne out by various research studies, e.g. Burden, 1980). By classifying emotional reactions which have been found to be common in parents, it reduces the likelihood of these reactions being perceived as inappropriate, pathological or chaotic. Moreover, being aware of the *sequence* of stages enables a professional to intervene in an appropriate and timely fashion.

Though useful, the Stage Model has also been criticised robustly (e.g. Wikler *et al.*, 1981). It assumes a 'right' and a 'wrong' way of adjusting, and that parents who deviate from this 'normal' sequence are psychopathological. For example, parents who do not go through all the expected grief reactions tend to be labelled as 'denying' the handicap. But many of the studies which report on 'stages' are methodologically weak (see review by Blacher, 1984b). It is now recognised that not all parents

Table 3.1 Model of psychic crisis at disclosure of handicap

Parent is told	Psychic crisis	Manifestations		Needs
	Shock phase	Emotional disorganisation: confusion, paralysis of actions, disbelief, irrationality	Can last from 2 minutes to several days	Sympathy and emotional support
	Reaction phase	Expression of: sorrow, grief, disappointment, anxiety, aggression, denial, guilt, failure, defence mechanisms	A process of reintegration through discussion	Listen to parent. Catharsis through talking out. Sympathy but honesty. Facts on causes
Frequent oscillation between phases	Adaptation phase	Realistic appraisal: parents ask 'What can be done?' This is a signal of readiness to proceed with 'How can we help?'		Reliable and accurate information on medical and educational treatment and future
	Orientation phase	Parents begin to organise, seek help and information, plan for future		Provision of regular help and guidance in treatment
	Crisis over			Appropriate provision of services

Source: Cunningham, 1979. Reprinted with permission of Baillière Tindall

necessarily go through these stages in this order. Some will go through more than one stage at once, or go back and forwards between stages (that is, *oscillate* between stages – see Table 3.1). Others may miss out a stage. Depending on the circumstances of the diagnosis, not all parents show a grief reaction, but may show relief instead (see p. 60).

Is there a final adjustment?

The idea of adjustment as a linear process, leading to a final stage of acceptance, has also been questioned. Professionals adopting a 'stage' viewpoint have tended to label parents who continue to show grief or anger over time as unaccepting or poorly adjusted and 'stuck' at a particular stage. This is commonly phrased as 'she's not yet come to terms with her child's handicap'.

But parents argue that this is not a helpful response from professionals. Some claim that they accept *their child*, but never fully come to accept the disability (Russell, 1983). Some talk of adjustment as a continual *cyclical* process: they may accept their child's condition at one period of childhood, but then find it more distressing and difficult at another period of the life-cycle (Wikler *et al.*, 1981). Examples include feeling positive about seeing one's child in a nursery group, but becoming more distressed when seeing one's child falling behind its peers at primary school, or accepting dependency in one's child when it is normally appropriate for peers, but becoming distressed and resentful when one's child is still dependent in adolescence.

The following Chronic Sorrow Model takes more account of the complexity of long-term grieving or recurring distress than the Stage Model.

The Chronic Sorrow Model

Chronic sorrow in parents is a natural reaction and its continued presence many years later is not pathological, according to the theory by Olshansky, 1962. It is argued that parents may experience periods of grieving at later stages of their child's life, without the parent being poorly adjusted. Chronic sorrow and *acceptance of a child's disability* can coexist alongside each other as part of the normal long-term process of parental adjustment. A parent who continues to feel sadness about a child's disability can still be competent and caring.

The Personal Construct Model

In contrast to the previous two models, this third model focuses on cognitive *interpretations* rather than emotional reactions. It proposes that parents differ in their reactions to disability because they bring different interpretations to the situation, and these interpretations stem from their previous expectations of themselves and their child (Davis and Cunningham, 1985, Cunningham and Davis, 1985).

Davis and Cunningham derive their model from the theory of Personal Constructs (Kelly, 1955) which postulates that people construct mental models in order to anticipate events. A basic assumption of the model is that all people are concerned to anticipate what happens to them and those around them. A principal need is to make sense of the world, to be able to make accurate predictions, so that they can then adjust adequately to their situation. To make the world meaningful in this way, each person constructs in their head a model of events; the mental model or 'construct' is built on the basis of the individual's experience. The mental model is used to guide their behaviour, and to interpret events or the behaviour of others on the basis of what is already understood of such events or behaviours.

Prospective parents build up a set of constructs during pregnancy about their future child and how they imagine their future parenthood and family life. Parents expect or at least hope for a 'normal' child. A diagnosis of disability leads to an *extreme crisis*, a situation outside their range of constructs, leading to *massive anxiety*. The parents may not have anticipated having a child with special needs, so their predictions about their child from the period of pregnancy are invalidated. The parents may know little or nothing about such children, in terms of causes or characteristics of the child's condition or its future development. If a prime motive of people is to understand and anticipate, parents in this situation must be highly vulnerable. They will be in a state of considerable *confusion and uncertainty*, experienced as numbness and shock.

They will also be drawing on their own previous construct of disability, which is generally very negative in Western society (see pp. 48–9) and may be filled with a 'nightmarish vision' of what their child will become (Ballard, 1979). Figure 3.1 shows the impact of diagnosis on personal constructs.

After initial intense reactions, this model predicts that parents may then set about rebuilding a framework to enable them to understand. They start to ask questions (to gain information for reconstructing their constructs). They need to know the causes of the disorder, what can be done about it, and what the future will hold, e.g. Will she walk? When will she talk? How will it affect our other children?

Gradually, most parents will reorientate themselves in terms of being able to *understand their situation* sufficiently well that they can set about the process of adapting to it. They begin to form a clearer idea about their child's condition and future possibilities. They may be ready to start assessing some of their current needs to help them care for their child.

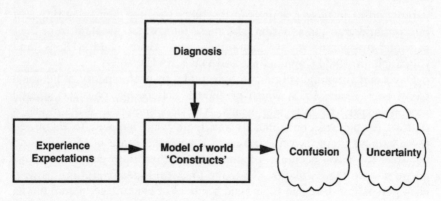

Figure 3.1 Impact of diagnosis on personal constructs

This model is also able to explain why for some parents diagnosis is a relief – a late evolutionary diagnosis confirms what they have suspected and felt confused about for a long time. 'At least we know what's the matter with her now – we knew there was something wrong all along ...' They can now start the process of adaptation because their own interpretations have been confirmed or clarified.

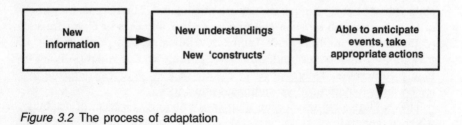

Figure 3.2 The process of adaptation

In perspective: the Personal Construct Model

This model has particular value in highlighting the importance of approaching each parent as an individual with their own perspective (their own set of understandings or constructs of their world), and this insight may be crucial for partnership work. '*If we are to work in a respectful partnership with parents we have to accept the reality of their interpretations and not oppose or ignore them*'. (Cunningham and Davis, 1985, p. 26). This recognition of multiple perspectives and individual diversity provides a sound basis for working in an anti-discriminatory way with diverse parents, and has been very influential in the development of the Negotiating Model.

Because constructs in the mind are viewed as developing through a dynamic process between internal organisation and external experience and interactions with others (and this model therefore embodies an *inter-personal* interpretation), it follows that certain experiences may facilitate (or undermine) personal adjustment for some parents. Counselling assistance from the professional may aid reorganisation of the parent's constructs. Either partner may need to change their constructs or perceptions as a result of their experiences with the other. Moreover, adaptation is not viewed as absolute, but relative to the parent's situation at the time. Readjustment will occur (and constructs be re-worked) if the child does not develop as expected or if new events occur, such as the diagnosis of further impairment or the beginning or leaving of school.

But various criticisms have been put forward of Personal Construct as a theory, though there is not space to discuss them in detail here. Briefly, one 'criticism is that the theory emphasises conscious thought processes and does not address itself to possible unconscious determinants of behaviour (cf. psychoanalytic theory). Secondly, it has been criticised as neglecting emotions (but Cunningham and Davis [1985] argue that the emotional reactions proposed in Stage theory can be re-explained in cognitive terms). Thirdly, from a methodological point of view, the theory is difficult to test for validity because of difficulty in observing and systematically measuring mental models of the mind (see Neimeyer, 1985).

The Model of Meaninglessness and Powerlessness

Two disturbing experiences on becoming the parent of a child with a special need are described by some parents: a sense of meaninglessness and a sense of powerlessness. Seligman and Darling (1989) draw on Symbolic Interactionist theory (a sociological approach to social psychology derived from George Herbert Mead, Charles Horton Cooley and others) to explain these reactions.

This approach suggests that beliefs, values and knowledge are socially determined through interaction and the ability of individuals to 'take the role of the other' or understand the meanings attached to situations by other people. This view of human behaviour focuses on social processes rather than on static characteristics of individuals (and is an *interpersonal* theory). When applied to families of children with disabilities, parental reactions would be interpreted within the context of their interactional histories prior to their child's birth and their experiences afterwards. Parents attach meanings to their experiences as a result of definitions they have encountered in their interactions with others, particularly with *significant* others (usually close family members and friends). How others define their situation will affect how they define it themselves.

Seligman and Darling claim that feelings of powerlessness and meaninglessness (both components of the sociological concept of *anomie* or
normlessness) are commonly experienced by parents of disabled
newborns. Although powerlessness is frequently experienced by all
parents of newborns in the professionally controlled setting of the delivery
room and the hospital, this feeling is intensified if events around the birth
do not proceed according to expectation and if concerns of the medical
staff are not revealed directly to the parents. The parent may pick up
unintentional cues from the staff that something is wrong, but be in a
helpless state of submission to professional authority. Feelings of meaninglessness may be deliberately created by medical staff withholding
information in the belief that they are protecting the parents 'who are not
ready to hear the truth'. The resulting uncertainty and suspicion on the
part of parents may, however, be more stressful than the news itself.

During the early months, the parents will be typically motivated by a
strong need to reduce their sense of meaninglessness and powerlessness.
Diagnostic information, when it comes, may relieve some of the stress
and sense of meaninglessness, although this sense may continue if the
parent is given only limited information. The feeling of powerlessness will
not abate, however, until the parent is able to begin to *do* something
about the child's condition.

By the end of the infancy period, most parents have resolved their
anomie. They may still be angry or disappointed by their child's disabilities, but they are beginning to understand them and feel more in control
of their situation. Their child's disability may begin to decline in relative
importance in their lives, and they can start resuming concerns with other
family members, careers, leisure activities. The extent to which a family
can return to a 'normalised' lifestyle will vary according to the nature of
the child's disability, the available social supports, and the positive viewpoints of significant others, as well as other factors.

In perspective: the Model of Meaninglessness and Powerlessness

This model has similarities to the Personal Construct Model: it emphasises
the way that diagnosis shatters previous understandings and expectations
of the parent and the importance of re-creating a framework of meaning.
Attention is drawn to the social interactional dimension of parental
reactions and the contributory role of 'significant others' (including professionals) to the process of adjustment. Importantly, difference in the
power positions of the parent and professional are seen as underlying the
parent's sense of powerlessness and anomie (destructive feelings that need
to be overcome in order to regain a real personal recovery and adaptation). This model and its predictions give further support to the case for
partnership and negotiation between the professional and parent; it would

suggest that moves towards more shared control would facilitate a parent's ability to resume a more 'normal' lifestyle.

Although these negative experiences appear to be widely experienced (e.g. Darling, 1979, Quine and Rutter, 1994), the extent to which all parents of disabled children go through them has not been established empirically. Because the theory focuses on interactions and does not address social structures (a common criticism of symbolic interactionism; see review by Meltzer *et al.*, 1975), further work will be needed on mapping the social and organisational structures and procedures that contribute to professionals evoking feelings of powerlessness in the parent.

Parents from ethnic/cultural variations

The literature on families of disabled children has tended to neglect or marginalise ethnic/cultural variation and professionals (generally from a middle-class and often majority cultural background) are inclined to adopt views and attitudes from their sector of society. The inappropriateness of this for working with the many social/cultural variations of a pluralistic society has been demonstrated by Milton Seligman and Rosalyn Darling (1989) in their review of cultural reactions to disability in the United States. Values important to a particular sector of society will affect the meaning they attach to disability. For example, moderate learning difficulties may be viewed as a devastating condition by middle-class parents and professionals (who share similar values of achievement and educational and occupational aspirations); but some working-class parents may not even define it as a disability (e.g. Holt, 1958, Seligman and Darling, 1989). The family unit is highly valued in sectors of minority Asian, Japanese and Chinese groups. Family problems may be regarded as private, and there may be a reticence to reveal coping difficulties to an outsider (see Seligman and Darling, 1989). Family counselling, rather than individual counselling, may be more appropriate for some families, also an awareness by the professional of how the family defines its own situation within the context of its social–cultural world.

Misunderstandings between parents and professionals of different social–cultural backgrounds are shown in assumptions and beliefs about the reactions of parents with ethnic minorities, that are frequently untested and rooted in ignorance, assumptions or hearsay (Shah, 1992). Examples of these include comments like 'the Asian male is the dominant figure in the household and all communications should be through him', or 'Asian parents see the birth of a disabled child as a punishment for sins or a test from God' (ibid.), or 'isn't it a pity that Moslem fathers reject girl babies if they have a disability', or 'Chinese people stick to their own and won't come out to parents' groups'. When stereotypical views are combined with negative valuing, they form the basis of prejudice against a minority group, but all stereotyping tends to exclude and to restrict an ethnic population. As Shah points out, there are some parents of the cultural group who will express and confirm assumed practices, but there will be many others who are not represented by them.

There are a number of major principles that Shah puts over, in her book on Asian families with children with disabilities, that need to inform any attempt to understand a parent from an ethnic minority. The first is the importance of recognising that disability 'creates similarly profound emotional, practical and psychological experiences for all parents, whoever they are' (Shah, 1992: 21) and the same kind of sensitivities, support and assistance that is offered to other parents should be extended to parents of ethnic minorities. The second is to realise the heterogeneity of any ethnic group and not to assume beliefs and practices for the individual parent and family. Although it is important to become informed and knowledgeable about ethnic/cultural differences, the religious and cultural practices of sectors of a specific ethnic group (and the possible meanings ascribed to disability in the group – see previously), the diversity *within* the group needs to be recognised and responded to. This means that the beliefs and practices of each parent can be understood only through learning from the parent directly. As Shah points out 'looking for differences where none exist or assuming homogeneity of feelings when differences need to be identified is a form of cultural racism'. The third point is that there are many barriers to communication and understanding in both directions and the professional will need to work hard and persevere at reaching a shared understanding (see Chapter 4). Listening to parents and consulting their views are the most valuable means of finding out about their experiences and feelings, the kind of services and assistance they need, how services can become acceptable to that particular ethnic group, and beginning to respond to and overcome their concerns and negative experiences in relation to using services and other wider community supports.

But even with greater cultural sensitivity of the professional, a parent may still prefer assistance from and work more successfully with a professional (such as an ethnic community adviser) from the same cultural background and, wherever possible, this should be offered as an option (e.g. Bangladeshi Parent Advisers at the Parent Advisory Service Tower Hamlets [p. 188] and the KIDS Family Centre [see Chapter 10]). But the quality of the relationship needs taking into account (as well as issues of gender, class and religious background) even when the professional and parent come from the same ethnic group. Sharing a common language is not sufficient to facilitate communication if the relationship between the two parties is not grounded in partnership practice (Davis *et al.*, 1994). I recall one home visit where a Vietnamese woman who had deserted her husband, because he had abused their disabled daughter, experienced the Vietnamese male interpreter as accusatory and disbelieving.

Trained interpreters may be required for assisting communication. But working through an interpreter is not easy and may make it difficult to build up an effective relationship between the professional and the family. Nevertheless, without an appropriate *partnership* relationship between the professional and the family, the help provided by the interpreter to the family will be minimised (ibid.).

Most of the conceptual models described previously suggest that many of the early intense negative reactions to disability can be resolved in time and parents may then resume a more 'normal' lifestyle. But some difficult and disturbing feelings and perceptions may persist in the longer term or recur at later dates for some parents (see following section).

LATER EMOTIONAL REACTIONS IN PARENTS – AND PROFESSIONALS

Using a *personal* approach to parental reactions, MacKeith (1973) drew up a classification list of negative feelings which could be found in parents at early and later periods in the life-cycle. This list has been cited frequently in the literature and includes the following:

- Protectiveness of the helpless, e.g. fiercely protective feelings towards the baby and child and wanting to protect them from any danger or discomfort or risks
- Revulsion at the abnormal, e.g. feeling a sense of unease, discomfort and revulsion towards people with a disability
- Inadequacy of reproduction, e.g. feeling that there is something wrong with themselves as parents because they have produced an 'imperfect' child
- Inadequacy of rearing, e.g. feeling that they are inadequate parents who are not able to look after their disabled child properly, or that it is their inadequacy as parents which has contributed to their child's behaviour/learning difficulties and problems
- Anger, e.g. feeling angry, bitter and cheated with 'life' and 'fate' for giving them a disabled child
- Grief, e.g. grief for the problems of the existing child or grief for the imagined child that was expected during pregnancy and never came, a sense of loss
- Shock, that is feelings of acute numbness, disbelief, unable to take in information, senses not working properly, sense of detachment and outside oneself, total internal turmoil

- Guilt, e.g. feeling guilty when things go wrong for their child, feeling that the disabled child is a punishment for something the parent has done in previous life
- Embarrassment, e.g. not knowing how to behave in a certain situation and worrying about what other people are thinking (such as not knowing how to tell friends and neighbours about the diagnosis, embarrassed about how the child is behaving in public, worrying about strangers' reactions).

Newson and Hipgrave (1982), discussing MacKeith's list, comment that parents of young and older children with disabilities do experience complicated and mixed emotions. Parents may wonder whether they are very odd in having such emotions, and if they think they are abnormal they may hide their emotions away from other parents and professionals. As Newson and Hipgrave point out, nobody can take away disturbing emotions altogether, but it may help parents to cope with them if they can understand them better. In particular, it may help if they are brought out into the open and discussed with other people who have gone through the same experience. It can be useful too for professionals to understand that they also experience a mixture of emotions, some of them not dissimilar from the parents' reactions (ibid., Cunningham and Davis, 1985), which can intrude on intervention (see further p. 50).

Redressing the balance: the positive reactions

But even though parents may experience some or all of the above feelings at some time in their child's life (and these feelings can recur at different times), many parents talk about many positive experiences and feelings too (e.g. Darling, 1979, Byrne *et al.*, 1988). Although the characteristics of some childhood disabilities may impede the formation of early parent–infant attachments (such as physical fragility, abnormal response patterns to parental nurturing efforts, no response to communication, unpleasant crying, delayed smiling, feeding difficulties, e.g. Waechter, 1977 and Blacher, 1984b), many parents grow in time to love and deeply value and cherish their child. 'The tremendous adaptive capacity of families is evidenced by the fact that given all the obstacles to the parent–child attachment present in the case of childhood disability, the vast majority do form strong attachments to their disabled infants' (Seligman and Darling, 1989, p. 38).

Caring parents who value and cherish their child may then find themselves at odds with other members of society (including some professionals and societal institutions) who continue to uphold the negative societal view of disability. There has been a tendency until recently for researchers and practitioners to focus on the negative and pathological reactions of parents (see Chapters 3 and 5), at the cost of recognising *the positive side* of being a parent of a child with special needs. This 'pathologising' of the parental experience is reflected in the strongly held view, until recently, that all parents of disabled children suffer from guilt (see MacKeith, 1973).

This assertion of the negative consequences of disability by the professional can be potentially destructive for parents and children, particularly in the longer term. It may strike dissonance with the parent's own viewpoint and experience. For example, parents resent being told not to feel guilty when they perceive themselves as not feeling it (evidence of widespread guilt has not been supported by empirical research either, see review by McConachie, 1986). Moreover, it is now understood from research that much of a parent's strengths and coping resources come from a positive attitude and orientation to their life situation (see Chapter 5); hence, ignoring the positive aspects of the child and the family's life with the child potentially undermines a parent's adaptation. Parents who strive to maintain a 'normal' relationship with their child and a 'normal' lifestyle may be criticised as 'denying the handicap' or being 'unrealistic', even though strong, cohesive family relationships are a strong predictor of family adaptation (see Chapter 5). A final point is that a negative approach by the professional upholds the prevailing discriminatory and devaluing attitude towards disabled people in society, which in turn contributes to the injustice of segregation and long-term disadvantage for the child and whole family.

So far, we have examined the diversity and complexity of the parental perspective, including positive and negative reactions to a child with disability. A developmental perspective has been shown to be useful in thinking about the changing reactions of parents over time and through different experiences. Some conceptual models have focused on the personal level and inner psychological reactions; others have focused on the social and interpersonal influences. Both seem to have an important bearing on the process of parental adjustment to disability. Although we have touched on possible parallels and differences between the parent's and professional's perspectives, we need to look further at how they might come together in a partnership relationship.

INTERACTIONS BETWEEN THE PARENT'S AND PROFESSIONAL'S PERSPECTIVES

Valuing the parent's viewpoint

One way in which professionals have traditionally maintained their expert power (see p. 6) is through their use of language, and one example of this is through *labelling*. Professionals have tended to talk of parents from their point of view. Parents have been labelled as 'unrealistic', 'denying', 'depressed', 'over-anxious', 'demanding', 'angry', 'not coping', 'dysfunctional'.

A main function of these labels and statements is to categorise. Parents of disabled children are treated as a separate group, and categorised in terms that may devalue and denigrate, pathologise or make blameworthy. The problem about this labelling is that it tends to place parents in a particular position, and thus restrict their options or subordinate them to the dominant power of the professional. It ignores the authenticity of the parent's standpoint, treats the parent and family as alien and 'other' and takes little account of the *relationship* and transactions between the parent and professional.

Devaluing the parent's perspective is contrary to the position advocated by the Negotiating Model (see Chapter 1), which is of the *equivalent worth* of the parent and professional's perspectives. Valuing and being willing to work with the parent's point of view is a crucial basis for successful negotiating. Some useful techniques for getting to appreciate the parent's perspective include active listening (see Chapter 4), perspective-taking and re-framing (see Chapter 6), as well as becoming more informed of the process of psychological adjustment in the parent and of the parent's role position and options. Role play has been used as a valuable training tool for enhancing insight into the parent's perspective, on the Tavistock Centre training course (see p. 28). But this process of reaching increased understanding and positive valuing is not always straightforward: we turn now to some potential problems.

Getting in touch with the parent

Various difficulties may get in the way of becoming attuned to the parent's perceptions and feelings. A first difficulty is not being able to discern these. Some parents may not want to reveal their feelings, and others give contradictory signals (such as saying that they are fine, but coming across as depressed). Some express feelings and views that are very different to the professional's, which may confuse the latter. One mother said, '*Well, thank God, he's only got Down's syndrome. It could be worse*' to her bemused health visitor.

Secondly, parents may express intense feelings (such as grief, anxiety, depression) which can overwhelm the professional (who then leaves the meeting feeling drained and emotionally burdened). The professional may find it anxiety-provoking and distressing to get too close to a parent who is in an intense emotional state. A third possible problem is that a professional may not pick up or understand what a parent is going through because they have not gone through such experiences and have had little experience of grief or trauma in their own life. The professional may lack the imagination or empathic intuition to have insight into the parent's reactions. Their own views, feelings and background as a professional may be very different from those of the parent.

Unfortunately a professional who finds it difficult to get in touch with a parent and is too distant from the parent's experience might respond in a number of unconstructive ways. They might adopt a number of defensive reactions against discomfort and anxiety, such as avoidance of the parent, detachment and lack of empathy, which may lead to responding in ways that are inappropriate for the parent. They may be inappropriately cheerful or give false reassurance, may selectively attend to or ignore certain cues, may rush into activity or advice-giving too quickly, robbing some parents of the chance to bear, and then manage, their own pain of their child's limitations (Daws, 1984). They may also judge the parent critically or discount or devalue the parent's reactions. Any of these responses may be experienced as unhelpful by the parent and may fail to meet the parent's real needs.

This strongly suggests that *developing empathy* is an essential skill and ability for working in partnership with parents. Supervision, peer consultancy and cultural advice from families and ethnic advisers may be important for helping a professional reach a greater understanding of parents, including those who are less familiar culturally. But in addition, assistance may be needed to help one look at one's feelings and reactions and to manage the difficult and anxiety-provoking feelings which can be evoked by greater empathy and closeness to the parent (see Chapter 12, p. 290). Lack of appropriate help could lead to the problem outlined below.

'Mirroring' the parent's reactions

Closeness between the professional and parent's experiences and viewpoints (e.g. when the professional also has a disabled child, or shares the same cultural or social background) may tend towards the professional identifying too closely with the parent's situation. They may 'project' themselves onto the parent's situation and presume certain reactions and viewpoints (which they may have had in the same situation), which may be invalid for the other person. They may find the parent's emotional reactions overwhelming and disturbing because they reactivate similar emotions in themselves.

If too closely identified with a parent, the professional's reactions may *'mirror'* the parent's. The potential for the whole professional system to 'mirror' the family has already been acknowledged in work with child sexual abuse (Dimmock and Dungworth, 1985). 'Learned helplessness' (Beck, 1976) in the parent may be mirrored by the professional feeling helpless and despondent; anger in the parent may trigger feelings of defensiveness, followed by retaliatory anger in the professional. One of the dangers of this kind of mirroring is that it can lead to a pattern of *circular causation* and *escalation*: the parent feels helpless, leading to the involved professional also feeling helpless and being unable to take constructive action to help the parent, which in turn reinforces the parent's sense of helplessness.

Any professional needs to tread a delicate balance between *empathy and understanding of the parent's perspective* and sufficient detachment to maintain *a separate professional viewpoint and perspective*. They need to be aware of the possible process of mirroring, its potential benefit for heightened empathy, but also its risk of negative knock-on effects.

SOCIETY, SERVICES AND PARENTAL REACTIONS

As the child grows older, not all of the parents' emotional reactions on issues to do with their child can be reckoned to arise directly from grief about the child's disability (as used to be believed, see p. 56). Their reactions may be a response to interactional and social experiences arising from having a disabled child (as was shown earlier). Even though parents feel positively about many individual professionals (Byrne *et al.*, 1988), surveys show widespread and fairly uniform dissatisfaction on aspects of their professional services. In fact, problems in contact with services were often felt to be of greater importance than problems arising directly out of the child's disability (Lloyd-Bostock, 1976). Parents have reported negative views and feelings on the lack of services or insufficient help; slow responses and delays; inaccessible, poorly coordinated or disorganised provision; and rapid staff turn-over and lack of continuity in assistance. With relation to individual professionals, they may feel negatively about poor communication, impersonal and insensitive intervention, lack of availability, lack of technical competence and lack of specialist knowledge (e.g. Lloyd-Bostock, 1976, Reid, 1983, Ayer and Alaszewski, 1984, Pahl and Quine, 1984, Ineichen, 1986). Complaints are made about generic service providers not being sufficiently well informed and parents having to become the experts on their children (Lloyd-Bostock, 1976).

In the Manchester Down's syndrome cohort study, Byrne *et al.* (1988) maintained that the professionals who failed to meet the parents' perceptions of their needs and their child's needs, or who did not involve the parents and show respect to them, were more likely to be perceived as unhelpful and to arouse negative feelings. This particularly applied to professionals who were perceived as having a specific teaching or advisory role and having skills to impart to the parent, such as speech therapists, physiotherapists, home teachers, and psychologists. Professionals who did not liaise effectively with other services and agencies were more likely to be experienced negatively; this especially applied to health visitors and social workers.

These findings throw a different light on professional attempts to help parents have more positive feelings and views about themselves, their child and their life experiences. Rather than working solely with the parent's feelings, assistance could as beneficially be targeted at changing the quality of professionals' interactions with parents, the quality and structure of service provision and its interface with the family, and the attitudes and opportunities (or lack of opportunity) offered by the wider society to children with special needs and their families.

To summarise, in this chapter we have considered the impact of having a child with special needs on the parent. The reactions and feelings of parents have been related to a changing process of inner psychological adjustment at the *personal level* and also to transactional experiences and social influences at the *interpersonal* level. The importance of recognising both aspects was highlighted in the diagnosis-giving period; although parents seem generally to experience intense and distressing reactions to the 'news' which have to be resolved individually, the transactions between the parent and professionals can serve to strengthen or undermine this adjustment. Conceptual frameworks of parental reactions and their under-lying mechanisms were presented to provide a basis for informed and supportive assistance. The importance of approaching each parent indi-vidually and not imposing assumptions was emphasised. As part of a partnership approach, ideas have been given for working towards height-ened empathy, sensitivity and appreciation of the parent. The potential risk of over-identification and negative 'mirroring' has also been discussed.

In the next chapter, we shall go a step further in looking at how the parental and professional perspectives can be brought together through practical communicational skills, such as active listening and negotiation.

PROFESSIONAL DEVELOPMENT EXERCISES

EXERCISE 3.1 MY VIEWS ON CHILDHOOD DISABILITY AND ON PARENTS' REACTIONS TO DISABILITY

(Exercise adapted from Dale and Woollett, 1989)

The following comments are genuine examples from parents who have a disabled child or a child with special needs.

Read each comment and then write down your immediate feelings on a separate sheet of paper (note, there are no right or wrong responses). Then write down what you might say in response (imagining that you were there as a professional).

1. Our child isn't different from any other child; we don't think of her as handicapped.
2. Sometimes I see a lovely baby; other times I see a monster.
3. If the tests show that my next baby is also affected, I'll go for an abortion.
4. I blame the school, he never had any good teaching.
5. We're thinking of having the baby adopted; we've never had this kind of thing in the family.
6. I feel devastated – this isn't the baby I was waiting for.
7. I'm going to give up everything for this child; he's going to need all my time and attention.
8. I don't think any parent should feel guilty about rejecting their handicapped baby. We all have a right to our own lives.
9. Our child is a joy and pleasure to us. We've never felt any different, right from her birth.
10. I'll never forgive that doctor. It's his fault that the baby's handicapped.
11. I wouldn't dream of sending him away from home to respite – it would seem like a rejection.
12. I don't want to do anything different for her than I've done with my two older children. They should all be treated the same.

Look critically at your responses: what do they reveal about your attitudes and views on childhood disability and on parents? Consider the potential implications (negative and positive) for your intervention with parents and children with disability. Write your responses to these issues on the separate sheet of paper.

EXERCISE 3.2 YOUR UNIT OR TEAM'S APPROACH TO DISCLOSURE OF DISABILITY

Consider your unit or team's policy and practice in giving a diagnosis or disclosure of disability/special needs, and of assisting parents through and after the disclosure. (Your unit or team may be involved in only part of the diagnostic procedure, and if this is the case, think about the extent and limit of your unit or team's responsibilities.) Look at each of the following questions and write down your responses on a separate sheet.

1. Is there a written policy, set of guidelines and established form of procedure?

2. What is the usual form of procedure?
   Who has responsibility for organising the procedure?
   Who breaks the news?
   How is it done? – where, with which members of the family, how?
   How is it followed up – by whom, where, in what way?

3. How is the actual disclosure linked to later support to the family? What kind of support is offered and by whom?

4. Does the procedure differ in a late diagnosis or 'evolutionary diagnosis' (i.e. where the nature of the child's condition emerges only as the child grows and develops further)? And how?

5. How do parents fit in with the general procedure? Who checks what the parents understand from the professionals? Are they permitted to negotiate and is their consent sought about intervention following the diagnosis?

6. In light of your reading of the Guidelines in Appendix 3.1,
   - are you satisfied with the procedure followed by your unit or team or would you like to see changes?
   - are you satisfied with the way that staff relate to parents or would you like to see changes?
   - are you satisfied with the extent and limit of your unit or team's responsibilities and how it fits in with those of other units, teams or other professionals?
   - what are the main changes you would recommend implementing?
   - what are some of the constraints prohibiting setting up these changes? Can they be overcome?

Summarise your conclusions in writing.

APPENDICES

APPENDIX 3.1 GUIDELINES ON GIVING A DIAGNOSIS OF DISABILITY

These general guidelines are a summary of the recommendations from various research studies, parental surveys and interdisciplinary reports. They would need to be applied flexibly to suit the individual needs, wishes and background of the parent and family and the particular circumstances of the diagnosis-giving unit.

It is recommended that telling should be:

1. done by a consultant paediatrician (if giving a medically-based diagnosis) and if possible with a specialist health visitor present (or similar professional who will be able to maintain regular contact with the family and make links between the hospital and community services). With education assessments of learning difficulties, telling should be done by the relevant senior professional who has been most involved in the assessment and is familiar to the family, such as an educational psychologist, a speech therapist.

2. done as soon as possible, except in cases of maternal ill-health. Even if staff are unsure of the exact nature of the impairment, telling should be done as soon as a disability is suspected. Parents should be given honest answers when they suspect something might be wrong. They should feel part of the process of diagnosis and go through it together with the professionals.

3. done with both parents together (unless they choose not to). Single parents should be accompanied by a friend or relative. A couple may want other relatives to be present too. A parent of an ethnic minority may need an interpreter and ethnic community representative (if chosen by the parent); this is essential if the parent lacks fluency in English.

4. done in a private place with no other professionals or other persons present (unless they are also involved in breaking the news), and where they will be undisturbed.

5. done with the infant present, except if very ill and in special care. This may not be appropriate for older children who may need to be told separately of their special needs. The baby should be held and talked about as a *person of worth*, not a problem, e.g. naming the child.

6. done directly, and parents given as much time as they wish to ask questions. A balanced viewpoint should be transmitted rather than a catalogue of possible problems; this includes positive aspects as well as some of the possible difficulties. Many parents talk about the importance of being given hope, including what the child may be able to do (not only the medical defects or what they will not be able to do). Questions need to be answered fully, but simply.

7. done with a sympathetic, caring, humane attitude. It is important to be in touch with where the parents are – they may be in a state of shock and unable to take in much verbal information.

8. done with an arrangement made for the health visitor or another key support person to see the parents again as soon as they want and a contact phone number to use, and reassurance that this professional will help to answer their questions and see them regularly. Where a diagnosis is made at birth, the community health visitor may be invited to meet the parents and infant in the hospital.

9. done in a private place where parents can be together immediately after the interview for as long as they need.

10. followed by an interview with the paediatrician and health visitor (or other professionals giving the assessment) twenty-four hours after disclosure. The parents may need at least two or three further meetings soon after the disclosure so that they can gradually assimilate all the information. It is advisable to check out what the parents have understood so far, so that the professional can pick up whether further information or clarification is needed. The parents may need help to ask questions.

In the case of an *evolutionary diagnosis*, where it is not clear immediately the exact nature of the condition, regular appointments should be made with the parent for review of progress and of results of investigations, to continue the process of understanding the diagnosis. Parents need to be given information about what is happening and kept fully in the picture. If parents are the first to identify a problem (as is often the case), it is particularly important that their own concerns should be taken seriously and not dismissed.

11. followed up with a written summary given to the parents, including information of the child's condition, details of further sources of help, and the name and telephone number of a key support worker (such as the health visitor for the family). It is advisable to write down other details if the parent asks for them to be written down. This summary needs to be translated into the parent's mother tongue if different from English.

12. followed up with an offer to have contact with another parent of a similar child (about half of their sample wanted this, Cunningham, 1983). Some parents find this very helpful, but others do not want to meet another parent with a similar child at this stage.

13. followed up with an offer to talk to other family members or advise parents on how to cope with other people's reactions (McConachie, 1991a). Parents can feel very isolated when faced with breaking the news to family and friends, and anxious about other people's reactions and may need help to tell others.

14. followed, in subsequent weeks, by coordination of support in the community with support at the hospital (or other agency giving the diagnosis/assessment) and to involve:
    (1) opportunities to go over the initial information given, and to discuss the implications of the child's possible future,
    (2) supportive counselling to be offered in the parent's own home,
    (3) information given on services and benefits.
15. followed by the introduction of the parents to a service offering practical advice and assistance, such as a Portage home learning service. It is beneficial to give parents some hope early on, and a view that there is something constructive they can do to help their child.
16. followed by the appointing of a key worker whose role is to help pace the flow of information to the parents, so that they are not bombarded with professional visitors in the first few weeks after diagnosis or later on.

(Derived from Cunningham *et al.*, 1984, Quine and Pahl, 1987, Cottrell and Summers, 1990.)

Chapter 4

Communicating and negotiating

I'm sorry, I haven't got time to talk to his parents today. ...

I get so frustrated ... the speech therapist never listens to me. ...

Because talking and listening are central to cooperation, communication issues are discussed throughout this book. But in this chapter, three forms of communication are given special attention because of their relevance for the partnership relationship and also for increasing the parents' and family members' wellbeing.

It is somewhat artificial to break communication down into discrete 'approaches', since communication is often a flowing two-way process with one 'approach' merging into another as each partner contributes and shifts the process along. But whilst over-simplifying the creativity and richness of dialogue, three 'approaches' have been parcelled out and examined separately in this chapter because of their significance for partnership work:

1. the transmission of professional expertise,
2. listening to the parent, and
3. problem-solving (guided and negotiated).

Negotiated problem-solving is of particular interest because of its integral role in the Negotiating Model (see p. 14). Dissent and disagreement between the partners is one possible outcome of negotiation, and this is discussed further in this chapter.

Communication proceeds within a relationship where each partner takes up particular role and power positions which affect the kind of communications possible and how these are received and interpreted. We start, therefore, with a brief consideration of the impact of relationship positions and transactions.

POSITIONS AND MESSAGES

Some of the role and power positions and differences between professionals and parents (and children) have already been discussed in Chapter 1 (pp. 4–8). Within this context any verbal message might signify something about the role relationship and their positions within it. How it is received by the listener might also reveal something about their interpretations and expectancies of the relationship.

The same message could have multiple meanings, depending on who communicates it and how it is 'read' and interpreted by the listener (as shown in the following example).

> When one professional announced, 'Now Bertram's three, he could start at the nursery class of the school for physically disabled children. It's an excellent school. Would you like to go and visit it?', the receiving parent 'read' this as meaning 'since I'm the expert and I'm telling you it's a good place, I'm strongly advising you to visit it.'
>
> A similar message to another parent might be 'read' as meaning 'it's a very good school, but I want you to feel happy about where your son goes. You must decide what you want to do.'

In this instance, the impact of the message in terms of its function to persuade or to share control was affected by how each parent interpreted their role relationship. There are a variety of possible ways of thinking about positioning in verbal transactions which could be useful for informing partnership work, such as the dimensions of conflict resolution described on p. 91. Discourse analysis has been used to show how language serves to underline power differentials. In an analysis of the exchanges between some educational professionals and a parent during an educational case conference, Marks (1992) showed how the verbal and non-verbal messages used by the professionals served to marginalise the mother and leave her out of the debate. Overly familiar references to her as 'Mum' (who must not be allowed to get 'upset') emphasised her subordinate and passive role.

We turn now to the first communication approach: the transmission of professional knowledge and expertise to the parent.

COMMUNICATING THE PROFESSIONAL'S VIEWPOINT

Professionals have specialist information which may be useful, if not vital, for them to impart to parents and other family members. They may have to inform a parent about the child's diagnosis and health, social and educational possibilities, and special educational needs. They will need to talk about services and treatment options. They may need to explain the purpose and procedure of an assessment; they may need to discuss a professional report. The parent will need to be adequately informed to make an informed consent to any procedure or intervention planned by the professional. Moreover, professionals have specialist skills which they may wish to impart to a parent, such as teaching methods, ways of managing child behaviour, or administering medical treatment.

Since the 1960s, there has been an increase in informing parents about professional decisions (e.g. medical decisions [Alderson, 1990]), and there are cited examples of individual professionals communicating clearly and sympathetically to parents (e.g. cardiac surgeons helping parents to make agonising decisions on whether to subject their child to high-risk surgical intervention [ibid.]). Notwithstanding this, the literature (and reports from parents) continues to portray individual professionals as having difficulty in communicating. Numerous surveys cite 'poor communication' by professionals as a major complaint by parents/patients, particularly the lack of information-giving (see pp. 51–3, 70). But even when professionals try to communicate, professional language is frequently misunderstood or forgotten later (see pp. 52–3).

A *communication barrier* may preclude the smooth transmission of expertise. This may be because of poor communication skills: the professional may believe that they told the parent everything, or assume knowledge and understanding in the parent, but make no attempt to find out what was understood or how the message was received. Lack of communication may also be a means of preserving expert power. In Marks' study (Marks, 1992) reported previously, lack of communicating the agenda and purpose of a case conference to a mother preserved the control over the proceedings with the professionals, who had already agreed the objectives in private.

In some situations, however, it may be difficult to make professional knowledge and expertise accessible without impoverishing the complexity or function of the knowledge. For example, to interpret the results of a standardised assessment may depend on understanding complex concepts like error margins and reliability levels. Similarly, understanding the possible outcomes of a life-threatening illness or high-risk surgery may depend on understanding complex probability concepts and balancing risk versus benefits (see further Alderson, 1990). The distinction between certain and uncertain knowledge may be difficult to get across to a parent, especially if they expect the professional 'to know' and interpret uncertainty as 'he's not telling me the truth'. Communicating professional knowledge may be even harder with parents of ethnic minorities and different social class backgrounds who may lack culturally shared ideas with the professional (see p. 63), and with children who have a different level of understanding.

But the barrier has to be crossed if a professional is going to pass across their expertise successfully. Poor communication, either intentionally or inadvertently, maintains the parent in a weak position. Lack of knowledge or miscomprehension keeps the parent ignorant and therefore powerless to participate in or intervene with professional activity or to help their child and family situation. Moreover, poor understanding and recall of the professional's messages can lead to dissatisfaction with the professional's intervention and less likelihood of complying with professional advice, which in the case of medical information may have serious consequences for the patient (Ley *et al.*, 1976, Nazarian *et al.*, 1974). Genuinely informed consent depends too on adequate understanding of professional information (Ley, 1989 and see p. 174). Therefore, making one's expertise accessible and sharing it with the parent should be an essential requirement of professional activity.

There is considerable evidence that professional communication can be improved, with beneficial effects for the parent/client. In an extensive review by Ley (1989), a number of studies were shown to have significantly increased patients' understanding and recall of communication from doctors by using a variety of communication techniques. These are included within the following list of guidelines. Although the guidelines are aimed primarily at adults/parents, they may also be of relevance to communicating with children, if the child's level of understanding and individual needs are taken into account. Children too need comprehensible information from professionals to give informed consent, to come to a realistic understanding of themselves and their disability, and to be equipped to deal with the challenges that face them.

Guidelines for practice

1. *Start with assessing the parent's emotional state.* Parents in states of shock, distress and anxiety may take in only part of the message. If the parent is in an acute psychological state, keep messages simple and brief, and meet again at the earliest opportunity.
2. *Be sympathetic, considerate and caring.* Remember that the affective style of your interaction may be as important for the success of the encounter as other communication skills (see Quine and Rutter references in Chapter 3).
3. *Invite the parent to present their own ideas, expectations and questions* and actively encourage their participation in the dialogue. The issue of relationships, power positioning and communication has already been touched on. Research on doctor–patient communications has demonstrated that many patients take a passive position in consultations and tend not to participate in the giving of information or the clarifying of the professional's messages (see review by Robinson, 1989).

4. Your message should be
   - *clear.* Be clear about what you want to communicate and use specific, rather than general statements.
   - *straightforward and direct.*
   - *simplified with shorter words and shorter sentences.*
5. To help recall,
   - *use primacy effects.* Information given first is remembered better.
   - *use explicit categorisation.* Categorise the material, list the category names to the parent before presenting the information, and then repeat the category name before each category of information is presented.
   - *use repetition.*
6. To help understanding,
   - *avoid technical jargon where possible.*
   - *include explanation.* Don't assume that the parent understands any of the technical terms or theories used. Explain in everyday language whenever possible or tutor the parent on the meaning of a technical term or concept. Note that language which appears to be the same as colloquial speech such as 'handicapped', 'slow learning' or 'learning difficulty', may be particularly prone to misunderstandings.
   - *check out whether the parent understands what has been told* at regular intervals.
   - *investigate how the parent 'construes' situations,* what 'constructs' they use, so that you can establish how they are interpreting what you are saying. A major problem in difficulties in doctor–patient communication has been shown to be a 'mismatch' between the doctor's and patient's views; the evidence available suggests that an important predictor of successful doctor–patient consultations is that the doctor offers advice and information which fits easily into the patient's pre-consultation belief framework (see review by Robinson, 1989).
   - *Help the parent to ask questions about what you have told them.*
   - *Use trained translators* to assist the communication with parents (or children) of ethnic minorities, where English is not the mother tongue. Even where English appears to be fluently understood and expressed, there may be subtle misunderstandings.
   - *Write down what you are telling them,* so that it can be considered further after the meeting.
   - *Hold a follow-up meeting* to find out how much has been understood and retained of what was discussed at the previous meeting, and to deal with further questions.
7. *Reflect on your reasons for 'editing'* any information. A desire not to share information may be justified as a 'need to be sensitive', but may serve other functions in the power relationship (Marks, 1992).

These guidelines highlight that the transmission of professional knowledge is a two-way, rather than one-way, process. Whilst offering information, a professional must also *receive* information, finding out about the parent's current emotional state, their understanding of the situation and of the professional's communication, and the gaps in their knowledge. This requires active inquiry and listening to the parent's responses and comments. So, although listening is considered as a separate topic below, it is also a key part of transmitting professional expertise.

LISTENING AND COUNSELLING

Listening to a parent is likely to be of major importance in the communication process (Davis, 1993, Dale, 1992). 'Not being listened to' ranks as one of the frequent criticisms of professionals by parents (see references on p. 70).

Listening is central to partnership work. Through listening, essential information from the parent about their perspective and viewpoint can be gathered. Listening also sends out messages to the parent (and other family members) that they are worth listening to and that their opinion has value for the problem-solving and decision-making process.

As part of a helping/counselling process, listening has other possible benefits for the parent and family with a child with special needs (Fost, 1981, Davis, 1993). With a listening helper, the parent (or other family member) may gain time and space to explore feelings and thoughts in ways that will help them to deal more effectively with their own life situation. Listening, as part of a counselling process, can help a person move forward in personal growth, overcome or cope better with specific problems, make decisions, or get through a challenging or crisis period (Nelson-Jones, 1983). This contribution is also very relevant for working in partnership; counselling methods have much to offer in helping a parent to participate as a partner (Cunningham and Davis, 1985).

In their model of the helping process, Hornby *et al.* (1987) suggest that listening fits into a three-stage process. A person being helped or counselled is first listened to, then helped to reach a greater understanding of their situation, and then helped to resolve their problems or take effective action (see Table 4.1).

Listening as a skill

From a skills point of view, listening appears superficially straightforward, but much more skill and insight are required than is at first obvious. As Table 4.1 shows, there are a number of different behavioural and verbal components to *active* listening, such as communicating attention, the appropriate posture and body language, and the judicious use of verbal

Table 4.1 Overview of helping model and skills

Stage	1	2	3
Skills	Listening	Understanding	Problem-solving
	open posture	summarising	brainstorming
	eye contact	information giving	clarifying options
	facial expression	identifying themes	evaluating options
	voice tone	expressing implications	developing plans for action
	no distractions	making connections	facilitating assertion
	attentive silence	noting contradictions	evaluating progress
	minimal encouragers	suggesting alternative interpretations	recycling the process
	open questions	suggesting new perspectives	arranging for further contract
	clarifying questions	suggesting tentative conclusions	referring on
	paraphrasing	self-disclosure	terminating contract
	active listening	you–me talk	
Aims	Exploration	Understanding	Action
	Acknowledgement	Analysis	Action

Source: Hornby et al., 1987. Reprinted with permission

acknowledgements and questions. These elements communicate to the parent that their viewpoint is being listened to and taken seriously. Apart from their value acknowledging the parent, they can also be used to help the parent to talk through to greater depth without being distracted or disrupted in thought.

Listening needs to be:

- attentive,
- accurate,
- empathic, and
- linked to messages back to the parent or family member that they are being listened to and understood.

Despite being an apparently 'gentle' intervention, listening can, however, arouse uncomfortable feelings in both the professional and the parent. A parent may feel uncomfortable taking up a professional's time by talking or frustrated that a professional is not coming up with a solution to their problem. A professional might feel an inner compulsion to *do* something to help and find it difficult to attend without interjecting and coming up with interpretations and solutions. Silence may arouse feelings of anxiety and discomfort in both parties. The professional may find it difficult to gauge whether it is appropriate to respond or not. Some difficulties from empathic listening have been noted in Chapter 3 (pp. 68–9). It is advisable to be aware of these potential difficulties and to monitor one's personal reactions which may hinder listening.

Active listening benefits from being practised as a professional skill (see Exercise 4.1, below).

Through talking and being listened to, a parent may be helped to reach a greater understanding and analysis of their own problem. This 'understanding' phase may follow the earlier 'listening' phase of the helping process (see Table 4.1), though the flow of this process is probably both forward and cyclical. Some of the communication skills involved in facilitating parental understanding are mentioned in Table 4.1. Useful further reading includes Cunningham and Davis, 1985 (Chapter 6) and Nelson-Jones, 1983.

PROBLEM-SOLVING

Although helping a parent to reach a greater understanding of their situation or problem may be sufficient on occasion, in other circumstances a parent may need help in working out a solution or remedy. The final phase of the counselling/helping process is known as *problem-solving* (see Table 4.1), and can lead to making a decision.

In Chapter 1, an important distinction was made between the Consumer Model and the Negotiating Model of partnership in terms of the balance of control of the professional's viewpoint and decision-making with the parent's viewpoint and decision-making. The difference between the two models is perhaps most obvious when comparing two forms of problem-solving:

1. *guided problem-solving* – the term used in this book to refer to the process of helping a parent reach their own solution to a particular problem (often one of personal concern) and
2. *negotiated problem-solving* – the term used here to refer to the process whereby a parent and professional strive to reach a decision *jointly* on a problem of mutual concern.

Although both kinds of problem-solving may be useful within partnership work (and there are many overlaps between the two processes, e.g. problems may be of personal *and* mutual concern, the means to resolve problems may be very similar, etc.), there are nevertheless important differences to draw out. As will be seen below, the two kinds have differing implications for techniques and process, the power relationship, the feelings aroused in parents and professionals, and the possible outcomes. It is these differences that strengthen the case for having a separate Negotiating Model to guide partnership practice, in addition to the Consumer Model (see Chapter 1).

Guided problem-solving

Guided problem-solving corresponds to the process of parent-centred counselling described previously. To get a clearer picture of the kind of situation where it would be relevant, imagine a problem along the following lines:

> Parent X raised this dilemma when his occupational therapist visited him at home: 'I want my daughter Melanie to attend your group at the hospital, but I can't see how to get her there by 9.30 on Tuesdays. That's one of my wife's working days, and I've got to get Eric to his nursery at 9 o'clock . . .'.

This problem was personal to this father (and family). Although the occupational therapist viewed it as the father's problem, she was willing to counsel him (by providing a sounding board, helping him look at his options and his feelings about them). With this help, he reached a viable solution for his family circumstances.

The contribution of the professional in guided problem-solving is to draw on counselling and problem-solving skills to help a parent work out their own solution to a problem that is concerning them (see Figure 4.1). Although the professional may have an interest in how the problem is resolved (the occupational therapist in the previous example was keen

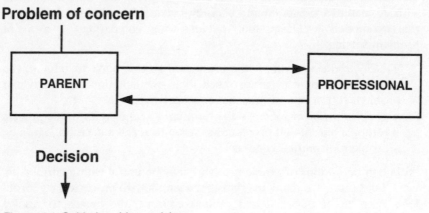

Figure 4.1 Guided problem-solving

for Melanie to attend the therapy group), a key element is permitting the parent to reach their own decision.

Guided problem-solving may be appropriate to use on many occasions in partnership work (Cunningham and Davis, 1985, Davis, 1993), the advantage being that the parent is helped to explore different options and to reach a decision which is realistic to their own family circumstances. The helping professional does not impose a viewpoint, although it can be offered to the parent if appropriate. The parent is given final control over decision-making, and this may enhance their sense of self-worth, efficacy and control.

General problem-solving skills

A parent can be helped to organise their problem-solving with structured problem-solving skills. As effective problem-solving has been shown to be associated with better parental and family adaptation in families of children with special needs (see Chapter 5), improving the parent's problem-solving skills may be beneficial. The following technique (adapted from Nelson-Jones, 1983) can be used with parents, preferably with reference to a present problem, or taught to parents for their own general use.

The steps of the process include:

1. defining the nature of the problem or dilemma,
2. generating alternative options to solve the problem (i.e. a brainstorming process),
3. collecting information about the alternatives (e.g. what they involve, how feasible they would be for the family),

4. examining the consequences of the alternatives (e.g. their impact on the child and family, what the family would feel about the different outcomes),
5. making the decision (selecting one alternative to pursue),
6. developing plans for action,
7. taking action,
8. evaluating the adequacy of the decision in light of the feedback.

NB: although using this approach can be helpful, other factors may be critical to the success or failure of problem-solving. For example, a person's general *orientation* to problems affects how they approach them (e.g. whether they wait for them to solve themselves, whether they act impulsively rather than taking a more systematic problem-solving approach, whether they find problems totally overwhelming) and how well they deal with them generally.

With the help of problem-solving skills, a decision may be reached to change something or to keep it the same. What is going to be changed may be on a personal level (how one thinks or feels about something) or on an inter-personal or outer level (referring oneself to a new service, changing a family routine, changing how one handles one's child etc.).

To sum up, guided problem-solving has an important contribution to make in helping a parent resolve their own problems, but it is not suitable for resolving all possible problems arising during partnership work. We turn now to negotiation as the other method for resolving problems jointly.

Negotiated problem-solving

Depending on their occupational role and job responsibilities, the professional will have (or will perceive themselves to have) direct responsibility for introducing their perspective into the final decision-making process. Decisions on diagnosis, child assessment, remediation, health intervention, school placement and education, or respite care, may all demand an active professional involvement in the problem-solving and decision-making process. Professional expertise in these issues is the rationale for the professional being involved in the first place. This active involvement (and interest) by the professional transforms the process and power balance of the problem-solving process. It cannot necessarily be delegated to the parent, and power over the decision-making either resides with the professional (as traditionally) or must be shared (if working in partnership). In order to share power, negotiation is an essential transaction for jointly resolving a problem.

Negotiation is the core communication approach for working in partnership because both parties' perspectives must be brought together to resolve some issue or problem of mutual concern. To see where this might be relevant, let us imagine a problem along the following lines:

At an introductory meeting between Parent Y and her daughter's physiotherapist, the physiotherapist wanted to assess whether the child, Clare, needed physiotherapy or not. Soon after their arrival, Parent Y stated that 'I don't think Clare needs physiotherapy. She seems to be getting on fine as she is.' The physiotherapist assessed Clare during the meeting, and reached an opinion that Clare was in need of regular physiotherapy.

In this example, both the parent and the professional had an interest in the final decision, yet each had a different opinion. The physiotherapist had carried out her professional responsibility to assess Clare and reached a decision that she would benefit from physiotherapy. Clare's mother was pursuing her parental responsibility of running her family life; she had decided to keep it as 'normal' as possible (by avoiding specialist treatment like physiotherapy) and believed this would be to Clare and the whole family's advantage. Each was carrying out their responsibilities as they saw fitting for their different roles, leading to (in this case) different viewpoints and preferences. Unless the two viewpoints could be reconciled, the two parties were either moving towards a confrontation or were tending towards divergence and separation.

Guided problem-solving would not be an appropriate process for handling this kind of problem, unless the professional decides to drop their interest and investment in the final decision and hand over the main control in decision-making to the parent. But if unwilling (or unable) to do this, a process of negotiated decision-making would be the only means of drawing together and resolving their different viewpoints cooperatively. This resolution would be essential for any further collaboration (see Figure 4.2).

Negotiation may be the hallmark of partnership work, but it places psychological, communicational, interpersonal and role demands on both the parent and professional. As Figure 4.3 shows, it requires not only a high level of cooperation, but also a high level of *assertiveness* (Thomas, 1975) on both sides, i.e. the willingness of each party to recognise that the other has legitimate views and wishes which will have to be taken into account in the negotiated settlement. It requires a shifting of positions and viewpoints and an altering of the traditional balance of power between the parent and professional (see pp. 5–7) to reach an agreement, and both personal and situational constraints will affect what is achievable.

By necessity, negotiation involves elements of dominance (when one partner imposes their wishes over the other) and resolution (Makin *et al.*, 1989), but with dominance shifting between the parent and

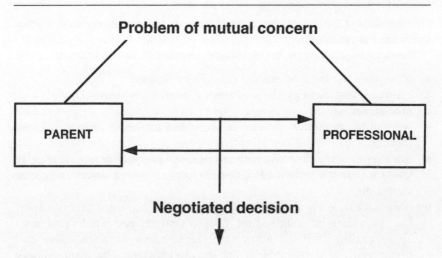

Figure 4.2 Negotiated problem-solving

professional (Cunningham and Davis, 1985). Both partners will require a sufficient trust of each other and openness and honesty to be explicit about their own perspective and wishes (but this may be unlikely in certain circumstances, see pp. 155, 157).

Negotiation as a technique

At the root of negotiation is *exchange*: two elements are brought together (in this case, the parent and professional's viewpoints or potential contributions) and then compared. Through comparison, one element may be exchanged for another or both may be combined or discarded. This process of bargaining or bartering may lead to resolutions such as 'If you do X, I will do Y', or 'We'll both accept X', or 'We'll both not do Y'.

Thomas' model of conflict resolution (see Figure 4.3) predicts that *problem-solving* is the best means of achieving a negotiated settlement. Consequently, a structured form of problem-solving (similar to the one on p. 86, but incorporating some additions and modifications) is introduced here as a technique to assist negotiation.

Because each negotiation is unique, it is unlikely to follow a set pattern (nor is this probably desirable). Nevertheless, to engage in joint problem-solving, the two partners need to go through at least some of the steps in the following negotiating sequence, but not necessarily all of them nor in the order presented. The process is not necessarily linear, but may be cyclical (returning to earlier steps before proceeding). A cycle may be especially relevant when two partners disagree and cannot easily reach a shared agreement or understanding (using a strategy to resolve a disagreement, then repeating earlier steps in the sequence until a joint agreement is reached).

The suggested steps of the negotiating sequence are as follows:

- *identifying the issue of mutual concern or interest,*
- *clarifying and defining the problem or decision to be resolved,*
- *brainstorming,*
- *generating alternative options to solve the problem.* This is reached through
- *listening to and acknowledging the parent's perspective,* e.g. getting to know a parent's preferred option, helping a parent assert their own viewpoint,
- *communicating the professional's perspective,* e.g. transmitting expertise, providing information on various options and what constraints are operating (NB To allow the parent room for manoeuvre and opportunity to participate in the decision-making, the professional's viewpoint would need to be presented as an option rather than as the sole or best solution),
- *evaluating the options in relationship to the shared problem or goal,* e.g. by collecting information about each partner's perspectives and preferred options, and considering the potential outcomes and consequences of each option,
- *making the decision jointly.* Two different outcomes of negotiation are possible:
  1. *the partners agree: they decide on the same option or reach a shared understanding and perspective on the situation,* and the parent consents to the option decided on, or
  2. *they disagree; they cannot agree on which option to pursue or they view the situation differently and cannot reach a shared perspective.* In this event, a strategy to resolve the disagreement may be adopted (see p. 93). It may be possible subsequently to re-enter the negotiation process and move towards a jointly accepted decision or understanding.
- *developing plans for action together.* If a joint decision is reached, the two partners may plan the relevant action,
- *taking action* by the relevant partner(s),
- *jointly evaluating the adequacy of the decision in light of the feedback.*

This sequence demonstrates how the two previous communication approaches mentioned earlier in the chapter (i.e. transmitting professional expertise, listening to the parent) come together during negotiation. In the last section, we consider the potential outcome of disagreement further.

HANDLING DISAGREEMENT

Disagreement may *precede* negotiation or be a possible *outcome* (see Negotiating Model, p. 14). In fact, if there were no difference in viewpoint initially, no negotiation would be necessary because consensus could be assumed. Even when disagreement signals a truly negotiating process, it may feel very threatening to the professional and arouse tension and anxiety. They may be concerned that the relationship will disintegrate or become confrontational if they were to make explicit their own viewpoint. Accustomed to having one's judgement respected and accepted, a professional may find differences of opinion difficult to handle. Parental challenges can make a professional feel less expert and less competent, and this may be particularly unsettling when working in conditions of insecurity (threat of job cuts, competitive tendering for professional services). In such a setting, a professional might avoid seeking the parent's viewpoint in case it raises questions of the professional's authority or leads to a confrontation with their employing agency.

On the other side, the parent is also likely to find disagreement threatening because they are generally in a less powerful position than the professional (see p. 6) or perceive themselves as such. They may be (or feel) powerless to oppose a professional's wishes even if they disagree with them. The professional might use domination to impose their wishes or use persuasion and pressure to influence the parent. They might threaten or use sanctions (such as withdrawing a service, refusing to offer alternatives, or penalising through reducing an intervention). In certain circumstances, they will be bound under law to enforce certain options or sanctions (see Chapter 11).

Because of the discomfort and difficulty of explicit dissent for both parties, either partner may take up a range of different transactional positions which avoid confronting or dealing with the disagreement. The general model by Thomas (1975) (see Figure 4.3) is useful for making sense of and recognising the various transactional and communicational positions that might be taken up when facing a problem of mutual concern (see Makin *et al.*, 1989, for discussion of application of the model). Cooperation and assertion are seen as two continuous dimensions which can be combined together to form a grid. The high and low on each dimension are considered here. In the grid point of *avoiding* or withdrawing, one or both partners take up a position of low assertion and low cooperation. The problems are ignored and nothing is done to resolve the differences. The partners may withdraw from each other or avoid each other. If only one partner takes up this position, then the other is likely to be in a reciprocal position of domination, forcing or imposing their wish on the first person. The grid point of *competing* or forcing allows two possible positions: one dominating and imposing their will and the

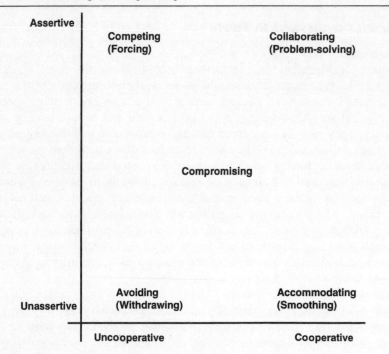

Figure 4.3 Dimensions of conflict resolution

Source: Thomas, 1975 (with amendments by Makin *et al.*, 1989). Reprinted with permission of John Wiley & Sons Ltd

other avoiding, or both asserting their differing viewpoints uncoopera-tively. Who wins the competitive contest of the latter is determined by which party can bring the greatest power to bear in the situation. This grid point is characteristic of parents in conflict with the local education authority over their child's special education.

Accommodating or smoothing is characterised by cooperation, but little assertion. If both parties take this position, then some agreement will be reached. This will not, however, make for a satisfactory or lasting agreement, as both sides will have avoided openly asserting their own needs and wishes. A 'false consensus' is the likely outcome. If one partner adopts this position, the other can either ignore the cooperation and force the issue to the conclusion which they want, or alternatively resume cooperation and go for a problem-solving approach, possibly believing falsely that the other person is also asserting their own needs and view-point.

It may not be unusual in current parent–professional encounters for one or other partner to adopt this latter stance. What *appears* as an equal collaboration obscures the fact that one party is not actively asserting their own viewpoint and wishes. The parent may go along with the professional's views, to 'keep the peace' and avoid being seen as 'troublesome' (this is a continuation of the traditional passive 'client' position). Alternatively, the professional may comply with the parent's views to avoid conflict and disagreement. This has been particularly noticeable since the implementation of the 1981 Education Act; some professionals support the parent's view whether they agree with it or not to avoid getting into a conflict position. If committed to partnership work, they may worry that assertion of their own viewpoint will be perceived as 'dominance' rather than 'difference'. That this position of 'accommodating' may sometimes feel unsatisfactory and cause dilemmas for the professional has been frequently voiced by professionals attending the Tavistock course (see p. 28), who wonder whether there is a place for the professional perspective in the partnership relationship and query whether they are able to pursue the child's best interests as they perceive them. Some feel they give in to the demands and wishes of assertive parents, at the cost of what they can offer less assertive parents and children (see Chapter 11, p. 272).

A relationship where the partners regularly take up positions of competing, avoiding or accommodating to deal with problems of mutual concern does not fit the definition of a negotiating partnership given on p. 14. But to take up the position of 'collaborating', assumed in the Negotiating Model, requires each partner being prepared and able to work with the challenge of possible dissent. Whether their relationship or encounter can sustain an open dissent without deteriorating into an antagonistic conflict (or one partner becoming compliant with or avoiding the other) will depend on a variety of factors.

These include their individual personalities (e.g. ability to assert themselves and handle disagreement), the quality and cohesion of the relationship ('When you've built a *relationship*, you can have anger, disagreements' (Ali Choudhury, pers. comm. on working with Bangladeshi families as a Bangladeshi Parent Adviser)), the balance of power between the parent and professional (e.g. the parent being able to express dissent without being sanctioned), the proximity of their interests (e.g. both being in a position to accommodate to the other party's wishes) and the possible outcome of the dissent (e.g. zero/sum or sum/sum, see p. 2).

In addition, the professional will need to be equipped to handle dissent. We end this chapter by looking at various strategies.

Strategies for managing disagreement

On the professional's side, an expectancy that disagreement is part and parcel of partnership work and a knowledge of constructive action to handle it may reduce feelings of defensiveness, hostility or impotence. To this end, a number of possible strategies for resolving disagreement have been outlined here, which can be used to prevent disagreement and conflict arising in the first place or to defuse it.

1. *Increase familiarity.* It does not take much to foster tension and disagreement between two groups of people, especially if one group is viewed as 'the Other' (Sherif *et al.*, 1961). Differentness, competition for scarce resources and sources of annoyance can all exacerbate tension and hostility (ibid.). Familiarity and trust can be increased through time spent together, opening channels of communication and building a partnership (see Chapter 2).

2. *Use of superordinate goals.* Dissent can be reduced by directing it towards a goal that both find acceptable (Makin *et al.*, 1989). The superordinate goal encompasses both of the two subordinate goals. For example, if the parent and professional have different priorities for the child's developmental progress, a superordinate goal is selected which includes elements of both their priorities. Instead of being forced to separate, they are bound through common interests. A variation of this is seen in situations where both parties join forces to fight a 'common enemy', e.g. instead of criticising the school, the parent joins the school in criticising the LEA for failure to support adequately the child with special needs.

3. *Re-framing.* Another variation of point 2 is using the technique of re-framing (see p. 134). Disagreement is rephrased in positive terms, e.g. different viewpoints are stated as alternative routes or strategies to the same common goal. The shared goal may need to be clarified.

   Re-framing can also be used to shift perspective (see p. 134): instead of viewing the problem from the professional's perspective, it is reframed from the parent's perspective, or in terms of the transaction between them. This can release a stalemate position and permit a creative, constructive response.

4. *Step-down.* One partner (either the parent or professional) drops their preferred option and concedes to follow the other partner's preferred option. The professional may decide to take a step-down position to the parent in the early days of 'joining' a family, until the relationship is sufficiently strong to allow challenge and dissent.

5. *Compromise.* The parent and professional reach a jointly accepted middle road between the professional and parent's preferred options.

6. *No change.* A 'no resolution' position is maintained, and the differences cannot be accommodated at present. The professional might shift to work on another area where there is no disagreement, or give further intervention which might alter the parent's viewpoint (or vice versa). But if no workable solution can be reached over time and the disagreement is sufficiently serious and intractable, then the relationship may enter a 'conflict' phase (see Chapter 1). This prevents

a partnership being built, in the first instance, or makes an existing partnership inoperative, either temporarily or in the long term. Possible strategies for resolving conflict are presented in Chapter 11.

In this chapter, we have examined the various ways that a professional might communicate with a parent to facilitate working in partnership and to assist a parent's own wellbeing and coping. One issue that has become apparent is the way in which different communicative approaches serve to shift the transactional and power positions of each partner, with different possibilities and consequences for the particular encounter and the parent–professional relationship itself.

In the following chapter, we move on to consider theoretical frameworks for understanding the whole family.

PROFESSIONAL DEVELOPMENT EXERCISES

EXERCISE 4.1 ACTIVE LISTENING

Try out listening actively to a parent you work with or to someone in your personal life.

Listen attentively. You should avoid adding extra comments, wherever possible, except continuation remarks like um-um, yes, I see, go on, really.

Observe how difficult it is to listen without interrupting, offering opinions, thinking about other preoccupations. What happens when you listen and don't interrupt? How does it feel to hold back on your own views and opinions?

After listening for a while, feed back what you have heard to the speaker and check it for accuracy.

Practise active listening with a number of people you have different relationships with, such as your spouse or close friend, your own child, a parent you are working with, your boss. Compare your different experiences of listening to different people. How easy or difficult is listening, depending on the role position of the person you are relating to and the nature of your relationship?

Write down your reactions on a separate sheet of paper.

EXERCISE 4.2 USING PROBLEM-SOLVING SKILLS

Consider a problem or decision that you are currently in the process of having to resolve.

1. Define the area for the decision or the problem to be resolved.
2. Go through all the steps of the problem-solving process (Table 4.1 and p. 86) in order to reach a decision on what action you wish to take.
3. Write out a plan for action – with a clear statement of goal(s), what steps are to be taken to attain the goal, and a realistic time schedule. Include how you will monitor and evaluate the effectiveness of your decision.
4. Consider any problems or difficulties that may arise in carrying out your planned action or decision. What help may you need to carry out your action or decision?

Write down your responses on a separate sheet of paper.

Chapter 5

Frameworks for understanding the family

Two months after the birth of Derek, his family were in a state of shock and disarray. His parents, Jim and Dawn, were acutely distressed by his condition of spina bifida with severe leg paralysis. Dawn was in a vulnerable post-natal condition of exhaustion and fatigue; disorientated and distressed, she was trying to cope with looking after Derek at home. Jim, usually a bedrock of strength, was weary and irritable, trying to keep up with work demands and worried about his wife's distress and fragility. His elderly parents, who had been looking after Jessie (their daughter) in the weeks following the birth, were exhausted by the demands of caring for an energetic 3 year old, and his mother had now come down with bronchitis. They were extremely shocked by the diagnosis, and though usually of great support and physical help to the family, were too distressed to be useful. Dawn, expecting to rely on them in the first hectic months after birth, found them suddenly too frail to give her the physical help she desperately needed. Jessie, now returned home, was confused and frightened by the distressed preoccupations of her parents. She refused to sleep in her own bed at night, and ended up sleeping in her parents' bed every night.

The arrival of a new baby has a massive effect on any family, but there is a qualitative difference when the baby has a disability or special needs. It has been likened to a 'family crisis' (Russell, 1983). Jessie, the 3 year old above, understood little about her brother's physical disability, but was highly affected by her parents' and grandparents' distress and their apparent distancing from her. As Dawn started slowly adjusting to Derek's condition with the sensitive attentions of her health visitor, her husband and the grandparents began regaining their own strengths which could then be drawn upon to help her care for the two children.

Each member had their own reactions to Derek's arrival, but their reactions (and how they coped with them) were bound up with the reactions of others in the family. A number of conceptual frameworks have been developed for making sense of this impact of the child with special needs on different family members and the whole family. In this chapter, we describe some of them and discuss their relative merits, in order to draw out some implications for working in partnership with families.

A first step is to consider the arguments for working with the whole family or at least adopting a 'whole family' focus.

ADOPTING A WHOLE FAMILY APPROACH

In Chapter 1, it was mentioned that the focus in the past was generally on the child with special needs, and this is still very commonplace (see p. 8). But there are now cogent arguments for shifting to a more family-focused intervention. The first is to do with promoting child development and adaptation in the child with special needs. Child development research has highlighted that the quality of interactions and relationships between the parents and the young child can accelerate the child's cognitive, linguistic and socio-emotional development. This has been demonstrated repeatedly for 'normal' children (e.g. Wells, 1981, Sroufe, 1983, Bruner, 1983) and also, to a lesser extent, with children with disabilities and chronic illnesses (e.g. Wasserman and Allen, 1985, De Maso et al., 1991). It can be deduced that efforts to help the parent relate to the child may be of greater long-term benefit for the child than efforts limited to the child (this is corroborated by research on the Parent Advisory Service, Tower Hamlets, see pp. 188–9).

The second argument is that research has shown that mothers, fathers, siblings and other members of the family may need their own support, counselling and guidance, and this has frequently been overlooked by service providers (probably because of the increased time and staffing resources required to meet their needs and the difficulty of justifying this indirect help to the child).

A further argument is that intervention that is going to be useful for the family will need to respect the way that the family organises and structures itself around having a child with special needs. A growing body of research is emphasising the importance of preserving the family's cohesion and internal organisation (see p. 111). This includes taking account of the 'whole lifestyle' of the child, their family background and culture (DoH, 1991a, Vol 6).

A final argument is to do with the way that the family operates as a 'system' (see Chapter 6). Although we have tended to assume (in practice and research) that a professional intervention affects only the targeted person, it is now recognised that any intervention might have extensive effects on others in the family, and they in turn may affect the outcome of the intervention (see further pp. 130, 139). In light of this, any intervention will need to be considered for its impact on the whole family.

A persuasive case has been made for shifting to a whole family approach, but this moves us naturally onto the question of 'who is *the family*'?

Who is 'the family'?

There are no easy answers to this question because the family is not a straightforward or static concept. The term 'family' evokes the notion of a stable married couple with dependent children with one or both parents fulfilling economic and nurturing functions. But the 'traditional' family structure of post-war northern Europe and the United States is being subjected to increasing change and strains through marriage break-up, cohabitation, lone motherhood, unemployment and new work patterns, and is increasingly less representative of many families' lives. It does not reflect the range and diversity of current family structures. For every two marriages in 1991 in the UK, there was one divorce. One-parent families nearly doubled between 1976 and 1991 from 10 per cent to 19 per cent of all families (HMSO, 1994). Instead of stability, some families will be in the process of breaking up or reconstituting and incorporating new members. Foster parents, step-parents, common-law partners, ex-boyfriends, friends, relatives may all play a key role in the child and family's life. Even estranged members who have left the home and play no active care role can still command a strong emotional 'hold' on the family.

Family patterns vary too across ethnic groups in Britain. The family structure of a stable, married couple with dependent children is still relatively common among households of Asian origin in the UK – Bangladeshis, Pakistanis, Indians and Chinese. It is least common among black families – more than half of Afro-Caribbean mothers are single parents (ibid., 1994).

Rather than assuming a particular structure, the professional will need to learn about the individual structure of each family. The family must play a key role in defining its members and relationships and who they wish to involve with the professional. But, irrespective of this, the Children Act 1989 also defines who has 'parental responsibility' for the child and therefore has a legal responsibility to be involved in decisions affecting the child (see Chapter 11, p. 262). Before you proceed, it may be illuminating to consider who you meet regularly from your caseload and why, and what is your knowledge of each family's structure and composition (see Exercise 5.1).

Theorising about the family

As part of changing trends in the way 'ordinary' families and disabled people are viewed in British and American society, families of children with special needs are undergoing changes in how they are viewed. Theories on the family are not static, but are linked to particular historical periods and socio-economic, cultural and political conditions and contexts. The dominant political ideology, the body of professional research and literature, popular and minority group culture, and the media all contribute (through complex and inter-relating processes) to preserving or generating particular theories and ideas of the family. Ideas on the family are not value- or ideologically-free, but serve to bolster or represent certain social and economic structures and functions (Riley, 1983).

One significance of this for the professional is that they are likely to be influenced by a particular theory (or theories) and this may impel them to work in a certain way. The implication of research for practice will be considered in the next section. There is a further repercussion for the family: how society perceives and socially positions the family with a child with special needs may affect the family's functioning and the possibilities open to it. Negative views of disability in society may, for instance, reinforce a sense of powerlessness and low self-esteem in the family as well as expectations of rejection of their child from friends and neighbours (Suelzle and Keenan, 1981). How the parent and the professional each think about 'families with children with special needs' may affect how they relate to each other.

The relationship between research and practice

The relationship between psychological research and practice is complex. Research ideas take time to filter down into qualificatory training courses and practice, with the net result that some theories continue to be in circulation in practice long after they have been disproved or challenged by later research. Apart from this time lag in research ideas entering professional culture, busy practitioners may have little time to read and keep up to date with a fast expanding research literature. The psychological literature is dense and not easy to penetrate. Moreover, the implications for practice may not always be clear, particularly when research findings are contradictory, inconclusive or based on generalisations of populations which cannot easily be applied to the individual.

Notwithstanding the fact that many of these difficulties do apply to using the extensive research literature on the impact of the child with special needs on the family, there are still important reasons for developing a more research-informed practice. Myths about families with disabled children abound, and it is vital that these are subjected to critical scrutiny. Recent research findings, as we shall see, are helping us to reach a far greater understanding of the ways that a child with special needs or chronic illness affects the family. They can be used to help inform service development and allocation, so that services are not just offered in a

haphazard fashion to people who 'appear most needy' or are more personally determined or have a higher social status (Black, 1980). Moreover,
they can help inform a more sensitive and appropriate intervention from
professionals to individual families.

The research literature on the impact of a child with special needs
(disability and chronic illness) on the family is extensive, and can be
discussed only briefly here. The interested reader might wish to turn to
Byrne and Cunningham (1985), McConachie (1986, 1991b) and Seligman
and Darling (1989) for reviews of the literature on families of disabled
children and to Eiser (1993) for a review on the family with the chronically ill child.

The Pathological (or 'sick' family) Model

One difficulty when thinking about the impact on different family
members is separating out what arises from having a child with special
needs in the family and what is to do with other problems and challenges
that might face any member and family, such as work problems, marriage
difficulties, financial problems. There has been a tendency in research and
practice to assume that any difficulties in a family member stem from
having a child with special needs in the family. This is known as the
Pathological Model of the family.

The pathological viewpoint has a long history. It goes back to ideas on
disability or mental deficiency as having an organic base that originate as
far back as the sixteenth century and possibly earlier in Europe. In the
eighteenth century, reproductive inadequacy and deficient organic material for reproduction was being associated with moral degeneracy and
sinful behaviours in the parents, and by the nineteenth century these
behaviours were being linked to hereditary disposition. As Joanna Ryan
points out in her historical account of mental handicap (Ryan and Thomas,
1981), this mixture of the moral and the biological was to persist
throughout the nineteenth century and well into the twentieth century.
The expression of feelings of guilt and blame continue to be expressed
by some parents to this day (see Chapter 3).

With the creation of the National Health Service in 1949, the field of
disability came under the organisation of medical services, and the organic
nature of 'subnormality' continued to be the main focus of attention.
Disabled people were treated as ill 'patients' requiring medically based
treatment. Medical ideas of 'pathology' were extended to families, who
were viewed as suffering mainly adverse effects from the disabled person.
The birth of a disabled child was seen as a 'crisis' or abnormal state and
this concept of 'crisis' was extended to the family. It was believed that
a family with a handicapped child became a 'handicapped family'
(Younghusband et al., 1970), and life with a disabled child would be

uniformly stressful. Disabled children were sent away to mental handicap hospitals 'for the sake of the siblings' who were believed to suffer harm if the disabled child stayed at home. Psychotherapeutic groups were set up for parents to help them focus on difficult and supposedly suppressed feelings (mourning over their loss, parental guilt, blame, over-protectiveness, rejection, over-anxiety) arising from giving birth to a defective child.

This model has been important for thinking about some of the adverse effects of a child with special needs on the family, and there is substantial psychological and psychiatric research to show that increased stresses and difficulties with mental and physical health are very common in this population as a whole.

Families under stress

Two issues need to be borne in mind when considering the research findings. Firstly, the studies were carried out on group populations and focused on reactions in the group as a whole, usually at one moment in time. Secondly, the concept of stress in the earlier studies was often poorly defined (Byrne and Cunningham, 1985). It can refer both to events or situations that impinge on a person, as well as to that individual's feelings and reactions. Until recently, the concept of stress was used to indicate a crisis arising from having a disabled child and was measured by levels of depression or stress in the family members.

Most of the early studies focused on mothers. They assumed that there would be some psychological impairment of family members (e.g. Evans and Carter, 1954, Holt, 1958). Many studies showed that mothers of children with disabilities did experience high levels of stress (Tew and Laurence, 1975, Bradshaw and Lawton, 1978, Butler *et al.*, 1978, Burden, 1980, Beckman, 1983). Mothers were shown to have 'critically' high depression after the birth of their child with severe disability (Burden, 1980). High stress levels have been shown in more recent studies too. In the Kent study of mothers of children with severe disabilities and learning difficulties, over half (59 per cent) showed 'critically' high levels of stress, indicative of depression; the parents showed higher stress levels on average than parents of normally developing children (Quine and Pahl, 1985). A study of 107 families of children with severe physical disabilities showed mothers to be at high risk of psychological distress, with a very high percentage (67 per cent) of mothers at 'critical' levels of stress (Sloper and Turner, 1993). Similarly, increased vulnerability has been shown in families as a whole with chronic childhood illness (Overholser and Fritz, 1991), in the emotional and behavioural development of children with chronic illness (Garralda *et al.*, 1988) and in their brothers and sisters (Tritt and Esses, 1988). But there have also been contradictory findings; a study by Gath (1977) did *not* find a greater difference in depression scores of mothers with children with Down's syndrome than in mothers of non-disabled children in the first two years after the children's birth.

Attempts to find cause–effect links between stress levels in the mothers and single factors, like socio-economic class and age of the mother, single versus two parent family, severity of disability of the child, size of the family, have been inconclusive, and researchers have concluded that vulnerability to stress is multi-faceted (Burden, 1980, Beckman, 1983).

Fathers

There has been much less research attention to fathers of children with special needs. Some evidence in Britain and USA suggests high levels of stress, depression and low self-esteem in fathers too (Cummings, 1976, Wishart *et al.*, 1981). Fathers who experienced higher levels of stress tended to cope by employing an escape-avoidance strategy (Houser, 1987, cited in Seligman and Darling, 1989). This may lead to a negative and debilitating dynamic in the family, with additional burdens of care falling on the mother as the father withdraws, and these added pressures arousing anger and resentment in the other family members (Seligman and Darling, 1989). But greater levels of stress were not found in fathers of children with spina bifida in an American study, compared with fathers of normally developing children (Kazak and Marvin, 1984), although mothers did show higher stress. Other studies have also found fathers to be less stressed than mothers (Goldberg *et al.*, 1986, Sloper and Turner, 1993), but there was evidence of psychological distress in a substantial proportion of fathers in the latter study. It is not clear, however, whether these reports of less distress in fathers are a distortion that reflects fathers' greater stoicism and difficulty in acknowledging and expressing their painful emotions in case they are perceived as a sign of weakness (Seligman and Darling, 1989). See further findings relating to fathers on pp. 130, 137.

Brothers and sisters

Earlier studies tended to predict that the experience of living with a brother or sister with a disability would be uniformly negative and lead to adverse psychological consequences. There is some evidence to support this position, though many of the earlier studies relied on mothers' reports rather than on direct investigation of siblings. Moreover, reports of apparently high levels of negativism, such as jealousy and rivalry, between siblings and children (e.g. with Down's syndrome, Carr, 1975) may not be showing anything substantially different from that between 'normal' children and siblings of a comparable developmental age (see Dunn and

Kendrick, 1982). Gath (1973) found a considerable rise in 'anti-social' disorder in older sisters of children with Down's syndrome. Sisters, especially older ones, may experience a conflicting pressure to achieve and to take on a parental surrogate role – they tend to do more of the childcare, babysitting and domestic work (Blacher, 1984b). Personal and clinical reports mention that brothers and sisters may feel resentful of their parents' preoccupation with the child with special needs and harbour aggressive and angry feelings (Featherstone, 1980, Sourkes, 1987). Lack of parental attention may be experienced as rejection (ibid.). But the sibling may be inhibited from expressing anger and displeasure towards the child with special needs by their parents (Miller, 1974). The presence of the child with special needs may affect the sibling's expectations for the future (they may be told by the parents that they will be expected to look after the child with special needs after the parents die). Moreover, siblings may have a very limited understanding of their brother's or sister's special condition and may construct a 'private view' based on fear, guilt and magical thinking (Sourkes, 1987). They may fear catching the illness or disorder, or of having caused the child's disability may fester. Apart from lack of information about disability, they may lack knowledge of how to handle their disabled sibling (Newson and Davies, 1994). Suggestion has been made that younger children in age position adjust less well to the presence of a child with special needs (Farber, 1960), while older siblings (with the exception of eldest daughters) experience better adjustment.

Nevertheless, other evidence suggests that adverse effects are not necessarily *inevitable*. Brothers and sisters of chronically ill children have been found to be well adjusted (Tritt and Esses, 1988). In Ann Gath's later prospective study of siblings of children with Down's syndrome (1978), no difference in emotional or behavioural disturbance was found between siblings of children with Down's syndrome and siblings of 'normal' children (see too Byrne et al., 1988). In the latter study, difficulties (when occurring) were associated with poor marital relationships, maternal depression and a poor maternal relationship with the child with Down's syndrome. Brothers and sisters have often been found to be well adjusted and mature and to show a responsible attitude that goes beyond their chronological age (Blacher, 1984b). They may show increased altruistic concern and tolerance towards others (Grossman, 1972) as suggested by their frequent choice of careers in education and human services.

Apart from thinking in terms of a unitary impact of the child with special needs, some studies have started to look more closely at specific behaviours within the sibling relationship, i.e. what might be causing difficulties and whether the dynamics of the relationship are any different from that which is commonly found between 'normal' siblings of comparable developmental ages (e.g. Dunn and Kendrick, 1982; Dale, 1983).

A direct interview study with ten school-aged siblings of a child with severe learning difficulties found no differences in conflict, embarrassment, amount of housework or playing with and teaching/helping the younger child, compared with ten control children (McConachie and Domb, 1981). Of the minority of siblings reported by mothers to have difficulties in their relationship in the Manchester study (Byrne *et al.*, 1985), the problems were frequently linked to particular behaviours of the child with Down's syndrome: aggressiveness, disruption at night-time, disturbance of the sibling's games and possessions. A number of children in the Nottingham and Leicester workshops for siblings of children with autism expressed feeling hurt by the autistic child's lack of empathy (Newson and Davies, 1994). But whether these behavioural and interactional difficulties were the cause of more general problems for the siblings in their relationship and personal adjustment is not very clear yet.

To conclude, it appears that some siblings fare well and others poorly, though our knowledge of the process of adjustment and aetiology of problems is still in its infancy (Seligman and Darling, 1989). What appears to be the case (see too ibid.) is that a variety of factors (including the nature of the child's disability, the behaviour of the child with special needs, the quality of relationship of the siblings, the openness of communication between the parents and sibling, the mental health of the parents and quality of relationship between the parents and child with special needs) intervene or mediate in complex ways to affect how a brother or sister develops.

The marital relationship

Within the Pathological Model, it was anticipated that having a child with special needs would lead to a great strain on the marital relationship. Looking at the effects of having a severely mentally disabled child on marital integration in 240 families, Farber (1959) found that the outcome was more closely related to marital integration prior to the presence of the child than to any effects from the child. Gath (1977) rated significantly more marriages as 'poor' in parents of children with Down's syndrome than among parents of non-disabled children. But an equal number of marriages were rated as 'good' in each group. No differences were found in the quality of marriage between parents of infants with special needs and parents of non-disabled infants (Waisbren, 1980), but at an older age (average 9.3 years) significantly less marital satisfaction was found in parents with children with mental disability than in a control group of parents (Friedrich and Friedrich, 1981). In Sloper and Turner's study (1993), 11 of the 14 divorced or separated mothers attributed the marriage break-up, at least in part, to their husband's non-acceptance of a physically disabled child.

In Gath's study (1977), marriages rated as 'moderate' or with overt disruption and hostility were more likely to have their pre-existing weaknesses magnified into obvious rifts. This adverse change in the relationship appeared to be closely associated with the initial shock of the discovery of the disability and at least one partner's failure to adjust to the child's condition.

Single parenthood

Vadasy (1986) has suggested that single parents of children with special needs will experience greater stresses than those in two-parent families. Problems of finance (see p. 117), social isolation and lack of personal support for single parents are likely to exacerbate stress. But the absence of support from a spouse may be compensated partly by support from other sources, such as relatives and friends (Dunst *et al.*, 1986).

To sum up, the research evidence has suggested that family life with a child with special needs may be highly stressful for family members, particularly for mothers (who have been most investigated) and also for some fathers and siblings. Nevertheless, this is far from being the complete picture, because there have been striking signs of variation between people in how stressed or adversely affected they were. Many brothers and sisters appeared to be adapting well, many marriages continued to be well integrated and strong, and some parents did not show greater stress than other parents without special needs children.

In perspective: the Pathological Model

Although this framework has been very important for alerting us to the incidence of stress and raised vulnerability in mothers and other family members, it has a number of serious deficiencies. The narrow focus on 'pathology' has been unable to explain the *variability* in stress levels seen in the studies reported previously. All difficulties around having a child with special needs are located *inside* the family, and no recognition is given of wider influences, such as the family's transactions with professionals, services and the wider society (see Chapter 3). It suggests that family life with a child with special needs is static, unchanging and uniform, i.e. *all* families will experience similar reactions and high stress levels and these will persist as the child gets older. But researchers have challenged this view. Gath (1974), for example, suggested that adverse effects were only found in families where the presence of a child with special needs was but one of a number of stresses on the family.

The Pathological Model encourages a view of families as *homogeneous*, and because they are assumed to have similar reactions and needs, these can be met by a uniform set of services.

The Common Needs Model

Around the late 1960s and early 1970s, a major shift in the care of disabled children from residential care to 'care in the community' (i.e. the child's home) occurred. Under the 1970 Education of Handicapped Children Act, children with severe handicapping conditions who until then had been classified as 'uneducable' and had been cared for in residential hospitals were now seen as eligible for education, and this contributed to a transfer of emphasis and responsibility from health to education. This led to thinking about the practical needs of parents for taking up their new or ongoing care role, and what 'community care' meant in material and practical terms (Wilkin, 1979). Researchers used survey methods to interview samples of parents, and the surveys revealed many common needs experienced by many parents. A consensus of views was also found regarding the services and their organisation, both in terms of the criticisms expressed by parents and in the changes they would like to see implemented (see review by Byrne and Cunningham, 1985).

Parents were found to be frequently socially isolated and restricted (particularly mothers), and having difficulties with the highly demanding care demands (such as night-time disturbance, physical care demands) and behaviour problems of their children (e.g. Hewett, 1972, Hannam, 1975, Glendenning, 1983, Ayer and Alaszewski, 1984). Mothers of children with severe learning difficulties carried the major care burden, with fathers providing the most support, followed by sisters (although the contribution of both was small) (Wilkin, 1979, Carey, 1982). Little significant help was received from relatives, friends or neighbours in day-to-day caring (Wilkin, 1979) and support from the social network was negligible in families of young children with special needs (Carey, 1982). This 'burden of care' was immensely demanding on family life and practical assistance from public services was needed to ease the burden. Instead of seeing the child as a pathology, unmet needs for services and material resources (*deficits*) were a major source of stress. This position can be summed up as a *needs-deficit* model. It is a viewpoint that continues to be widely endorsed by many parents and professionals in the childcare field.

Common needs reported included day provision during school holidays and weekends, baby sitting services, help with transport and financial help (Lonsdale, 1978, Wilkin, 1979, Carey, 1982) and the need for a link person between the family and health, social and education services to coordinate and mediate (Bayley, 1973, Lloyd-Bostock, 1976, Reid, 1983, Ayer and Alaszewski, 1984).

In perspective: the Common Needs Model

This model has been very helpful in focusing on the *practical* and material needs of parents and families and practical solutions to remedy these needs. It remains relevant today because of the continuing shortfall between families' perceived needs and the available service provision and resources for families in society (with distressing consequences for families). It has helped bring about a reconceptualisation of children and families with chronic illness or disability as 'ordinary people in exceptional circumstances' (e.g. Seligman and Darling, 1989, Eiser, 1990).

The model has been criticised for its tendency to assume that all families have *similar, homogeneous needs* (whatever their family resources and circumstances). This view predicts that similar service provision would be suitable for all families and that each family would benefit in a similar way from the same set of services. Recent research challenges this viewpoint (see Stress/Coping Model, below).

The Stress/Coping Model

An alternative framework for thinking about the impact of the child with special needs has been developing since the 1980s. The impetus for this shift in conceptual focus has come from a rapidly expanding set of studies whose findings do not fit comfortably into the two previous frameworks. The Stress/Coping Model developed in the mental health and family health literature has been particularly productive for linking these diverse findings together.

Variability in stress and vulnerability

Unlike earlier studies on the family, recent research has used a different methodology (called 'multivariate' or multi-factorial) where multiple measures are taken of the family to look at variation between families in their reactions to having a child with special needs and variation in possible causal factors. The main finding coming out of this approach has been of the *variability* in coping within and between individuals and over time (see reviews by Byrne and Cunningham, 1985, McConachie, 1991b). Many families cope remarkably well and show no apparent difference from ordinary families in the community on a whole variety of measures (Byrne *et al.*, 1988). After going through a very difficult process of adjustment and reorientation, many families of children with Down's Syndrome (in the Manchester cohort study) regained a varied, rich and 'ordinary' life and showed great strengths in coping with everyday pressures. On average, the mothers were not more stressed than urban mothers of normal children. Family relationships were generally reported to be satisfactory, and the majority reported excellent relationships between siblings (ibid.). In the Kent study of mothers with children with severe learning disabilities (Quine and Pahl, 1985), not all mothers showed higher stress levels than normal. Instead of a 'pathological' model, it is more appropriate to think of these families as 'ordinary' families having at times to face specific crises around having a disabled child (Seligman and Darling, 1989). But although many regain ordinary family life, a minority of families remain highly vulnerable and have many difficulties in coping.

In the Manchester cohort study, a minority of families (30 per cent) did experience 'critically' high levels of stress and were particularly vulnerable. A substantial minority expressed dissatisfaction with some part of their daily lives and relationships. Some families seem more vulnerable to stress than others. Burden (1980) found that the birth of a child with a disability places tremendous stress on most families, and the likelihood of emotional problems increases greatly in the early days after diagnosis. But whether the parents developed severe problems in the long term seemed linked to other critical experiences going on in and outside the family and also the parents' own personality.

Risk and vulnerability

What distinguishes those families who cope quite well from those who remain particularly vulnerable? Attempts to find simple links between stress-evoking events or features of the family and stress reactions have been inconclusive in the past (see p. 103). As an alternative research strategy, a multivariate approach using a range of variables (including primary ones and mediating ones that can moderate the effect of the primary ones) to predict coping and adaptation has been adopted in recent years. This strategy has identified factors which are highly predictive of high levels of stress and a perceived poor quality of life in parents. Although this does *not* imply that stress will be *inevitable*, it does suggest that the presence of these factors in family life constitutes a 'risk' for stress reactions. This has been shown across a variety of groups, such as families with children undergoing bone marrow transplant and with children with sensory or physical disability (Sloper and Knussen, 1991). The risk is likely to be increased if other risk factors are also present, or if some of the protective factors described on p. 111 are missing. The risk factors include:

1. Features of the child

   - behaviour problems in the child;
   - night time disturbance with the child, including difficulty in settling the child at night;

- multiple impairments in the child (a combination, possibly including incontinence, immobility, poor communication skills, a sensory impairment);
- communication problems in the child;
- serious problems with the child's physical health;
- more severe learning difficulties in the child;
- problems with the child's appearance;
- high excitability in the child.

2. Parental and family characteristics

- social isolation in the mother, lacking a close friend, not utilising available social support;
- socio-economic hardship – unemployment, no car, poor housing, low income, money worries, lack of maternal employment;
- poor parental education;
- high levels of strain from current life-events (see p. 115);
- marital dissatisfaction;
- poor coping strategies by the parent – a low use of practical coping methods; a high use of passive acceptance in dealing with child-related problems, and wishful thinking;
- lack of active recreation and leisure in the family;
- lack of strong moral-religious emphasis in the family;
- lack of family cohesion and closeness;
- families who have difficulty adjusting to the child and where the mother–child relationship continues to be poor. Poor mother–child relationships may reflect poor family relationships generally.

3. Service characteristics

- a high number of unmet needs

(Quine and Pahl, 1985, Byrne *et al.*, 1988, Sloper and Turner, 1993).

Note that many of these parent and family characteristics are also found in mothers with high levels of stress and vulnerability in the general population (see Brown and Harris, 1978, Lazarus and Folkman, 1984). It should be noted too that much of the research with families of children with special needs has been undertaken with mothers. There is evidence that the risk factors for fathers are not necessarily the same as for mothers. Behaviour problems in the child and unusual caretaking demands like regular night-time disturbance and severe health problems have been especially linked to high stress in mothers, probably because of the very heavy care demands placed on them. A perceived strain of recent life events and financial problems have been particularly associated with life dissatisfaction in fathers, as has a low communication skill level in the child and in boys (e.g. Beckman, 1983, McKinney and Peterson, 1987, Frey. et al., 1989, Sloper et al., 1991). But financial hardship and communication difficulties in the child have also been linked to maternal distress in Sloper and Turner's study (1993).

Resilience and coping

Irrespective of social or cultural background, there are many individual families who seem to cope very effectively. It cannot be assumed that these families do not have many problems and stressful events in their lives. But what seems to distinguish them from other families is that they have a greater resilience in the face of adversity and crises and greater ability to handle stressful experiences. 'Protective' factors are those which have been associated in the research literature with lower levels of stress and a greater satisfaction in life for mothers and fathers of children with special needs (there are some differences between mothers and fathers). They appear to confer resilience to stressful events and to increase coping ability. These include:

- a supportive social network, i.e. friends and relatives that are experienced at being supportive (but note, social networks can be a source of stress as well as support; parents with a highly supportive network felt more positively about their child, but also expressed more symptoms of stress [Waisbren, 1980]);
- support from and friendship with other parents of children with special needs (see too Bristol, 1984);
- an ability to acquire social support, e.g. being able to ask for help from friends, being able to participate cooperatively with professionals;
- satisfaction with the marital relationship;
- a cohesive, adaptable family system, including open communication between the members and harmony in parenting;
- utilitarian resources, e.g. employment (including maternal), adequate finance, adequate housing, having a car;
- a positive outlook, e.g. comparative appraisals like 'Well, Sandra's not as badly off as others; at least she can get around in her wheelchair', and positive beliefs like 'I know that we were meant to have a special child ... she's brought a lot of love into our family';
- a practical coping style, e.g. 'I'm alright as long as I get out one evening a week, have a good laugh and let my hair down ... it makes the rest of the week bearable';
- problem-solving skills for tackling problems;
- health and energy of individual family members;
- few unmet needs for help from services.

(Sources include Nihira *et al.*, 1980, Bristol, 1984, McKinney and Peterson, 1987, Frey *et al.*, 1989, Sloper *et al.*, 1991, Sloper and Turner, 1993).

Developing a Stress/Coping Model

Reviewers like Crnic *et al.* (1983) in the USA and Byrne and Cunningham (1985) in the UK have proposed using a conceptual model of stress, coping and family ecology to understand why families cope so differently. The Stress/Coping Model that has been most commonly used to make sense of the research findings is the model by Lazarus and Folkman (1984). Helen McConachie (1994) has drawn on this model in her summary of research studies of families of children with special needs (see Figure 5.1).

The stress/coping model highlights a complex relationship between the events causing a family stress (stressors) and the actual stress levels in parents and the family's ability to cope. Families differ greatly, not only in what stressful events they have to cope with, in how they organise themselves and in the resources that they have, but also in how they perceive the challenges they face (ibid.). The same event will have different meanings and effects for different individuals (i.e. perceptions act as 'mediating' factors between stressors and final stress levels in parents). This is graphically illustrated in an earlier study by Bradshaw

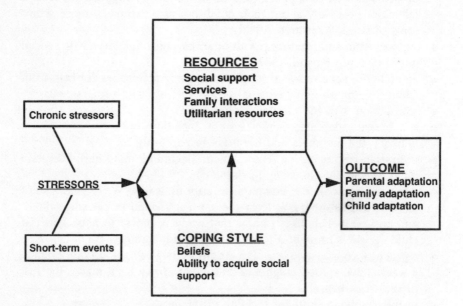

Figure 5.1 Stress/Coping Model
Source: McConachie, 1994. Reprinted with permission

and Lawton (1978). They showed that there was no straightforward relationship between objective factors such as a family's standard of housing,
their frequency of social outings, or their child's level of self-help skills
and a parent's level of stress. Stress was predicted instead by the mothers'
feelings and perceptions about these stressful factors, that is, whether she
considered the house was unsuitable, felt socially restricted, or felt that
the child was difficult to manage.

Coping strategies

Families differ in the ways in which they cope with stress; they show a
variety of *coping strategies*. Coping strategies are actions, behaviours and
thoughts used to handle and overcome a stress-evoking situation. They
may be used for solving problems raised by the situation and/or for
reducing stress linked to it. The following examples show some of the
variety of ways in which parents deal with stressful events:

- denying the diagnosis so as not having to face up to it;
- using respite facilities to give themselves a break from childcare;
- seeking help from friends and relatives;
- thinking positively (for example, the mother of a child with severe
  learning difficulty who said, 'Well, at least she's not got a physical
  handicap. I don't think I could cope with that . . .');
- changing one's way of viewing the situation (changing beliefs, values,
  etc.). For example, one mother said, 'Now I know he's always going
  to be slow, I've stopped worrying about why he's not doing this and
  that . . .';
- active information-seeking, e.g. seeking a second opinion, reading relevant books, asking questions;
- constructive problem-solving, i.e. identifying a problem and pursuing
  a realistic and effective means of solving the problem;
- passive acceptance of any treatment programmes offered (handing
  over responsibility to others or avoiding challenge or confrontation);
- withdrawal from a stressful situation, e.g. withdrawing from contact
  with the hospital, wishful thinking, avoiding other family members (as
  in some fathers, see p. 103).

Although all these coping strategies may be of some short-term benefit,
it has already been shown in the previous sections that some will probably be more effective than others in the longer term. Strategies which
have been associated with a positive adaptation in parents and their
satisfaction with life include *holding a positive belief and thinking positively* and *using constructive problem-solving* (such as planning, making
social contacts, etc.). This contrasts with less adaptive approaches, such
as avoidance of problems or wishful thinking (see review by Beresford,

1994). The implications of this for partnership work are discussed further on p. 122.

In perspective: the Stress/Coping Model

The main value of this model is that it draws attention to the *diversity* between families and their individuality, and moves away from an assumption of 'pathology' or one 'right' way of responding. Families vary widely in their resources, stresses and coping styles, and there is a complex interaction in each family between these and how well adapted they are as individuals and as a family. This model encourages a very flexible approach in practice, and some of the implications for partnership work with families are discussed further on pp. 119–25.

Research derived from this model has helped identify 'risk' factors which make families more vulnerable and 'protective' factors which potentially make families more able to cope with stress and crises. This information can be used to inform the professional so that they offer specific services and assistance that may be especially beneficial for the individual family. Some practice guidelines are given on p. 123 and in Chapter 7.

One concern is that it could lead to an over-emphasis on 'coping', thus removing attention from the real vulnerabilities and stresses of some individual family members (Eiser, 1993) and creating an added sense of failure in 'those who cannot cope'. Furthermore, experience shows that some people *cope* even in the face of harsh disadvantage and deprivation. By highlighting the individuality of family responses, it could remove responsibility from the State and society for the 'common' experiences and positioning of families of children with special needs in society. Responsibility may be taken away for providing adequate services and provision to combat the discrimination and disadvantage faced by all disabled people and their families (see Equal Opportunities Model, p. 117).

FAMILIES WITH OLDER CHILDREN AND ADOLESCENTS

Adopting a developmental perspective

Within the earlier frameworks, research tended to be restricted to one age period in the family life-cycle or to draw on a sample of parents of children of mixed ages and assume that stress reactions would be similar whatever the life stage of the child and family. The importance of adopting a lifecycle and developmental perspective when considering vulnerability has been suggested by various findings.

The experiences of a family may be affected by the child's age, their disabling condition, and the stage of the lifecycle they are going through.

For example, behaviour problems in the child (which have been associated with a poor outcome for mothers) may be more difficult to cope with for parents of children with learning difficulties in middle childhood (Sloper *et al.*, 1991) than for parents of young physically disabled children (e.g. Sloper and Turner, 1993). Lack of mobility in a physically disabled child may be much easier to bear in preschool years than in later childhood, when the child would be expected to be mobile.

How the child behaves at a particular stage may affect how the parent responds to the child, and this in turn may affect how the child is at a later stage, suggesting a cyclical influence in the parent–child relationship over time. Behaviour problems in the child were found to decrease later when mothers had shown positive adjustment to the child (with the initial level of behaviour problems controlled in the study) (Sloper *et al.*, 1988). Other interactional effects between family members may also develop over time. In one study, the fathers' adjustment to the child at year 1 was found to significantly predict the mothers' adjustment to the child at three years (Frey *et al.*, 1989).

Different periods in the lifecycle bring different tasks that have to be accomplished and create differing demands on a family. Living with infants and preschool children, a family will have to organise itself around heavy caretaking demands and shared family activities; a family with adolescent children may need to organise around increasing separation between family members and more independent family activities. Movement from one period of childhood and through specific lifecyle events, such as the birth of a child, starting school, entering puberty, requires periods of transition and change for family members.

Although change can lead to periods of growth opening up new and exciting challenges and possibilities, it can also be demanding and cause anxiety and uncertainty (especially if the change is unpredictable, unwelcome and unfamiliar, and if the rate and degree of changes are excessive). Changes require new behaviours to accomplish new tasks and new responses to changing circumstances. Any period of crisis and change may overload the family's existing coping resources, making the family particularly vulnerable.

Caplan (1964) distinguished times of potential crisis in the life of any individual, i.e. 'normal crises' at times of transition, e.g. going to school, leaving home, starting work, marriage, birth of the first child, death of parents, retirement, and also crises which were not common to all, such as the birth of a child with special needs, death of a spouse or child, marital break-up, loss of one's job or house, unemployment. Wikler *et al.* (1981) point out that in periods of transition for the child, such as starting school, leaving school, entering puberty, preparing for guardianship and residential placements, the parents may experience recurrences of earlier grief and distress and be in particular need of help. Dora Black (1987) identified many specific periods and events that may be difficult or demanding for the family of a child with special needs and may arouse anxiety and stress, such as when the parents realise the implications of the impairment for the child and the family; when a decision about school placement has to be made; when a decision about future pregnancies has to be made and during subsequent pregnancies; when the prospect of promotion or job change involves moving away from the family, neighbourhood and professional supports; if there is a significant deterioration in the disorder or if the child dies; when the child fails to negotiate a normal developmental stage; if another child in the family develops the same or another disorder; if the child requires an operation. As Black pointed out, since these periodic crisis periods are additional to those normally experienced by every family, the likelihood of two or more hazardous times concurring is high.

The needs of parents of adolescents and adults with disabilities have rarely been considered, although their needs and difficulties may be very different from those of families with young children (Byrne and Cunningham, 1985). A number of studies have identified considerable anxiety in parents, because their young people were unemployed as adults or passing their time in inappropriate occupational activities (Hirst, 1982), or they were concerned about the future when they could no longer cope as parents and where and how the young adult would live (Card, 1983). Card (1983) described the often painful and distressing adjustment parents must make to a new and more separate relationship with their adult son and daughter. Even though parents were concerned about future provision, most wanted to keep their young person with them for as long as possible and preserve their relationship, and this could cause conflict with professionals who desired to develop independence in the young person.

A Change/Life-cycle Model

A *change/life-cycle* model recognises that the family is a developing, dynamic unit, and that children and families change over time, their needs and resources change, and service provision must provide a continuity and flexible adaptation to help families through changing periods. Services have often been criticised for lacking continuity (see p. 70), particularly at transition periods from preschool into school, or from school into adulthood when the existing service personnel tend to fall away and are either not replaced or followed by new staff. Different life-cycle events and periods in childhood present different challenges, demands and opportunities for the child and their parents.

This model suggests the importance of looking at *change* over time, but few studies have included this in their design (McConachie, 1991b).

Parents of teenagers and young adults report being less supported by formal and informal networks than parents of young children (Suelzle and Keenan, 1981) even though their needs for support and guidance may be just as great (Hirst, 1982, Wikler *et al.*, 1981, Suelzle and Keenan, 1981).

THE FAMILY IN SOCIETY

Disadvantaged families

Many studies in the United Kingdom have shown the particular pressure placed on families by the additional care needs of children with disabilities and special needs (see p. 107). In many families, parents (especially mothers) carry an enormous burden of care. The recent OPCS studies (1989) found that disability imposed considerable additional costs on all the caring families. Even when families had a member in employment, earnings were likely to be significantly less than for similar families without a disabled child. Additional costs for heating, laundry, clothing and food were particular strains on low incomes, with many women unable to work because of the care needs. Single parents were significantly worse off (75 per cent relying wholly on state benefits). Only 4 per cent of the families received respite care, although 50 per cent felt that both their own and their child's health were adversely affected by limited opportunities to go out or to give time equally to all family members.

As Phillippa Russell (1993) has pointed out, increased pressures of care and the vulnerability of disabled children and their families have to be put in the wider context of social and demographic change in UK society. Poverty has been increasing sharply in families with children in the UK (Bradshaw, 1990) and many families are under great strain. Within this backcloth of increased vulnerability, one would expect the stresses on all families of children with special needs to be rising.

Equal Opportunities Model

This viewpoint argues that disabled people (and their families) are disadvantaged in their access to resources and opportunities as a result of discrimination against disabled people and their lack of means for gaining access to opportunities. Disability is viewed primarily as a psycho-social/ political issue rather than a medical one (even though there are medical implications). Thus, disability only becomes a 'handicap' in certain social conditions (e.g. the wheelchair-bound child is handicapped when there are no ramps, adapted toilets or lifts). The economic findings of the OPCS studies (1989) revealed the economic disadvantage of families with a disabled child, and unemployment and other adverse socio-economic factors are likely to put special strains on families. Lack of paid employment of the mother and inadequate financial resources have been strongly associated with a poor outcome for mothers (high stress and a poor perceived quality of life) (Sloper and Turner, 1993). Their children are more likely to develop behaviour problems (as are non-disabled children under these circumstances) (Byrne *et al.*, 1988). The emphasis from this model is on altering services, attitudes in society and institutionalised discrimination, to overcome the disadvantage for disabled people (and their families). Socially disadvantaged families need better housing, improved employment opportunities and a reduction of financial strain. Income support, financial benefits, and priority applications for housing may all be critical. Mothers may need assistance to take up paid employment through a wider availability of flexible childcare schemes and a service intervention from professionals that can accommodate to working mothers (e.g. better coordination, flexible home visiting times). Adequate respite and leisure activities for the young person and employment opportunities for the young adult with special needs are required to remove some of the care burden from the family. Increased opportunities for social and educational integration of disabled children (and their families) would open up greater acceptance of people with disabilities in society and also reduce their social isolation. It would follow too that the social and economic disadvantage and discrimination against members of ethnic minorities would add to a double disadvantage for these families, if they have a child with special needs (see Shah, 1992).

This model has very widespread support by adults with disabilities, campaigning groups on behalf of the civil rights of disabled people and many ordinary people in Britain, as shown in the enormous support for the Civil Rights (Disabled Persons) Bill (which came before Parliament in May 1994 and was defeated at its third reading).

Services which improve families' lives

One way of helping families overcome their disadvantages is to offer good-quality services that can meet some of their needs for assistance. But contrary to professional assumption, involvement with professionals can actually exacerbate stress in parents (Harris and McHale, 1989). Stress may be aroused by service provision that is poorly structured or badly coordinated, or where service needs are unmet (Sloper and Turner, 1993).

A number of 'quality' services have demonstrated, however, that professional assistance can provide accessible and relevant help that may be a beneficial and important addition to families' lives. For examples of services that have been well appraised by parents and found to be beneficial, see pp. 51–2, 183, 188, 200, 283. Research on these projects and other services has gone some way towards identifying important,

and possibly essential, components of care and effective service provision
for families with children with special needs. Many of the features identified in these projects have been demonstrated at the KIDS Family
Centre, Camden (see Chapter 10). All families with children with special
needs may need external support and assistance at some time during the
childhood years, and a comprehensive support system should be set up
as a right for all families with a child with special needs across the age
range. A model of a support system (the KIDS Family Centre) is described
in Chapter 10. At this Centre, the role of the named worker was developed for responding to the *fluctuating* needs of families for support
assistance across the childhood lifecycle, and to support families through
stressful periods. It fits in with the position of the Equal Opportunities
Model that all families with children with special needs may need additional assistance, or positive discrimination, to help them overcome their
disadvantaged position.

In the final section, we draw on the Stress/Coping Model and associated research findings to consider some implications for practice.

IMPLICATIONS FOR PRACTICE

The most important point to make first is that it cannot be assumed that
any research finding will necessarily apply to the individual parent and
family. Any factor in the family circumstances that has been shown to be
a 'risk' or a 'protective' factor in a group of families may not necessarily
have a negative or positive effect in the individual family (because other
factors may be mediating and altering the influence). The value of these
research findings, as analysed below, is that it alerts us to the *possibility*
of increased risk or increased protection from stress if some of the identified factors are present in the family.

Diversity and individuality

Probably the most useful contribution from the Stress/Coping Model is
to emphasise the diversity and individuality of families. Families will have
a wide range of resources, stresses and coping styles. There is no clearcut
'normality' or 'abnormality': what works for one family in their coping
approach may not work for another. This implies that one can learn about
all these factors and *what they mean* to the family only from the family
directly. It suggests the importance of a flexible approach to each family
and the inappropriateness of imposing indiscriminate assumptions on the
family (cf. Pathological Model).

It also suggests that each family will need an individualised package of
services that fit in with the family's own current needs, and their particular strengths and coping resources. A 'link person' will be needed to

coordinate service input to the family, and to establish that the timing and mixture of services offered is appropriate for the family's present circumstances (Byrne *et al.*, 1988, Quine and Pahl, 1989, Sloper *et al.*, 1991). What kind of assistance and how much is required will vary with each family and at different times, and this can be established only through negotiation with the family (see Chapter 7: Assessment of Family Needs).

A 'holistic' approach to the child and family

Another key element coming out of the Stress/Coping Model for practice is the predicted contribution of many different aspects of family life to how a family is adapting. Although specific child issues may be affecting the parents and family (such as behaviour problems, night-time disturbance), these will interact with many other influencing factors (such as the parents' positive or negative outlook on life, their general beliefs, material/utilitarian resources, and coping styles). Concern about the well-being of the family will require a 'holistic' approach to a much wider set of issues than has traditionally been the case. This demands a family-focused intervention by the individual professional, and a multi-agency, coordinated framework of service delivery.

Drawing on risk and protective factors

Specific factors have been shown to predict highly how well parents and families are adapting to their life situation, and this has a number of implications for practice. The professional would be advised to be alerted to whether these factors may be affecting an individual family, because of their potential effects on the family and also for deciding what intervention might be helpful. Any finding can be used to inform the professional, but whether an intervention will be appropriate for the individual family can ultimately be decided only in negotiation with the family. Chapter 7 shows ways of bringing the professional's knowledge (the 'professional perspective') into the assessment of needs with the family (see p. 156).

The family cohesion

Two elements of cohesion have been shown to be good predictors of positive parental and family adaptation: firstly, support from one's spouse and a strong marital relationship, and secondly, cohesive harmonious relationships in the family, with open communication. Both features seem to give a family strength and ability to withstand the negative impact of stress.

Of concern is the fact that a professional's preoccupation with the child (and possibly one parent) could inadvertently weaken family cohesion in the longer term. In various ways, support from the spouse can be under-mined or overlooked. In many home visiting schemes, the mother of a preschool child is visited regularly whilst the husband is at work. This might lower the father's confidence and skills in handling his child, compared with the mother's developing skills. A risk factor for stress in fathers has been shown to be having a child with low communication skills, especially if it is a boy. Fathers may benefit from guidance in communicating and playing with their child, so they become more confi-dent in relating to the child (McConachie, 1986, 1994).

Professional intervention can, nevertheless, support and possibly build on family cohesion. To bolster the family's cohesion, the professional would need to be aware of and to respect the family's ways of organis-ing and managing their internal resources to deal with the demands that are facing them. This requires taking time to get to know about the family's structure, culture and organisation; particular efforts will be needed to get to know about a family from a different ethnic/cultural background. The professional may have a role to play in supporting family cohesion and reducing family tensions by bringing the family together and facilitating their shared understandings and joint decision-making on issues affecting the child with special needs and the whole family. Support intervention could be structured around thinking of the family as a 'system', and considering the interactions and communi-cations between different family members and how they affect each other (see Chapter 6).

Support and assistance to one family member may in some situa-tions enhance family cohesion. Stressed fathers tend to withdraw from other family members and not support their partners (see p. 103). Fathers' groups, where fathers meet regularly for social support, have been asso-ciated at a later evaluation with lower stress and depression in fathers and higher satisfaction regarding their social support in fathers *and* in mothers. Mothers reported increased family cohesion (Vadasy *et al.*, 1986b).

In some families, there may be special stresses and difficulties in com-munication in their relationships. In research, some siblings have been shown to be prohibited from expressing negative affect and anger to the child with special needs by the parents (see p. 104). Difficulties can arise with grandparents who are grappling with their own reactions to the child and taking a major support role in the family. When their own parents were involved, fathers of young children with special needs tended to do more with their child and feel more competent, but both mothers and fathers registered higher stress (Waisbren, 1980). A suggestion for help has been of training in assertiveness skills for family members, to help them communicate and assert their personal needs within the family (e.g. Schilling *et al.*, 1984, Ferraro and Tucker, 1993).

Mothers too have been shown to be at 'risk' if they have difficulties communicating with their child with a disability (Sloper and Turner, 1993). This suggests that mothers could be helped by early intervention services putting a greater focus on mother–child interaction.

Coping strategies

The professional will need to be aware that a variety of different behaviours by the parents and other family members can function as *coping strategies*. A parent who does not attend her clinic appointments at the hospital may, for example, be using a coping strategy of trying to reduce stress by withdrawing from a stress-evoking situation. Because these strategies may play an important role in their coping with the stresses of having a child with special needs (or with other stresses), it is advisable to start from a position of respecting and accepting the family members' own strategies. Intervention should aim to work constructively with and not confront or undermine these coping methods. It would not, for example, be appropriate to expect a father to attend frequent meetings with the professionals if the family's survival depended on the income generated by his long working hours.

Nevertheless, it may be helpful to introduce the family gradually to other methods of coping when they lack coping resources or their existing strategies have outlived their usefulness or are not proving very effective. Research and clinical experience show that parents fare better with some ways of coping than others (see pp. 110–11). In one family, for example, the parents' denial of their child's diagnosis was useful in the early days because it reduced acute stress levels, but in the longer term it became detrimental because it prevented them carrying out necessary actions and problem-solving around their child's disability. It stopped them receiving assistance which might have been useful for the child and themselves, because they turned away all offers of help.

Introducing a family to another strategy would need to be done carefully so as not to discount the validity of their current way of coping. But as a longer-term objective, intervention should aim to increase parents' feelings of control over events through *constructive problem-solving* and to instil *positive views about their situation* (these are strategies which have been associated with effective coping, see p. 111 and McConachie, 1994). Parents can be helped to view their child and situation more positively (e.g. positive comparative appraisals, identifying positive characteristics in the child). Cognitive behavioural therapy has been suggested as an approach in helping parents reframe their ideas about their situation, such as learning to tell themselves that 'I can find a solution to this; asking for help is a strong thing for me to do' (ibid.). In addition, parents can be taught problem-solving skills (see Chapter 4); they may need help to use practical coping techniques (i.e. what they can *do* to improve their situation). Parents can also be given counselling help to support and encourage their coping efforts, such as help-seeking strategies.

Strengths in the family

A variety of factors have been linked with wellbeing and adaptation in the parent and family, such as a strong marital relationship, paid employment for women, leisure/recreational activities in the family, and a religious-moral framework (see p. 110). The professional can help a family build on its strengths by acknowledging them and helping a family to identify and utilise them effectively. This also helps the professional and family to place the professional's contribution or other professional assistance into perspective. It is important that service intervention does not undermine a parent or family's strengths. For example, a woman who gains strengths from her job but feels guilty when she fails to attend all clinic appointments with her child might benefit from a reorganisation of appointments to fit in with the days she is not working.

Vulnerability and vulnerable families

Knowledge about 'risk' factors (see p. 109) helps the professional to become more informed about possible sources of stress within the family, though whether these factors (or any other ones) are actually causing stress will depend on what they mean to the individual family. The professional may help the family consider how these sources of stress can be reduced or minimised, if possible. Some areas may be beyond the bounds of the professional's responsibility, such as economic problems, but the professional can help by providing an intervention which makes realistic demands on a family's resources, and is sensitive to the competing demands for time and energy on the family (Dunst and Leet, 1987).

The professional may also have a direct contribution to make towards helping the minority of families who are especially vulnerable and will have specific needs for extra services. The professional will need skills in identifying those families who are very stressed and in need of urgent assistance. Knowledge of 'risk' factors can help in this process of identification.

For example, families with children with more severe learning difficulties and behaviour problems may be highly stressed. Extra help might involve identifying and assessing the child's behaviour difficulties and setting up behaviour modification/management programmes in consultation with the parents, or increasing parental responsiveness to the child's cues and parental consistency in management. These families may need generous access to day- and night-time relief/respite schemes to have a much-needed break (Byrne *et al.*, 1988).

Parents with children with severe physical and health problems are likely to be very restricted in their leisure and social activities and will also need generous access to respite care with skilled carers, who can cater for the very special needs of the child, as well as needing assistance from well coordinated and integrated service provision (ibid.).

Byrne *et al.* (1988) found that the most vulnerable families were those where the mother–child and general family relationships were poor. In this group, the child was likely to be perceived as difficult, to be attention-seeking and socially intrusive, and to show behaviour problems. Extra help might include intervention to help 'restore the emotional bond'. Parents may need help to understand their child and its behaviour in a more positive way. They may need help to interact positively with the child and experience more warmth and closeness. In families with poor family relationships, it will be important that any intervention takes the whole family system into account (see Chapter 6); family therapy may be especially useful for families with poor relationships (ibid.).

A fourth group of vulnerable families is where the parent is socially isolated and lacks support from their spouse, relatives and friends (see following).

Socially isolated families

Informal social support has been shown in the research to be highly important for family wellbeing; a parent's *satisfaction with social support* is a highly predictive factor of positive adaptation. Parents who can turn to relatives, friends, or organisations of parents of disabled children are likely to have greater wellbeing and family adaptation than those who are very isolated and unsupported. For some families, informal support is well provided for and the involvement of professionals is of secondary importance and may even obstruct their opportunity for social relating. Frequent appointments may deplete parental resources and prevent a parent having time to visit friends, get to know other parents, or take up employed work.

Apart from ascertaining that any intervention does not undermine the parent's own sources of support, professionals can also assist with developing the family's support networks. In the longer term, this helps a family shift from dependency on professional support to more 'normalised' support in the community (Seligman and Darling, 1989). It is useful to know that informal support can generate stress as well as give assistance. Support networks that are close-knit and dense (i.e. closely interlinked, with many of the people knowing each other, as against a loose network) may not only foster a sense of cohesiveness and support, but also create stress (Kazak and Marvin, 1984). This may be because the members are more prone to 'burn-out' (Kazak, 1986). In such circumstances, families may be helped by 'opening up' their network to include new sources of support, such as being introduced to the 'link family' schemes of social service departments (McConachie, 1994).

Parents' groups for parents of children with special needs can be a source of valuable support (e.g. Crowe, 1979, Hatch and Hinton, 1986), although parents vary in when and whether they find them helpful. The acceptability of the 'differentness' and the 'disability' connotations of these groups or any centre for children with special needs will vary across parents, some of whom will prefer a more integrated setting or will not feel ready to enter 'the world of disability' (see Chapter 10). But there is research evidence that families with low support in and outside the home may particularly appreciate access to social groups, parent groups and parent and child opportunity groups (see Chapter 10), and these parents may appreciate being helped and supported by professionals in their initial mixing with other parents. Other family members may benefit from support groups, e.g. for siblings (Ferraro and Tucker, 1993, Newson and Davies, 1994) or for grandparents (Vadasy et al., 1986a).

Groups for families of a particular ethnic group may be especially valuable in combating isolation and extending the support network. The weekly group for Bangladeshi mothers of the Parent Advisory Service (see p. 188) has enabled mothers to meet and support each other (Davis et al., 1994). Many of these mothers had been extremely socially isolated, living in very poor-quality housing (often high-rise flats), lacking an available extended family and further segregated through fear of racial abuse. They tended rarely to leave their homes and the weekly support group was often a lifeline.

Professionals can provide a useful role in helping parents locate support groups or set up such groups (Linder, 1970, Evans et al., 1986). In the Southend-on-Sea Group Therapy Scheme (described in Pugh, 1981) and the KIDS Parent Support Link Project (NCVCCO Under 5s Initiative), professionals worked in partnership with parents in running parent befriender schemes for parents with young children with special needs. The value of parent-to-parent support, where a 'matched' volunteer parent, who is prepared, trained and backed up by professional staff, can offer practical and emotional support to a needy family, has been demonstrated in Home Start schemes (Van der Eyken, 1982). This fits in with the concept of 'resource exchange' proposed in the Empowerment Model of partnership (see p. 13).

In summary, in this chapter, the main theoretical frameworks for understanding the impact of a child with special needs on the family have been discussed and their relative merits considered. The Stress/Coping Model and associated research findings have been shown to lead to a range of implications for professional practice.

In the next chapter, we look at practical ideas for working in partnership with the whole family.

Chapter 6

Working with the whole family

This chapter explores some practical ideas for working in partnership with the whole family group. Since most thinking on partnership work has focused on the one-to-one relationship with the parent, methods of working with the whole group are at a more rudimentary stage of development. As we will see in this chapter, the Negotiating Model can be applied to working with the whole group, but there are some particular challenges for the professional and the family. Ideas from family systems thinking will be drawn on to consider family functioning and the impact of the professional on the family and vice versa.

TASK AND BOUNDARIES

In the previous chapter, a case was made for not 'pathologising' or assuming any unusual problems in families who have a child with special needs. Although some families will be very vulnerable or going through a very stressful period, many families are adaptive and show great resilience and strengths in dealing with the exceptional demands around disability. It is particularly important then that the privacy of the family is respected and involvement with the whole family (or part of it) is undertaken only with the members' consent. Moreover, there are many ways in which families will need to draw on professional assistance for helping them with their child with special needs (such as medical treatment, therapies, education), and these joint tasks should not be viewed as 'problems' of the family. In this sense, family work in partnership is different from family therapy, though many of the insights and approaches from family therapy can be usefully applied in any family work, including with families of children with special needs (see further Berger and Foster, 1986, Black, 1987, Seligman and Darling, 1989).

To keep the boundary clear, an early task in any family work is to establish and agree upon roles and boundaries, and to explore mutual expectations and understandings (see Chapter 2). Roles and boundaries will need to be established and agreed on, and you may need to ask your-self the following questions:

- What is my role?
- What is my primary task/the objectives of my intervention?
- What are the boundaries/limits of my intervention?
- What constraints inhibit what I can do in my present role position?

Exercise 6.1 enables you to reach a clearer understanding of your own role with respect to these questions. In Chapter 2, we looked at the process of defining a shared objective or task, clarifying responsibilities and creating realistic expectations of what can be achieved, and then reaching a joint 'contract'. This process can be adapted for use with both parents or the wider family group.

Boundaries can be very difficult to preserve in family work, especially if visiting a family at home and/or being closely involved with the family. Certain professionals, such as the Portage home visitor, the day nursery staff, the physiotherapist, or health visitor, may be very closely involved with the family and get pulled into many family issues and concerns. A difficulty will be knowing where to draw the limit of one's involvement; it may be difficult to stick to one's professional agenda (such as teaching the child, carrying out physiotherapy). Alternatively, one's role constraints may prevent one giving the help that is really needed. This issue of balancing the different needs within the family is discussed further on p. 132. But suffice to say here, extra care is needed to clarify and preserve the limits to one's intervention. At the same time, the question of when to be flexible will need addressing.

It is a common experience in family work that the presenting concern or issue does not remain the only concern or is the most significant problem, and the professional and family will need to be prepared for renegotiation of the initial 'contract' at later periods.

We turn now to considering the application of the Negotiating Model for family work.

APPLYING THE NEGOTIATING MODEL

Access and consent

The first step in working with a whole family is to gain access and to meet the various family members. Exercise 6.2 provides an opportunity for examining which family members are usually met in your own caseload practice. Nevertheless, access or presence cannot be assumed to signify consent to participate. Anyone who does home visiting knows the diffi-culty of knowing who to involve or who wants to be involved, if they find themselves having to clamber over the dog, compete with the blaring TV, and sandwich themselves on the sagging sofa between three generations, all apparently uninterested or fiercely glaring. Sometimes only the dog or the pet iguana shows a willingness to get involved!

A clear invitation will need to be extended to all relevant family members to become involved and to participate, and their willingness to collaborate must be established. Securing consent has to be negotiated individually with each family member, including children and siblings. But in some families, it is a lengthy process finding out who wants to get involved or not, and the professional will have to contend with this ambiguity and uncertainty.

It is likely in a partnership approach that the decision to get involved and consent issues are kept mainly in the control of the family in the initial period. But it may become important to involve other family members or the whole family in some situations, such as an assessment of family needs, or a decision on respite care or a residential holiday. If one parent feels it is appropriate to keep out the siblings or the other parent, one can accept their convictions, whilst at the same time suggesting definitely that the presence of the other family members would be useful for you to get a clear picture of the situation and the family's needs. As Emilia Dowling explains in her article on using a joint systems approach with families and schools, this shifts the emphasis from '*you* as an *expert* offering help to them, as *them as experts* in their knowledge of a given situation helping *you* to understand it better' (Dowling, 1985, p. 20).

Who referred? Whose concern?

It cannot be assumed that there is a consensus in the family of what help or whether help is needed from the professional. A first step in defining the problem is to find out

- Who is concerned?
- What is the concern about?
- What are the expectations of those concerned about the professional's intervention? (Dowling, 1985).

One parent may have been referred for respite help, not necessarily with their partner's agreement. Or a home teacher may have referred a family to a family centre because the parents are very depressed and isolated, and one parent is much clearer about the reason for the referral and the function of the family centre than the other parent. A GP may have referred the child for a specialist developmental assessment at the hospital, and neither parent fully understands what the concern is about.

The professional will want to explore with the family the referral, the background to the referral, and the nature of the problem or issue as seen by various members of the family, and their expectations regarding the professional's intervention (see Chapter 2). This starts clarifying whether there are shared expectations and understandings not only between the parents themselves but also between the parents and the professional.

In family work that lacks the tight boundaries of 'therapy', family members may come and go in their contact with the professional. In some home visits, the father is present as well as brothers and sisters, or a grandparent or friend; at other times, only the mother or a childminder will be there. Sometimes the father will turn up at the hospital appointment; at other times the mother will come. This makes it much more difficult to ascertain shared objectives, tasks, and 'contracts' with the whole group. Because of this, it may be necessary at key transition periods, such as starting or terminating a service, beginning a behavioural modification programme, changing a medical regime, or holding a family assessment meeting, that the professional extends a firm and clear invitation for all relevant members to attend (see Dowling, 1985) so that shared understandings and decisions can be reached and objectives set.

Without establishing consensus, beginning a new intervention with one or two members may come up against resistance from others in the family. A behavioural programme that aims for consistent parental management to reduce a child's behaviour problems or a night-time programme to reduce night-time waking will be undermined if one parent refuses to respond to the child in the same way as the other parent. A Makaton signing programme with a child with delayed speech will not be very effective if one parent refuses to use the signs, and communicates differently to the child from the other parent.

Another reason for involving both parents is that one parent may be a valuable support to the other parent in carrying out any intervention programme. The importance of support from one's spouse was discussed in Chapter 5. There is evidence that while fathers may not at present play a leading role in caring for their child with special needs, they may perceive their role as supporting their wives, and their presence and support may be vital for the mental wellbeing of the mothers (Nagy and Ungerer, 1990, see review by Eiser, 1993). In Nagy and Ungerer's study of mothers and fathers of children with cystic fibrosis, mothers who received considerable social support from their husbands reported better mental health. Therefore, involving fathers (or getting their commitment to a programme) may help mothers to have the internal resources to carry out an intervention programme. Moreover, fathers who are involved are likely to carry more responsibility for the general household chores and care of the non-disabled children (Klein and Simmons, 1979), and this allows mothers to have the time and energy to give extra help to the child with special needs.

The next section provides some guidelines for applying the Negotiating Model to working with the whole group. Means of working with the different perspectives of the family in order to negotiate and reach a decision on family needs are discussed further in Chapter 7.

Guidelines for practice

1. *'Join' the family* (see too Chapter 2). This requires joining the family culture, accepting and blending in with the family's organisation, experiencing how the family interacts and communicates together, and following the family's path of communication (Minuchin, 1974). The 'joining' process is particularly important for becoming familiar to and trusted by all members of the family, and may require having meetings when all or most members are present.
2. *Get to know about the whole family*, its composition, its cultural style, its beliefs, its ways of interacting and communicating, who carries which responsibilities, etc. This requires looking at a family in a multi-dimensional way. The dimensions for classifying a family in Table 6.1 may be useful for this (and Exercise 6.3 for trying out the classification system).
3. *Support the family's coping methods.* You will need to learn about the family's concerns and preferences, its resources, its stresses and how it deals with them. Any intervention will need to respect the family's coping strategies and not undermine family cohesion (see Chapter 5); this includes looking at the impact of any programme on all family members in terms of stress, energy and time (McConachie, 1994).
4. *Show respect.* All members of the family need to feel equally respected and to be able to retain the privacy of the family boundary.
5. *Seek active consent from all family members* if you are going to do any direct family intervention, including from children and siblings (but see p. 175). Try to involve all members in decision-making and activity, but respect the family structure if it inhibits this (see later in chapter).
6. *Stay neutral.* Avoid making an alliance with one member or colluding with one member's preferences. A neutral position is especially important when members are disagreeing or showing differences in their concerns and needs.
7. *Enable each member to contribute* through listening, asking questions and seeking further information and through helping them to participate in joint activities. The child with special needs and their siblings may need particular assistance to join in group discussions and activities with the professional.
8. *Acknowledge each member's viewpoint.* Listen to each member carefully and non-judgementally; you need to find out how each person understands and conceptualises their situation and the family situation.

Working with the whole family group requires being prepared for and committed to working with multiple perspectives.

9. *Share your perspective with the family*, if appropriate. It may be appropriate to share your view of what might be helpful for the family, or your knowledge of family reactions (e.g. to stressful events). This contribution is discussed further on p. 136 and in Chapter 7.

10. *Use negotiation and assist negotiation.* The professional may have a role to play in helping members communicate and negotiate with each other, as an independent 'third party'. The aim would be to draw together their different perspectives to reach some joint resolution on a decision, to help them coordinate their actions or reach a greater understanding of each other's viewpoints. Decision-making between the professional and the family must also proceed through negotiation, and this may be time-consuming if seeking informed consent with each member (see p. 173).

11. *Be prepared for disagreement.* There may be disagreement within the family, or between the professional and family/individual family members. The professional can sometimes play a useful role in helping disagreement between members come to the surface and provide a 'containing' function which allows them to work on resolving their disagreements together. Disagreement needs to be worked with constructively, using strategies to resolve the disagreement (see p. 93) wherever possible. (But see following sections and *Conflict within the family* on p. 141.)

12. *Recognise the potential impact of the professional on the family system or of the family on the professional (and professional network)* and monitor the consequences of this two-way influence (see p. 142).

Balancing different needs

Different members of the family will have differing needs, and family work requires a willingness to be flexible and to respond to these differences. But in practice this can lead to an uncomfortable pull between competing needs. Home teachers will be familiar with the predicament of whether to listen to the parent and respond to their concerns or whether to continue with the professional agenda of teaching the child with special needs.

The structuring of any meeting with the family must allow time for different members to express their concerns and preoccupations, whilst retaining sufficient time to continue the agreed task objective. Many Portage home visitors allow about twenty minutes for the parent to discuss wider family issues within each meeting, so that the parent knows of the regular space for talking but also of the boundary with the teaching period.

Table 6.1 Multiple dimensions of the family

FAMILY STRUCTURE

a) Membership	e.g. child with special needs, single parent/ couple, siblings, grandparents, non-related carers
b) Cultural style	e.g. ethnicity/culture/religion, socio-economic status, geographical region
c) Ideological style	e.g. beliefs, values, 'family culture'
d) Resources/stresses	e.g. informal social support, good marital relationship; utilitarian — economic, housing, employment, service provision/facilities; coping strategies, vulnerability factors, e.g. physical/ mental illness, isolation, severity of child's disability

FAMILY INTERACTIONS   interaction patterns, sub-systems, communication patterns, cohesion and adaptability, organisation of tasks, family routines and traditions

FAMILY FUNCTIONS

Interaction and activity in the family to fulfil the following functions:

economic	generating income, paying bills
domestic/health care	preparing food, transportation, medical visits
recreation	hobbies, recreation for the family
affection	mutual concern, nurturing, meeting needs of individual members
educational/vocational	learning/stimulation, play, career choice
socialisation	transmission of social values, norms, culture, friendships, development of self- and family-identity
negotiating life-cycle events	

FAMILY LIFE-CYCLE

Developmental stages of family childbearing, school-age, adolescence
Adaptation to child with
special needs

Crisis/transition period	e.g. diagnosis, formal education assessment, leaving school

Source: adapted from Seligman and Darling, 1989

Because of the many different aspects of family life that may be affecting a family at any period of time and the importance of taking a 'holistic' view (see Chapter 5), it is ideal if space is permitted within each meeting to review where things are for them as a family and as individuals.

Differing perspectives: the professional and the family

We have discussed earlier in the book the possibility or likelihood of the professional seeing the family situation or the particular issue of concern in different terms from the parent and family. In Chapter 3, the tendency to label some parents and families in negative or stereotypical terms, such as 'the over-protective family', 'the dysfunctional family', 'the un-cooperative family', or 'the Black mother' was discussed. This distancing or objectifying process can get in the way of empathising with and seeing a situation from the parent and family's perspective(s) and reaching a basis of understanding for moving forward cooperatively. It can also reflect a failure on the professional's side to take account of the *relationship* and transactions between the family and the professional, which may be contributing to the family's reactions.

Re-framing

Construct theory predicts that there are multiple ways of viewing the same situation, person or relationship, depending on the viewpoint from which it is seen (Kelly, 1955). Re-framing is a technique that can be used to change the conceptual and/or emotional setting or viewpoint in relation to a situation, and to place it in another frame which fits the 'facts' of the same concrete situation equally, or even better, and thereby changes its entire meaning (Watzlawick, 1974). This can change the 'entire personal significance' of the situation in question. Re-framing has been used as a crucial strategy in family therapy (structural family therapy, Minuchin, 1974). The Milan school has developed the notion of 'positive connota-tion' (positive re-framing) as part of their systemic approach to problems (Palazzoli *et al.*, 1978).

Re-framing can be used to help shift from viewing the parent from the professional's perspective to imagining the same situation from the *parent's* perspective. The parent's behaviour, for instance, might be des-cribed in terms of what it means for the parent (what its function is, why it makes sense to the parent) (see examples in Table 6.2). By gaining an understanding of the function and value of the parent's behaviour *to the parent*, the professional may be surprised to find themselves gaining more empathy and respect for the parent.

A further re-frame can then be developed by making a link between the *parent* and *professional's* perspectives (i.e. what it is about the professional that makes the parent behave in this way, or what it is about the parent that makes the professional behave in a particular way). This can be called a 'transactional re-frame'. Any difficulties, if occurring, may no longer be seen as purely residing in the parent; they are now seen as something going on between the parent and professional or professional network (see Table 6.2). It may be useful to use the re-framing technique to consider the following two examples: from the parent's perspective, and a transactional re-frame (what it is about the professional that contributes to the parent behaving in a particular way):

1. A couple with a recently diagnosed infant with Down's syndrome were never at home when professionals arrived on home visits; they avoided any contact with professionals. The father had a criminal record and was very suspicious of anyone 'in authority'. He did not want any professionals coming into his home, and insisted that his wife was absent (or feigning absent) when a professional came to the door.

2. A mother had difficulty coping generally; her home was dirty and untidy, the children were often in dirty clothing, and her unemployed husband spent long periods in bed. The family aroused considerable anxiety in the whole professional network involved with them. Concerns were felt about the child's developmental delay, her lack of progress, and also the parents' inability to provide adequate childcare. In her involvement with her professionals, the mother continually 'played one off against the other'. She was always praising one at the expense of another, or saying that another disagreed with this one's plan.

Table 6.2 Re-framing perspective

The professional perspective	The parent perspective	The transactional perspective
'the demanding parent'	I want the best for my child	What is it about me, the professional, that is obstructing and gets in the way of this parent getting what they need?
'the hostile parent'	I don't feel valued, I don't feel respected	What is it about me, the professional, or what I represent that makes this parent feel threatened?
'the manipulative parent'	I don't feel in control	What is it about this professional network which makes the parent have to try to take back some control?

In some circumstances, this technique can be surprisingly freeing, permitting a new way of viewing the parent or family situation and leading on to finding positive and constructive ways of moving forward with the parent and family (or at least having a greater understanding of why a behaviour and pattern is continuing). It may also ensure that the professional starts taking responsibility for how they are relating to the parent and family, particularly those which they are experiencing as 'difficult' or 'uncooperative'. This may involve considering what one represents in one's role to the particular parent and family, and to acknowledge the limits and possibilities of one's role position for the family.

Transactional re-framing can also be used to help the family explore and gain greater appreciation of different members' perspectives within the family and their relationships with each other and with the professional and network system.

Differing priorities

Even without negative labelling, the professional carries professional expertise and responsibilities that may make them see a particular family situation differently from the family. For example, they may view the family as urgently needing respite care, but the parents may be resistant to this idea. In one family, the mother referred herself to a family centre because of concerns about her adolescent daughter at school, but when the Family Adviser had made a couple of home visits she became aware of (what she viewed as) greater family difficulties (marital problems, and an 'enmeshed' or over-involved mother–daughter relationship that excluded the father and sibling). The dilemma for this professional working in partnership was whether to act quickly on the parent's presenting concern, or to pick up on these other family difficulties, or to wait and see if they were eventually raised by the family.

Within a negotiating dialogue, the professional may judge it appropriate to take the initiative and introduce their perspective on occasion (e.g. identifying a particular family issue or creating the context that enables the family to identify various difficulties). The sensitivity, timing and appropriateness of this can be assessed only within the particular relationship and established role task and boundaries of the professional with the family. But to move forward on any family issue evoked by the professional requires an explicit consent from the family, so that the privacy of the family boundary is respected and the members are continually in control of any movement forward.

Reconciling the differing priorities of the professional and members of the family may be possible through using some of the *strategies for managing disagreement* given in Chapter 4.

In the following section, we turn to some particular problems that may arise when trying to use a Negotiating Model approach with a whole family.

Challenges for negotiation

These questions have all been raised during our training course:

- 'What do I do if the mother wants to get involved, but the father doesn't?'
- 'How do I work with a couple where the two of them can't agree over anything, even whether we can meet together?'
- 'I think the sister should be involved in this decision on boarding school, but her parents refuse to allow it.'
- 'Craig's in foster care; his mother visits him weekly – who should I work with?'
- 'I don't know anything about Vietnamese families; they don't speak any English and I don't know who to talk to in the family.'

When problems surface during negotiations with a family, they appear frequently linked to aspects of the family's internal organisation and dynamics (e.g. disagreement in viewpoints, hierarchical structure, confused membership of the family) or to do with unfamiliarity with this kind of family (e.g. from a different ethnic/cultural background, uncertainty about family roles and cultural appropriateness).

Opposing perspectives

Although many couples share decisions about their child with special needs (61 per cent of families with children with Down's syndrome in Byrne *et al.*'s report, 1988) and many agree on most decisions (61 per cent in Byrne *et al.*'s report, and 67 per cent in Carr's study of families with young children with Down's syndrome, 1975), a substantial proportion may disagree when making joint decisions. Byrne *et al.* found that disagreements were generally about discipline, decisions about schooling, and decisions about short-term care. Moreover, most families of their sample had some differences in child management (one parent being felt to be stricter than the other).

It is not uncommon with anxieties over their child to find two parents polarising in viewpoint: one taking up a view of optimism about the child's future and the other being pessimistic, or one being positive that a service will help their child and the other being sceptical and disbelieving ('he'll catch up . . . you'll see'). It has been found in research that mothers tend to understand more about the medical condition of their child than fathers (Nolan *et al.*, 1986), probably because they have more contact with the medical staff. They have also been found to be less optimistic than fathers of their child's prognosis (when the child is chronically ill), and to express greater anxieties and concerns (Banion *et al.*, 1983). If mothers and fathers differ in their understanding of the child's condition, and their beliefs about the prognosis and limitations, this has implications for their perceptions of and behaviour towards their child, as well as acting as potential causes of disagreement between them (Eiser, 1993).

Although these different viewpoints may serve a valuable balancing function in some families (with each parent holding onto a different but valid perspective on the child's condition), an extreme polarisation can have an estranging effect on a couple. Opposing views also raise particular difficulties for the professional in negotiating with the family: can the professional reconcile them or should he or she work with one to the exclusion of the other (and what will be the effect of this on the parents' relationship)?

In families where the parents (or other members) have differing perspectives on the child, it may be beneficial for one parent to be given additional information and knowledge from the professional if they have missed out on receiving accurate information. Another strategy may be helpful too. To show that they both have valid views, Daws (1984) recommends that each tries to hold onto their own position and put it together with the other's so that this results in a combined moderate view, e.g. that a specific service could facilitate the child's natural development. The professional's role in validating the two separate perspectives and then bringing them together in combination can help reduce the polarisation (and resulting distress). A positive re-frame and identifying a super-ordinate goal (see *Strategies for managing disagreement* on p. 94) can help reduce dissent, e.g. 'You are both concerned about how best to help your son, but your husband is protecting you from getting too hopeful and being disappointed and you are holding onto his hope in what your son can achieve.'

Poor communication

Family members may not be accustomed to talking directly to each other over problems and negotiating decisions together. As Eiser (1993) points out, whether parents can communicate with each other when there is a child with a disability or chronic illness will affect the way in which they both view and make sense of their child's condition, their emotional responses to the child, their ability to share the practical demands around the child and integrate these successfully into their everyday lives. In this sense, there are some very special communicational demands for couples with a child with special needs. A major source of disagreement is likely to be over the burden of care for the child that generally falls on the mother's shoulders (see p. 107) and also not being able to discuss responses and feelings about the child. Couples complain that they have little leisure or time alone together, and mothers have reported feeling very alone in some families (see review in ibid.). Communication can be especially compromised when one parent blames the other for the child, especially when the child has an inherited condition and the problem is all seen as 'to do with your family' (ibid.). In a minority of families, messages and signals may be very negative and aversive (frequent criticism, nagging, shouting, hitting) and communication may be very impoverished or non-existent.

In some families, the professional may be able to facilitate communication between family members, by holding an interview with all the members, directing questions to and listening to different members, and modelling communication with all members. This may be very useful for the couple on their own, so that they can explore their differing or similar understandings and feelings with the support of an outsider. Family members can be brought into joint problem-solving and/or a joint task to do with the child with special needs or another family issue (e.g. choosing a leisure activity for the whole family, teaching a skill to the child with special needs). In joint discussions, a technique of circular questioning from family therapy can be helpful for enhancing an awareness of each other's perspectives and understandings and also exploring misunderstandings. One member is asked how they think the other member views the situation, and this member is then asked how they think a third member views the situation. Less assertive and less vocal members of the family, such as the child with special needs, and siblings, may need to be enabled to contribute to family discussions.

Hierarchical organisation and power issues

Minuchin (1974), in family therapy, has considered the structure of the family in terms of its hierarchical organisation, boundaries, sub-systems, and alliances. Each family has a hierarchical organisation, and can be divided into sub-systems, e.g. parental, marital, sibling, which are groupings of relationships within the family. A family can be divided into generational sub-systems: grandparents, parents, children. Sub-systems can also be arbitrarily assigned according to emotional closeness and involvement, e.g. a closely involved father and son sub-system. Each family will have its own 'executive sub-system' for making decisions. The professional will need to find out who makes the decisions, and how these are carried through in the family (whether by consulting, or imposing, or not carrying them out).

The hierarchical organisation in some families may prevent one of the two parents from having equal access to the professional and taking an equal part in the decision-making. One parent may dominate and take control over decisions and resources. In some families, one parent functions as the 'gatekeeper' controlling access to the family (such as the father in some ethnic minority families). The lines of authority may be blurred or confused in some families; for example, which of the two men in the house is the child's real father? does the live-in boyfriend have any authority? is the mother-in-law in charge? A strong cross-generational alliance between a mother and grandmother, for example, may exclude a father from the family decision-making. The professional may not know who to involve in the decision-making.

There is another quandary for the professional working in partnership (and also within the legal framework of the 1993 Education Act and 1989 Children Act, see Chapter 11). The movement towards involving children in decisions affecting their lives has to be carefully balanced with the importance of supporting parents in their parenting role. Minuchin (1974) and other clinicians have pointed out that for families to function well a hierarchical structure is needed where parents (or other responsible adults) are in charge and can wield a flexible, rational authority. For children to feel secure and know who is in charge, they need to have appropriate limits and rules set by their parents and have them enforced consistently. The professional needs to be careful not to undermine this authority, in pursuit of the child's autonomy. At the same time, this authority has to be flexible enough to allow the child to grow and become increasingly independent; the professional will have to tread a careful path between supporting the parents in their authority and at the same time helping the parents and children to negotiate with and accommodate each other's needs (ibid.).

Role division and assignments

Role divisions and assignments in the family also affect who can or wants to join the professional in decision-making and activity. Where there is a rigid split between childcare and economic responsibilities, only the parent with childcare responsibilities will be expected to get involved with the professional. In the Manchester cohort study, 32 per cent of families left the decision-making on the child to the mother (as against 3 per cent leaving it mainly to the father) (Byrne et al., 1988). In some families, siblings are assigned the role of caring for other children in the family, including the child with special needs. The professional may be in a dilemma whether to support this, because this role assignation has been shown to place some siblings at greater psychological risk (see p. 104).

The issues of working with an unequal power structure are complex and warrant more discussion than can be given here. They include looking at one's own value judgements and ideological commitments, as well as thinking about one's impact on the family as a professional (see later in the chapter). It is worth knowing that family therapists from the structural therapy school emphasise the need to make an alliance with those in power, if change is to be brought about in the family. As a suggestion, *it is often worthwhile gaining trust with the more dominant members of the family* by working with them and respecting and accommodating the existing power structure of the family. If the professional tries to bypass the more dominant members, they may find them resisting and using their internal power within the family to exclude them. If they work within the existing structure, they may find it possible over time to extend their involvement to other family members as they become more trusted and familiar. Choudhury (pers. comm) reports a similar strategy and experience as a Bangladeshi Parent Adviser working with Bangladeshi families (where she often had to gain trust with the father of the family before gaining access to the mother).

Conflict within the family – a limit to partnership?

When disagreement *within* the family becomes extreme and dysfunctional, the family as a whole may not be able to cooperate together and in partnership with the professional. One parent, for example, may be very hostile to the other parent being involved with the professional. A father and mother may intensely disagree over family issues. One parent may actively undermine the other parent's decisions and actions. The expressed needs of the child or sibling may be ignored, disputed or thwarted by the parents. The child may be manipulated as a go-between or pawn between the parents, or used as a scapegoat for family problems. Conflict may be expressed through extreme negative communications and emotions, physical violence, extreme detachment or paradoxical contradictory behaviours.

There are no hard and fast rules to exactly when it becomes impossible to work with a family in conflict and dysfunction, since each family situation is different. In some families, the internal conflict prevents some of the family members from working cooperatively with an external professional, but it may be feasible to work with the remaining consenting members. Depending on what the professional's role and responsibility demands, they may be able to proceed with some members if others refuse contact. If not (e.g. where there is statutory child protection intervention), the reasons for this must be stated clearly to all relevant family members.

It is easy to get sucked into the system of conflict, and be manipulated into taking one side against another. A practical approach is to try and stay outside the family system, take a neutral stance, and apply the principles of working in partnership with the family as far as possible (see previous guidelines). Supervisory help and support from experienced colleagues who are not involved with the family (see Chapter 12) is advisable. As the following example shows, it is wise to try and balance control between the professional and different family members, even when members are in conflict with each other (or with the professional), so that each member is helped to be in as much control of any intervention as possible. If this is overlooked, the dissenting parent is given little opportunity to develop a partnership relationship with the professional in the future.

> Example. *In one family, a father refused to meet any professional after his daughter had been diagnosed with cerebral palsy. He was in a very distressed state and hostile towards the idea of any professional visiting his home. When a social worker came to visit from the local child development team, he refused him entry. His wife, however, felt in great need of help and support and she later phoned the social worker and asked for his assistance. In the discussion that ensued, the social worker acknowledged that she had a right and need to seek her own help. He expressed his viewpoint that if she did this without agreement from her husband it could lead to greater conflict between them and also greater hostility from her husband to professionals in the future. He felt that it would be advisable to try and obtain her husband's cooperation. She agreed to the social worker writing to her husband. A letter was sent which acknowledged that the husband might not want anybody to visit his daughter at home. He was asked whether he would prefer the social worker to meet the mother and daughter at home or at the child development centre. The father sent a message back to the social worker that he was willing for him to visit his daughter at home. Regular home visits proceeded, and two months later, the father spontaneously turned up at one of the visits and met the social worker for the first time. From then on, he became more actively involved with the social worker.*

In situations of extreme within-family conflict and dysfunction, the professional may have to acknowledge with the family that it is not possible to work with them in partnership, at least over this particular issue of concern. The family may be willing to be referred for specialist help, such as family therapy or marital therapy.

THE IMPACT OF THE PROFESSIONAL ON THE FAMILY

Although often unaware of it, the professional starts having an impact on a parent and family from the earliest contact. From the first meeting onwards, the professional may have an impact on the family structure and system. As already noted in Chapter 2, the first meeting acts as a *punctuation* which marks a shift or transition in the existing family system. The mere presence of the professional may lead to the family looking at their present circumstances and 'taking stock', or the referral itself may be a consequence of some preceding change in the family system and family situation.

With later intervention, the professional may continue, intentionally or accidentally, to have an impact on the family. They may inadvertently undermine the family's strengths and coping ability, rather than build on them. For example, an occupational therapist set up a programme of independent skills learning with an adolescent boy. She could not understand why his mother was so resistant, and put it down to acute anxiety about her child's greater independence. She did not realise that the mother gained her strength and coping ability from her role in the family of 'looking after her dependent son', and had a strong investment in preserving the status quo in the family.

A number of family systems concepts can be usefully applied for thinking about the impact of the professional on the family system. Although these effects may not always or generally occur, it is useful to know of some of the potential consequences of intervention in some family circumstances. A professional can, probably unintentionally, intensify some already present difficulties in family relating.

If the professional works exclusively with one parent, they may create or reinforce *splitting* between the parents. A home adviser worked successfully with one mother and developed a close, familiar *alliance* with her; the father, who had not been involved in the programme, felt cut off and excluded. His role in the family felt usurped by the home adviser and there was increased distancing between the two parents. In cases of marital conflict, the professional may take sides and form a *coalition* with one partner against the other; they may, for example, take on the wife's viewpoint and criticise and blame the husband.

In families where the husband and wife believe that all their problems arise from having a disabled child, and avoid recognising or taking responsibility for other sources of stress (such as marital conflict, employment difficulties, mental health problems), *detouring* may occur. If the professional involved also focuses on the child as the main problem, this may reinforce the detouring. In some families the professional might get drawn into a *triangulation*, where the child with special needs is used by the parents to blame and fight each other in a marital conflict.

The professional may reinforce or change existing patterns in the family, such as those of hierarchy and dominance. If working with the woman only, they may reinforce a role position and division in the family of the woman as the main caregiver. If referring all main decisions to the husband, they may reinforce the man as 'the head of the family'. Ignoring the sibling and child's viewpoints maintains their position as subordinate to the adults of the family.

The act of partnership work predisposes the professional towards developing more equable, negotiating relationships with each parent and other family members. But if this is achieved practically, the professional may well have some structural impact on families, especially those with internal inequality. For example, a professional worked over a long period with a woman who was in a subordinate position to her husband. Through the respectful, enabling nature of the intervention, the woman grew greatly in confidence and self-assurance and became increasingly dissatisfied with her position in the family (leading to increased tension and conflict between the wife and husband).

Because the professional may have power over resource allocation and service delivery, they are in a position to potentially wield power to enforce change in the family structure and process (such as only being willing to give the family respite care if all members of the family turn up to a family meeting to discuss it). Although there may be strong grounds for encouraging change in the family system, using power to enforce change does not tally with a partnership way of working.

The professional needs to be aware of their potential impact on the family through 'joining' and working with it, and to consider whether the form of intervention is having, intentionally or inadvertently, a negative or positive effect on the family as a whole.

THE IMPACT OF THE FAMILY ON THE PROFESSIONAL NETWORK

The influence between the professional and the family is not one-way, as the family may also be having an impact on the professional and wider professional network. The process of 'mirroring' between the individual parent and professional has been previously discussed in Chapter 3 (see p. 69). It is not uncommon for a *split* family in extreme difficulty to be 'mirrored' by a fragmented, split professional network (different professionals may be working closely with different family members, but not communicating with each other, or different professionals may be siding with different members of the family and refusing to accept the other professionals' or family members' perspectives). The latter is particularly seen in child protection work, where part of the professional network may accept the child's accusations of abuse, and another part disbelieves the child. Splitting in the family may be 'mirrored' without the professionals being aware of this. In some situations, the parent or other family member actively manipulates the professional. When a mother says, 'Oh don't bother to write to him; you won't get him involved', she may be encouraging the professional to stay in alliance with her and exclude the father.

The family's responses or ways of dealing with their situation may set off similar responses (or 'mirroring') in the professional and professional network. An angry, hostile family is often met by angry, defensive reactions in the professionals involved with the family. A family's anger with a paediatrician can set off similar feelings towards the paediatrician in other professionals working with the family.

Another form of reciprocal influence between the parent and family is that of 'circular causality' (see too p. 69). The second family example on p. 135 gave rise to a neat circular causality. The professionals involved with this family were very concerned about the child; they made frequent home visits and demanded that the child be taken to the day nursery every day (and they monitored this). The family felt low self-esteem, criticised and taken over by the professionals. To regain some control over the network, the mother played one professional off against another. This intensified the professionals' concern and distrust of this mother (they became disbelieving of anything she said) and they became even less confident of her ability to look after her child.

Because of the incidence of 'mirroring' and reciprocal influence, it is useful for the professional and the professional network to be aware of possible links between how they are reacting and what is going on in the family. A valuable insight from the concept of reciprocal influence is that neither side is 'causing' the problem, so neither is to blame for the difficulties. But because both sides are contributing, the possibility for change lies on either side. A 'mirroring' process can be valuable if it helps draw parallels between the professional experience and the family's experience (as an aid to empathic understanding of the family, and also on occasion to be offered as helpful information to the family). Where, however, the process becomes destructive is when it reinforces patterns which may be detrimental for the family.

To summarise, the focus of this chapter has been on the family as a system, with a network of inter-relationships and mutual influences within the family and between the family and the professional. Understanding the structure and process of the family system has been shown to be important for not disrupting family cohesion and undermining internal coping mechanisms when intervening, and also for considering the consequences for the rest of the family system of working with part of the family only. Ways in which other family members might affect the possibilities of intervention with one member have also been discussed. Various challenges for working in partnership with the whole family have been explored, particularly inequality or disagreement in the family which blocked negotiation between members or between members and the professional. Practical approaches for dealing with some of these challenges have been suggested. One point that emerges is that partnership is not always feasible with the whole family, but may still proceed with part of the family, leaving the door open for others possibly to get involved at a later date.

In the next chapter, we move on to thinking about a comprehensive assessment of family needs in partnership.

PROFESSIONAL DEVELOPMENT EXERCISES

EXERCISE 6.1 HOW I VIEW MY PROFESSIONAL RESPONSIBILITY

Use a separate sheet of paper to write your responses to the following statements and questions.

I am responsible firstly and foremost for:

I view my client as:

My goals of intervening are:

What constraints/conflicting responsibilities or interests get in the way of working on behalf of my client(s)?

I view the boundary of my responsibility as:

Is your professional group or team in agreement with the above?

EXERCISE 6.2 GETTING TO MEET DIFFERENT FAMILY MEMBERS

Consider a small group of families (4–6) in your caseload (select them in alphabetical order of their surnames). Review whether you take as full an opportunity to meet all family members as possible.

1. Using a separate piece of paper, write down your responses to the following questions for each family:

    (1) Who are the significant members of this child's family?
    (2) How many of them have you met?
    (3) Who do you meet regularly?

2. On the basis of these responses, jot down a brief response to the following questions. You may want to think about each family individually or consider the whole group/your whole caseload.

   (1) Could you improve on this – and meet more family members?
   (2) Do you meet each child mainly in the clinic/hospital/school/ nursery/outside the home?
       Does this affect whether you meet the whole family?
   (3) Could you alter your way of working to ensure that you meet other members of the family?
   (4) What constraints prevent you meeting other members of the family?
   (5) In what circumstances might it be inappropriate to try to meet all family members?

Consider the implications of this for working in partnership with individual family members and the whole family.

EXERCISE 6.3 DESCRIBE YOUR OWN FAMILY

1. See how many of the dimensions in Table 6.1 (p. 133) you can use to describe the current structure and pattern of your family (your family of origin, or your present family). Write your responses on a separate sheet of paper.

2. Then use the same set of dimensions to see how far you can describe the current structure and pattern of a friend's family.

Write down your responses, and then compare the two structures and patterns. Write down any points you have learned from doing this exercise.

Chapter 7

Assessment of family needs

Assessing family needs in partnership with the parents and family members is a relatively recent development in professional work, and it is useful to start with a brief exploration of the changing thinking and legislation underpinning this practice. Until recently, the 'needs' of children with special needs and their families were decided upon mainly by *expert opinion* (i.e. what professionals and service providers viewed as necessary) and by *supply* (i.e. what was available in services and material resources). The new movement towards involving parents and users in the assessment of needs heralds a major shift towards a *demand-led* definition of needs based on *what users and consumers say they need*. At least two strands of practice and law have driven and reflected this change in practice. First, we will consider significant developments in the United States, before reviewing the British angle.

A BRIEF REVIEW OF RECENT HISTORY

The United States

Fuelled by the school desegregation cases of the 1950s, parents of children with disabilities brought a series of court suits challenging the exclusion of their children from educational services. This contributed to the passage of the notable Public Laws 94-142, The Education for All Handicapped Children Act of 1975, which stated that each state that sought federal aid was required to provide a free and appropriate education for all children, regardless of the nature and severity of their impairments, and to provide individually appropriate services in the least restrictive environment, and amongst other requirements, '*to ensure parental due process rights in the assessment of, planning for and delivery of service to the child*'. The law initially covered children from 5 to 21 years.

In 1986, the law was amended (PL 99-457, the Education of the Handicapped Act Amendments) and its coverage was extended to include children from birth to 5 years. In these laws (under Part H – Handicapped Infants and Toddlers), 'parent involvement' and Individual Education Plans (IEP) of PL 94-142 were replaced by the concept of family-based intervention and Individual Family Services Plans (IFSP) for each *child and family* served. The IFSP had to include a statement of the family's strengths and needs, and of expected outcomes for the child and for the family. Part H applied only to the under-two's, but it was expected that its philosophy would extend across the age range so that comprehensive family support would be planned with a long-term perspective (Turnbull, 1988). As with PL 94-142, all fifty federal states opted to participate in this programme.

The main concept behind an *Individual Family Services Plan* was that assessment and service planning for the individual child and family should be *needs-driven*, i.e. service planning should be according to *what the family needs*, rather than slotting them into available services. This should lead to developing an individualised care package that was tailored to the individual family, within the resources that were available.

The catalyst of new legal responsibilities for professionals arising from Public Law 99-457 led to a ferment of research activity to refine models and develop tools for family assessment. Until then, diagnostic tools had been developed primarily to assess the *child* with special needs rather than the *whole family*. Professionals now found themselves poorly equipped to know what to assess or how to assess. They turned to or became involved in setting up research studies focusing on the impact of disability on the family, family coping strategies, and the family's role in shaping the service delivery process (e.g. Crnic *et al.*, 1983). A variety of measures were developed to assess family strengths and family 'needs' (e.g. Questionnaire on Resources and Stress, Friedrich *et al.*, 1983; Dunst and Leet, 1987; Family Support Scale, Dunst *et al.*, 1984; Parent Needs Survey, Seligman and Darling, 1989).

United Kingdom

A few years later, influenced by these American developments and changing thinking and practice in the UK, the Children Act 1989 was passed by the British government (see further details, Chapter 11). Amidst many other requirements, the legislation spelled out that Social Service Departments' provision for children with disabilities should involve an *initial assessment of need*, a continuing process of reassessment, and a review of the plan for the child. This empowerment to assess for needs would complement the new requirement in law for Social Service Departments to provide services for disabled children and their families (see p. 263). Accompanying guidance and regulations emphasised that multi-disciplinary agencies (with Social Service Departments as the lead agency) should develop clear assessment procedures for children in need within agreed criteria which took account of the child and family's needs and preferences, racial and ethnic origins, their culture, religion and any special need relating to the circumstances of individual families. Through the process of assessment, the outcome

> should be a holistic and realistic picture of the individual and family being assessed, which takes into account their strengths and capacities, as well as any difficulties and which acknowledges the need to make provision appropriate to the family's cultural background and their expressed views and preferences.
>
> (DoH, 1991a, Vol. 6, p. 9)

The Act empowered Social Service Departments to combine assessments under the Children Act with those under other legislation (see p. 264).

Care management

The idea of a 'family plan' or individual 'care management' was again emphasised in the policy guidance of the White Paper: *Caring for People: Community Care in the Next Decade and Beyond*, Chapter 3, Care Management and Assessment, 1990. This report stressed that care management in its most comprehensive form should involve an assessment of the user/family's circumstances and the design of a 'care package' in agreement with the user's carers and relevant agencies, to meet the identified needs within the care resources available. An important feature of the care management process (as in the US Public Laws mentioned previously) was that it should be based on a *needs-led approach within resource availability*. Responsibility for assessment and care planning should be separated from service provision, in order to focus on needs, and where possible the two separate tasks should be carried out by different staff. This was to ensure that people were not merely fitted into existing services, but that services would be adapted to individual needs. This separation would also enable any discrepancies between assessed needs and available services to be identified.

Because of the multiple service providers required to meet the majority of special needs, recent legislation and policy guidance papers have stated that care management approaches should be undertaken in a multi-disciplinary approach. Moreover, they all underlined that parents/carers and children/users ought to be viewed as major contributors to the planning process.

ASSESSMENT OF FAMILY NEEDS

These recent developments concur that the assessment of family needs should be based on the following principles and objectives.

The *assessment of family needs* should aim to identify the current needs of a particular family at a particular period. It should be *individualised* (recognising each family has its own needs) and *time-specific* (recognising that needs change over time). A comprehensive assessment should focus on both family resources and strengths as well as needs, and help to provide a balanced appraisal of *strengths and deficits*. It should be *family-focused*, and should strive to consider the needs of each family member and the whole family as a system. The cultural needs and preferences of each family should be taken into account.

The assessment should form the basis for establishing whether any additional services and resources could be useful for the family, or whether any changes should be introduced at this period of time. It should also aim to help a family utilise its own informal resources to its best advantage. As each family's needs change over time, assessment should be seen as a continuous process, with further assessments taking place at later dates.

Although these principles were generally agreed upon, there was one potential problem that was not generally acknowledged in the legislation and reports (nor recommendations given on how to resolve it). That is, in the possible scenario of disagreement between the parent/child and professional, who should *define* the needs and who will *accept* the definition?

NEEDS – WHO DEFINES, WHO ACCEPTS?

Rooted in the legislation and reports was the assumption of a consensus in viewpoint between the parent and professional. For example, the Children Act Guidance and Regulations, in a section on planning services for the individual child, states that 'partnership and consultation with parents and children on the basis of careful joint planning and *agreement* [my italics] is the guiding principle for the provision of services. . . .' (DoH, 1991a, Vol. 6, p. 14). This tends to suggest that the professional who is joining in assessing the needs and/or allocating service provision will readily agree with the parent's viewpoint.

Nevertheless, circumstances may arise where the professional and the parent differ in their judgement of what the child or family needs. How should any difference of opinion be resolved? Should or can the professional always concede to the parent's view (as would be expected in a *demand-led* assessment)? (See also the Consumer Model of partnership, p. 12.)

It was mentioned at the beginning of this chapter that needs can be defined in at least three different ways. Differing definitions may be used, for example, by the different interest groups of the National Health Service: the purchasers, the providers and the consumers (Schwartz and Lees, 1994). The purchaser may have particular concerns about 'supply' and what needs can be met within the available level of resources and services, or in determining the actual level of resources. The provider may depend on expert opinion and research to decide on the service provision to meet families' needs. The consumer may have their own opinion of their particular family's needs. That the consumer's viewpoint (or needs) may not necessarily coincide with the professional's (or provider's) is emphasised by Kat (1992) when he distinguishes between 'need' and 'demand': *need* is '*what people could benefit from*' and *demand* is '*what they ask for, or what their health professional prompts them to ask for*'.

The professional may influence the consumer to request (or not request) certain services, which may not necessarily correspond to their own or their child's real needs. There are different kinds of needs of consumers which have differing implications for service providers (and may affect how they respond to the request). In a paper on measuring individual needs for care and services, Brewin (1992) viewed needs as

1. lack of health or wellbeing,
2. lack of access to particular forms of care,
3. lack of specific activities by health carers.

The first and third reflect 'needs for care' and lead to requirements for specific activities or interventions to help with disabling reactions or symptoms (they may or may not require specific services). The second one clearly reflects 'needs for services' and leads to institutional requirements (i.e. agencies to deliver the interventions). How well the provider can respond to the latter will depend on the supply available.

This brief discussion alerts us to a possible discrepancy between the professional and parents' viewpoints and interests during a joint assessment of needs. In the next section, we will use the Negotiating Model (see p. 14) as a framework for assessing family needs in partnership. It will be suggested that the joint assessment procedure can proceed cooperatively and satisfactorily, but in some circumstances it may be more problematic than has been presumed.

ASSESSMENT OF NEED IN PARTNERSHIP

The assessment procedure should be carried out through a negotiating partnership with the family, according to the Negotiating Model. Priority aims for the professional would be to facilitate the parent and family's own identification of needs and problem-solving, and to ensure their shared control through the assessment process. Additionally, the professional may want to bring their own viewpoint and contribution into the assessment procedure, and a negotiation process would be needed to draw together the different perspectives.

Setting up the assessment

Before proceeding with the assessment interview, all family members would need to be given the opportunity to participate. Informed consent should be obtained, if possible, before advancing with the participants; they would require sufficient information about the process and possible outcomes of the assessment. Although it may be desirable to involve the whole family (though note the issues concerning respecting the family's own structure and decisions on participation in Chapter 6), the assessment could proceed with one or two members only.

The assessment may take place during a single interview or over a series of meetings with the family. It could be carried out within ongoing work with a known professional or might form part of an introduction to a new worker. Mutual expectations should be clarified at the beginning to avoid any later misunderstandings and disappointments (see further Chapter 2). Confidentiality boundaries need to be established too, e.g. what information may be shared with colleagues, what may get written in the child/family's file.

The interview should be carried out in a relaxed, semi-formal manner so that each family member is put at ease as far as possible. During the interview, the professional needs to show a genuine concern, interest and commitment to finding out what family members want and need, and how these needs can best be met.

Eliciting the family member's viewpoint

During the assessment process, the professional will want to help the parents and other family members express their needs as they perceive them. This is often the 'brainstorming' phase of the negotiation process (see Chapter 4). At this stage, the professional's main contribution is to encourage participation and listening; any expression of needs should be treated respectfully. But it may be useful to add *structuring questions*, which will help organise or focus a family member's contribution. Open-ended questions can be used to raise certain topics and assist a family in making a balanced assessment of their own deficits, strengths and needs. Some examples are listed below.

1. Questions which help the family acknowledge its strengths and coping abilities and positive orientation:

- *How do you feel you are getting on?*
- *What has been going well recently?*
- *What do you feel has been achieved recently?*
- *What have you found most helpful for you . . . your child?*
- *Which services have been going particularly well for you . . . your child?*

2. Questions which guide the family to start exploring its needs:
   - *What kind of help do you feel you need now as a family?*
   - *What do you see as the next challenge or problem facing you as a family, and how can you be helped to deal with it?*
   - *What do you want to change most?*

OR (to get round the problem of the family saying that they do not need any help because they do not want to appear uncoping)

   - *You seem to be getting on well, but is there something that could make life better for you?*

A useful question for getting a family to think creatively about its own needs is:

   - *if you could chose three things for yourselves as a family, what would they be?*

3. Questions which help a family to think about their desires and aspirations or concerns for the future:
   - *Where do you see yourselves in six months' time/a year's time/ a few years' time?*
   - *What do you hope for you and your family in a year's time/a few years' time?*

NB Thinking about the future can be difficult for any family, but may especially arouse feelings of anxiety, distress and depression in parents of children with special needs. This kind of question should be used with discretion and sensitivity. But it may be helpful for families with an adolescent youngster who must start planning for the future. It can sometimes be useful for families with younger children, as it may elicit expectations and aspirations, as well as fears.

The checklists mentioned on p. 149 may be useful for helping the family identify and explore their needs. Before using them, you need to explain their purpose to the family and obtain consent for their use.

Two further issues need thinking about when seeking the perspectives of the parents and family members. Firstly, the internal structure and dynamics of the family may inhibit the participation of some family members (see Chapter 6). Various techniques to help less assertive or less vocal members become involved in discussions and to increase open communication and problem-solving within the family are given on p. 139.

The viewpoint of the child with special needs (as well as of brothers and sisters) is often overlooked. But remember also the importance of respecting the family's internal structure (see pp. 121 and 141).

Secondly, the role relationship of the professional and parent/family members (and the organisational or socio-political contexts in which they are operating) may affect and inhibit open communication between them. This is discussed below.

Constraints on the parent: lack of trust and difficulties in being honest

The idea of assessment in partnership suggests that parents will be willing to share their personal needs and concerns openly with the involved professional. Some parents talk of their difficulty in being honest with professionals. The priority needs of some parents (to do with poverty and reliance on benefits, unemployment, and poor quality housing – Dunst and Leet, 1987) may be difficult to discuss publicly. Furthermore, within periods of resource scarcity, some parents are concerned that if they say positive things about their child and their home life and focus on their coping ability, they will not be given priority for services. One mother said, 'If I tell the doctor or the social worker that I'm coping, I won't get any help. ... When the person for respite care came to visit me at home and met X (child's name), I showed her all the things we were doing together. I wanted to show all the good things about him. . .I didn't get any respite help after that!'

Another factor which may inhibit parents from being honest is their perception and/or experience of professionals being partial and giving one-sided information. The professional may be perceived or experienced as representing the employing authority's interests and giving only information supporting the authority. One father said, 'When I met the educational psychologist he told me that the only suitable school for X (child's name) was ... School. I believed him and accepted this until I met another parent who lives nearby, and her son with the same condition goes to a school out of borough. Now I can't believe the professional any more ... he tells me only schools which the borough is willing to pay for. You can't trust them.' Another mother said, 'You can't talk to them honestly – they surround themselves with a mystique and you feel intimidated. They're not open with you and you don't want to risk being honest with them.' The previous experience of other professionals may hinder some parents from trusting a new professional.

Establishing rapport and open communication may be especially laborious with parents from an ethnic minority. Many constraints may affect the parent's willingness to be open, such as a distrust of service providers, the apparent reluctance of some professionals to listen, an experience of stereotyping and prejudicial attitudes, and an experience or fear of racial inequality and racism in service delivery and provision (Ballard, 1979, Shah, 1992).

Some of the implications of these constraints on parental communication for professional practice are discussed further on pp. 158–9.

Sharing the professional's perspective

Apart from listening to the family members, the professional may want to share their own viewpoint, when appropriate. Help may be needed by the parent in working out what they or their child needs. If the KIDS Family Centre research project (see Chapter 10) can be taken as representative, it appears that many parents of infants with special needs may not know what they need initially. Forty per cent of the fifty parents interviewed said, looking back retrospectively, that they had no idea of what they were looking for when they first came to the Centre. Other writers have also queried whether assessment of needs should be left fully to the parent: is a parent who expresses no needs in regard to helping their child with special needs better off than a parent who expresses some needs (Sheehan and Sites, 1989)? Sloper and Turner (1992) found that mothers of young physically disabled children who adopted a coping strategy of passive optimism, e.g. 'I go along with fate', and did not take an active approach in obtaining help, were in turn provided with more limited appropriate help by their local services (and were more likely to have unmet needs). Moreover, is a parent always in a position to best represent their child's needs (Appleton and Minchom, 1991)?

The professional has a perspective and expertise which they may want to bring into the negotiating process to help the family explore and evaluate different options. They could draw on their own observation and assessment of the particular family's needs. They could contribute to the family having a broader view of their needs and a more effective understanding of how their needs could be met, particularly if the professional is informed in the following areas:

1. knowledge about general and local service provision;
2. knowledge about which kinds of services and intervention are especially beneficial for particular kinds of families and personal circumstances;
3. knowledge about general family resources and strengths;
4. knowledge about potential risks and vulnerabilities in families.

Frequent attention has been paid to the fact that many parents lack and have not been given adequate information about what is available (e.g. 59 per cent of parents with severely physically disabled children felt that they had been given inadequate information in Sloper and Turner's study, 1993). Under the Children Act 1989, local authorities have a duty to publicise information on all relevant services for families of disabled children in the authority. But in addition to social services, all professionals (whatever their agency) need to be informed about relevant services available in the locality (statutory and voluntary, general and specialist) and for the child's particular age group, and the system of referral to each service. It is useful too to know of services available in other areas, e.g. specialist centres which may be relevant to the particular family, other services which could be set up in one's own locality. The professional can help a family learn about different forms of service intervention by assisting them in visiting the provision and weighing up whether the provision meets their needs and preferences.

As shown in Chapter 5, recent research is beginning to inform professionals about the kinds of services and intervention which may be particularly beneficial for certain kinds of families and personal circumstances. Drawing on this knowledge, the professional may want to recommend a service or form of assistance that they view as especially helpful for the particular child and family.

Moreover, the professional may have a view on which existing or past services have worked effectively with this child and family, and may want to share this appraisal with the family or utilise it to guide their intervention.

Recent research is also beginning to inform professionals about those aspects of family life which might act as resources and strengths (see Chapter 5). A family may be unaware of what could be used or what is providing a strength and resource, and may not be using their potential strengths to the maximum benefit. The professional can guide them towards more active or effective use of and reliance on their own strengths and resources.

Furthermore, research is beginning to provide information on risk factors which may make a family more vulnerable to stress and difficulties in coping (see Chapter 5). The professional may want to explore with the family whether any factors are causing stress and to recommend forms of assistance which may be especially helpful for vulnerable families under stress (see Chapter 5). Parents can be alerted to aspects of their lives that they had not been aware were causing them strain; they can use this information to guide them in their own assessment of their circumstances.

Constraints on the professional against negotiating

Just as constraints on the parent may inhibit their communication (see previously), the scope of negotiation on the professional side may also be confined by constraints. These can be on the personal level, e.g. assumptions of what the parent wants and needs getting in the way of finding out what the parent really wants and needs.

This is shown graphically in the mismatch and misunderstandings around respite care needs and Asian families with children with special needs. Because of the evident low take-up of respite care services by Asian families, some social workers *assume* that Asian parents do not want respite care because 'their children are looked after by the extended family' and so do not bother to suggest respite care or explore the parents' feelings and concerns about it (Shah, 1992). Shah points out that many Asian families desperately need and would benefit from respite care, but are ignorant of respite care (it has never been properly explained to them) or fear that their own cultural-religious needs would be overlooked (dietary needs, female carers for girl children, etc.).

Role constraints (and the context in which the professional is working) may also limit their communication and negotiations. One social worker was instructed by her managers to recommend only one respite scheme to families, the family link scheme in the borough. The authority was not prepared to pay for the residential respite centre in the neighbouring borough that some of the parents wanted to use, particularly those with multiply disabled children. A home teacher from a voluntary agency felt a hidden pressure to recommend her own home learning service to new parents, because the service was threatened with a financial cut in its grant, especially if few families were using it (the grant-funding body evaluated 'success' in terms of the numbers of families using a service). These kinds of role constraints and pressures may prevent the professional being honest or giving broadly balanced information.

Being coerced or obliged to offer only one form of intervention or provision creates particular difficulties for the professional wanting to work in partnership. Even in these conditions, it is feasible that the provision or intervention could be negotiated with the parent if the professional was honest to the parent about their role constraints. The provision would have to be offered as an *option* that could be refused (and other alternatives to be sought independently by the parent). But having to balance agency interests with parental interests and being committed to a negotiating way of working could nonetheless place the professional in a difficult and uncomfortable position (which might be untenable to maintain on occasion).

We have discussed some of the constraints that may be prohibiting some parents from communicating freely. This is not to imply that these constraints will always be functioning or that they cannot be overcome in some circumstances. Certain approaches by the professional might achieve this. For instance, the professional would need to demonstrate honesty and work hard at building trust in the parent. They would need to show a willingness to negotiate with the parent even if limited by role constraints and employer pressures. This includes giving the parent full space and support to give their own viewpoints and feelings, without having them influenced by the professional. They would need to demonstrate to the parent that they have presented a full picture and real alternatives whenever possible, even if they are not those most favourable or preferential to the parent. Time and space would be required to permit an open discussion between each partner. The parent in turn would need to feel a shared control over the decision-making process.

Working within resource deficits

In periods of resource scarcity and lack of sufficient services, the professional may find it particularly difficult to communicate openly with the parent. They may even avoid working with the family because they feel they have nothing to offer. They might feel wary of arousing expectations that cannot be met or anxious of becoming the butt of the parents' frustration and anger. Their own reactions of helplessness, anger and frustration may 'mirror' those of the parent. But even in a climate of scarce resources, the professional can still make a useful input, assuming that they have sufficient time to work with the family. The family may have internal resources and strengths that they can draw on to help their situation, and the professional may be valuable in helping to identify these. The professional can also corroborate that the family has particular needs, and they may lend their weight towards obtaining assistance or empower the family to be proactive in getting help. Some useful strategies for empowering the family in this circumstance are listed in Appendix 7.1.

Decision-making through negotiation

The assessment process can be conceptualised as a negotiating transaction, with the parent/family members' viewpoints and the professional's viewpoint being brought together and explored as options for evaluation and consideration, leading up to the final decision and plan for action. Each party has a crucial and important contribution to make towards the final decision (see further on negotiation in Chapter 4). Decisions may be reached on what are the family's current needs, those serving the highest priority, how they might be resolved, and who would be responsible for carrying out any relevant action (see Figure 7.1). For the final decision or outcome of the negotiation to be mutually accepted, both will need control and ownership over the decision.

Reaching a decision on priority needs

One or more priority needs may be identified. It can be helpful to draw up needs and resources into two columns on a sheet of paper (see

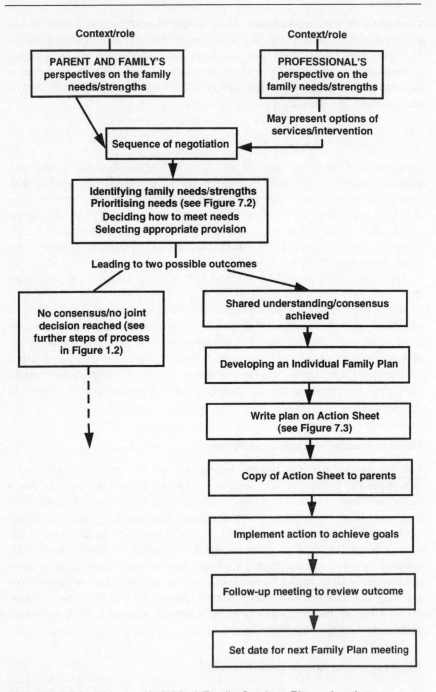

Figure 7.1 Developing an Individual Family Services Plan using the Negotiating Model

Appendix 7.2, Example Family Assessment Sheet), so that a family can weigh up their assets and deficits and be helped to draw on their available resources to help resolve their current problems, where possible. Because the constellation of each family's needs, resources, and problems are unique, workable solutions are likely to be individual to the particular family.

For example, three different couples expressed a similar need for more leisure time, and they all wanted someone to look after their child while they could go out as a couple. But after being assisted to look at their own needs, strengths and resources, each family came up with a different solution:

Family 1 decided to take up a place for their child on a local authority respite scheme.

Family 2 decided to draw on the willing help of a friendly neighbour to look after their child.

Family 3 decided to extend the existing help from the child's grandparents and put their child's name down for a local authority respite scheme.

Some needs may be appropriately met by linking a family to an external service – such as a playgroup, physiotherapy, holiday play scheme, medical treatment, housing aid centre, and so on. Other needs can be assisted by helping the family utilise or develop further strengths and resources which are internal to the family and the family's social network – such as receiving practical help from a friend, rearranging family routines so that the father can more actively help in childcare, etc.

Selecting appropriate services

A rational approach to service selection is to start with helping the parent appraise their existing or past service provision, so that they can evaluate what has been effective for their child and family. The professional may want to share their own appraisal too, if appropriate, and can then help the family resolve whether to proceed with or terminate existing services, and take on new services. The parents' expectations about particular services may need to be explored before linking a family up to a service. The family can be helped to think about any consequences of changing their existing service input, including the impact on the child and family.

For example, two parents met with their Home Learning Service Adviser to consider the effect on their family of joining a new service, the Developmental Play Group at the Centre. They came up with the following:

1. their child would need to become accustomed to playing and learning in a new setting;
2. they would need to get used to meeting other parents and disabled young children;
3. they would have the additional burden of getting their elder daughter to her playgroup as well as getting their child with special needs to the Centre early in the morning.

The latter was seen as the only negative consequence, and the parents resolved to overcome this practical problem.

We have already discussed the possibility of differences and dissent between the parent and professional's viewpoints and interests. This is particularly likely during negotiations on service selection, because the professional may have a direct investment in what the parent opts for. For instance, the professional may have to prioritise which families will get a service (weighing up the varying needs of a group of children or a group of families). Though a parent wants to use it, the professional may decide not to offer the service because they view this family as less needy compared with others. Moreover (as said earlier), the professional may be subjected to various constraints that limit the options they can offer, possibly to the parent's chagrin. Another source of disagreement may be a parent wishing to terminate a service which they view as unhelpful, even though the professional believes it is helpful for the child (or family).

If they cannot reach an agreement, the professional working in partnership would need to resort to strategies for resolving the disagreement (see p. 93) before being able to reach a negotiated decision.

The strategy of *step-down* (i.e. with the professional conceding to the parent's viewpoint, at least for a period of time) may have certain advantages in some circumstances. Firstly, it demonstrates a respect for the parent's preference, and keeps the parent in as much control of the service selection as possible. Secondly, the professional may not, in fact, be in a position to judge which families have greater needs than others because vulnerability and coping is affected by multiple factors (including the parents' perceptions of stressful factors – see Chapter 5). Thirdly, some parents are unable to decide whether they would benefit from a particular service or not until they have had first-hand experience of it.

Through direct service experiences (either taking up a new service or terminating an existing service), the parent may gradually come to a different viewpoint which may possibly correspond more closely with the professional's viewpoint.

If the professional and parent both continue to take up strongly held and polarised positions on needs and service options to the extent that no further joint decisions for action can be reached, then the partnership may enter a conflict phase and joint assessment of needs becomes un-viable (at least for the time being). (See discussion on p. 273.)

Selecting goals

Assuming that a consensus has been reached on the priority needs, the final stages of the assessment are to agree on goals and action to achieve the goals and to draw up an *Action Plan* (or *Family Plan*) with the family. Planning and decision-making should be done in collaboration.

It is essential that goal selection is done through negotiation so that the parent (and child, if appropriate) retain shared control and the goals fit in with the family's priorities and concerns (otherwise their commitment to pursuing them may be low). Goals selected should be realistic in their scope; in general, short-term goals are more likely to be achieved or perceived as attainable than longer-term goals. It may be advisable to break down long-term goals into short-term steps. Families with multiple and recurring problems may need help to select one or two priority goals to work on, rather than trying to tackle all the problems at once.

Once identified, goals need to be stated precisely so that the parent (and child) and professional know what is being aimed for. Because of their differing viewpoints and understandings, it is best to avoid vague statements which are open to multiple interpretations. For example, the parent, child and professional may have very different ideas of what 'becoming more independent' means for the child.

To reduce misunderstandings, goals should be described, as far as possible, in specific behavioural statements which refer to explicit behaviours which can be measured and which both agree on. A useful formula is to describe the goal objectives in terms of *who* will *do what* and *when*, and also to acknowledge any *setting* criteria (i.e. under which conditions this will apply or disapply).

Examples of clear goal statements are as follows:

1. Judy and Mac Floyd (the parents) will visit Appletree School in November with Greg Nightingale (social worker).
2. Delroy Smith (social worker) will offer four weeks of home visits on a weekly basis starting from June 16th to help Marie O'Connelly look at issues around her daughter's new diagnosis of muscular dystrophy.

In contrast to these clear statements, 'fuzzies' are incomplete or partial statements that are vague about *who* will *do what* and *when*. For example,

1. Jacob needs to be statemented under the 1993 Education Act.
2. Jane needs to learn some self-help skills.
3. Kit (the physio) is going to visit the Boston family.

It is important to remember that goal statements are not 'tablets of stone', and they can be rewritten or discarded in response to unexpected reactions and altered needs. But they have many advantages: they may help a parent (and child) have a greater control over family events and professional intervention, by tackling problems through structured problem-solving; they make explicit each parties' responsibilities and what can be expected of the other, and accountability is thereby built into the Action Plan; they give direction to the professional intervention and thus allow accountability to the professional's managers and colleagues, and because they are specific and measurable, they can be evaluated for success.

Writing a Family/Action Plan

Action or Family Plans can be written on a standard form which makes clear what will be done by whom; this is the written formulation of the mutually agreed decisions. An example Action Plan is given in Appendix 7.3.

A review date should be set to review whether the action has been completed, goals achieved, and anticipated outcomes reached. The timing of the review date should allow sufficient time to carry out the goal-related activity, whilst avoiding too long a delay between completion and review. At the review, it may be useful to look at what has been learned through pursuing the goal and to praise the parent and child for successful goal activity. Successful goal attainment can be rewarding and motivating for both the parent and the professional, and can help build the family members' confidence and competence in dealing with their family issues.

SETTING UP INDIVIDUAL FAMILY SERVICES PLANNING IN THE TEAM

Developing an individual Family Plan (*Individual Family Services Planning*) involves not only the kind of negotiation transactions and sequence of actions described previously in this chapter, but also extensive requirements at the organisational level. Many children with special needs will require support from a wide range of agencies and their need for services will often be a continuing need throughout childhood and into adulthood. The ongoing process of assessment, monitoring and review with each family is very draining on staff time. Experienced staff are required, who are adequately skilled and supported to carry out this often demanding and stressful family assessment work. Because of the resourcing demands, comprehensive and regular assessment on a broad scale for all eligible families in a locality can be sustained in the longer term only if underpinned by an adequately resourced and organised delivery structure.

The question of which professional and which team are best positioned to set up and deliver the service is challenging, in view of the connection between the role context and role constraints and difficulties for the parent–professional communication suggested earlier in this chapter. This recognition of a possible contradiction between the service delivery and the assessment of needs is given brief mention in the Children Act Guidance and Regulations (DoH, 1991a, Vol. 6). It is suggested therein that the responsibility for assessment and care planning should be separated from the service provision, and if possible have the tasks carried out by different staff.

Other conflicts of interest or responsibility may also prevail. The Children Act proposes that Social Service Departments act as a lead agency in the assessment of need, but this would be alongside other assessments by other agencies and under other Acts. The Guidance document asserts that developing an individual package of care may require a wide diversity of service provision and will necessitate close liaison and negotiations with service managers and budget holders across a range of agencies (social services, health, education, voluntary and independent sectors). But any possibility of competing interests between the different agencies and budget holders, the impact of these interests on the parent and child, and the difficulties in resolving them are not discussed (see, however, Chapter 12).

The assessment could be carried out by one worker with continuing responsibility for managing the coordinating and provision of services, or these responsibilities could be shared by different workers. But 'it should be emphasized that where responsibility is given to a single care manager, that care manager should be from the agency *most relevant* to the current needs of the child with a disability, and that this agency may change over time' (DoH, 1991a, Vol. 6, p. 10, my italics). No mention is made, however, of the possibility that the agency most closely involved with the child's current needs may sometimes be in conflict with the parent.

This issue deserves more discussion than can be given here, but a few points are worth making. Firstly, it is feasible that in some circumstances a professional who is more independent of agency interests and relatively impartial for the purposes of the assessment (e.g. working for a non-statutory agency or working for an authority other than the one required to provide the planned service) may be more suited for assessing in partnership with a family than a professional who is more tightly controlled by agency purposes. Secondly, in principle some multi-disciplinary or multi-agency teams with representation from health, social services and education (such as some district handicap, child development or community mental handicap/learning disability teams) may have a greater flexibility and freedom to negotiate than a single disciplinary or single agency team, and may be in a stronger position to collaborate across discipline and agency interests for the individualised and multi-service package required by each child with special needs and their family. Some of the features of team structure which have been shown to foster inter-disciplinary cooperation and collaboration are considered in Chapter 12.

Within the organisational and team setting selected for the assessment of family needs, a range of policies and operational procedures will need to be developed. The guidelines in Appendix 7.4 provide a basis for setting up suitable structures and policies.

In summary, this chapter began by describing briefly the recent history and events leading up to Individual Family Services Planning or partici-patory assessment of needs. One issue that was claimed to be overlooked in the legislation and governmental reports was the possibility of a signif-icant difference between the professional and parents' viewpoints and the difficulty this might present for partnership work. This was expanded on in the discussion on differing definitions of 'need' shown by different interest groups. A process for assessing family needs in partnership with the family was described. The Negotiating Model was promoted as a conceptual framework for a realistic practice within the constraints and possibilities of present-day parental and professional role contexts. Examples were given of contextual circumstances which might prohibit the professional and parent communicating and negotiating freely and might therefore potentially undermine a negotiating partnership.

In the next chapter, we extend our consideration of working with families in partnership to participation in developmental services.

PROFESSIONAL DEVELOPMENT EXERCISE

EXERCISE 7.1 PERFORMING A FAMILY NEEDS ASSESSMENT

1. Carry out a comprehensive family assessment with one of the families you are working with, to establish their current needs and which services would suit them best at present.

2. Plan in advance of the interview some of the kinds of questions you may wish to ask and issues you may want to explore with the family. Consider too how you might involve different members of the family.

3. Write down after the meeting your responses to the following questions:
   - What was the process of the assessment?
   - What were you were thinking and feeling during the process?
   - What do you think different members of the family were thinking and feeling during the assessment?
   - What needs were identified by different members of the family? Was there agreement within the family? If not, how was this handled?
   - What did you feel were the needs of the family? Were they the same as those perceived by the family?
   - Did you use a Family Assessment sheet (see Appendix 7.2) to balance resources and strengths in the family with family needs, in order to reach a decision on priority needs? How did this work with the family?
   - How did the negotiation proceed, and how successful was it?
   - If there were any differences between your viewpoint and that of family members, how were these handled?
   - What was the outcome, what decisions were made, and was a Family Plan written down?
   - Was a review meeting set?

4. Write down what worked well from your point of view, how it felt as a partnership, and any difficulties. Were there any unresolved issues, and how do you intend to deal with them in the future?

5. Consider any lessons learnt from doing the assessment, and also whether there is anything more or any changes you would like from your agency to assist you in future family-needs assessments.

APPENDICES

APPENDIX 7.1 WORKING CONSTRUCTIVELY WITHIN RESOURCE SCARCITY

A context of resource scarcity may lead to pressures on the parent and professional that work against creating a collaborative partnership (see pp. 155 and 158). The following strategies may possibly assist the professional to work constructively with the parent and empower them to take proactive steps in the situation.

1. *Be honest about what you can and cannot achieve*, to permit realistic expectations in the parent and a demarcation of your own role responsibilities (see Chapter 2). As long as you have executed your responsibilities to the best of your ability, you may have fulfilled your side of the 'contract' with the family.
2. *Be prepared to listen to the anger and frustration of the parent*, without being defensive. Through being listened to, parents are permitted to vent their feelings and have them acknowledged. This may assist them by helping them feel less desperate and overwhelmed by their situation, and also confirm that their feelings are rational responses to an unsatisfactory situation.
3. *Inform parents about who is responsible for resource allocation* i.e. where the power lies in service planning, funding and resource allocation. Knowledge empowers parents to direct their anger and frustration to the appropriate executive personnel, the appropriate level of management, and the appropriate level of political power.
4. *Enable parents to develop their collective strength* to effect change. Help parents meet each other, set up their own groups, have access to voluntary groups, invite relevant speakers. Professionals can help parents run their own groups, tutoring them in skills of self-assertiveness and groupwork (see p. 125).
5. *Use Individual Family Services Planning as a formal channel of feedback to managers and service planners*. IFSP builds into the process of assessment the dissemination of information of service shortfall and family needs to managers and policy makers (see Appendix 7.4). Family assessment should make explicit what families in an area perceive as their needs.

APPENDIX 7.2 EXAMPLE FAMILY ASSESSMENT SHEET

Name of family:

Name of professional:

Date:

STRENGTHS AND RESOURCES   NEEDS

PRIORITY NEEDS

1.

2.

3.

APPENDIX 7.3 EXAMPLE ACTION PLAN

Name of family: CHONG (Mr and Mrs CHONG, child Li)

Name of professional: Eve Phillips

Date of meeting: 6 June 199-

WHAT NEEDS TO BE DONE (GOALS)

1. Li and his parents will be prepared for Li's new respite care placement.
2. Li will attend the respite care home successfully three times.
3. Any early difficulties of the respite care will be sorted out with Mr and Mrs Chong.

WHO WILL DO WHAT WHEN

1. Eve will visit the Chong family at home twice before the first respite care stay. Issues around the separation will be discussed. Eve will help Mr and Mrs Chong work out how to prepare Li for his first stay.
2. Eve will keep in touch with Mr and Mrs Chong with a phone call after each of the first three respite visits.
3. Eve will make one home visit in the month following Li's first respite stay to help Mr and Mrs Chong sort out any difficulties.

WHAT WILL HAPPEN (EXPECTED OUTCOMES)

Li and his family will be prepared for the respite care separation, and Li will become well settled in his new respite home. Any initial problems will be dealt with and resolved.

DATE OF REVIEW MEETING 18th August 199–.

APPENDIX 7.4 GUIDELINES FOR SETTING UP AND MANAGING INDIVIDUAL FAMILY SERVICES PLANNING

1. Agreement needs to be reached within the service/team/agency that an IFSP system is to be used. This may include looking at whether existing multi-disciplinary teams can be utilised or developed for creating or sharing assessment systems.
2. Identify or describe the specific system to be used, including the recording or monitoring system. NB No specific assessment procedure is laid down in the primary legislation or regulations of the Children Act 1989.
3. Local policies and guidelines on the status of parents and families in decision-making should be made available, including how best to involve parents and children in the assessment process and ensure that they have shared control over the process.
4. The role of the Named Worker, Key Worker or Care Manager (i.e. the individual who will be carrying out the Family Assessment and/or who is responsible for managing the care package) with the family needs to be clarified. Who will take on the role of the Named Worker and how this fits in with their other responsibilities or those of other workers must be decided upon. It is essential that sufficient caseload time is allocated for Named Workers to carry out this responsibility, and that adequate staffing is available for running the service.
5. The role of a Coordinator of the system (if appropriate) should be clarified.
6. A Named Worker should be named by or assigned to each family.
7. A regular Team Meeting for review of Individual Family Service Planning is to be arranged.
8. *Staff organisation* requires that:
   - all staff members understand the system,
   - regular and adequate time is available for staff to prepare for, attend and follow up IFSP meetings,
   - support is built in for Named Workers.
9. Inform other relevant agencies of the system. Ensure that the system fits in with and does not conflict with the existing assessment arrangements of other agencies/teams.
10. Sort out *practical arrangements*, e.g.:
    - venue of Team Meetings,
    - where Plan records will be kept,
    - whether copies will be made of documents, for whom and when,
    - who will provide administrative and secretarial services,
    - to whom copies of the Action Plan will be sent.

11. Arrange for a regular report on the Unmet Needs of families and to whom it will be sent, e.g. to service managers so that they know about shortfalls in service provision.
12. The frequency of IFSP meetings with families and the regular Team Meeting will need to be agreed.
13. The system of documentation needs to be agreed.
14. The Named Workers will require a list of existing services, resources and amenities in the locality, so that options are clearly known.
15. Published information needs to be available and accessible to all potential service users and carers, including those with any communication difficulty or difference in language and culture. The information should set out the assessment procedures to agree needs and ways of addressing them, and the standards by which the assessment will be measured (DoH 1991a, Vol. 6, p. 14). Information must also be available on the types of services available in the locality, plus the criteria for the provision of these services.

(Adapted from a system of Individual Planning by Sperlinger, 1990, pp. 127–128)

Chapter 8

Participating in developmental services

Specialist knowledge and expertise provide the rationale for the professional's role status and authority. We might therefore expect some reluctance from professionals in allowing parents to enter areas of their expertise, partly as a result of believing the parent to have little to offer, and partly because of wanting to preserve their authority and status. In this chapter, we will examine to what extent parents can or do participate in two areas of professional enterprise: developmental assessment and education. We will consider what has to be shared to achieve a negotiating collaboration, including informed consent. Although focused on specific tasks and approaches, many of the principles and issues raised will have a wider application for any disciplinary involvement with parents and families.

INFORMED CONSENT

The issue of consent has been raised as a key element of partnership work throughout the book. But in practice consent is an illusive concept; it is often taken for granted in professional interventions and assumed implicit in many routine interventions. It is a socio-legal concept (of central significance in any ethical code of practice, in any statement of the client's rights, and in the legal framework within which practitioner/client interventions are carried out [Barnett, 1985]) and it works on the psychological and interpersonal levels of functioning. In the kind of open, uninhibited dialogue envisaged by the Negotiating Model, a cooperative movement forward should be on the basis of freely given consent or agreement by the parent. But, as we will see here, what constitutes consent and how it is obtained is far from straightforward.

Consent is commonly defined on a continuum from 'acquiescence to or acceptance of something done or planned by another' to 'accordance (or harmony) in opinion, feelings, etc.' (*Collins English Dictionary*). The ideal of partnership would be to strive towards active accordance rather than passive acquiescence or compliance. But the process of obtaining consent may be complex. In the 'helping' professions, it is difficult to inform without persuading, to inform without provoking anxiety, and to inform without being prescriptive or directive (Kennedy, 1994). In an arena characterised by time pressures, competing demands and uncertain outcomes, certain dilemmas are forced upon the professional, such as whether or not to act. There is an ever-present tendency to overreach oneself in the client's 'best interests' or to avoid situations that arouse discomforting feelings for the parent/patient or professional (Daws, 1984, Barnett, 1985).

Barnett identifies three elements in thinking about the levels and type of consent given by clients:

Educated consent

This requires communication of full, clear and relevant information with regard to all types of intervention, and the client must be given the opportunity for open, unpressurised discussion. 'Educated consent' is best achieved in an atmosphere of sharing, where the client is an active, and possibly dissenting, partner in an ongoing relationship (see too Daws, 1984). Barnett notes that the professional may feel a need to exercise 'editorial control' in order not to overwhelm the client with detail, or over-emphasise the drawbacks and alternatives. A dilemma is whether to spell out risks and raise what may be unnecessary anxiety. But if these hazards do occur, the client may feel the professional has been dishonest and cheated them of full information (Alderson, 1990, Eiser, 1993).

Consent by choice

Informed consent involves voluntariness, without manipulation or coercion by the professional. But in everyday interaction, some degree of persuasion is likely. The issue for the professional in partnership must be to strike a balance between:

- reasonable persuasion versus unreasonable pressure,
- authoritative guidance versus authoritarian control,
- caring versus paternalism.

Consent via competence

The client must be capable of understanding the professional's communication and be capable of weighing up the possible consequences of intervening (or not intervening). But how do we ascertain their competence to make such a judgement?

This issue is brought into stark relief by work with or for children. They are judged different in competence from adults under the law (criminal), yet we are exhorted in recent legislation (Children Act 1989, Education Act 1993, Code of Practice) to consult them. Most children are referred via a concerned adult, and we may have to reconcile competing demands (between children and adults and/or between adults) with achieving consent. The pressure may be on adults to undertake psychological assessment and treatment where early intervention may have a major impact on future functioning (e.g. with medical treatment adherence problems) (Schwartz and Lees, 1994). Usually it is an adult who makes the decision for the child or young person and who defines the initial needs and goals for them (ibid.). One question for the professional working in partnership with parents and children is: how to ascertain the wishes and feelings of children in the light of their age and understanding, given that the limits of a child's consent are necessarily different from those of an adult (Kennedy, 1994)?

Kennedy (1994) describes two further elements that need considering in addition to those above:

Consent is dynamic

Consent is not a one-off 'legal' binding agreement between two or more parties. It is an ongoing agreement in which the wishes of both parties are the subject of regular review and where disagreement can be a necessary feature. The nature and level of consent will fluctuate over time and needs frequent clarification and acknowledgement. A process of dialogue and joint activity may be necessary before consent is reached in the first place.

Consent and confidentiality

For trust to be sufficient for work in partnership to proceed, clients need to be confident that information about them will be safeguarded. The limits of confidentiality need to be made explicit and should be regularly reviewed (see, too, pp. 240–1).

Partnership work requires striving towards informed consent from parents and children, but the professional will have to grapple with possibly perceptible differences in degree or quality of consent within or between clients, as well as tolerate high levels of uncertainty and ambiguity (ibid.). These challenges are particularly apparent when seeking consent and involving parents in child developmental assessment, as will be shown in the following section. For further consideration of the issue of consent, see Alderson, 1990 for a detailed discussion of the moral and practical dilemmas facing parents (and professionals) over consent to high-risk medical treatment on behalf of their child.

CHILD DEVELOPMENTAL ASSESSMENT

In the past, the parent has generally been disregarded as a biased, unreliable witness. Commonly, parents have been believed to see their 'geese as swans' and to attribute unreal or exaggerated achievements to their child. Parents have been considered as getting in the way of objective child assessments, because they might distract or pressurise the child to perform a particular action. To minimise this 'confounding' influence, parents have usually been excluded from standardised assessments.

Parents as a resource for assessment

In 1976, however, a landmark paper by Elizabeth Newson argued persuasively for the immense contribution parents can play in the assessment process.

> We start from the basic assumption ... that parents in fact have information to impart: that parents are experts on their own children. This is not to say that what they know of their children is in any systematic or integrated form: one cannot ask the parent to bring along to the clinic an ordered case-history of the child. ... Nonetheless, they know more about the child, on a very intimate level, than anyone else does; the fact that their knowledge may be diffuse and unstructured does not matter, so long as it is available. It is the professional's job to make it available; structuring can come later.
>
> (Newson, 1976)

This intimate, detailed knowledge comes from having to constantly observe and learn about how the child behaves at home and elsewhere. Parents learn extensively about their child's behaviour, habits, likes and dislikes, moods, relationships and friendships, and from this they anticipate how their child will behave in particular situations (Wolfendale, 1990). This rich source of information becomes one, *amongst a variety of other sources*, to be included in the assessment process, and can be used as independent information for confirming or comparing with the test results and behaviours observed in an assessment situation. The parent is often the first person to pick up that 'something is wrong' with their child, and this suggests that parental concerns should never be trivialised or dismissed (as has often been the case).

In her assessment clinic at Nottingham University, Dr Newson developed a method of assessment for incorporating parents as a major resource. The child's developmental status was explored by a professional playing with them in a carefully structured playroom. During this play-based assessment, the parents sat with other observing professionals behind a one-way screen. One professional would interview the parent while the observations proceeded. A picture would be elicited from the parents of the child as it has been in the past and is now, using the observations of the child in the clinic as a visual aid. The combined team utilised their observations to build up a detailed, rich description of the child's behaviour and performance. 'Observing of the child and the interviewing of the parents were . . . done in conjunction – so that each could contribute valuably to the other' (Newson, 1976).

As Dr Newson pointed out, the professional needs skill in order to extract this information from the parent, including the use of a structured interview approach. Various techniques and practices are described in Newson, 1976 (see Appendix 8.1). In addition to the Nottingham assessment practice, other procedures have been developed to help parents participate in the assessment process, such as using checklists together (e.g. Portage checklist), or aids to help the parent (or older child) make their own 'profile' of the child (the 'ALL ABOUT ME' checklist by Wolfendale, 1980).

Quite apart from helping parents participate and share their expertise, the issue of shared control and negotiation will need to be addressed if the Negotiating Model of partnership (see p. 14) is to have any relevance to child assessments.

Control over the assessment process

It is pertinent to inquire which aspects of the assessment process are open to being negotiated and consented to. How informed is the parent of the whole procedure? Is dissent permissible?

An assessment has a purpose and agenda, a set of tasks and a procedure, and an outcome. The purpose may be overt (e.g. to establish whether the child has language delay) or covert (as in telling the parent the child's developmental status will be assessed, but not the child's behaviour problems and their possible association with parental neglect). The procedure itself may or may not be open to negotiation; for example, the format of standardised psychological testing cannot be altered otherwise it loses its validity. The professional may not necessarily divulge their own uncertainty or concern about a particular impairment at the outset of the assessment, or the likelihood that the child will be recommended for placement in a particular school as the result of the assessment. On some occasions, the professional may judge that, in the interest of obtaining 'naturalistic' data, it would be preferable that the parent (and child) are not told what the procedure is striving to measure.

Without much information on the possible outcome or consequences of the procedure, the parent may not be in a position to make a judgement on the assessment. It is evident that the parent will not always be equipped to give the degree of 'informed consent' envisaged by Barnett (see previously), and the professional may have to contend with the ethical dilemma of exerting the kinds of 'editorial control' shown in the previous paragraph. One consequence of this editing of information and not giving the parent an opportunity to discuss and negotiate is to put the assessment firmly in the control of the professional. This lends itself to one notable danger: lack of power on the parental side rapidly becomes experienced as being under the authoritarian control of the professional *if the outcome is viewed as unsatisfactory by the parent*. Given that the purpose and agenda may be unstated and that the outcome is often unwelcome or surprising and may give rise to diagnostic labels that categorise (with often long-term and disadvantageous consequences), it is easy to see why the assessment process is so frequently experienced as stressful and alienating for the parent.

Unless actively brought in from the first signs of concern and kept fully informed throughout the assessment, the parent is not necessarily going to accept and share the same diagnostic/outcome viewpoint as the professional. And as Robert Sheehan points out in his review (1988), the majority of empirical studies show that parents (usually mothers) overestimate their child's performance compared with a trained diagnostician. Without a consensus viewpoint on the child's condition and needs, it is unlikely that a common basis can be established for further joint action and remediation. The groundwork is also laid for adversarial conflict.

To prevent this happening, the professional's concerns need to be communicated honestly to the parent (including their uncertainties), and the parent also needs to feel as much control over the procedure as possible (e.g. being informed fully and asked to consent before each major step proceeds). Influences that bias this consent process need to be minimised. To this end, Pryzwansky and Bersoff (1978) suggest a number of methods for gaining consent to educational psychological assessments (these could be applied to other forms of assessment too):

1. giving correct information on the intent to assess, the rationale for assessment and the devices to be used (including any disadvantages or risks from agreeing to an assessment),
2. giving time to consent,
3. giving the names and addresses of other persons and advocacy groups to consult for advice and information,
4. giving parents the opportunity to bring anyone with them to the consent conference,
5. abstaining from any threats concerning loss of rights if the parents refuse to consent,
6. reminding the parent that they have the right to revoke consent if they choose to do so.

A consensus viewpoint is more likely to be attained through open dialogue and negotiation, bringing together the parent and professional's perspectives and understandings. This includes respectful listening to the parent's viewpoint, and responding seriously to any concerns expressed (see further Chapter 4).

Dissent and resolution

Active negotiation must permit the possibility of dissent, according to the Negotiating Model. Considering the discrepant ways that parents and professionals might view the child's condition and the general developmental process (see later in chapter), the likelihood of misunderstandings and disagreement may be strong, particularly in situations where assessment is one-off and the professional lacks familiarity with the family and their priorities and concerns.

In some circumstances, a disagreement in viewpoint derives from differing role responsibilities (and interests) of the parent and the professional. A parent may, for instance, not want to accept the professional's conclusion because they feel implicated in the child's emotional/behavioural problems. A teacher would not want to accept a parent's allegation that their child's behaviour problems at school stem from poor classroom organisation.

There may be multiple reasons for reaching disagreement in assessment, and it would be simplistic to suggest a single remedy for overcoming it. But the strategies for resolving disagreement on p. 93 begin to address some possible routes to reconciliation, as shown in the two following examples. The third example shows how the lack of using a resolving strategy can rapidly lead to a breakdown in partnership or prevent a partnership growing between the parent and the assessing professional(s).

Example 1. A 15-month-old boy was diagnosed by the Child Development team as having brain damage and global developmental delay (neurological cause unknown). His parents could not believe this diagnosis, and continued to retain their view as 'slow for his age, but nothing wrong with his brain. He's all there. ....'

The paediatrician of the team listened to the parents' view and said he understood why they felt as they did. This diffused some of the anger and confrontation expressed earlier by the parents. The paediatrician then used a strategy of *re-framing* (p. 134); he acknowledged that both the parents and the CD team recognised that the child was slow for his age and both wanted to help him progress forward (establishing a superordinate goal, see p. 94). He suggested that, because of this, the family be referred to the local Portage Home Learning Service. He added that using this service would allow the parents to see for themselves after

6–12 months whether the child had ongoing global delay (and brain damage) as viewed by the CD team. This again acknowledged that the parents' viewpoint was currently different from the professionals', in a way that made the parents feel more validated and respected. The parents consented to this referral.

> *Example 2. A parent brought her 5-year-old child to her GP because she said he was hyperactive and she wanted him investigated for dietary allergic reactions. The GP contacted the boy's school, and the head teacher expressed her view that the boy did not have pervasive hyper-activity, but had behaviour problems at home because his mother had great difficulty controlling him.*

The GP came up with a *compromise* strategy. She agreed to have the boy tested for dietary allergic reactions, but also suggested that he was seen by the clinical psychologist attached to the GP service. She told the mother that psychologists were often able to help children with hyperactivity and could devise helpful behaviour programmes for handling him at home. The parent did not feel blamed for her son's problems and agreed to the referral to the psychologist.

> *Example 3. A 12-year-old boy was assessed by the local educational psychologist as having special educational needs (general developmental delay and emotional/behavioural problems). His mother disagreed and viewed his problems as 'all starting when he went to his new school ... his teachers can't get through to him ... He's never been backward. ...'*

The educational psychologist continued to recommend that he be sent to a smaller school for children with emotional-behavioural problems and moderate learning difficulties and wrote this in his report for the formal assessment procedure under the 1981 Education Act. The parent continued to contest this viewpoint strongly, and went into active conflict by formally appealing against the LEA statement.

As the first two examples suggest, to overcome dissent the professional may have to strike a difficult and delicate balance between working with the parent's viewpoint without losing sight of the professional's viewpoint. They must strive to work constructively with the parental viewpoint, without colluding in ways that might be detrimental to the parent and child (e.g. fuelling false hopes in the parent that the professional's diagnosis is erroneous). As the third example highlights, if no attempt is made to reconcile the diverging viewpoints or if there is no possibility of bringing them together, then disagreement may shift into conflict (see further p. 273).

The possibility that the parent and professional may not always be able to reach a jointly agreed view on the child in an assessment situation fits in with the Negotiating Model. It also argues for a different model of parental involvement in assessment than earlier conceptions gave, that all parents and children will benefit from parental involvement in assessment (Sheehan, 1988). Sheehan (1989) proposes that a more diversified model will be required that can take into account:

1. differing interest and skill levels of the parents,
2. the purpose of the assessment (and whether this is consistent with parental involvement), and
3. the instruments to be used (and whether parental involvement is appropriate).

We move on now to apply the issues of participation, negotiation and consent to remediation and education.

REMEDIATION AND EDUCATION

Parents of children with special needs have been actively brought into remediation and education (particularly at the preschool stage) to complement and consolidate gains made by the child in an educational setting, and also to help parents in their handling of their child. Since the early 1970s, parents have participated in a variety of programmes (such as the Portage home teaching programme and behavioural modification workshops at the Hester Adrian Research Centre). There have also been numerous experiments of involving parents with schools, but there is not space to discuss them further here (for reviews, see Wolfendale, 1983, 1987).

The reported aims and assumptions of these programmes have included

● to transmit professional skills to parents, so that they can assist in their child's learning,
● to give parents techniques for handling their child's behaviour appropriately (this may serve a preventative function against future difficulties),
● to increase the generalisation of child skills across settings (e.g. from school to home) and their maintenance over time,
● to improve parent–child relationships (e.g. by helping parents gain positive feedback from their child through participating in their child's growth and learning, or helping parents gain positive/realistic expectations of their child's development and potential),
● to give parents social and emotional support,
● to equip parents for participating in other services, such as nursery, school, and improve family-service relationships,
● to increase efficiency by using parents to take over or supplement the educator or therapist role (rather than relying on scarce specialised professional resources).

(See, for example Yule, 1975, Lillie, 1975.)

Within an Equal Opportunities Model (see p. 117), some practitioners are beginning to conceptualise their work with the parent as a means of indirectly empowering the child with special needs, e.g. by helping the parent to value the child and to increase the child's autonomy (giving the child choices, helping the child to say 'No').

The parent's need for help

Although parents make observations of their child's behaviour, they will need to *interpret* and *understand* the child's behaviour. This enables them to decide on what is the most appropriate way of handling their child, and whether circumstances around their child should alter. This can be very difficult for all parents, but particularly so for parents of children with special needs, who may find their child's behaviour puzzling and unpredictable and have few sources of information to turn to for advice. A parent may be uncertain about how a specific behaviour fits into the child's wider developmental process – is it short-term, will it change of its own accord, is it to do with their level of maturity or their disabling condition? Professional intervention and expertise has a potentially important and valuable contribution to make in this situation, by providing expertise and techniques for helping the parent understand and handle their child more appropriately.

Some present-day programmes that involve and assist parents are grouped in this chapter under four different theoretical orientations. They will be considered for what they offer to parents, and also for the extent to which parents are involved in them. This is not an exhaustive summary of the available approaches and programmes involving parents, but it sums up some of the main ones in current use. It is beyond the scope of this book to give more than brief mention of the extensive literature on the effectiveness and outcomes of these programmes or the methodologies of associated research studies.

Behavioural orientation

The Portage programme

The Portage programme was first developed in Wisconsin, USA, in 1970–1, as a peripatetic learning programme for children with moderate developmental difficulties, in order to overcome the problem of the large geographical distance between families (Shearer and Shearer, 1972). It was introduced into Britain via a pilot study in Winchester in 1976 (Smith *et al.*, 1977). Following the success of the early evaluation studies, the service spread rapidly in prevalence across Britain (and internationally) until there were well over 100 services functioning in the UK by the mid-1980s. It remains the most widespread parental participation programme in Britain today, and its great popularity is a testimony to its acceptability and feasibility for parents and service providers.

The classic version of the model has a number of distinguishing features: its curriculum and teaching methods, the form of relationship between the 'home teacher' and the parent, and the structure of the Portage team (see Chapter 12). It draws on behavioural psychological theory and techniques; parents are trained to observe, quantify, record and change the child's behaviour by structuring tasks, shaping and giving reinforcement (or motivating) contingencies. Portage programmes have been staffed by professionals from a wide variety of disciplines (or non-professionals and parents in some programmes). All home teachers are prepared through a short training course. Managers and clinical supervisors have often been drawn from psychologists, because of the model's base of behavioural psychology. Details of the team structure and organisation are given in Chapter 12. In regular home visits, the parent is helped by the teacher to set up an appropriate teaching activity with the child, which they then apply during the week. Further details of the home visit are given in Appendix 8.2.

The relationship set up between the parent and home teacher has many of the elements of *partnership* asserted by the various conceptual models described in Chapter 1. The parent is treated respectfully as a partner to the teaching programme. Their expertise and knowledge of the child are shared with the professional's in the observational assessment, direct teaching, and the feedback of the child's progress. But there are also some potential limits which fall short of the negotiating partnership of the Negotiating Model (see in the following section).

Because of the familiarity and close contact with the child and their family, Portage home teachers often act as the family's preferred 'named worker' or 'key worker' (as envisaged by the DES Warnock Report, 1978) and provide enormous support and assistance. Many parents develop a very trusting, familiar and negotiating relationship with their Portage visitor (see Appendix 8.2). The Portage programme has also been adapted to a variety of settings outside the home (see Hedderly and Jennings, 1987).

With regard to achievement and outcome, many early studies reported a high child success in achieving the behavioural targets (see review by Cameron, 1986a). But this early acclaim was then superseded by the more restrained reports of better controlled research studies, which found a moderate child progress, particularly in children with moderate developmental delay (see reviews by Cameron, 1986, Sturmey and Crisp, 1986). The least progress was seen in children with cerebral palsy, visual impairment, severe developmental delay and those of a higher age

(Barna *et al.*, 1980, Bidder *et al.*, 1982). Numerous positive benefits for parents have been identified (see summary of research in Appendix 8.2) and the programme seems to be particularly effective in what it offers to parents.

These positive results must, nevertheless, be evaluated within the context of some criticisms and limitations of the programme. Criticisms have been levelled at the curriculum of the programme (particularly the developmental relevance of the Portage checklist, see Appendix 8.2). In terms of teaching approach, the child is viewed as a passive recipient of external events and this provides the rationale for a one-way structured teaching approach. This approach is contrary to many recent developmental advances, which have viewed the child as learning through actively participating in *social interactions*, exploring their own world, engaging in problem-solving, and regulating their own learning environment. Some of the implications of this are considered further under *Negotiating remediation* (see later in the chapter).

Another set of criticisms is that the programme often embodies a *transplant* relationship (see Chapter 1) with the professional 'transplanting' skills to the parent and expecting the parent to comply with this. The professional may come across as more competent and capable than the parent, or they may convey the expectation that the child's success depends on the parent's teaching efforts, or that there is only one effective method for teaching the child. All these could in some cases lead to a reliance on the professional for assistance or a lack of confidence in other ways of interacting with the child. A related concern is that the high frequency of home visits intensifies dependency on the home teacher; in one study, less frequent visits were found to be more effective (Sandow and Clarke, 1978).

The Portage programme works on the assumption that parents are willing and capable of participating actively in remediation and teaching, but this has been challenged (e.g. Turnbull and Turnbull, 1982). It is not clear whether parents always want to be involved or whether they should act as 'teachers' to their child. Cunningham and Davis (1985) have suggested that this may not even be feasible for many parents because of their special relationship with their child. The child may interpret their parent's teaching efforts as the corrective behaviour of an angry or displeased parent, whereas similar behaviour by an outside teacher would be construed as normal and appropriate. Moreover, the willingness of a child to comply with formal teaching approaches will vary according to the child's developmental level; compliance will be much higher in early infancy or later childhood than in the late infancy and preschool period. A final point made by Cunningham and Davis is that if the parent adopts a very didactic teaching style with their child, this may inhibit the child's development of self-efficacy and control and instead create a highly dependent relationship (with the parent–child relationship possibly 'mirroring' the professional–parent relationship).

Do parents want to participate?

Findings from the interview study of the KIDS Family Centre (see Chapter 10) suggest parents *vary* in their motivation to participate (Dale, 1986). The home learning service at the KIDS Family Centre was one of the most widely used services and received the most positive appraisal across the highest percentage of users. But there were variations in actual partic- ipation; some chose to follow a highly structured programme with daily teaching activities and a standard recording sheet, whereas others preferred a less structured service with suggested teaching activities to try out when time was available and a more open recording of general obser- vations of the child's progress with the task. When it came to involvement in the teaching programme, a majority (65 per cent of N=43) felt fully involved in using the checklist, but only a minority (35 per cent) felt fully involved in goal-planning and in designing the weekly activity (14 per cent). The majority of parents were satisfied with their degree of involvement and did not wish to increase or decrease their level of participation. Many of the mothers were happy to delegate the final responsibility of decision-making and design to the professional staff. Moreover, a sizeable proportion (48 per cent) would have liked to share the day-to-day teaching of their child with someone else, given the choice. Twenty-three per cent would have liked more help from a professional (the remaining 25 per cent referred to non-specific helpers, other family members or volunteer visitors).

When probed further about whether they felt that teaching their own child fitted in with their parenting role, a small proportion (7 per cent) felt it did not fit in (reasons given included lack of time, competing demands of work and home responsibilities). The majority (63 per cent) felt it compatible with parenting; they were willing to teach their own child. But a further 23 per cent gave a qualified response: the compati- bility of the two roles depended on the age of the child. The older child might be more responsive to a professional teacher than to the parent as teacher (see too Cunningham and Davis on previous page).

A similar desire to share the teaching responsibility was expressed in the Manchester Down's syndrome study. Many mothers using the early home-based intervention felt 'they were not doing enough' and were relieved when their child joined a preschool or nursery class and the responsibility for teaching became shared (Cunningham, 1985).

Behaviour management

It was mentioned in Chapter 5 that behaviour difficulties in the child may be especially stressful for parents. Parents are therefore likely to benefit from being taught skills in behaviour modification that can minimise or overcome behaviour difficulties and problems. Similar to Portage, this approach draws on behavioural psychology and has been mainly developed by psychologists (though staff from other disciplinary backgrounds have been taught to apply these methods). Parents are taught the principles and techniques of operant learning theory (see section on Portage) in order to increase or decrease the child's motivation to perform a particular behaviour. Many studies have demonstrated that parents can be effective in decreasing sleep difficulties, eating problems and conduct problems and in increasing and teaching independence and self-help skills, as well as changing other behaviour. (For reviews on the effectiveness of these programmes, see O'Dell, 1974, Yule and Carr, 1980, Cunningham, 1985, Clements, 1985.)

Although parents may find the professional's expertise very helpful (particularly if an intransigent behaviour problem is at last removed), there is again the potential limitation for the parent of a one-way transplant approach with the professional (see p. 22). But Newson and Hipgrave (1982) have shown that a negotiating approach can be successfully combined with a behavioural approach, in order to establish behavioural goals that are relevant for the parent (and the child) (see p. 196).

We turn now to the second teaching approach which focuses on the parent–child relationship and interactions.

Interactional orientation

Unlike the previous approach, where the main target of change is the *child* (although the parent or carer's pattern of interactions are considered important for reinforcing or modifying particular child behaviours), this second approach emphasises the importance of the *parent–child* relationship. Instead of within-child goals, *interactional* goals are aimed to enhance the impact of the parent's behaviour on the child's social/ emotional, cognitive and language behaviour (Fraiberg, 1971, Bromwich, 1976).

An infant with a disability may be at a particular risk, from an *interactional* perspective. If the infant's actions and attempts to communicate are experienced as puzzling or unrewarding by the parent, the parent may become less responsive to them. For instance, the parent of a blind infant may construe the expressionless stillness of the baby's face as meaning that the baby is not enjoying or reacting to their advances (rather than understanding that the baby is responding acutely through highly attentive listening). Getting little reward from the baby, the parent may reduce their interactions and become distanced emotionally, and the baby's further development may be seriously hampered by this lack of response.

The interactional model could potentially be of great value for supporting and guiding parents to find alternative pathways for inter-action that can circumvent or overcome the problems created by the infant's unusual responses or particular deficits. An example of this approach is the programme proposed by Affleck *et al.* (1982). This programme aims to facilitate the parent–child relationship by setting out to increase parental responsiveness, positive attitudes, joint play, warmth and closeness, increased parental confidence, control and problem-solving. Parents are helped to set up learning situations which increase the child's exploration and regulation. Comparing this intervention with two groups of mothers of children with learning difficulties, the authors found that the mothers with the *relationship-focused support* were more emotionally and verbally responsive to their child, more responsive during interactions and participated in more reciprocal activities (mutual imitation, social games) with their child.

This approach, although not disseminated in an organised form like Portage, may fit in comfortably with some parents' priorities and perceived roles. It conveys a very different view of the child and their disabling condition than the Portage model, in that the child is seen as an active participant, striving to make sense of events and to regulate and control their social and learning environment, and this may have a long-term effect on the parent's relationship with the child and on their aspirations (Cunningham and Davis, 1985).

One consideration to be made, however, is that because the focus is on the parent–child relationship rather than on the child, this focus could be perceived as threatening by those parents who already feel insecure in their parenting (although, equally, it could be particularly beneficial for this same group). A careful explanation and negotiation would be needed for this group.

Play and cognitive orientation

A third approach, which focuses on involving parents to increase the child's internal cognitive processes and problem-solving rather than to teach discrete skills and tasks, has also shown promise. The cognitive psychology approach, emanating from the tradition of Piaget (1950), considers how an individual child explores the world, solves problems and processes information. It has been utilised to assess and help a child with special needs make their own adaptive transformations to reach common developmental goals. Interventions which promote play at home have been shown to increase short-term language development (Martin *et al.*, 1984). This approach encourages parental flexibility and creative responses to the child and an increased sensitivity to the child's own mental constructions and interests. It may lead to more flexible parent–child interactions and a greater shared understanding between the parent and child as a basis for communication.

Counselling orientation

In the fourth approach, the main objective has been to increase parental wellbeing, understanding and ability to cope, as a means of improving general family functioning and the quality of the parent–child relationship. 'Insight' and 'reflective' approaches have worked on enhancing the parent's understanding of their own and child's reactions, emotions and needs. Attitudes, expectations and feelings have been explored, usually in small discussion groups in a climate of trust and openness. Parents have been encouraged to take control of the agenda of these discussions. In a review of these reflective counselling groups, Hornby and Singh (1982) concluded that these groups did appear to lead to changed attitudes in parents and a better ability to manage their child (but the flawed methodology of the studies prevented any firm conclusions).

Another counselling intervention has been the one-to-one counselling support relationship set up with families of children with special needs in the Parent Advisory Service, Tower Hamlets, London. Unlike the other interventions mentioned previously, building a negotiating partnership with the parent was an integral part of this service model. The Parent Advisers (who were drawn from a range of different disciplinary backgrounds) received an initial training in counselling methods before partaking in the service. Working-class white and Bangladeshi families received regular home visits from their named Parent Advisers. Both groups of parents, but particularly Bangladeshi parents, showed considerable benefits from this intervention, compared with control groups who did not receive this service and had standard local authority/health services.

> Respect from a trained counsellor, who visited regularly, built up a trusting, familiar, caring relationship, and who listened and communicated well ... appears to have provided the circumstances or support to facilitate increases in maternal self-esteem. This was associated with increased sense of confidence, effectiveness, positive feelings and wellbeing.
>
> (Davis and Rushton, 1991)

This model compares very closely with the Named Worker service at the KIDS Family Centre (see Chapter 10). Of particular interest is the finding that the children showed greater developmental progress during the period of the programme than a comparison group where the children had standard services from another local authority, although they received no direct remediation from this programme.

To sum up, all these approaches seem to have had positive benefits for parents and for children and to have contributed to a productive collaboration between parents and professionals. A primary value may have stemmed from the quality and form of *relationship* built up between the training professional and the parent, which seems to have borne many of the features of a partnership. None of the approaches seems inherently superior to the others (Gray and Wandersman, 1980, Bricker *et al.*, 1984), and they may all have valuable contributions to make in particular circumstances (though it should be noted that there have been few attempts to systematically compare them for their relative effectiveness, see review by Cunningham, 1985). Most of the methods seemed to have an impact on the child's current difficulties and the parent's attitudes and behaviours, especially when the target behaviours were specific, within the child's present level of functioning and when the programme was well structured and goal-oriented (ibid.). The more diffuse or severe the child's difficulty, the less the impact and the greater the need for individualised programmes. What seems to be emerging from the research literature is that the various approaches seem to benefit different types of parents and families and probably at different times in the family life-cycle (ibid.).

The professional will need to be open-minded and eclectic in selecting orientations that appear to suit the perceived needs of the particular child and family (until we have more definitive comparable studies available). Different approaches can also work alongside each other, e.g. counselling support for the parent may be given in conjunction with a behavioural programme to tackle the child's behaviour problems. The final selection of a programme would need to be reached through negotiation with the family, taking account of the broader family issues affecting the family (see Chapter 5).

We turn now to the case for building negotiation into the intervention programme with the parent.

Negotiating remediation and education

Since most research has focused on the child or parent outcomes of these programmes (e.g. the targeted behaviours of the child), we know relatively little about the extent of negotiation during these programmes (and whether this affects the outcomes). Negotiation is probably very variable, depending on the personalities of the people involved, how the professional perceives their own role and agenda, the nature of the programme material, and the ability of the partners to negotiate. But as the following section unfolds, it should become clearer that negotiation may have a very important contribution.

Selecting a programme

Throughout the book, a strong case has been made for negotiating any service intervention with the family (e.g. Chapter 7: *Assessment of family needs*). Similar arguments apply to selecting a developmental intervention. Nevertheless, the professional may find themselves in a difficult and uncomfortable position if trying to help the parent reach an informed choice or consent (see issues discussed previously). Should they tell the parent that the effectiveness of an approach is not proven – would this weaken the parent's confidence in the programme? What if the most favourable or favoured intervention for the family is not available in the locality? What if the parent chooses the option that is least suitable for the child or family (as viewed by the professional)? The issue of 'interests' has also been raised in Chapter 7; will or can the professional negotiate, if they are not disinterested (their job position, for example, may depend on sufficient families choosing to use their teaching intervention)?

Negotiation within the programme

As will be argued in this section, the effectiveness of any programme may be compromised and the type and level of parental involvement requested may be inappropriate, unless a number of issues concerning the parent are explicitly explored and negotiated within the programme.

The parent's understanding of the child

How the parent construes their child's condition, how positive or negative is their view of the child, and how much of the child's behaviour and performance they attribute to the child's condition may affect the success or otherwise of a remedial intervention involving the parent. For example:

> Gail tended to see much of her child's behaviour in a negative light and attribute it all to her child's disabling condition. She felt very negative about her child and was insufficiently motivated to get involved in the home learning programme.

The parent's understanding about general child development

Intervention programmes work on the assumption that children learn and develop, and that parents can act as facilitators and educators to assist the child in their development and learning (e.g. Filkin, 1984). But parents do not necessarily view development in the same way, and their own view may affect their enthusiasm for involvement and how they perceive the effectiveness of the programme.

Neither of the following sets of parents shared the commonly held assumption of professionals that *both* the child's condition and maturation processes and the learning opportunities and assistance to the child affect the child's developmental outcome. Their different attitudes and expectations had very different consequences for their involvement.

Usha believed that her daughter was unlikely to change much because she had autism and this stopped a child learning and changing. Therefore she felt it was a waste of time for her (or the teachers and therapists) to try and help her child to grow and change.

Derek and Bridget saw themselves as parents (and other teachers and therapists) as having a major influence on their son's learning and progress. Their son has Down's syndrome, and they had read about the importance of early teaching help to infants with Down's syndrome. Also, their Home Adviser gave the implicit impression that change in the child was all down to the teaching intervention. As a result, they viewed any lack of progress in their son as stemming from inadequate efforts by themselves, and this reinforced their feelings of guilt and inadequacy.

The parent's concerns, priorities and aspirations

Goal selection is a primary task in a teaching programme. In the Portage model, it is common for the professional to select one of the next steps in the Portage checklist which follows the child's current performance level. But following an instructional sequence may not necessarily fit in with the child or parent's priorities and needs.

Goals differ in their value for parents and children, and these values may not always correspond to the professional's (Sturmey and Crisp, 1986). Some goals are very significant for parents and caregivers, such as reducing behaviour problems in the child (Gardner, 1984) or increasing self-help and communication skills (Geiger *et al.*, 1978). A straightforward cognitive task like 'sorting red and yellow buttons' may seem unimportant to parents, especially if it lacks an obvious functional purpose for everyday living. Unless the goals and skills have an intrinsic value and meaning to the parent, they are unlikely to be maintained once the programme has finished or to be generalised to other tasks (see Kazdin, 1977 – a study on behaviour modification).

How well the short-term and longer-term objectives fit the parent's own goals, values and aspirations will affect their motivation to participate and to continue with the same approach after the programme has formally ended. One parent, for example, may be content for the child to stay as she is as long as she is happy. Another may be hoping that the child will catch up with his peers and is teaching him frenetically with this objective in sight. Motivation will also be affected by whether the parent understands the purpose of what the professional is trying to achieve.

The parental role(s)

Some parents are not comfortable with taking up a didactic teaching role (Turnbull and Turnbull, 1982) or with the demands of a structured programme, especially if their child is unresponsive and little progress is made (Holmes *et al.*, 1982). Families with multiple and chronic stresses and low resources may find the burden of teaching their child further compounds their problems (Dumas and Wahler, 1983, Pugh, 1987). The success of a programme will be affected by whether the role position required of the parent fits their own preferred or possible role positioning.

Broader family issues

Some of the possible effects of the broader family system on a professional's intervention (and vice versa) were discussed in Chapter 6. Unless these are taken into account, an intervention programme may fail. Many of the early programmes developed for children at the Honeylands Family Support Unit, Exeter, were found not to be implemented at home (Rayner, 1978); subsequent home visits revealed that the team's lack of knowledge of the parents' resources and emotional difficulties was responsible. It appears that some intensive home-based programmes can place intolerable burdens on some families (see *The parental role(s)*, above), and it has been suggested that centre-based services, such as day nurseries and respite care, may be preferable for highly stressed families. They provide a break for the family and teaching can be carried out by relatively unstressed professionals (Sturmey, 1987). In light of this, the choice of service option and timing and level of involvement should be negotiated as part of a wider assessment of family needs and resources (see Chapter 7). This includes looking at the wider family culture and beliefs and the relevance of the teaching programme for the particular family (particularly with families of ethnic minorities).

Since all these factors may come into play, considerable communication and negotiation may be needed to reach a mutually understood and agreed set of objectives and procedures. But such negotiation may also depend on a self-reflexive and internally examining approach from the professional. Unless the professional is aware of their own assumptions and theories, they may not discern any differences and mismatch with the parent's.

Exercise 8.1 provides an opportunity to practise this self-reflexive or self-examining approach and to look at how your own assumptions and theories conform with or diverge from the parent's.

Now that we have established the potential value of negotiation, let us turn to the next section, which opens up a discussion on the more paradoxical situations of dissent.

Negotiation and dissent

Some professionals have strongly invested interests in preserving their own control and expertise and in maintaining the 'expert' power (see Chapter 1); in some contexts, it may be especially threatening to let go of professional power (see p. 91). But even when the professional is willing to share control, the negotiation process can get into difficulty.

How far can the professional let the parent define the content and direction of the programme? In a paper at the National Portage Association conference in 1985, Gillian Pugh said 'I am constantly struck by the conflict between the need to give guidance and enforce a structure, and the wish to respond to the parent's needs' (Pugh, 1987). Conflicting needs or purposes had been previously highlighted by Sandra Sandow at the 1982 Portage conference. She commented that if the parent is to have true power they must have more than the right to agree to the tutor's suggestions. But she also queried 'Can the professional take a back seat if the selection of objectives seems inappropriate or even perverse?' (Sandow, 1984).

In such a situation, there may be occasions when the professional judges it appropriate to follow the parent's wishes and preferences even when they differ from their own priorities for the child, because of the potential benefit for the parent and child of being more in control of their lives. Nevertheless, there will be instances when following the parent's preferences arouses concern in the professional (see following example).

A mother of a 4-year-old daughter, who had severe learning difficulties (and verbal memory and verbal expressive skills in advance of her non-verbal conceptual abilities), was receiving a Portage-style home learning service. During the first two months of using the service, the mother showed little interest in practising any of the teaching tasks suggested by the Home Adviser. It seemed that she saw little relevance in any of the activities, and her concern was in her child appearing as similar to her peers as possible. To this end, she was very keen to teach her child the kind of activities that other 4 year olds were doing. The Home Adviser, not finding any other objectives of interest to this mother, decided to let the mother take full control of selecting some teaching goals. The mother taught her daughter to count from 1 to 10 by rote learning, to recite part of the alphabet, to memorise the name labels for a large number of picture cards, and to copy a few capital letters. After a number of months, the Home Adviser became increasingly concerned as the girl's repertoire became more and more limited to verbal imitative learning (for which she received much attention and praise from her mother). Her speech became very echolalic, and she showed a reduced interest in exploring and manipulating toy materials. Little progress was shown in her conceptual understandings.

The dilemma for this or any professional is can they proceed with a teaching intervention which they disagree with (and for how long?), bearing in mind that they are sharing the responsibility for the content and direction of the teaching programme? Because of the continuing responsibility of the professional and the direct consequences for the child of the teaching programme, the professional may not feel that their role position allows them to follow (or continue to follow) the parent's differing preference.

Negotiation therefore places a heavy onus on the professional. To maintain a shared responsibility for intervening with the child (as implied by the Negotiating Model), they cannot necessarily follow whatever the parent suggests. At the same time, they would need sufficient information and knowledge of the principles and processes of child development to *know how and when they might flexibly alter the programme and when it would be inappropriate* within the standards set out by the programme and counterproductive for the child's developmental progress. This might need to be communicated to the parent, and the understandings of underlying principles shared. Uncertainties may need to be communicated too, particularly when it is not clear how an intervention brings about change. Negotiation that leads to an educational/remedial programme that can work for *both* the parent/family and the child requires a high level of professional skill and judgement about child development/learning and family interactions and resources, as well as the confidence and ability to communicate these to the parent.

In the following example, a professional strove to combine her professional expertise in negotiation with the parent.

Valerie, a single mother, was very keen to start toilet training her 2½-year-old son (who was severely developmentally delayed and had recently started walking). She wanted to work on the Portage goal of 'sits on the potty or toilet seat for 5 minutes'. The Home Adviser viewed that the boy was not ready to start toilet training; he showed no interest in the toilet, no bodily awareness of urinating, he was very involved in his new mobility skills and was reluctant to sit still when directed. Apart from believing that premature training would be counter-productive for the child (and could lead to an aversion to being placed on the potty), she also knew from experience that this mother became very dispirited by any failures in the teaching programme. In view of this, the Home Adviser explained some of the processes involved in learning to use the toilet and the behaviours that she would expect to see before she felt he would be ready to start learning. She advised that they observe his toilet-related behaviours over the next few months, and mean-while work on a possible prerequisite of getting him to sit still when directed to do a brief play activity each day. Although disappointed, Valerie accepted the explanation, and agreed to work on the alternative task.

Because of the expertise required for negotiation in remediation/education, doubt is shed on whether relatively untrained staff can carry out this kind of work (particularly when children have complex and severe learning difficulties). Without this expertise (or at minimum, regular supervision from a suitably qualified staff member), the risk is of pursuing the parent's wishes in ways that might sometimes be detrimental for the child's developmental progress or, conversely, of rigidly following a structured programme and not adapting it to the individual child and family.

To permit negotiation within remediation, intervention programmes will require a curriculum that includes guidance on how procedures should be used and what can or cannot be altered to preserve the quality standards. Although the Portage checklist has accommodated considerable flexibility in use, the weakness of its theoretical rationale (see p. 201) provides little basis for knowing what can and cannot be validly changed or what level of expertise is required by its users.

There are no necessarily neat solutions for resolving disagreement between the parent and the professional during remediation. But the Negotiating Model at least predicts and prepares the professional for the possibility of differing viewpoints. Working in partnership during remedial/educational intervention requires not only skills for negotiating and strategies for resolving dissent (see p. 93), but also, ideally, a relationship that can 'contain' some dissent and mutual challenge without falling apart. The trusting, familiar and long-term relationship built up between the Portage home adviser and the parent would seem especially conducive for this kind of partnership work.

The final section of this chapter suggests some ways for moving towards consensus.

Moving in the same direction

Over time and through a process of sharing experiences and experiments, discussion and negotiation, the parent and the professional may move towards developing a programme that accommodates each partner's current understandings, priorities, values and aspirations. This demands a remediation that is flexible and tailored to work for the individual parent and child, and a professional who is respectful of the parent's own viewpoints and values. The professional may retain a longer-term goal of aspiring to work with the parent and child in a particular way (e.g. increasing parental responsiveness to the child's communicative acts), but may be willing and able to start from the parent's position.

Neither partner's viewpoints and interpretations are likely to be static and unchanging (see Chapter 3). As the programme proceeds, each may alter their viewpoint and shift closer to that of the other. Joining in practical activity around the child and making decisions together could help to create trust and greater mutual understanding.

Planning priorities with the family

Newson and Hipgrave (1982) present one possible approach for planning a remedial or behavioural programme that takes into account the family's priorities and recognises the possibility of differing perspectives. The parent is helped to see that the child's perspective and priorities may not necessarily coincide with the parent's, and that 'balance' and compromise may be required to meet the competing needs in the family. This allows the professional to introduce their own perspective on the child and family in a less threatening or overpowering way – as one further perspective to be introduced into the balancing equation.

The authors suggest writing up a *balance sheet* of three columns with the family. The family take an active role in identifying:

1. *positive behaviours* – the present characteristics and skills of the child which can be built on,
2. *negative behaviours* – the ones that prevent their progress or create stress for the family,
3. *in-between behaviours* – which have good and bad points, and therefore require partial change to make them more positive.

Using the balance sheet to weigh up the positive and negative behaviours, the family and professional can work towards establishing a set of *urgent needs*. The family would consider the following questions (taken from Newson and Hipgrave, 1982) to help them identify the urgent needs for the child and themselves:

1. What new behaviour would be most useful to my child? Why?
2. What behaviour has s/he now that would be most useful *to her/him* to change?
3. What new behaviour in my child would be most helpful *to me* in coping with her/him? Why?
4. Which of her/his present behaviour do I most need to change, for my own sake? Why?
5. Taking all these together, the area of most urgent need for us as a family is ... what?
6. Is there anything that would make it difficult to start with this? What can we do about that?

In summary, this chapter has explored the issues of parental participation, negotiation and consent in child assessment and remediation/education. Differing forms of participation in current types of assessment and remediation have been described. Although a persuasive case has been put forward for building in negotiation and consent of the parent in both forms of activity, some ethical and professional dilemmas of sharing the control of the procedures have been identified.

In the next chapter, we examine the ownership and control of information on the child and the family and how this affects the working relationship between the parent and professional.

PROFESSIONAL DEVELOPMENT EXERCISE

EXERCISE 8.1 COMPARING THE PARENT AND THE PROFESSIONAL'S VIEWPOINTS

Select one family in your caseload (who you feel has different views or values from your own) to consider. On a separate sheet of paper, write down your responses to all the questions.

1. How do you view the child with special needs? Write a paragraph describing your view of the child.

2. How do you view the child's development – how they are developing, what are their possibilities for change and learning, what will help them most to change and develop, what gets in the way of them developing and progressing?

3. What is your greatest concern for the child, the parent(s) and the family?

4. What is your highest priority for the child, the parent(s) and the family?

5. What do you hope for most for this child, the parent(s) and the family?

6. Where do you see yourself fitting in – what is your contribution to meeting the concerns, priorities and aspirations listed?

7. Now imagine that you are one of the parents. How do you think you would respond to each of the above questions from your point of view?

    Write down your responses on a separate sheet of paper.

8. Compare your and the parent's viewpoints. Write down where they converge or differ. What are the implications for working together in a joint intervention (such as education/remediation) and for your partnership relationship?

APPENDICES

APPENDIX 8.1 ELICITING CHILD OBSERVATIONS FROM THE PARENT

The following guidelines for helping parents share their knowledge and observations of their child are taken in abbreviated form from Newson, 1976 (see too p. 176).

1. *Ask the right questions.* A case history needs to be taken from the parents in a relaxed, but not casual way. Questions need to be framed effectively so that they make sense to the parent, fit in with the parent's way of seeing things, and can elicit richly detailed and significant descriptions of the child, e.g. 'Has [child's name] ever surprised you by telling you something you didn't think [child's name] could tell you?' (this gives parents an opportunity to talk to you about their child's best efforts and gives insight into their expectations).

2. *Teach parents to be good witnesses.* Asking parents the right questions helps parents to become more aware of the nature of evidence. This may be done by starting off with a general question about some topic and then raising more specific questions, or helping parents to see that the child's understanding is dependent on a particular context.

3. *Giving parents a job to do.* In addition to the demanding role of providing information through the assessment, parents can be asked to investigate topics at home (e.g. making detailed notes of a sample of speech).

4. *Give parents tools*, e.g. one-way screens (to join an interviewer in jointly observing the child during an observation assessment), video cameras to help the parent record some behaviour at home (under optimal familial conditions, or very disruptive behaviour that only occurs at home). Video can be used sometimes to help show what is going on between the parent and child during the problem time.

5. *Give back information.* The final part of the professional's responsibility is to make information available to the parent in a clear, structured form, so that the parent understands the outcome of the assessment, what possibilities lie ahead, and the implications for remediation.

In the Newson clinic, this includes brief summing-up discussions directly after the observation assessment, and then compiling reports that dovetail together the professionals' observations and the information from the parents. The parents are the first to receive the report because they are regarded as the most essential recipients of the information.

APPENDIX 8.2 THE PORTAGE HOME LEARNING PROGRAMME

Structure of the home visit

The home teacher visits the family on a regular basis (usually weekly or fortnightly) at home and sets up a structured teaching programme. The home teacher and the parent jointly assess the child's current level of developmental achievements with the Portage checklist, and the teacher uses this as a basis for deciding on a set of teaching goals. The home teacher demonstrates how a longer-term goal can be broken down into smaller achievable steps. From here, the home teacher sets up a play/teaching activity to help the child attain a particular step and shows the parent how to carry out the activity through modelling and verbal feedback. The parent tries out the activity in the presence of the home teacher, and is shown how to fill in a standard recording form. In between visits, the parent is expected to continue the teaching programme on a daily basis with their child. At the next visit, the home teacher reviews the child's progress with the parent, and then decides whether the child is ready to move onto the next stage of the teaching programme.

The structure of the home visit can be successfully divided between child-focused teaching and support/counselling time for the parent. Many practitioners have had to move beyond the child-focused structure to take into consideration broader family issues, such as the emotional and social adjustment of the whole family (e.g. South Glamorgan Home Advisory Service, Revill and Blunden, 1979).

Effectiveness for parents

There have been many positive findings of the effectiveness of the Portage system. Families from a variety of social class, ethnic backgrounds and other differences in family circumstances have been shown to be enthusiastic users of Portage-type home learning services (Bardsley and Perkins, 1985, Dale, 1992). Research studies have demonstrated that parents can learn to use the Portage teaching methods successfully (Shearer and Shearer, 1972). Reports of parental consumer satisfaction have been largely positive (e.g. Revill and Blunden, 1979, see review by Sturmey and Crisp, 1986). Home learning services have been valued by parents for the help in promoting their child's development and for the support they provide for parents (Sampson, 1984, Dale, 1992). In a postal questionnaire, parents voted overwhelmingly for their Portage Home Visitor as 'the most useful person in meeting my child's needs before school' (Rennie, 1987: 71).

Other reported benefits include a reduction in maternal and parental depression (Holland and Noaks, 1982, Cameron, 1985) in comparison with parents not receiving a home-based intervention service (Burden, 1980), greater acceptance of their child and more positive attitudes about themselves as parents compared with other parents with children with special needs/disabilities (Sampson, 1984). Further benefits include low rates of divorce and children received into care (Cameron, 1985). Individual parents report of greater confidence in dealing with professionals, improved child's attention span and attitude to learning, teaching the parent to break objectives down into small steps to teach the child, preparing the child for school (Rennie, 1987). A frequent comment one hears is 'Portage was the first "positive" programme we received, positive in that our child began to "achieve" instead of always being "unable"' (ibid.).

In their review study of Portage research, Sturmey and Crisp (1986) point out that many of the research studies are flawed in their methodology (lack of control groups for comparison, poorly designed measures to assess consumer satisfaction, e.g. response acquiescence to questions on the questionnaire). The positive findings must therefore be interpreted cautiously.

Criticism of the teaching programme

One criticism is the weakness of the Portage checklist, which underpins the developmental curriculum of the programme, although it is very popular (probably because it appears easy to use, gives a strong direction, and constructively builds on the child's functional behaviour and skills, i.e. what they can *do*). But criticisms have been raised of the lack of a theoretical rationale for the items that have been selected (mainly from old IQ tests and outdated developmental checklists) and the way in which they have been ordered in the instructional sequence (ibid., Kiernan, 1987). The child with special needs is viewed as developing in a similar sequence to the normally developing child, but this may not be appropriate for the wide heterogeneity of children with special needs (especially those having to use compensatory pathways to reach particular developmental goals – e.g. children with physical disabilities, visual impairment, communication disorder). The checklist also suffers from poor psychometric properties, and lacks testing for reliability and validity.

Chapter 9

Information and control

Until recently, access to records regarding the child with special needs was restricted to professionals. The professional held on to their expert knowledge by deciding which information was relevant to record, by controlling its distribution, and by using it to make decisions that determined the child's future. In this chapter, we shall consider some implications of this control over information for the partnership relationship, and ways in which this control is changing (or not). Three issues will be considered: record-keeping, review conferences, and liaison and communication between professionals. Some possible routes forward for partnership work will be examined.

RECORD-KEEPING

Access to records

The legal situation

A series of legislation over recent years has given individuals access to their records in health, social services and education. These include the Data Protection Act (1984), which gives individuals access to personal records held on computer, the Access to Personal Files Act (1987), which allows access to manual records held by local authorities, and the Access to Medical Reports Act (1988) allowing individuals to see, correct and refuse permission for health records to be sent to employers or insurance companies. The Access to Health Records Act (1990) gives patients or their authorised representatives the legal right to see entries in non-computerised medical records made on or after November 1991.

The Access to Health Records Act aimed to strengthen patients' rights, by emphasising that the rights could be denied only in certain circumstances (see Appendix 9.1). But it has been argued that any real increase in rights is debatable since the rejection criteria are vague and ambiguous, the overall decision to allow access continues to remain that of the individual health professional (as prior to the 1991 Act), and the client has no way of knowing whether they have seen the whole or only part of the health record (Stallard and Hudson, 1994).

Changing practice

At the fieldwork level, there are signs of a growing openness regarding access to professional records, as shown in the trend of recent years towards patient- and parent-held records in maternity and child health services. Many of the main professional associations, e.g. the British Medical Association (1990), the British Psychological Society (1992), have produced briefing papers on the Access to Health Records Act, but the details of its implementation have been left to local procedures and interpretation. Since the majority of professionally written records are 'held' by the corporate body of which the professional is the employee, the legal requirements of access must be implemented at corporate level. The ease of accessibility appears variable. In some health authorities, access to health records is through a lengthy bureaucratic process, which has to be initiated by the individual applicant in writing. In some social services, the applicant may have to pay to see their records.

When it comes to actual practice, there is some evidence of changing perceptions and behaviours in professionals, but also of confusion and uncertainty. A study of seventy professional staff members in a hospital psychiatry department, three months after the Access to Health Records Act came into operation, found that although all were aware of the Act, few had had formal discussions on it within their teams. On the whole, the staff viewed the Act positively, because it made them more thoughtful about what they wrote and also removed patients' anxieties about what was written in the case notes; 52 per cent had told at least one patient about the Act. Nevertheless, many staff showed reservations and reported no change in their behaviour (52 per cent had not changed the content of their notes; 48 per cent had not informed any patient of their new right to access) (Butler and Nicholls, 1993).

In another study, a few years after the implementation of the same Act, thirty-five clinical psychologists (mostly Heads of the psychological services for their area) were randomly selected from different health districts and sampled for their reactions (Stallard and Hudson, 1994). The authors found that a significant majority did not routinely inform their clients about their right to access to their health records. Only 40 per cent reported being aware of their local procedures for implementing the Act. Most reported that no one had requested to see their psychological records since the Act came into operation. A few individuals had requested access to part or all of their record (and this had been granted in most cases, with a few refusals, e.g. a grandparent requesting to see their grandchild's record, a disputed custody case in which personal information relating to one parent was included). Many had no formal procedures for deciding who would agree access to a multi-agency record, who would grant access when working jointly on a case, or for resolving access issues when more than one family member was included in the 'family record' or for dealing with confidential issues regarding the child (see Appendix 9.1).

Both studies revealed very variable professional practice following the implementation of the Act. Stallard and Hudson (1994) suggested that a model of more openness would seem desirable whereby clients are routinely informed of their rights to request access, all written correspondence is shared with them, and procedures are established whereby requests are considered by more than one person. They concluded that it does 'appear that there is a long way to go before a true, open and honest model of partnership between clients and professionals can be established' (ibid.: 27).

Successful examples of record-sharing

On the parent/client side, however, the evidence to date suggests a very positive response to seeing personal records. Record-sharing appears to have positive outcomes for the client and the professional–client relationship. Where patients have been given copies of hospital clinic letters sent to the general practitioner, their reaction has been very positive and their communication with the doctor improved (Gill and Scott, 1986). Reviews of Ley and Morris, 1984 and Ley, 1988 confirm that the majority of people would like written information about their medication and other aspects of their health care. An article in *Community Care* reported favourably on a trial where written social work reports were given to clients (Mittler, 1986). Parents of children attending a child psychiatry clinic found it very helpful to receive copies of letters sent from the consultant psychiatrist to the general practitioner (and GPs also reported positively) (Richards, 1994).

Positive reactions have been shown too by parents of children with special needs. Parents of children with developmental problems are routinely given written assessment reports at Charing Cross Hospital. This is in the form of a letter to the parents compiled by the paediatrician, which incorporates the findings and views of the team and follows a final discussion of the assessment with the parents. Weighing up the advantages and disadvantages of giving written assessment reports, the late Professor Hugh Jolly (1984) stressed the value to parents of reducing their anxiety, increasing their understanding, and aiding their communication with professionals. At the Warwick Child Development Centre (Partridge, 1984), the practice has been for a key worker to deliver a summary report to parents by hand. This report would contain extracts of some, but not all, of the original reports prepared by assessment team members. Receiving the report proved to be popular with parents.

At the Wolfson Centre, London (McConachie *et al.*, 1988), the parents of twenty-five children seen consecutively were sent the same report as that sent to other professionals, following an assessment by a paediatrician, therapist and/or psychologist. In all cases, each professional knew that the report would be sent to the parents. Parents were interviewed about their reactions to the reports. Similarly to the other findings, parents' reactions to the written reports were overwhelmingly positive. Only one said it was not useful. They particularly found it useful for jogging memory ('too anxious at the time to take it all in'), and for looking back and reading again in the future to see if progress had been made. The few instances of unfavourable reactions in the study appeared connected with a lack of acceptance by the parents of their child's need for assessment.

Resistance to change

Although most parents/clients seem to like receiving copies of reports and letters, the apparent lack of enthusiasm of the corporate bodies and professionals for routine access (in that clients are not invited on a routine basis to see their files) suggests some unresolved tensions on their side. Any radical change in practice (such as changing the organisation and keeping of records) is likely to be very uncomfortable for some professionals (Stallard and Hudson, 1994). But other reasons for discomfort and reluctance to change might include the following (they were all issues that had to be confronted by the KIDS Family Centre when initiating an open access record system, see Chapter 10):

1. a difficulty for the individual professional (and team) in reconciling the multiple and competing requirements of record-keeping, and a belief that access weakens the value of the record. Some professionals participating in the Tavistock training course (see p. 28) have made comments like 'I don't feel I can write now what's really going on in the family' or 'it's easy to write about positive things, but not what the problems are with the child';
2. uncertainty and lack of direction at the individual and team level in how to organise and change the method of record-keeping and deal with some of the complex issues raised by open access (see Appendix 9.1);
3. a desire to preserve professional autonomy and possibly privilege, and not relinquish control over information;
4. the time-consuming and difficult task demands of open access record-keeping.

Other constraints may operate on the authority/agency level, such as an interest in preserving 'whole-authority' control by maintaining control over information (it may not be in the authority's interest for some information to become public knowledge) or practical difficulties in storing and releasing files for access.

These different constraints may all have to be addressed and dealt with individually, but one of them has been selected here for further discussion. The demanding issue of reconciling the competing and multiple requirements of record-keeping must reach some kind of workable resolution if the professional is going to be able to communicate the objectives of the record to the parent. The importance of clarifying objectives for proceeding with partnership work has already been discussed in Chapter 2.

Competing requirements of the 'record'

The parent who views the record or participates in the record-keeping will need some understanding of the purpose or function of the record, why an issue is being recorded in a particular way, to whom the record is communicating. But the professional cannot communicate this unless they are clear about the objectives themselves.

Under the Access to Health Records Act (1990), a health record is defined in Section 1.1 as

> any record containing information relating to the physical or mental health of an individual who can be identified from that information, or from that and other information in the possession of the holder of the record; and has been made by or on behalf of a health professional in connection with the care of that individual.

By including 'all identifiable information', the Act covers letters, formal assessment reports, summaries of consultation, personal letters written to the professional, video tapes of family or individual sessions, written records of telephone conversations, summaries of supervision sessions and working notes (including hypotheses, personal opinions and responses to clients). The client can therefore request access to both formal and informal notes on themselves which may be stored in one or more file.

Some of the possible requirements and objectives of the formal and informal notes in a record might be as follows:

1. *to provide a report of the diagnosis/assessment and treatment progress* for the child, parent and family and professional (including results of medical and diagnostic investigations, formal assessment reports, goal setting/achievement, summaries of consultations);
2. *to provide a record of intervention with different family members* for the particular family member and professional;
3. *to act as an aide-memoire* for the professional of their involvement with the child and family (including working notes, personal opinions, hypotheses);

4. *to record concerns*, e.g. suspicion of abuse, risk factors;
5. *to preserve continuity* between departing and new professionals in the team;
6. *to transmit information to other professionals* and coordinate multi-disciplinary involvement with the child and family (correspondence, written notes of telephone conversations, summaries of interdisciplinary meetings);
7. *to ensure a record of accountability* of the professional's intervention for managers/employers and the family, and provide an 'insurance' for the individual. Records may be required for defence of professional liability and expert witness material. NB The courts can serve a subpoena on all professional records and private casenotes (Access to Health Records Act, 1990).

It can be seen that these objectives and requirements are not necessarily mutually exclusive, and a written document may serve multiple purposes at the same time. A critical dilemma that will have to be resolved for the individual professional, team and employing agency is whether each of these objectives can be pursued sufficiently if the client is to have complete and routine access to their whole file. Information that is essential for supervision purposes, for example, might be inappropriate for direct disclosure to the individual parent/client. Recording concerns about the child could be immensely distressing and threatening for the parent, and occasionally place the child at risk. Those hypotheses that might usefully guide the professional's problem-solving and interventions could also be inappropriate for sharing or discussing prematurely.

The potential difficulty of accommodating the individual's right to access and the professional's duty to maintain up-to-date, accurate and comprehensive records highlights again the ongoing challenge for partnership work. The parent and professional may have differing responsibilities and interests that are not always easily reconciled (see further Chapter 1). But unless there is an openness in record-keeping, it is difficult to see how a professional and parent can proceed with an open and negotiating dialogue. This demands facing up to and addressing this problem as constructively as possible, although there are likely to be no perfect solutions and the professional and agency will have to grapple with ongoing compromises and tensions in their record-keeping. Chapter 10 describes some of the lessons learned and issues tackled at the KIDS Family Centre in pursuing a policy of routine access to records.

The process of moving towards routine access requires an ongoing commitment and efforts by the staff and their organisation to work on some of these challenging issues. The Royal College of Psychiatrists (1992) has recommended regular case note audit to keep the practice of record-keeping high up on the professional agenda. In Chapter 10, the importance

of specific training, supervision and team decision-making on this subject is identified. Decisions reached at team level will need to fit in
with local policies and procedures established by the record 'holder' and
authority/organisation, and will require authorisation at middle and senior
managerial/corporate level. Finally, the parent too will need help in
reaching a greater understanding of the multiple objectives of record-
keeping and some of the difficulties in reconciling all of them. They will
need to understand the process of record-keeping and where they fit in.

Negotiating record-keeping

So far, we have been talking about the possibility of routine access for
the parent. But from the Negotiating Model perspective, this viewing of
a report or record is an essentially passive process. It lacks the element
of shared control and negotiating that is seen as critical for partnership
work. At the KIDS Family Centre, we moved beyond routine access to
a more collaborative method of negotiated record-keeping, where the
parent took a much more active role in negotiating the written account.
Some of the challenges and problems of this are discussed in Chapter 10.

Not all parents would want to be involved in a negotiating recording
process all the time (and it would not be appropriate for interventions
where the parent was not directly involved, such as medical treatment of
the child, direct teaching of the child). Nevertheless, it has apparent
benefits for the parent and the professional and their relationship. A
summarising dialogue at the end of each meeting (as a basis for the written
record) permits each member to establish how they and the other have
construed the events of the meeting; it allows the checking of mutual
understandings and decisions, or differences of opinion. The parent is
less likely to feel marginalised, helpless or distrusting, because they are
not excluded from the recording process. The record is less likely to be
perceived as biased or inaccurate. There is also less risk of infringing
privacy and causing a breach of confidentiality if all family members are
involved in the recording process and giving consent to the record (but
see Appendix 9.1).

The one exception to negotiated record-keeping must, however, be in
cases of child protection intervention, when the child's welfare must come
first (see Chapter 11). How this situation was confronted at the KIDS
Family Centre is shown on pp. 246–7.

Language use and records

The issue of language use (which has been discussed elsewhere in this
book) is particularly salient when we consider the conditions of access to,
and participation in, recording. It also raises again the question of the

objective of the record. The choice of language can serve to exclude or involve the parent in the written material; its *intelligibility* is a pertinent issue. All three studies reported on pp. 204–5 expressed concern about how best to ensure the parent's understanding of technical terms in reports. In McConachie *et al.*'s 1988 study, eleven parents mentioned one or more technical terms that they had not known, but several had asked their health visitor or family doctor to explain. A revealing study by Cranwell and Miller (1987) investigated parents' understanding of reports (written by several groups of professionals) provided as advice for formal assessments under the 1981 Education Act. Of particular interest was the intelligibility of language used for parents.

Their analysis revealed that 244 words and phrases were identified on one or more occasion as problematic, in the 67 reports and 19 statements provided by the LEA. The most difficult words and phrases for parents are shown in Table 9.1.

They also asked parents to make a guess at what the words and phrases might mean. Some of the guesses were as follows:

symbolic play   –   he'll sit on his potty and won't do anything.
gestures   –   is that guessing?
rote learning   –   I should think it means she writes it down on paper.
cues   –   Well, the only cue I know is a snooker cue.
unassertive   –   is it aggressive or noisy?
pastoral care   –   the only pastor I know is our pastor.
peers   –   sounds like a Member of Parliament when you think of Peers or Lords – they've made it too political.

In other instances, terminology was also the source of additional worries and anxieties:

developmental –   the develop bit's OK, but I felt worried about the mental part of it.
gross motor   –   it was the gross motor bit that really worried us.
coordination   We thought it was something to do with brain damage.

This study showed succinctly that many commonly used technical terms are frequently misunderstood by parents. It brings us right back to our earlier question of the purpose or objective of the record. Clearly, if a main function of the record is to communicate with the parent, then these reports failed abysmally. But their function was to communicate information to the local education authority (for the child's formal assessment), and again we are confronted with the contradictions of the multiple requirements of recording. Professional advice to the local education authority had to be technically specific if it was going to be successful in securing extra specialist provision for the child; but the report was then likely to be less comprehensible to the parent (Kennedy, pers. comm).

Because of the multiple purposes of many written reports (e.g. a copy of a report from a hospital paediatrician to a general practitioner might be communicating complex medical information as well as trying to keep the parent informed), it is likely that many professional documents cannot stand on their own as a communication to the parent and family without *additional* oral explanation (of the meaning of the language, of why the report has been written in such a way, of the purpose of the message for the sender and for the receiver). Oral communication will be even more critical for parents who are not fluent in English or are lacking in literacy skills.

For developing a more respectful and egalitarian relationship with the parent, the *acceptability* of the language in the record must also be of significance. In a recent examination of fifty sets of psychiatric records, it was found that between 80 to 84 per cent contained at least one moderately or extremely offensive comment, as rated by two professionals or patients respectively (Crichton *et al.*, 1992). Concern over this was expressed by the Royal College of Psychiatrists in their guidance on the Access to Health Records Act (1992); they emphasised the importance of avoiding 'offensive pejorative comments' and encouraged case note audit on this problem. The British Medical Association (1990) has advised that 'personal views about the patient's behaviour or temperament should not be included [in records] unless they have a potential bearing on treatment'. Richards (1994), in the study mentioned on p. 204, commented that professionals tend to use clichés when time is short and this can lead to language which is offensive to patients.

The issue of style moves us on to considering methods of recording for open access and negotiated record-keeping. Richards (see previously) noted that letters which go to parents take longer to write than usual because one has to think harder about how to describe situations in a way which, while it does not conceal their seriousness or possible consequences, offers some positive ideas about how they can be dealt with. Further discussion of the methods of record-keeping at the KIDS Family Centre is pursued in Chapter 10, but one method is given here, to show how the format of negotiated report-writing was undertaken at the KIDS Family Centre. This method is very similar to that reported in Newson, 1976. What emerges is how time-consuming it is to actively involve a parent in report-writing (the following procedure demands an interval meeting with the parent to discuss the draft copy of the report). Nevertheless, the overriding advantages of this method are that the parent understands what has been written, their views are included, and they are more likely to be satisfied with and to support the assessment statement and recommendations of the final version.

Table 9.1 Most difficult words and phrases for parents

Individual words and phrases in order of total numbers of misunderstandings	Total no. of times misunderstood	Total no. of times used	Per cent of times misunderstood
peers/peer group	17	22	77
self-image/concept	13	16	81
description of child's functioning/description of functioning	11	39	28
*year level expressed as 3 yr. 8mth level, etc.	10	17	59
visual (acuity, cues, defects, discrimination, memory, sequential memory)/ visual motor	10	18	56
cognitive (development, functioning, skills)	8	9	89
social (skills, interaction, reasoning)	8	15	53
gross motor (coordination, development, skills)	8	22	36
fine motor (control, function, skills)/fine movement	7	10	70
expression/expressive (language, vocabulary)	7	16	44
*standard deviation written as −0.2 S.D., etc.	6	6	100
2–4 word level (etc.)	6	8	75
auditory (association, memory, reception, skills, sequential memory, work)	6	7	86
Derbyshire Language Scheme	5	7	71
mean scale score	5	6	83

*mainly from 3 reports

Source: Cranwell and Miller, 1987. Reprinted with permission

Guidelines for negotiated report-writing

1. *Start with deciding on the purpose and status of the report* with the parent, to whom it will be sent, what it is trying to achieve, and whether a report is appropriate and necessary.
2. *Write a first draft report* including your observations and viewpoint on the child and initial conclusions.
3. *Show the draft report to the parent*, explaining the content and the implications. The parent is encouraged to comment on the professional's report, including any statement or phrase they do not understand or with which they disagree.
4. *Discuss any difference of view and work towards a resolution.* Through negotiation, a decision may be reached to reject or amend a section of the report. Differences of opinion may get resolved in other ways (see p. 93). If not, differences of opinion may be spelt out in the same report, or two separate reports may be compiled (but see p. 179 for further consideration of dissent in the relationship).
5. *Invite the parent to add their own perspective.* The parent may add comments on the child's abilities or special needs, their priorities and preferences for particular intervention. As in item 4, a shared perspective and understanding may be reached, or 'the parent's viewpoint' may be added in a separate paragraph or report.
6. *Compile the draft report into a final report* after the meeting, taking into account the outcome of the consultation process with the parent. Then send the first final copy to the parent. Subsequent copies of the report may be sent to other professionals with the parent's consent.

NB The differences in power and status between the parent and professional (see Chapter 1) tend towards the professional's viewpoint being taken much more seriously by other colleagues. The sections on *Enabling* and *Advocacy* in Chapter 11 explore ways of increasing the influence of the parental contribution.

Before we move on, it may be helpful at this point to examine the ease of access to records and reports for parents in your own work practice (see Exercise 9.1).

In the next section, we will consider parental participation in review conferences.

PARTICIPATION IN REVIEW CONFERENCES

In the recent past, the extent of parental participation in review conferences varied according to agency setting. Reviews with parents (and children) were not unusual in educational settings, but were traditionally much less common in health or social service settings (particularly since reviews often included child protection issues). In these settings, review conferences typically lacked parental participation or, at most, parents were brought in *after* the objectives for the child had been decided and their presence was perfunctory. Parents were informed about the decisions made, but were not invited to participate in their formulation. This situation has changed rapidly in recent years; with the added impetus of the Children Act, parental presence and participation in social service case conferences are now becoming the norm.

Although parents are generally invited to review conferences, their practice and how parents are involved varies markedly, according to local policy, the kinds of issues being dealt with, the numbers and personalities of participants, and their very different outcomes (Marks, 1992). In some, the atmosphere may be confident and relaxed, whilst others can be disinformative, mistrustful and anxious affairs (ibid.). Parents may feel intimidated and threatened by the collective power of the professionals, and find it difficult to convey their own viewpoint. If personally assertive, they fear being viewed as 'aggressive', 'troublesome' or 'demanding'. They may discern a hidden or pre-agreed agenda, to which they are not party. Professionals may also find the conferences personally threatening, with the exposure of having to work openly with colleagues from other disciplines and agencies and also the anxiety of potential disagreement with the parent.

In a discourse analysis study of one educational case conference, Deborah Marks (1992) showed how these different forces can come together to create a situation where an appearance of apparent amicability and agreement between the parent and professionals may belie some underlying and unacknowledged tensions. In this study, the author/observer was able to converse with the professionals prior to the meeting and then observe the meeting from the position of the parent. Although she had learned of a serious difference of opinion between the mother and the professionals from the professionals prior to the meeting, this was never acknowledged during the meeting. Instead, a series of strategies and devices were used by the professionals to bring the parent smoothly round to the professionals' perspective without any resistance or 'upset'. These included:

- intentionally not informing the parent of the purpose of the meeting or its agenda (so she did not get 'upset');
- using factual devices of an 'outside' authority (e.g. a medical report) which undermined the mother's right to speak;
- discussing one issue as if the mother were absent and thus absenting her from this part of the discussion;
- showing defensive reactions if the mother queried anything.

The professionals' proposal (that the child be sent to the local learning difficulties school despite universal recognition that he did not have learning difficulties) was presented as the only option. The mother was silent during most of the meeting and her viewpoint was not consulted (although it was known prior to the meeting that she strongly opposed this option). The author/observer noticed that the tone of the meeting became much more conciliatory once the mother had accepted, albeit unwillingly, the professionals' proposal.

In this conference, although the professionals were attempting to agree the most appropriate educational provision for the child, the author concluded that there seemed to be a price in failing to acknowledge the agenda of the meeting to the mother and of denying conflicts, ambiguities and uncertainties in favour of presenting a united professional front.

> It undermined current emphasis on involving parents in their child's education. The image of a case conference as a collaborative forum in which professionals and parents meet and democratically debate the issues of educational provision, seems to disguise a more paternalistic process. The mother left the meeting without the benefit of any clear discussion of the precise nature of her son's difficulties at the school.

> (Marks, 1992, p. 17)

Before proceeding further, it may be useful to look at Exercise 9.2 to assess the extent of parental participation in review conferences held by your team/agency. It would be advisable to distinguish between review conferences (such as child development assessment meetings, family needs planning meetings) and case conferences on child protection issues, though you may wish to consider the latter separately if you work in child protection.

Because of the many different influences and counterinfluences that are likely to come together when a group of professionals work alongside each other and with parents (see too Chapter 12), review conferences are likely to be unstable affairs with unpredictable sequences and outcomes. Marks (1992) suggested that one of the ways of making them less personally threatening for all concerned was to ensure a specific outcome through a formal organisation rather than relying on an open and exploratory approach. The following guidelines have been developed to ensure an explicit and organised process for involving parents in the decision-making.

Guidelines for including parents in review conferences

The following guidelines are adapted from Turnbull and Strickland, 1981.

Pre-conference communication

Send a written notice to parents stating the purpose of the review, and informing them who will be attending. Arrange a mutually convenient time and location: this may imply early evening, and at the parents' home.

The written notice should be personal, and might include a set of questions for the parents to consider (see following). Alternatively, the parents should be visited by a professional to help them prepare their own perspective before the conference.

Examples of questions which might be included:

- what skills would you most like your child to learn?
- what do you see as your child's strengths and weaknesses?
- what methods have you found effective in teaching your child, and in managing any difficult behaviour?
- to what extent does your child play with children in the neighbourhood?

Encourage a single parent to bring a friend or relative for support.

Initial stages of a review conference

Delegate one person to greet the parents and introduce them. Consider how many people are necessary at the meeting (the number is often overpowering for the parent). A parent needs to be informed of any 'pre-review' meeting set up to assist the professionals, to which the parent has not been invited. Discuss with the parent the purpose of the review conference, the agenda and the time available. One professional may assume the role of 'parent advocate' – directing questions to the parent, reinforcing comments by the parent, requesting clarification of information, encouraging active participation by the parent.

Negotiation during the review conference

When transmitting the professional viewpoint, be clear and specific and explain technical terms. Present options for consideration where possible (such as different forms of remedial provision), and discuss these options in the light of the child's needs, raising the pros and cons of each (from the professional's point of view).

Invite the parent to share their own viewpoint and listen to it respectfully. For example, ask parents for their insight on their child's progress, and any special concerns they have. Bring together the parent and professional's perspectives and explore how they fit together. Try to resolve any differences of perception or opinion there and then, e.g. if the parents consider frequent physiotherapy is necessary but the therapy staff feel ordinary physical education at school will be sufficient. Negotiation skills and strategies for resolving disagreement may be needed (see Chapter 4).

Deciding on future goals

These can be drafted in advance of the conference meeting, but should be reserved as a frame of reference for parent–professional *discussion* and negotiation. Parents can react by approving, amending or rejecting the recommendations if they are proposed tentatively.

Conclusion of the meeting

The designated chair person should summarise the decisions made, future actions (e.g. review procedure, methods of communication) and persons responsible for implementing the decisions. For example, this might include reviewing the role of the key-worker with the family during the next few months.

In the next section, we will look at the transmission of information between professionals and where parents can or might fit into this process.

COMMUNICATION BETWEEN PROFESSIONALS

The professional network can be viewed as a communication system with information flowing between professionals in all directions (see Figure 9.1). Professionals frequently confer with other members of their team or members of external agencies about children and families they are working with. The importance of interprofessional communication and cooperation for a coordinated, integrated childcare practice has been repeatedly acclaimed by numerous childcare reports and legislation (see p. 281). Though essential for a coordinated input, which many parents desire for their child and family, some of the more negative impacts of this interprofessional communication on the parent have received less attention. In practice, parents frequently have low control over the communication flow and their consent for the transmission of information is infrequently or inconsistently sought. This has various implications for partnership work, as will be shown in this section.

Where are the boundaries of confidentiality?

Although professional associations, local authorities and trade unions supply policies and guidelines on confidentiality, the precise limits or boundaries are often vague. Parents are often unclear about the extent

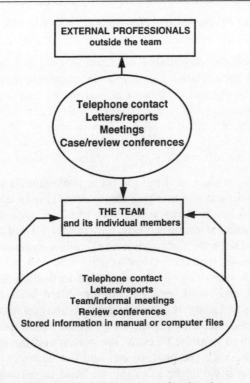

Figure 9.1 Communication network between professionals

of transmission of information. For example, they may know that hospital records are confidential (Patient's Charter), but not know the specific health workers who have access to their child's record. Some assume a greater flow of information than is actually occurring and get frustrated by any failure of transmission (e.g. 'I get so fed up having to tell my story again and again every time I meet a new professional. ...'). Others are suspicious and disconcerted by a professional knowing information which they had not given directly to them.

Professionals too may lack a clear idea about the boundaries of confidentiality. The outer boundary between the professional system/lay person is generally recognised, but inner boundaries *within* the professional system may be less apparent. Professionals chat informally over the telephone, in the corridor, over a cup of coffee about a family with another involved professional. A question to be asked is: when does liaison with other colleagues become a breach of child/parental confidentiality?

The importance of this issue of consent over the communication flow is recognised in various professional associations' codes of conduct. For example, Section 4.2 of the British Psychological Society's *Code of*

Conduct, Ethical Principles and Guidelines (1991) stipulates that members should

> convey personally identifiable information obtained in the course of professional work to others, only with the expressed permission of those who would be identified (subject always to the best interests of recipients of services . . . and subject to the requirements of law) except that when working in a team or with collaborators, they shall endeavour to make clear to recipients of services . . . , the extent to which personally identifiable information may be shared between colleagues.

Omitting to inform parents about the other professionals with whom their case is discussed (and not securing their consent) may convey disrespect of personal and family privacy and may result in such discussion being viewed as a breach of confidentiality. The perceived and actual power of the professional network system over the family is potentially heightened, possibly adding to feelings of low control and low self-esteem in the parents (though, paradoxically, it might lead to positive feelings of being well supported and cared for by a well-organised body of professionals for some parents). Lastly, the partnership relationship is compromised by the lack of shared control over the information transmission. Thus, there may be some detrimental effects for the parent and family as well as for their relationship with the professional and the whole network.

It follows that it would be advisable to build in parental consent (and child consent where feasible) for liaison and inter-professional communication. An example of translating this policy into practice at the KIDS Family Centre is described in Chapter 10.

Various obstacles may, however, need to be overcome before this consent procedure can become effective practice. One concern is the negative effect of *reducing* the flow of information between colleagues, given the well-documented difficulty of achieving inter-disciplinary and inter-agency coordination in the first place (see p. 281). To create a fragmented service delivery in the pursuit of a successful parent–professional partnership would be of dubious value for the child or the family. How this issue was confronted at the KIDS Family Centre is discussed further in Chapter 10. A less obvious cost may result from removing some of the support network of the individual professional. Family work is frequently very demanding and can be very distressing, and talking with colleagues may give space for releasing and sharing feelings (as well as testing out hypotheses and gaining information and ideas). Unless the increase of parental control over the information flow is compensated by an adequate professional support system, reducing this outlet could increase feelings of isolation and lack of support.

A further problem to be explored is the fine art of balancing the parent and child's interests. A parent might refuse consent over information which must be urgently transmitted for the child's benefit. This is particularly concerning with relation to child protection or child illness (see further, Alderson, 1990). The Code of Conduct mentioned previously (see p. 218) adds the proviso that the professional (referring to the psychologist) should

> in exceptional circumstances, where there is sufficient evidence to raise serious concern about the safety or interests of recipients of services, or about others who may be threatened by the recipient's behaviour, take such steps as are judged necessary to inform appropriate third parties without prior consent after first consulting an experienced and disinterested colleague, unless the delay caused by seeking this advice would involve a significant risk to life or health.
>
> (BPS, 1991, Section 4.3)

These potential problems need to be resolved through team discussion and decision-making. To reach a concerted approach to parental consent and inter-professional communication, the team and agency will need to draw up a policy document on the issue and agree on a set of related procedures (such as consulting an experienced colleague in exceptional circumstances where consent may have to be overlooked). Appendix 10.1 shows an example policy document on confidentiality which includes an exemption clause for child protection.

DEVELOPING THE PROFESSIONAL VIEWPOINT

Although we have looked at arguments for increasing parental participation and control over domains that have traditionally resided with the professional, there is still a case for preserving separate areas of joint professional decision-making that do not involve parents. The argument for this derives from the Negotiating Model and its recognition of the *separateness* and complementary importance of the professional and parental perspectives and responsibilities. Professionals need to work together to solve problems and develop their own viewpoint. This process should be conceptualised as distinct from the process of negotiated decision-making with the parent (though there may be many occasions when the two pursuits will be combined in a single meeting).

A lengthy process of problem-solving with other colleagues may be required before reaching a viewpoint which can be shared with the parent. For example, a group of multi-disciplinary professionals may collaborate before reaching a child diagnosis; or a group of professionals may work on solving how their varied interventions can be coordinated successfully (as in a 'pre-review' meeting before a review conference with the parent). Although on occasion it may be helpful for some parents to observe this inter-professional problem-solving in process, the function of this kind of meeting does not require the parental presence or involvement. And for some parents, the observation of uncertainty and differences of opinion between professionals might be detrimental to their confidence in the professional support system.

In order for the parent not to feel excluded and distrustful of such meetings, and to minimise the risk of breaching parental and child confidentiality, however, the purpose and membership of the meeting should be discussed with the parent in advance (see example policy in Appendix 10.1). If the parent has a desire to attend, this should be accommodated if possible.

Of crucial importance for a partnership approach, the professional problem-solving meeting cannot be used to make *final decisions* for action in relation to the child and family. It can, however, be a forum for developing draft goals and recommendations which would then be introduced into the negotiation process with the parent and family as the 'professional perspective' (see p. 16).

To summarise, in this chapter, we have examined the balance of control between the parent and the professional over the content, recording and distribution of information. Three main areas of storing and transmitting information have been considered: record-keeping and report-writing, review conferences, and inter-professional communication. Although the balance of power has been shown to lean mainly towards the professional, evidence of changing practice and shifts in power have been presented with guidelines for increasing parental participation and control.

Some of these issues are explored further in the next chapter, which describes a model of service delivery, the KIDS Family Centre.

PROFESSIONAL DEVELOPMENT EXERCISES

EXERCISE 9.1 ACCESS TO RECORDS AND REPORTS

This is an opportunity to explore the extent of access parents have to written information about their child and themselves. Consider your individual practice and that of your department/team/agency, and answer the following questions on a separate sheet of paper.

1. Do parents receive copies of reports? (Never/Sometimes/Always)

2. Do they receive copies of letters sent to other professionals? (Never/Sometimes/Always)

3. Are the copies of reports given to parents the same as those given to other professionals? (Yes/No)

4. When/why would you not give a report to parents?

5. Do parents have open access to their records? (Yes/No)

6. How easy is it for parents to view their records?

7. Do you inform parents routinely that they can see their records? (Yes/No)

8. Do they regularly see their own records? (Yes/No)

9. What do you see as the main advantages of an open access record system?

   What do you see as the main difficulties or obstacles to overcome in maintaining an open access system?

   How are these overcome in your own practice/organisation?

10. How can parents/children be helped to gain from an open access system?

11. Does your team/agency have a written policy and procedures on parental access to records? (Yes/No/Don't know)

    What is it?

    Do parents know it?

12. On the basis of your responses to the above, assess on a scale of 1–5 (1 = no access, 5 = easy access, regular viewing) the ease of access to records in your work practice/agency. Do you feel this is satisfactory, or would you like to see changes?

EXERCISE 9.2 PARENTAL PARTICIPATION IN REVIEW CONFERENCES

Consider child-related review conferences held in your own work setting/team/agency. Then add your responses to the following questions, writing your replies on a separate sheet of paper.

1. Does your team have a written policy on parental participation in conferences? (Yes/No)

2. Does it follow set procedures with all parents? (Yes/No)

3. Are parents invited to all conferences held on their child? (Never/Sometimes/Always)

4. Do they sit through the whole conference or only part of the conference? (Part/Whole/Varies)

5. When/why would you not include parents in a conference?

6. What do you see as the main advantages of including parents in conferences?

7. What are the main difficulties or disadvantages of including parents in conferences?

   How might these be (or are being) overcome?

8. How are parents helped to participate in the decision-making of the conference?

9. How are children helped to participate in the decision-making of the conference or to have their views consulted?

10. On a scale of 1–5 (1 = no participation in decision-making, 5 = full negotiated decision-making), allocate the score which shows the extent of participation of the parent in the decision-making procedure of the conference (and also the child).

    Is it variable? What causes this variability?

APPENDICES

APPENDIX 9.1 ACCESS TO HEALTH RECORDS ACT 1990

The Act stipulates that access would not be granted if, in the opinion of the holder of the record, this would disclose 'information likely to cause serious harm to the physical or mental health of the patient or any other individual' or would disclose 'information relating to or provided by an individual other than the patient who could be identified from that information' (Section 5.1). The other exemption clause was for the part of the health record made before the commencement of the Act on 1 November 1991.

Three areas require consideration when working with children and families (the following notes are derived from Stallard and Hudson, 1994):

Rights of access if the child is under 16 years old

People with 'parental responsibility' under the Children Act 1989 have the right of access to a health record where the client is a child under 16 years of age. Divorced and separated parents do not lose parental responsibility, and local authorities can acquire it. This continuing responsibility (and right of access) may, on occasion, cause problems or a conflict of interests for the child if, for example, they have discussed difficulties during a visit to one parent or alleged abuse. Access of one (or both) parents can be prevented if the child is 'capable of understanding' the request or, if not, whether the record holder considers it not in their 'best interests' (Section 4 of the Act, p. 11).

Stallard and Hudson point out the practical problems of implementing this, because of the ambiguity of these terms, which are open to differing interpretation. They recommend that good practice entails a procedure where such matters are discussed and agreed jointly with at least one other colleague, preferably not involved in the case.

Confidentiality and the child

In some instances a child may see a professional for individual sessions, which could involve discussions on relationships and sexual matters. Under the Act, the parents would be able to apply for access to their child's health records, and this lack of confidentiality could lead to distress and distrust of adults on the part of the child. The guide to the Act acknowledged 'there will be a need for the rights of the child to confidentiality to be balanced against the parental responsibility to ensure that only accurate and non-prejudicial information is recorded about the child'

(p. 7). Section 5.3 states that access to any part of the record can be denied if, in the opinion of the record holder, it would disclose 'information provided by the patient in the expectation that it would not be disclosed', and that this information should be recorded separately in the health record.

Stallard and Hudson highlight that the difficult tasks of deciding this for those children not 'capable of understanding' and of balancing parental rights against those of the child for confidentiality will rest ultimately with the appropriate professional. They suggest, as a way of safeguarding the rights of children, that children should be informed of any requests for access to their health record and be asked whether there is any information that they do not want disclosed. Where this is not possible, the procedure described in *Rights of access* (see above) with at least one un-involved colleague would be useful.

Family records

Identifiable information about other family members may be recorded in the child's file; this is especially likely when working in partnership with parents and families. Under the Act, the child can apply for access to their health record upon reaching the age of 16 years, and would there-fore become privy to such information. This might include information which the parent has shared with the professional, such as experience of abuse, details of the parentage of the child, the parents' relationship, but which they do not want disclosed to the child. Stallard and Hudson (1994) write that the complex issue of family records is not considered in the Act, but Section 5.1 of the Act does prevent access that would disclose 'information relating to, or provided by, an individual other than the patient, who could be identified by that information'. They suggest that this might lead to the practice of keeping separate records for each indi-vidual within the same family. This is already undertaken by some Social Service Departments, but is complicated, time consuming and difficult, and clinically unacceptable (it prevents an overview of the family or recordings of interactions between family members).

They suggest an alternative practice of keeping combined records, but access would have to be by agreement of all those involved. This could be negotiated with the family during their first contact with the profes-sional and a 'contract' of access agreed and signed (although this lacks legal standing). Another alternative is that the family is shown the profes-sional's notes at the end of each session, which they in turn could sign and specify anything they wanted recorded separately. These suggestions fit in with the KIDS Family Centre's approach (see Chapter 10).

The KIDS Family Centre: a model of service delivery

> Acceptance and adaptation take a considerable period of time and we were impressed by the work of voluntary organisations like KIDS ... in working sensitively over a period of time with families of children whose special needs have been newly diagnosed.
>
> (ILEA Fish Report, 1985)

In this chapter, a model of service delivery which has been developed specifically to meet the objective of working with families in partnership will be described. Three features will be focused on:

1. the operation of a named worker service,
2. shared control and information,
3. diversity of parental participation.

The KIDS Family Centre, Camden, London, was set up in 1979 by KIDS, a charitable voluntary organisation. It continues to maintain its independent existence, whilst receiving the main proportion of its funding from the London borough of Camden. The Centre is a family support centre available to all families with a child with special needs (disabling conditions, and conditions associated with long-term learning difficulties) residing in the borough. Most children using the Centre have moderate or severe long-term learning difficulties, associated with mental, physical or multiple disabilities and/or sensory impairments.

The Centre promotes the principle of equal opportunity and positive discrimination in its policy documents, i.e. that all families with a child with severe special needs may need extra support at some time in their lives in order to help them overcome some of the difficulties and disadvantages facing families with disabled children and to take up a more equal, integrated position in their local community. Moreover, 'those involved in the regular care of children with special needs require specialised support and practical help in order to enhance the children's potential and wellbeing' (KIDS *Annual Report*, 1987/8). To translate these policy statements into practice, the Centre has committed itself to providing a range of service provision that can be of assistance to special needs children and their families in a long-term way throughout the childhood period until early adulthood (19 years).

The other dominant policy principle of the Centre is to work in *partnership* with parents and families, and through this has arisen a set of policy documents and operations for putting *partnership* values into practice. The Centre aims to involve parents fully in decision-making and activity around their own child and family, and also to involve parents in policy formation affecting the Centre.

The ensuing description of procedures and practice emanates from the period of 1982 to 1988, when I was a full-time member of the Centre staff. The Centre has continued to evolve and change since that period in response to changing needs and contextual circumstances. In the mid-1980s, the Centre was staffed by a multi-disciplinary team of professionals (staff included preschool and primary school teachers, a nursery worker, social worker, occupational and speech therapist, and a clinical child psychologist/Centre Director [myself]) who worked on an *interdisciplinary* basis (see p. 283). The team was accountable to the main governing body of the KIDS agency (whose membership included professional advisers, members of national voluntary organisations, and parent advisers) and met regularly with the local Advisory Committee (composed of representatives from Health, Social Services and Education, and up to four parent advisers) which served an advisory function.

Services provided by the Centre in 1988 included a home learning service (modelled on a flexible Portage-type scheme, see p. 182) for preschool children and their families, Centre-based developmental play sessions for parents and preschool children, and a named worker attached to each family with either a preschool or school-aged child for support, advice, information provision and counselling. Additional services included parent group meetings, outings and workshops for siblings, leisure outings for the whole family, and a parent-to-parent befriending service (the Parent Support Link project). The breadth and variety of service provision at the Centre stemmed from parental wishes for particular services and also a recognition on the staff side that families have *diverse* requirements (Dale, 1992). The Centre aimed to offer a flexible, personal range of services tailored to each individual child and family, enabling families to select those which best met their own requirements and preferences.

THE NAMED WORKER SUPPORT SERVICE

The period referred to runs from 1983 to 1988. During this time, all families using the Centre were linked to a named member of staff, who acted as their 'named worker' (in line with the role recommended by the

DES Warnock Report, 1978). The service aimed to provide support, counselling, guidance and advice to parents and the whole family through regular long-term contact. The two main functions included:

1. an advisory, networking service facilitating the family's external relations, and
2. assisting the family and child in dealing with their own problems and challenges around disability and special needs in the child.

These functions were pursued within an active partnership relationship developed between the parent, family and named worker.

All members of staff participated in the named worker service. In addition to their original professional training and qualification, they were expected to have a basic and developing knowledge and expertise in child development, learning techniques and disability issues. They received further training in Portage home learning methods and in counselling to enable them to fulfil their responsibilities on this service. In-service training was provided in communication, negotiating, partnership and record-keeping skills.

Role and context

The organisational independence of the KIDS Family Centre as a voluntary agency affected how the named worker could operate and also how they were perceived by parents. Although there were constraints and boundaries imposed by the agency on the role of the named worker, the staff were not subjected to some of the conflicting pressures apparent for local authority employees (e.g. reconciling serving the parent and family as 'client' whilst acting as a public servant serving the aims and interests of the employing authority). Many parents talked spontaneously about the value for them of having a worker whom they perceived as 'impartial' and independent, because the worker was not associated with or restricted by the policies of a local authority employer. They often said that they trusted the information and advice from the KIDS staff because they viewed it as less biased or one-sided than that of local authority staff.

Nevertheless, being outside the statutory system had disadvantages and limitations too. The professional staff had much less power than statutory professionals in obtaining certain service resources in the statutory sector for parents and children. They could also be discounted and marginalised, e.g. not receiving referrals systematically, because they were outside the statutory network. To overcome these possible problems, staff had to work hard at developing and maintaining close cooperative contact with other professionals in Health, Education and Social Services, and this was time-consuming.

Introductions

When first linked up to a family, each named worker had to spend time and be committed to developing a relationship with the family. They introduced themselves in a manner which established the framework for a partnership relationship (see Chapter 2). Additionally, a 'contract' needed to be agreed upon by the parent and professional so that each party was clear about what was expected from themselves and from the other (see p. 42). The process of becoming familiar and getting to understand each other took time and could not be hurried for either party. The timing and pacing of sharing information about the family rested primarily with the parents and family members; how much they chose to reveal and when was kept mainly under their control. Nonetheless, the professional also had to gain basic information from the family (with their consent), before they could proceed further and provide a service. This included information on the child's condition and special needs, members of the family, other service/professional involvement, and a brief developmental history of the child. It was important to know the background to and reason for the referral, and also the family's prior experience of services. One stipulation before offering a service was that the KIDS staff member would need to make contact with any other professionals involved with the child and family, to inform them about the new involvement from KIDS and to seek their views on any proposed service delivery. Consent for this was rarely withheld.

The professional's main approach at the beginning was to be *available*, open and honest, to listen to the family, and to set the foundation for a trusting, sharing relationship.

Venue of visits

The majority of families chose to have their named worker service in their own home, but the venue was always negotiated with the family. Some families preferred to make initial contacts in a more 'neutral' place, such as the Centre, a nursery or school, or with another known professional present. Regular meetings enabled the parent or family and worker to become familiar with each other and build up trust and acceptance.

Periods of assistance

Families sought emotional support, practical guidance, information and advice, counselling, and enabling assistance/empowerment from their named worker. Assistance included early pre- and post-diagnosis support and counselling, helping families link up to other agencies and services and resources, information on financial benefits, practical help (including behavioural programmes supervised by the psychologist in the team, and independence skills programmes at home), guiding parents through the 1981 Education Act formal assessment procedure for special educational needs, and other advice and support. Help was often needed during transition and change periods, such as entering or leaving school, the arrival of a new baby. Support was also sought in periods making the family more stressed and vulnerable, such as child hospitalisation, parental illness, or internal family conflict. Changes in the child, such as when the child's behaviour became a problem or the child entered a new stage of development, might also lead a family to require help in making some necessary readjustments. Parents also sought help over specific problems, e.g. lack of respite care or breakdown in respite provision or difficulties in relationships with another professional or service. Help with siblings was frequently requested.

Many of these issues might traditionally have been dealt with under conventional *casework* of social workers (see Evans *et al.*, 1986), but the majority of these families had very little or no social worker contact (other studies also report low contact with social workers, e.g. Ayer and Alaszewski, 1984, Cunningham and Sloper, 1977b).

Types of assistance offered

Depending on the circumstances, the named worker offered a support, listening and counselling intervention (see Chapter 4). They offered information and advice and might transmit expertise on child development, special needs, and behavioural management. They might assist the parent in methods of handling the child. Parents were also helped to look at the needs of other family members, such as siblings, fathers, and at how the overall family was coping. The named worker helped link the parent and family to other resources and services, and offered help in liaison and networking. They drew on communication and negotiation skills (see Chapter 4) to help parents participate in discussion and decision-making. They aided parents and family members in developing problem-solving skills, and becoming more confident or effective in using their own abilities and resources.

It was important that the named worker had a clear idea of the limits of their responsibilities and competence. They had to assess whether the family might benefit from specialist or other help beyond what was appropriately provided within the named worker role, such as developmental remediation and education, social work assistance, psychotherapy and 'depth' counselling, marital counselling, family therapy, and then negotiate with the family whether they would take help from another source.

The description of one named worker's day illustrates the variety of assistance that might be required.

Example working day. A named worker began by making an occasional telephone support call to a family with a school-aged child; the parent reported that life was running smoothly at present. Then she spent half an hour writing up notes on the previous day's home visits and telephone calls. Then she made a lengthy home visit to a very distressed couple who had recently learned of the diagnosis of their child's retinoblastoma and severe visual impairment. She then visited a single mother and her 8-year-old daughter to counsel them over the girl's negative feelings about being seen publicly with her severely disabled younger brother and recent refusals to go out publicly with him. After lunch, she phoned a parent to monitor how she was progressing with a behavioural programme on night-time problems, which she had set up with the parent (under supervision from the psychologist). Next, she met up with a parent at a local school, to support the parent who was very nervous about visiting the school for the first time. She ended her working day with a regular home visit to a family who were highly stressed and battling with recurrent problems (a conflictual divorce process, housing problems, financial difficulties and aggressive behaviour in their child with special needs) and making heavy demands for support. Her main help recently had been to visit them regularly and to offer a listening, supportive contribution. Today, she hoped to help the family identify some priority need and to set a specific goal objective for them to work on jointly.

This 'typical' day shows the diversity of situations confronting a named worker. The highly variable needs of families require the named worker to be very flexible and adaptable in response. The nature of the role is multi-faceted and therefore very demanding for the professional concerned.

Goal-setting

Alongside developing support through the relationship, it was essential to pursue goal-focused objectives in order to preserve direction in one's intervention and prevent long-term dependency on the professional's involvement. Short-term goals were decided on together, and activity to reach them was planned and implemented (see earlier, p. 163). Joint decision-making and negotiations between the parent and professional underpinned the partnership. Additionally, it was important for the professional to develop the relationship as an 'enabling' one, and to regularly review whether the parent and family were being helped to use their own resources and abilities and become more independent in coping.

Record-keeping

Written records were kept of the intervention by the professional with each family. The record sheets had a standard format, which included date of meeting, who was present, purpose of visit, past goals/actions achieved, issues discussed between named worker and parent/family members, any other observations, future goals set/action to be taken, and date of review meeting/next visit. What was to be written down and put in the file on the child and family (stored at the Centre) was negotiated with the family at the end of the home visit. Parental consent was sought on what was going to be recorded. This sheet was often combined with a Goal Plan, which recorded systematic goal-setting. Some of the demanding issues and challenges experienced by the staff in open-access record-keeping are discussed further on pp. 237–40.

Help with the formal assessment process

Almost all families undergoing the Formal Assessment procedure under the 1981 Education Act for special educational needs requested and/or took up extensive support and guidance from their named worker. Many parents found the assessment process to be a baffling and anxiety-provoking experience. Regular support was needed to help them cope with delays and uncertainty whilst the decision-making was proceeding.

Without guidance and assistance from the KIDS staff, many parents would have been inadequately informed and equipped to participate and take up their own responsibilities and rights. Many lacked information and assistance from any other source. The named worker intervention ensured that each family was enabled to take up the full possibility for participation under the 1981 Act legislation (see p. 250). Families frequently commented on their appreciation of the support during this period, and also their preference for support from an 'independent' named worker who was separate from the LEA. The need for support often extended far beyond the initial 'statement', to the child's entry into school and settling-in period, and then through to yearly reviews of the child's placement and special needs provision. Later reviews often aroused further anxiety, as the child's placement and provisions for special needs were again subjected to scrutiny.

School-aged children and families

Through the experience of running the service, it became apparent that many families with school-aged children (including adolescents) continued to need access to a named worker. Those who had received it during their child's preschool years were frequently reluctant to give it up when their child entered full-time school at five years. It was noteworthy how few families received support and assistance at home from their wider professional network system once their child entered full time school at five years. Health authority staff often withdrew at this period. This fits in with Suelzle and Keenan's study (1981) which found that the amount of professional support available to families decreased with the increasing age of the children with disabilities. They found that the parents of teenagers and young adults were less supported than families of younger children.

Although some families welcomed this new independence from professional assistance and the shift to a more 'normalised' lifestyle with greater involvement in the more integrated structures of society (ibid.), others found the withdrawal difficult and felt isolated and unsupported. In particular, families whose children were being integrated into mainstream school placements often felt alone with their school (and home) concerns, especially if there were no other parents with children with severe special needs at the school. Apart from the minority of families receiving social work input from the social services or local special school, most families lacked any equivalent named worker from another agency. School staff were not generally able to offer a support relationship to the family at home.

Although some families chose to withdraw from the named worker service when their child entered school, others continued to need regular or occasional intermittent help (for example, over concern about their child entering puberty, generalising their child's learning at school to the home environment, the setting up of suitable after-school leisure pursuits, developing appropriate independence behaviour in their child, behaviour problems at home).

After the Centre had been running for about ten years, it became increasingly difficult to resource the staffing required to meet the named worker needs of the school-aged children and families. Each year infants were joining the service from below, but many families with older children were still requiring occasional and sometimes intensive help from the service. In light of this, a separate support service with its own staffing, called the Family Project, was set up in the late 1980s specifically to serve families of school-aged children.

Frequency of contact

Frequency of contact varied with each family according to jointly assessed need. This was negotiated individually with each family. The frequency of visits was written into the initial and subsequent 'contracts' set up with the parent, putting the relationship onto a contractual level. Nevertheless, staff still needed to have some guidelines on frequency of intervention, and a policy document for the service was developed by the whole staff team. The frequency of intervention was generally more frequent for preschool than school-aged children's families, in response to the greater need for support of families of young children (Suelzle and Keenan, 1981). As a general guideline for families with school-aged children, it was recommended in the document (KIDS Family Centre Named Worker Service Policy Document, 1987) that families would receive three to four visits (fortnightly or monthly) when getting to know a family. This would be followed by regular visits on a three-monthly basis (except during a particular crisis or planned intervention period, when it might be weekly, fortnightly or monthly for a specified time-limited period). After a period of time, it would be reviewed whether the family would be ready for less regular contact (two six-monthly home visits a year). More frequent visits would be resumed if a new problem required more intensive assistance and if help was to be offered. (This was decided through negotiation with the named worker.)

In families with preschool children, the named worker service was combined with the KIDS home learning service (which most families elected to receive). The home adviser on this service also served a named worker function. Contact in this service was more frequent (weekly or fortnightly visits during the first year of service, fortnightly visits during the second year, and monthly visits during the third and later preschool years). The frequency of contact and joint participation in teaching activities in the child's early years built up a very positive and strong relationship between the family and home adviser.

The point of termination of the named worker service (either for an agreed period of time or for the long term) was negotiated with the family.

Supervision and peer consultation

The taxing emotional and psychological demands of being a named worker made it imperative that the providers received ample support and supervision themselves. Moreover, the challenges and dilemmas of implementing a partnership approach into practice necessitated discussion and joint problem-solving with other committed peers. Many different issues were explored in supervision, but one recurring issue was the difficulty of maintaining a personal/professional boundary. Both the intimacy of a long-term relationship and the collaborative nature of the partnership could make for difficulties in preserving and working with separate parental and professional perspectives. It was sometimes difficult to resist getting over-involved and possibly transgressing professional boundaries, and this required regular monitoring. The complexity of working with the whole family and preserving a partnership relationship with all members was also frequently considered (see further Chapter 6).

All staff, whatever their experience and status, received regular supervision and consultancy assistance. Supervision was provided by the clinical child psychologist in the team (who was also the Centre Director), and regular peer consultation was provided by fortnightly team meetings to discuss ongoing work with named worker families. The Centre Director had regular consultations with an external psychologist. The well-integrated inter-disciplinary team played a key role in instilling mutual support, open communication and guidance between the professionals of the Centre. It also permitted careful coordination of intervention and accountability between staff members at the Centre.

Service resource planning and allocation

Diversity and lack of predictability in the demands and needs of families and the long-term requirements for support had particular repercussions for service planning and resource allocation. It was difficult to make accurate prediction of the specific workload time needed by a particular named worker at any moment in time. To overcome this problem with some rational planning, an 'average' unit time was allocated to each family of a two-hour home visit (plus travel/liaison/report writing time/peer consultation time) i.e. 3.5 hours once every two months. Using this unit measure of 0.44 hours per week, it was possible to calculate how many families could be held on a named worker's caseload (depending on what proportion of their working week was allocated to the named worker service). For instance, a named worker with a caseload of fifteen families, visiting them on average once every two months, needed seven hours (approx. one working day) per week for the named worker service. It was found that variation in excess of the allocated time in some families was balanced by under-usage in others. Notwithstanding this, it was found necessary to have a spare capacity time available of four hours per week (i.e. half a day) for unexpected crisis periods which could befall any family and which often used an inordinate amount of professional resources for a limited period of time or for intensive short-term planned intervention.

In 1988, 62 families received the named worker service (using 28 hours of staff time per week, spread across four team members); another 35 families with preschool children received the named worker function through the Home Learning Service. A team of five full-time staff were able to provide regular named worker support to approximately 100 families (in addition to the range of other family support services listed on p. 226).

This resource allocation worked reasonably well until the numbers of families requiring the named worker service outweighed the existing staffing level. Parents and staff were becoming increasingly frustrated that the staff could no longer provide the frequency of a regular named worker service. The staffing level was unable to expand due to funding constraints, even though there was an increase in service user demand. As a result, the service changed format and staffing level in 1989 by separating families of school-aged children from those of preschool age. Two full-time staff were employed to provide an advisory/counselling and support service (the Family Project) to families of school-aged children, in addition to developing groupwork with parents and siblings. The two members (at the time of writing) carry a caseload of 25–30 families each (with about 65 families using the service in one year, at a cost of £52,000 in 1993-4) (Woodley, pers. comm).

The KIDS Family Centre research project

One of the measures of service audit was to set up a research project which could provide a 'process feedback loop' whereby those who were at the operational end of the work could establish what they were achieving. A feedback system was developed to allow staff to receive consumer feedback on the quality of their work. An interview question-naire was designed by the author, in consultation with the staff. The questionnaire aimed to establish which aspects of the Centre and its services were working most successfully for parents, and how they expe-rienced and evaluated the practices of partnership pursued by the staff. A variety of family measures were employed to investigate the relation-ships between parental appraisals and individual family circumstances. In 1986, an outside interviewer was employed to interview 50 parents of preschool children (selected in alphabetical order) who had all been using the Centre for at least one year. Mothers were interviewed (the original intention had been to follow this up with interviewing fathers, but this was unfortunately never achieved, due to research funding limitations). The interviews took place in the parent's home and generally lasted ½ to 2 hours, and the questionnaires were then analysed 'blind' (without the names of the parent interviewed) by the author (see further details in Dale, 1992). Some of the findings are discussed later in this chapter, but one striking result was the very positive appraisal of the general quality of support care.

The value of support

When asked what they appreciated most about the Centre, 40 per cent of the mothers interviewed referred spontaneously to *emotional support, care and concern* for themselves (and their child) from the staff at the Centre (ibid.). (Note, a similar proportion remarked spontaneously on practical guidance and concrete advice for themselves and their child. This fits in with the conclusions of other studies that parents want practical advice and guidance as much as being listened to and supported, e.g. Hewett, 1970, Bayley, 1973, Wilkin, 1979). Many expressed the value of having someone/somewhere to turn to, being helped to cope, being less alone. Examples of their comments include:

'the fact that they care for us both'

'the understanding, the support, the homely feeling'

'makes a very difficult situation liveable'

'they are available – they come and visit, see you in the home, they care'

(Dale, 1992)

Sizeable proportions of parents also appreciated the availability and approachability of the staff (e.g. 'there is always someone here when I need them') and the partnership with the staff (e.g. 'they make me feel as an equal – I do not feel less capable', 'the way they listen', their 'attitude towards parents as human beings') (ibid.).

A caring approach is a *personal* one; those cared for feel that the professional is sincerely and genuinely committed to their welfare. Other studies have also established that high priorities for parents are that the professional knows the child and family well, has a sympathetic, patient approach (Sandow *et al.*, 1987), is available, approachable and gives time to the family (Ineichen, 1986, Byrne *et al.*, 1988). The named worker role seems particularly suited to offer these contributions and qualities.

Even though a named worker service carries heavy workload and resourcing implications, there were many perceived benefits from running such a service for families. Parents felt supported and valued; they appeared to become more confident and competent. They were assisted in tackling problems and stress-evoking events constructively, and many expressed the view that the help from KIDS made them feel more self-esteemed and positive about themselves, their family and their child with special needs. These benefits of support and counselling from a named worker have been demonstrated objectively in a research study on the Parent Advisory Service, Tower Hamlets (see p. 188, where parents were shown to have increased self-confidence and coping abilities and more positive attitudes towards their child and family, and these benefits were shown to be even higher for ethnic minority Bangladeshi families (Davis and Rushton, 1991). At the KIDS Family Centre, parents were facilitated in their relationships with external professionals, so that they could participate in an informed and assertive, but constructive, manner. Perhaps one of the indicators of the growth in individual strength and empowerment was the mushrooming of collective parent initiatives over recent years, such as the Parent Support Link Project (the parent-to-parent befriending service), a parent-initiated training video for medical students, a parent-run forum, and vocal parent campaigns against threatened service cuts.

In the recommendations of the Fish Committee, it was reported that

> there is a need for a designated person, outside the education authority, to provide appropriate information; talk through any problematic issues; and to make the parent feel confident and comfortable at any time ... we had clear evidence that many parents needed an extra resource in order to be able to assume the role of 'partner' rather than 'client'.
>
> (ILEA, 1985)

In her article on the KIDS Family Centre, Gillian Pugh wrote that

> this is a role which KIDS staff seem to fill admirably. They are able to get to know the families well and can provide a link between them and the many other professionals whose paths they cross ... parents feel that they can approach staff about any issue that troubles them, and that they will be listened to. For those who have been involved in making a statement under the requirements of the 1981 Act, the key [named] workers have enabled them to make a real contribution and to feel confident to negotiate the final decision on placement.
>
> (Pugh *et al.*, 1987)

Apart from specific service design and operation, the Centre staff also had to resolve complex issues to do with sharing control with parents.

In the next section, we examine one general area of this shared control: the recording and communication of information on the child and family, and consider some of the related procedures and dilemmas arising from them.

INFORMATION AND CONTROL

Using an open record-keeping system

One method of operationalising the partnership policy into practice was to give parents routine open access to their records and to enable them to participate in the decision-making on recording. Parents were informed about the record-keeping system and their possible involvement in the recording process before being offered any service (see policy document in Appendix 10.1). Their consent to the procedures of the Centre formed the initial 'contract' (a contractual agreement to abide by the main policies of the Centre, but of no legal standing) when joining the Centre.

Each child had a written file, which included all written documentation of the Centre staff's involvement with the child and their family as well as correspondence received from external professionals. The parents of the child were regularly invited to view their file. The only written material excluded from the file were notes of supervision sessions between the staff and clinical supervisor of the team. These were maintained in the supervisor and staff members' private files and information was labelled by the initials of the child/family's names to remove identification. These notes were to guide individual staff in their professional practice, and the staff member's notes were destroyed when they stopped working with the particular family.

Deciding what to write down in the record was openly discussed between the staff member and parent and formed an integral part of the negotiation process and intervention. It required an explicit discussion of what had gone on between them at a meeting and what should be recorded and how. Although this was time-consuming, staff became accustomed to building this into the end of the meeting with the parent. They found that it became not only a procedure for sharing control and bringing their perspectives together, but also a useful exercise in 'meta-awareness' or reflecting on the thinking and action of the session, which could lead to new insights and understandings for the parent and professional. The child could also be brought into these discussions.

Parents did not generally resist documentation of any intervention because they were already sharing control of the intervention. Many parents approved of the staff's written records and profiles which grew out of a process of joint activity and negotiation by the parent and staff. In particular, the lengthy joint involvement in the Home Learning Service and the familiarity of the staff with the child led to developmental reports that parents felt were very representative of their child. Nevertheless, the staff member and parent did not always share the same interpretation of a situation, such as differing in their view of the severity of the child's learning difficulties. This required careful and sensitive recording: for example, giving a detailed description of the child's current skills and abilities without spelling out their degree of delay if the parent did not seem ready to accept this information yet.

Apart from being time-consuming, this practice of negotiated record-keeping required ongoing and sometimes challenging problem-solving and decision-making by the staff. There was a definite tendency for staff to record information about the child or their goal-oriented action with a family rather than their counselling discussions on family issues. Parents might discuss marital problems, psychological/mental health problems, sibling difficulties, financial and housing problems, and domestic violence, and these issues could be difficult (if not impossible on occasion) to record in an open access record. Staff were hesitant about encroaching on the parent and family's privacy and undermining the trusting relationship they had built up. Some discussions were never recorded because of the concern that the parent may be inhibited from engaging in further such discussions in the future. Moreover, open recording highlighted the problem of working with one parent rather than the whole family system or couple as the right to privacy of absent family members could be compromised by working with the one family member present. Mothers frequently discussed problems about absent partners which they did not want recorded. The bounds of confidentiality had to be considered regarding discussions on siblings, partners and the child, where consent had not been sought or could not be given (see Chapter 9).

Some issues that were censored by the parent were felt by the professional to be important for recording. The staff member might recommend that some issues remain unrecorded until the absent person they referred to could be informed and their consent sought. Alternatively, some matters could be recorded if first re-framed into more acceptable terminology. Instead of writing that 'Ms X criticised her husband for his lack of help with Carly', this might be re-framed as 'Ms X discussed some current difficulties in carrying out the physiotherapy programme at home, including her husband's lack of time to be involved'. The professional had to weigh up whether something was better recorded or not, and what would be the consequences of either option for the parent and child or the parent–professional relationship or the ability of the professional to assist the family.

> For example, one parent requested that a staff member not record their joint observations that the child (who had muscular dystrophy) had deteriorated in developmental skill level. She was concerned that this information would be sent out in the next developmental report to external professionals, and would be used as evidence to stop maintaining him at a mainstream school. The staff member explained her own viewpoint of the recording, which in this case was that the information should be recorded because it was needed to inform her remedial intervention with the child. She suggested a way in which the information could be transmitted to other professionals, incorporating the parent's wishes. The parent considered this carefully, and then gave consent to the recording.

There were no universal rules or solutions, and the professional had to use their judgement to decide on individual cases. A procedure of joint decision-making with an experienced colleague in the team who was not directly involved with the family (if possible) or with the clinical supervisor was used to resolve challenging dilemmas.

The staff team had to develop consensually accepted procedures and protocols for recording their parent/family work that were not likely to jeopardise their partnership with parents, yet would meet the professional/ agency requirements for accurate record-keeping. It proved helpful for the team to use a series of record sheets which contributed to a systematic, standard and regular form of recording. In addition, in-service training in record-keeping, individual supervision by the clinical supervisor, and occasional team workshops to design and audit recording methods all assisted in the acquisition of open record-keeping skills. Through experience, staff became able to record greater amounts of information systematically without alienating parents, and more confident about their decision-making of which information to retain in writing and which to discard.

Inter-professional communication and consent

The KIDS Family Centre Policy Document on Confidentiality is shown in Appendix 10.1, and some of the experiences of implementing it are discussed below. One of the practices of the Centre was to hold a regular peer consultation meeting of the staff team members. This forum enabled staff to be kept informed about each other's intervention with children and families, thus permitting a coordinated support approach to the whole group of families using the Centre. It also acted as peer supervision, enabling members to guide and assist other members of the team. It provided a means of accountability, such that the intervention of members was made known to other members of the team. In addition, it contributed to team-building, fostering collective policies and approaches to working with families and children.

Parents were not invited to these meetings. They were not perceived by the staff (or parents, as far as was known) as conflicting with the committed policy stance on confidentiality and parental consent (see Appendix 10.1). Parents knew that information shared with one member could be shared with the rest of the team, and they often assumed that matters discussed with one member would be known later by other team members. It appeared that this added to their perception of the staff as a collective and interchangeable support entity (see p. 287), at least for many families (though the full impact was difficult to ascertain). Nevertheless, this policy probably had an impact on the control of parental communication. Parents were in control of what they shared and did not share, and in light of team-sharing of information may well have selected accordingly.

Greater difficulties were found in meetings with external professionals outside the agency. Regular meetings were held at the Centre between the Centre staff and therapists from the local child development team. These inter-professional meetings were very helpful and constructive from a professional stance; they helped establish cooperative relationships across agencies and also coordinate the professional intervention with families. It was efficient in professional time to run through all the shared families at the same meeting, but there was not always time before meetings to go through with each family what information would be transmitted (and thus secure parental consent). Moreover, one might learn information on the family from the external professionals which the parent would not have wanted transmitted. The Centre staff tried to overcome this difficulty by regularly reviewing with families, whilst working with them, what could or should be conveyed to which relevant professionals, so that they were preparing in an ongoing way for these meetings. During the meeting itself, one of the problems explicitly focused on was *which material about any child or family could be transmitted in either direction without breaching parental/child confidentiality.* This joint problem-solving served to raise consciousness in and remind colleagues of the importance of parental and child privacy, control and consent.

Similar difficulties and dilemmas were experienced in telephone conversations through which a great deal of inter-professional communication took place. Although the KIDS staff tried to be diligent in discussing with the parent and securing consent before telephoning an external professional, it was less easy to control what the other professional might say to them. The parent may not have given consent on the other side. Moreover, an external professional could ring unexpectedly and request certain information from the staff before the staff member had an opportunity to ask consent of the parent. In these situations, the staff member might feel a conflict of interests – to communicate openly with the external professional and maintain good inter-professional relationships or to preserve parental confidentiality and control at all costs. Some external professionals were irritated by refusals to provide information on a family without first talking it through with the family, and in some cases perceived it as staff 'possessiveness' over a family or 'collusion' with the family. It was also perceived as wasting scarce professional time.

There were no easy solutions to these dilemmas. In general, however, the staff at the KIDS Family Centre have continued to strive to pursue a practice of maintaining parental confidentiality and consent, although it is often time-consuming and demanding for inter-professional communication. Over time, external professionals have become more respectful and understanding towards the Centre staff's practice and more willing to communicate in a compatible manner. The practice has possibly had a knock-on effect of changing the practice of external professionals. There is no doubt that the information flow between the Centre and external professionals is potentially slower and more consuming of staff resources when parental consent and control is continually being sought (a disadvantage of the partnership model of working). To offset this negative impact, staff have worked hard at, and been publicly noted for, initiating regular and effective contact with external professionals (with parental consent). They are perceived in the locality as developing cooperative and productive relationships with external professionals, and playing a leading role in assisting cooperative relationships between *parents and their whole professional network*. These effective relationships between parents and their professional network justify the extra time spent on seeking parental consent, because they reduce the likelihood of waste and unproductive professional activity when there is a lack of parental cooperation.

In the final section, we examine the diversity of parental participation at the KIDS Family Centre and some of the findings on this issue from the research project.

DIVERSITY OF PARENTAL PARTICIPATION

The KIDS Family Centre offered an unusual opportunity to investigate parental preferences for parental participation services. By providing a range of different services involving different levels and types of parental–professional collaboration and a policy of free choice, it was possible to do a within-group comparison of who selected what (though we were not able to investigate those parents in the catchment area who were eligible, but chose not to enrol at the Centre; estimates of the time suggest that about two-thirds of eligible families were using the Centre [Dale, 1992]).

In the research study (see p. 235), it was found that the parents of preschool-aged children varied in what they chose to use (ibid.). The most popular services were the named worker service and the Home Learning Service at home (both were used by the majority of the sample). The parent- or family-focused services at the Centre (Parents' Meetings, Parent Social Events, Family Outings, Sibling Workshops) were used by smaller proportions, but still by a third to nearly a half of the parents (depending on the service). Although all the services were used by sizeable proportions, there were definite patterns in usage and appraisal which suggested that *some services were particularly welcomed by a certain kind of parent* (ibid.).

Family background variables were strongly associated with what parents chose to use and with their ratings in terms of helpfulness for the parent and for the child (ibid.). For example, the Developmental Play Sessions were more likely to be used by mothers whose husbands played a low role in caretaking, who were not part of an ethnic minority, who had been referred originally to the Centre by a professional, and who perceived themselves as 'willing to enter the world of handicap'. The mothers who found this service most helpful for themselves and for their child were more likely to be working class and to perceive themselves as very sociable. The Parents' Meetings were also particularly likely to be used by mothers who perceived themselves as 'willing to enter the world of handicap', but those who found them most helpful tended to have self-referred themselves to the Centre. Appreciation of the Parents' Social Events was strongest in those rated as needing the greatest degree of professional support.

Empowering disadvantaged families

One of the earlier criticisms of parental involvement services was that they would overburden and deplete the already limited resources of families who were disadvantaged socio-economically. This has been supported by studies reporting a bias towards more middle-/upper-class families participating in parental involvement services (Hargis and Blechman, 1979) and to a higher drop-out rate in socially disadvantaged and less educated parents (Rickel *et al.*, 1980). But contrary to these findings, the experience at the KIDS Family Centre was of particular appreciation of certain services by some families who were more disadvantaged. Working class mothers who had poor support from their spouses and few other people to share in the care of their child (but were also sociable and willing to enter a specialist centre for children with special needs) were more likely to use and appreciate the Developmental Play Sessions, the Sibling Outings and the Family Outings.

It seemed that certain kinds of services and low-key ways of encountering professionals could have an *empowering* effect. These services gave some disadvantaged parents access to new or wider social, leisure and learning opportunities and to a new peer community. The Lothian Regional Educational Home Visiting Scheme (Raven, 1980) and the study of Homestart (Van der Eyken, 1982) had also highlighted the need of mothers with low social support within and outside the home to engage in social events. These opportunities may have gone some way towards alleviating their individual personal and social disadvantages, and this might explain their particular appreciation by these parents (Dale, 1992).

It is worth emphasising two important issues from this research into service usage, because of their implications for service development and provision. The first was the apparent relationship between what parents chose to use at the Centre and personal/family factors (such as the parent's personality and attitudes, marital satisfaction and support, socio-economic resources). This neat 'fit' could only have been achieved through letting parents choose from a range of possible service options. But though free to enter or to discontinue the service, individual users varied in how beneficial they found a service; the degree of perceived benefit was again related to personal circumstances and family background. From this complex interface between services and personal/family background factors, we drew out a pointer for future professional practice. It seemed vital to incorporate a broad *family focus* in one's negotiations with the parent, when offering a service and monitoring its acceptability and perceived benefits (see Chapters 6 and 7).

The second issue was of parents' attitudes towards the so-called 'world of handicap'. As Gough *et al.* (1993) point out, it has rarely been examined in research on families of children with special needs, but in our research study it was very salient in distinguishing between different kinds of service users. Parents who did not seek to 'avoid' the world of handicap were more likely to join in group services at the Centre (this has been subsequently replicated in a research study in Glasgow (ibid.) using the same attitudinal measure of 'world of handicap'). Those who avoided the group services included those who wanted to keep their family life as normal as possible and did not wish to be involved with other families with disabled children (similar to the 'family-oriented' group of parents in Seed, 1988). There were others who were very isolated loners who felt they could not presently meet other people; they included a number of mothers with mental health problems. The KIDS Family Centre was able to provide a network of support services for those who sought out group experiences and support and were willing to offer support to others. For those who wished to avoid 'the world of handicap', services at home were valued as resources to enable them to lead as normal a life as possible. Home-based services also gave personal, private support to parents who could not face meeting others at this stage. It is likely that the parents' attitudinal orientation is a reflection of different facets; it may reflect the parent's present state of adjustment to their child's disabling condition (Gough *et al.*, 1993), the life-cycle stage of the child and family, or the parent's ideological beliefs about integration and normalisation of children with special needs and their families (Seligman and Darling, 1989). This orientation is unlikely to be static, varying with parents' changing needs and expectations of services (Seed, 1988).

Participation as a process and interaction

Individual participation in services was not static, but changed over time because of changes in each child, parent and family (linked to different stages of adaptation and life-cycle, differing life tasks, changing needs, resources and values and preferences) as well as the match or mismatch between availability of service provision and family needs. Even though the two parents discussed below started with a similar choice of service and level of involvement, their differing needs were paralleled by diverging service usage over time. The apparently neat match for each family might not have been achieved without the active facilitation and sensitive negotiations with their respective Named Workers.

Example 1. Mother A chose to use only the Home Learning Service at the KIDS Family Centre in the first years of her child's life. She was a busy working mother with a full-time career job who wanted to keep her child's and her own life as 'normal' as possible. Her child had severe cerebral palsy affecting all four limbs. She had a live-in nanny, a husband with a busy career, and an active social life. It suited her to have the Home Learning Service at home late afternoon, on her return from work, and she found the support and counselling very helpful. The nanny helped carry out the teaching activities with the child. This mother did not want to use any other services at the Centre and did not feel the need at this time to mix with other parents and children with special needs. When the child was 4 years old, she entered a local school for children with physical disabilities, and the mother reduced her contact with the Centre.

Example 2. Mother B was a single mother recently arrived from a Middle Eastern country, with a traumatic history, who had one child (with brain damage and severe learning difficulties). She was socially isolated, now lived in a high-rise council block after a year in homeless accommodation, and was very shy. In her early days with the KIDS Family Centre, she used only the Home Learning Service and was very nervous about coming to the Centre. With the active help of her home adviser/named worker, she was introduced to the Developmental Play Sessions and started attending them. She made friends with one or two other mothers and joined them in going on a Family Day Outing organised by the Centre staff. Then she started to attend other social events at the Centre, attending with the mothers already known to her. After a period of time, she became an actively participating parent and gained considerable support and confidence from her friendships. She began to extend her social involvement in the community, and eventually took up a part-time job locally (five years after her initial involvement with the Centre).

The low involvement of parents from ethnic minorities in the Developmental Play Sessions was picked up from the research study, and responded to by alterations in service design. A new Bangladeshi member of staff was appointed to work closely with Bangladeshi families; the combination of this new worker and new transport arrangements led to Bangladeshi families starting to attend the Developmental Play Sessions at the Centre.

In summary, this chapter has presented a description of the practices of the KIDS Family Centre, which was set up specifically to work in partnership with families of children with special needs. Various practices and procedures have been discussed, to illustrate how partnership methods were put into practice and some of the dilemmas and challenges arising from sharing control with parents. Diverse patterns of participation were also explored.

The following two chapters look at partnership work within the wider context: firstly, the legislative framework, and secondly, the professional's organisation.

APPENDICES

APPENDIX 10.1 EXAMPLE POLICY DOCUMENT ON CONFIDENTIALITY

(adapted from extracts from the KIDS Family Centre Policy Document: Confidentiality (1988)

This document was open to staff members, professional colleagues and parents. Parent users received a more user-friendly version, in the form of an introductory leaflet. Parents were asked to sign their agreement to the leaflet before entering into receiving services. Some additional features have been added here.

Our objectives

We aim to

1. provide services to each child and family of high professional standard,
2. respect each child and parent's rights to privacy,
3. involve family members as full partners in whatever we provide to them so that they are fully active in all decisions and actions involving their family.

What we commit ourselves to doing

1. All identifiable information on any child and family is *confidential*. No identifiable information on any child or family will be discussed with any person outside the Centre team, except with other colleagues of relevance to the Centre's involvement with the family and after securing parental consent.
2. No written information on any child or family will be shown to any person outside the Centre team, except to other colleagues of relevance to the Centre's involvement with the family and after securing parental consent.
3. Any information given by a child or parent to one member of the Centre team may be shared with all members of the Centre childcare

team. This team meets regularly to help each other offer the best kind of service to the children and families using the Centre.

4. Parents are invited to be present at any review meeting held on their child at the Centre and to take full part in it. Parents are key partners at the meeting, and their participation is strongly welcomed.

5. The staff may also need to meet with or telephone other professionals outside the Centre from time to time to coordinate or discuss their involvement with a particular child and family. The parent's consent would be sought before such a meeting was held, and the parents would be informed of who would be present. Parents have a right to attend the part of the meeting when their child is discussed, if desired.

6. Written records on the child and family are open only for inspection by the child's parents and other members of the Centre childcare team. Parents are regularly shown the content of their file, and negotiate with the staff over what is kept in the file. The secretarial staff have access to the file for filing purposes.

7. Reports and correspondence pertaining to the child and family from external professionals are stored in the family's file. External professionals are informed in advance that any correspondence on the family will be stored in an open-access file.

8. Communication with other professionals outside the Centre about the child is undertaken only with the parents' consent. The information to be shared with or sought from other professionals is discussed with the parent before making contact with the professional. The main issues discussed are fed back to the parent, verbally or in written notes in the child's file.

(NB It is essential, however, that the other professional has given consent to this, and knows the nature of what is being written down.)

Exception to 8. In the exceptional case that we have significant concern that a child is at risk of being emotionally, physically or sexually abused or neglected, we are duty bound in law to inform the local authority Social Services of our concerns. In such circumstances, parental consent will not be sought. We will inform parents of our action, and the general nature of our concern, before making contact with the Social Services.

Chapter 11

Legislation and partnership

How far a parent goes in participating with a professional, and how much right and power they have to participate, has depended until recently on the *discretion* of the individual professional. The professional has decided whether the parent should be involved or not, and the parent has had no recourse to law if they disagreed with decisions made or felt inadequately consulted.

Legislation by the State authorises whether partnership is an integral, statutory part of public life or merely a voluntary, private relationship between a parent and a professional. The Education Act 1981 was seminal in giving parents explicit *legal* powers to participate in the procedure of special education decision-making. As a result of this and two other significant legislations, the Education Act 1993 and the Children Act 1989, partnership has begun to shift into a statutory relationship between the parent and professional. This chapter explores some of parents' new rights in law and some of the achievements and problems arising from this legislation. The issue of child rights is considered briefly. Routes to empowering parents are discussed, as well as the possibility of conflict and options for resolution.

EDUCATION ACT 1981

The Committee of Enquiry into the Education of Handicapped Children and Young People, chaired by Mary Warnock, was set up in 1974, and its full report of the Committee's recommendations, *Special Educational Needs*, was published in 1978. This followed the earlier DES Plowden Report (1967) and DHSS Court Report (1976) which highlighted the need for collaboration between parents and professionals in education and health care, and drew on contemporary ideas of good practice. Major innovations for the education of children with special educational needs (S.E.N.), requiring changes in perception and practice, were proposed in the Warnock Report. Children with disabilities were not to be differentiated from other children in educational terms, unless if on an individual basis they required any special educational provision additional to that of their peers (so S.E.N. were defined in relation to peers and in relation to the learning/social setting). The Report was heralded as a major step forward in the thrust towards integration of children with special needs into the mainstream education system.

A central section of the report was headed 'Parents as Partners' and *partnership* was a fundamental theme in all its recommendations. The Committee urged 'great recognition and involvement of parents wherever possible as the main educators of their children during their earliest years', and called for improved working relationships between school and home, professionals and parents. 'Parents, it cannot be too often stressed, must, wherever possible, be treated as equal partners in the educational enterprise' (Warnock Report, 1978). A *named worker role* was proposed to support parents and help them participate in their child's education and take up their potential role as partners.

The 1981 Education Act was the government's response to the Warnock Committee Report. In addition to introducing the concept of 'special educational need' and a range of associated changes for the education of children with special educational needs, the Act instigated a number of new rights for parental participation in special educational decision-making. Parents were to be given a new role in the assessment of their children for special educational needs.

Assessment under the 1981 Act

The Warnock Report (1978) outlined five stages of assessment of children's special educational needs. These were progressive and depended on the severity of the problem. The first three stages were *school based* and covered both the 18 per cent identified by Warnock as having special educational needs at some time in their school life (transitory special educational needs) and the 2 per cent of children with long-term needs and/or most complex needs. The final two stages were to be concerned with this latter group of children for whom formal statutory procedures would be necessary. Stages 4 and 5 became the procedures in Section 5 of the Act and were variously known as: Formal Assessment, Section 5 assessment, and Statementing procedures.

In the guidelines accompanying the introduction of the 1981 Act (DES Circular 1/83), it was recommended that parents should be made aware of concerns about their child some time before a Section 5 assessment was discussed, and that they should have access to the records of any actions taken to help their child leading up to that period.

Parents' rights under the 1981 Act

The Act came into force on 1 April 1983, and enshrined new parental rights and responsibilities. Before the Act, parents' wishes were not considered on a regular basis and professionals decided where a child with a 'handicapping condition' would be educated. Under the Act, parents were now empowered to be involved in the total assessment process. Parents could request an assessment, which the local education authority had to comply with if the request was deemed 'reasonable'. They were permitted to contribute their own views to the assessment as 'parental evidence'. They had a right to be present at the assessment and they had the right to see and comment on the draft statement of special educational needs if one was drawn up. They also had the right of appeal if they disagreed with the final statement of special educational needs. Their appeal in the first instance was to be made to their LEA Appeal Committee, and then, if still unresolved, to the Secretary of State.

The Act was heralded as breaking new ground in the movement towards integration; it placed LEAs under a qualified duty to integrate children with special educational needs into mainstream schools. This duty was qualified, amidst other constraints, by the requirement to take into account the wishes of the child's parents.

Although the spirit of the Act was for 'parents as partners' and the expectations of parents and professionals were initially high, parental rights were weakly articulated in the Act and many problems ensued once the Act was in operation.

Problems in practice

Alongside the introduction of the Act, Circular 1/83 (DES, 1983) was distributed with guidelines for teachers, headteachers, governors, and education officers to help them implement the Act. One section emphasised that 'parental involvement in assessment provides the opportunity to reach an *agreed understanding* of the nature of the child's learning difficulty' (my emphasis). The success of section 5 of the Act appeared to depend on parents and professionals reaching a shared understanding and consensus, which in turn depended on effective communication and a common set of assumptions (Sandow *et al.*, 1987).

As has already been argued in Chapter 1, however, the different viewpoints, roles and possible interests of parents and professionals were likely to lead to diverse priorities and understandings. Thus, the ease or possibility of reaching a consensus of belief and objective was always likely to be more problematic than envisaged by Circular 1/83.

This has been borne out by a detailed case study in a London borough (ibid.). When the responses of parents and professionals to the Formal

Assessment procedure were compared, great difficulty was found in reaching an 'agreed understanding' (ibid.). Conspicuous differences in expectations and priorities (and also the professionals' understanding of parents' priorities) were apparent, which paved the way for much disagreement and misunderstanding. For example, parents especially valued professionals having regular contact with their child and getting to know their child well (rather than receiving occasional expertise from a less familiar professional). They particularly wanted individual attention to their child's problem based on real familiarity and close knowledge of the child. In contrast, professionals rated regular contact with the child as a low priority (for themselves and for parents). Instead, they presumed that parents most wanted specialist expertise and advice, and above all, a guaranteed solution to their problem. There was little evidence that either the parents or professionals were shifting in attitude towards accepting and building a partnership.

The authors suggested that the professionals' expectation that parents wanted, above all, an immediate solution was likely to lead to a tendency to offer something positive and comforting to the parent, rather than to enter into a process of dialogue and negotiation. The child was likely to be fitted into whatever facilities were available, in the easiest and quickest way.

> To indicate uncertainty, to ask parents to share the problems and questions associated with identifying the difficulty, goes against the grain. Yet it is only by doing so that true partnership is offered. Anything else is not partnership, but collaboration. 'Parents as collaborators' is an unattractive phrase, but this may be the role into which they are forced if the professional idea of partnership is one in which people who are perceived as inadequate or vulnerable are persuaded to take up the proffered options without fuss, thus satisfying their need for 'something to be done' without, contrary to the intention of the Act, actually taking part in the decision.
>
> (Sandow *et al.*, 1987)

Underlying these different expectations and viewpoints were real and perceived power and role differences between parents and professionals in terms of decision-making and resource allocation (see further Chapter 1), which were neither acknowledged nor addressed in the 1981 Act. This was demonstrated in a study commissioned by the Department of Education and Science on the implementation of the Act (Wedell *et al.*, 1987).

To study the process of the implementation, five LEAs were investigated in depth using a 'case study' approach (ibid.). One part of the study explored the recognition of the rights of parents by the LEAs. Difficulties in communication between parents and professionals or administrators appeared to arise when the latter were faced with dilemmas about identifying the nature of the child's problems or about the availability of appropriate provision. Parents reported that they tended to be met by defensiveness and evasion in these situations. The authors wrote that the general impression emerging from the research findings was that parents felt that efforts were made to involve them in the statement procedure, but that their participation in decisions was limited.

This imbalance in decision-making and resource allocation led at times to irreconcilable differences in objective and interest. For example, it was clearly in the interest of some local educational authorities with over-stretched resources to try and breach or circumvent the provisions of the 1981 Act so that they were not duty-bound to provide extra provision for special educational needs. There are reports of this happening (e.g. Leader, *Times Educational Supplement*, 9.8.91). Some LEAs avoided carrying out formal assessments, some avoided writing statements, and some avoided delivering the appropriate special needs provision. Parents found themselves having to fight for what they felt were essential provisions for their child and having to appeal against the LEA's decision or action. For the professional caught between the interests of the parent and the LEA (such as the educational psychologists employed by the LEA), there were many problems in trying to reconcile the conflicting pressures.

A few years after implementation of the Act, a House of Commons Select Committee set up to review its effects reported continuing piecemeal parental participation and that many parents were not contributing to the assessment process. One of the most common difficulties experienced by parents was 'inadequate or unclear information about the local education authority's assessment procedures and about the range of special education provision available' (House of Commons Select Committee Report, 1987). Without information, parents remained marginalised and unable to participate in the assessment decision-making process.

Circular 22/89 was the DES's response to the Select Committee findings and it replaced Circular 1/83. It played down the earlier concept of *partnership* because 'time and experience have shown that in the absence of a balance of power between parents and professionals, the notion of partnership is unrealistic and misleading' (DES Circular 22/89).

Instead, it recognised that parents and *pupils* needed to be empowered with greater *rights*, and recommended that they have greater rights to information and involvement in the formal assessment process. This included parents being given fuller and more accurate descriptions of their child's needs in statements, parents and children being more fully involved in the assessment procedure, and parents being given full information.

Although Circular 22/89 spelt out recommendations for good practice, they were not legal *requirements* and were not therefore binding. It was left to the discretion of individual LEAs how they responded to the Circular's recommendations.

Difficulties in the implementation of the 1981 Act were again reported in the Joint Audit Commission and HM Inspectorate report *Getting in on the Act: provision for pupils with special educational needs: the national picture* (1992). The report criticised the length of time taken to complete an assessment and issue the statement, and saw this as the principal reason why the process was not valued by parents. 'All of the LEAs take longer than the six months recommended by the Department for Education and Welsh Office and the median is 12 months' (ibid.).

Other problems identified in the Audit Commission's Report and the House of Commons Select Committee Report (1987) included:

- lack of clarity about what constituted special educational needs and also about the responsibilities of LEAs, schools, parents and children,
- wide national/local variation in implementation of the 1981 Act,
- lack of incentives for LEAs to implement the 1981 Act.

THE 1993 EDUCATION ACT

The 1993 Education Act was the government's response to the Audit Commission and HM Inspectorate report and also to the changing context in which special education was being conducted. In the fifteen years that had passed between the Warnock Report and the 1993 Act, various trends had started to have a major impact on the context and delivery of special education. These included an increased awareness of children with special needs, increased consumer self-awareness and power (e.g. 'chartering' initiatives, open enrolment and parental choice of schools in 1988 Education Act), deregulation of the public sector, increased central governmental control in education (e.g. National Curriculum and funding arrangements), greater professional accountability and appraisal, and the growing strength of the voluntary and private sectors. The most significant contextual changes included increased autonomy of schools, through local management and delegated budgets for local education authority (maintained) schools and through self-governing status for grant-maintained schools. As decision-making and control has increased at the level of the school, in turn the role of the LEA has been dramatically reduced.

Part III of the 1993 Act deals with special educational needs and supersedes the Education Act 1981. It retains many of the features of the 1981 Act, but also introduces a 'Code of Practice' with guidelines. The Code has been generally welcomed and is seen to embody good practice rather than introducing major innovation. Local education authorities must 'have regard' to the Code, but it is essentially guidance and most of it is not binding. In light of the context of increased delegation of budgets and managerial responsibilities to schools, it is significant that some of the Act (and Code of Practice) defines more precisely LEAs' *and schools'* responsibilities towards children with special educational needs. The role of the school in the education of children with special needs is greatly reinforced through, for example, the broadened brief of the Special Educational Needs Coordinator.

The Code reiterates the five stages of identification and assessment of special educational needs first introduced in the Warnock Report. The Code emphasises the need for early recognition of a child's special educational needs and the importance of a range of partnerships in finding the best way to meet those needs (such as early multi-agency links and cooperation). It emphasises the full involvement of parents throughout the five stages of assessment, and parental rights are strengthened through a clearer definition of 'partnership'. The Code breaks new ground by exhorting, for the first time, schools to seek out the ascertainable wishes of the *child* or young person about their education.

The Code sets out criteria for proceeding to a statutory assessment by the LEA, and for the issuing of a statement. The criteria were developed partly in response to the wide variation across the country identified by the Audit Commission, and were intended to ensure greater consistency by LEAs. Regulations (Schedules 9 and 10) set out a statutory time limit of six months on the conduct of a statutory assessment and the issuing of a statement; this was to rectify the lengthy periods (sometimes years) of waiting by parents in the past. Although welcomed by parents, it is not clear whether this new administrative requirement will be effectively reconciled with the expectation that parents work in partnership with professionals (with its associated time and resource demands) or the kind of comprehensive assessment which requires much familiarity with the child and family. Regulations also ensure greater specificity in the drafting of statements, which will need to be more detailed and individualistic with clear educational goals.

Section 160 of the 1993 Act replaces Section (2) and 2(3) of the 1981 Act with a change to the wording on parents' wishes. The qualified general duty to integrate does not apply if it is 'incompatible with the wishes' of the child's parent. This new wording aroused considerable concern that parents were being given a 'veto' on their child's integrated placement and raised questions about the circumstances in which parents and children might not be in agreement (Stobbs, 1993). However, Section 160 sets out a general duty and Schedule 10 sets out the procedures to be followed in the case of the individual child. Under Schedule 10, parents have a new right to express a preference for a particular maintained school; the LEA is then under a qualified duty to name the preferred school in the child's statement (the qualifications being as in 1981: the appropriate provision for the child, the efficient education of other children, and the efficient use of resources).

> This creates a significant shift and effectively puts the onus on the LEA to show why the child should not be placed in the preferred school. Schedule 10 may prove to be a powerful tool in the hands of parents who are seeking an integrated placement for their child, and also for those parents seeking a special school placement for their child.
>
> (Stobbs, 1993)

The main addition to parental rights in the Act is nine new grounds on which parents can appeal against their LEA's decisions and actions, and the right of appeal to the new Special Educational Needs Tribunal. This new independent Tribunal, which is composed of one legal representative and two lay people (one with knowledge of special needs and one with local knowledge), is established by Section 177. Parents who have requested a statutory assessment will be able to appeal against the decision by the LEA not to carry this out (S. 173(2)). This is in addition to the grounds for appeal which existed under the 1981 Act, against a decision not to issue a statement and against the content of the statement itself. Parents have welcomed the new Tribunal because it is more accessible and its decision will be binding on the LEA. But there is also widespread recognition and concern that it will possibly lead to a more litigious resolution of disagreements between parents and LEAs (Stobbs, 1993).

In an article on the 1993 Act, Wright (1993) described the Act as representing a conceptual shift, *'replacing partnership with conflict as the model of problem-solving in special education'*. In the absence of new procedures to foster openness and trust between parents and LEAs (such as the continuing lack of right of parents to receive copies of the professional advice gathered during assessments which lead up to a LEA decision not to issue a statement), parents may have only one recourse left for participation, that is through formal appeal and challenge. Parents, for example, could use their parental right to appeal to the Tribunal when an LEA refused to issue a statement following assessment. The Tribunal would have the power to require disclosure of all the professional advice obtained by the LEA. The parent would subsequently become informed, but only through having taken up a position of conflict.

This greater possibility of conflict, and some of the anxieties this has aroused in government and professionals, may possibly be minimised or reduced by various means (at the time of writing this has not yet been established). In her article on the Act, Phillippa Stobbs welcomed the new governmental funding for parent partnership schemes, which could help parents play a more meaningful part in the assessment of their child by informing and supporting them. 'They can help to bring about negotiation where confrontation may otherwise arise and some schemes have worked with LEAs to make their information and procedures more parent-friendly' (Stobbs, 1993). A second approach which has been suggested is for LEAs to adopt as local policy a set of binding principles and practices which would make up for the failings of the legislation itself (Wright, 1993). For example, LEAs could commit themselves to sending parents copies of all the professional advice concerning their child automatically, as soon as it was obtained, regardless of the actions they proposed to take on the basis of that advice (ibid.). They could also adopt a policy of always naming a school for the child in the final statement. Measures such as these, locally adopted, would help create trust and release pressure on the Tribunal from parents having to appeal for access to information (ibid.).

Constraints on professionals

Other constraints have limited the efficacy of the Education Acts for supporting parent–professional partnerships. Both have imposed lengthy and complicated bureaucratic procedures on professionals. Many professionals involved in Formal Assessment have found the changes in their own jobs very stressful, with extra paperwork, formality and time pressures (Sandow *et al.*, 1987). The 1993 Education Act imposed major new bureaucratic responsibilities on professionals without direct central resourcing through financial support and training. No allowance was made in extra resources for the statutory requirement of completing the assessment process in six months. These bureaucratic demands probably spill directly into the individual parent–professional relationship. One way of keeping the workload manageable may be to confine one's contact with parents to the minimal task of giving them information (ibid.). Professionals who lack time may be unable or unwilling to communicate with parents and negotiate decisions.

The 1993 Act has brought no change in the funding arrangements for special education, so LEAs may continue to be caught between the requirements of the law and the limitations of their budgets. Constrained in the options they can provide to the child with special educational needs, some LEAs may instruct their professional employees to tell parents what is 'best' for their child (which may be what is cheapest or most convenient to offer). Without room to manoeuvre, the professional from the LEA might avoid seeking and hearing the parent's views and entering into negotiation.

These constraints are likely to compromise the intervening professional in their willingness, ability or power to set up a negotiating partnership with the parent.

Negotiation and education decision-making

Even with these limitations, however, the 1981 and 1993 Acts have opened up new possibilities for participation in education decision-making. There are many examples by repute of parents and professionals working successfully together in effective negotiation and reaching a mutually acceptable decision and solution. But parental participation as a partner is likely to depend on the individual professional's steps to empower and assist the parent. The parent needs to be informed of their rights and duties in law and of the formal assessment procedure and its possible outcomes, and to be supported and assisted through the procedure (see Table 11.1).

The Negotiating Model has a potentially useful contribution to make in guiding the professional's intervention. By starting with a recognition of the possible differing viewpoints and interests between parents and professionals (and the LEA), it avoids the illusory concept of 'shared understanding' common in much of the early thinking of partnership during the introduction of the 1981 Act. The possibility of dissent and disagreement is built into the Model, encouraging the professional to be prepared for and committed to working with and resolving disagreement. The greater clarification of what constitutes a negotiating partnership allows for a clearer understanding of the conditions under which part-nership work is temporarily, or in the longer-term, inoperative, thereby engendering a more realistic view of what is feasible or not in the current (or future) context. See further Chapter 1 (p. 17).

Use of this model has been demonstrated throughout the book, but a few points regarding education intervention are relevant here. When participating with the parent, the intervening professional must be willing to listen to the parent's perspective on their child's needs, how they believe these needs could be met, and their educational preferences. The parental perspective should be sought through open, uninhibited discussions, and then brought into active negotiation involving an exchange of the professional and parental perspectives. The professional may want to share how they see the child's needs and the kind of provision that they view as desirable to meet these needs (as well as what is available). They should be willing to share uncertainties, dilemmas and information about short-falls in actual provision. Information should also be given of other constraints operating, for example, that only one suitable form of provi-sion is available, or that only one is likely to be financed by the LEA (for possible constraints on trust and honesty for the parent and profes-sional, read pp. 155 and 157).

Accepting the validity of their different viewpoints lays the way open for active discussion, exchange and negotiation, particularly if there is room for manoeuvre and debate between the parent and professional.

Table 11.1 Formal assessment and partnership

What parents need to know	What professionals can do
Parents have the legal right to request a formal assessment	● Inform parents
Parents need to know what the advantages and disadvantages of formal assessment are	● Explain the situation carefully and objectively ● Offer other sources of help ● Make arrangements for parents to consult other sources
Parents should become involved as soon as professionals are aware of a child's special needs	● Get in touch with parents ● Hold meetings with them
Parents should know that a formal assessment is being proposed before the 'letter' arrives	● Discuss the matter with parents ● Reach the decision jointly
Parents need to fully understand the letter proposing formal assessment and its implications	● Deliver the letter in person ● If the need arises, arrange for a person who speaks the family's language and understands their culture to be present
Parents need to know they have the right to make a contribution to the assessment and at what stages they can do this	● Make it clear that this is a right ● Positively encourage parents to put their views forward ● Take account of these views ● Explain – if necessary – why these views have had to be set aside
Parents need advice and information throughout the assessment process	● A telephone helpline, video, taped material, leaflets may be helpful ● Attach a named worker to the family ● Parents need to know who is the LEA's named person and what is their role
Parents need support	● Set up opportunities for parents to meet each other through parent groups, parent befriending schemes ● Attach a named worker to the family
Parents need honesty	● Their fears regarding special education need to be addressed ● Explain what statementing means ● The link between statement and special provision should be made explicit

Table 11.1 continued

What parents need to know	What professionals can do
Parents need to have a clear idea of the stages of the assessment	• Give them a flow chart showing all the assessment stages, with names and positions of the people involved as well as of relevant voluntary groups • Make sure this chart is available in languages other than English when necessary
Parents need to be present	• Inform them in good time of meetings • Make them feel welcome • Show that you feel their contribution is as valid as others
Parents need support at meetings	• Ask them if they wish to be accompanied by a person of their choice (relative, friend, interpreter, trusted professional, etc.)
Parents may need to be empowered to be heard	• An independent advocacy or befriender scheme should be available to help parents write their contribution
Parents need to know what has been proposed or agreed	• Give them a draft report of the statement and explain it in person, so they can challenge it if necessary • Take appropriate measures to ensure that the report is accessible to non-English speakers and that their comments are taken into account • Explain the reasons for delays
Parents need to know they have the right to appeal, and the grounds on which they can appeal	• Inform them • Help them to weigh up all the aspects • Be supportive, whatever their decision
Parents need to know about annual reviews	• Write up review procedures in an information booklet • Give proper notice • Explain the purpose of the review • Encourage the parents to make a contribution in writing • Encourage them to attend the review meeting. If necessary, take measures to ensure that non-English speakers are fully aware of the review procedure and its implications

Source: adapted from Cameron and Sturge-Moore, 1990, ACE, 1988, and Elfrida Rathbone Education Advocacy Scheme guidelines.

The purpose of the negotiating process should be to take on board agreements and disagreements and work towards some kind of workable, mutually agreeable solution (see Chapter 4 on negotiation skills and strategies for resolving disagreement). If, after repeated attempts to resolve any disagreement, the two perspectives or positions of the parent and professional remain opposing, then the parent needs to be informed of their options in dealing with the conflict (see later in this chapter).

Assisting parents from ethnic minorities

All the recommendations of Table 11.1 are relevant, but further issues warrant consideration for families from ethnic minorities. The scope for misunderstanding and disagreement is even greater between parents and professionals when neither party necessarily shares the same language, cultural values and understandings.

To overcome some of the potential disadvantage and discrimination facing parents from ethnic minorities whose mother tongue is not English, a bilingual trained interpreter should be brought into the initial decision-making process of whether to assess a child formally or not. This interpreter would need to be conversant with the procedure so that they can explain fully the purpose, the format of the procedure, and the parents' rights, so that the parents are fully informed before their consent is sought. In particular, families need to understand the *legal* nature of the educational assessment. An interpreter would be needed at each stage of the procedure with non-English speaking parents to ensure that they are adequately informed and able to participate and negotiate in the decision-making. Wherever possible, medical and psychological assessments should be done by a mother-tongue speaker or with a competent mother-tongue speaker present (Cameron and Sturge-Moore, 1990). Parents may need access to an interpreter and scribe to help them write their contribution to the assessment. (NB Using other members of the family or their informal social network as interpreters is not appropriate because of the potential impact of this on the balance of the family system, the potential infringement of parent and child privacy, and the risk of biased, inaccurate information being transmitted to the parents.)

Writing a parental profile

The opportunity to contribute written 'evidence' during the assessment procedure is the main way that parents can transmit their views about the situation, problems, educational and emotional needs of their child to the LEA, but the KIDS Family Centre experience was that almost all parent users, whatever their social or cultural background and level of education/literacy, needed help and support to write their contribution (see p. 231). With such help from the staff, almost all parents sent in a written letter or report or decided to add their viewpoint to the staff member's report.

Sheila Wolfendale (1985), through piloting a procedure for developing parental profiles, found that the provision of broad headings (developmental/skills area) were a better aid to helping parents write their own profile at home than nil headings (a blank sheet) or an abundance of items to be ticked. This led on to the development of another format, the developmental checklist for parents of preschool children called 'ALL ABOUT ME' (Wolfendale, 1990). This checklist differed from traditional formats in combining developmental headings with open-ended items, which allowed for the parent to add comment and detail.

> A vivid picture of the child at home can be provided, the accuracy of which is not the prime concern. The information itself can be used as the basis for a dialogue, to explore parental and professional perceptions, disparate or shared attitudes and aspirations for a given child.
>
> (Wolfendale, 1985: 26)

The ALL ABOUT ME record can also be used to exchange information between parents and teachers/nursery nurses and as a basis for curriculum development and programme planning.

Before moving on to the other main legislation, it may be useful to review how your own agency assists parents through the Formal Assessment procedure (see Exercise 11.1).

THE CHILDREN ACT 1989

The Children Act 1989 became operational on 14 October 1991, and was described as 'the most comprehensive and far-reaching reform of child law which has come before Parliament in living memory' (Lord Chancellor, 1989). It followed recommendations made by a series of committees over the previous ten years, including the House of Commons Social Services Select Committee (Children in Care Report, 1984), the Review of Child Care Law (1985) (leading to the White Paper, the Law on Child Care and Family Services, 1987), the inquiries over the tragic deaths of Kimberley Carlisle, Jasmine Beckford and Tyra Henry, and finally the Cleveland Inquiry (1987).

The Children Act strives to reform the law relating to children and to achieve a better balance between the duty to protect children and ensure that their needs and safety take priority and a recognition of parents as key agents in the upbringing of children. The main principles espoused in the Act include:

- the welfare of the child is the paramount consideration in court proceedings,
- wherever possible, children should be brought up and cared for within their own families,
- parents continue to have parental responsibility for their children, even when their children are no longer living with them. They should be kept informed about their children and participate when decisions are made about their child's future,
- parents with children in need should be helped to bring up their children themselves,
- this help should be provided as a service to the child and family.

Parental responsibility and the family

The role of the parent has been conceptualised in a new way under the Act. It introduced the concept of *parental responsibility* to replace the phrase 'parental rights'. The notion of parents' rights over children, as if they were property, has been superseded by the concept of parental responsibility with its association of parental duty and obligation towards children. The term sums up the collection of duties, rights, powers, responsibilities and authority which a parent has in respect of the child and the child's property. Parental responsibility can be allocated to people carrying out these duties other than parents, such as grandparents and step-parents. Both parents retain it after divorce and when a child is being looked after under a voluntary arrangement with a local authority. If unmarried, mothers have parental responsibility but a father can acquire it by agreement with the mother. A person with responsibility cannot surrender or transfer it and can only arrange for someone to act on their behalf.

The family is defined broadly to include relatives and non-relatives where relevant; it can include any person who has parental responsibility for the child and any other person with whom they have been living (Section 17 (10)).

Parents in partnership with the local authority

Such arrangements are intended to assist the parent and enhance, not undermine, the parent's authority and control.

(DoH, 1991a, Vol. 6, p. 14)

In order for parents to fulfil or to retain the parental responsibility described previously, the Act sets out, for the first time in law, support options as a preventative function against family breakdown or difficulties. The Act establishes the basic principle of the value of *supporting families*, so that family breakdown should be minimised through the detection of need and early intervention.

The Act imposes a number of duties upon local authorities such as identifying children in need living in their area and providing a range and level of services to secure the health and development of these children and to promote the upbringing of such children by their families. They have a new duty to help families through support services, e.g. advice, guidance and counselling, cultural or recreational activities, home help including laundry facilities, assistance with holidays, family centres, day care for under 5s, accommodation (respite care), and out-of-school activities. An important aim is to provide local authority services in a way that is non-stigmatising and facilitating for families, 'on the basis of partnership and cooperation, and not as a mark of personal failure' (Hansard, Co. 156, 18.5.89).

Parents should be able to choose from a range of available services, and the notion of *working in partnership* with parents is given precedence, with services being, wherever possible, adapted to their expressed needs and wishes.

The legislation also underlined the need for professionals to take account of culture, race and 'any other relevant characteristics' when assessing a child's wellbeing and needs and the competence of their parents and families to care for them. Cultural differences in child care and parenting practices should be given due consideration when assessing a child and family's needs.

Children with disabilities: possibilities and limitations

The new category of children 'in need' includes children with disabilities (Section 17 (10)), thus the Children Act has major implications for any practitioner working with children with disability and their families. Combining children with disability with all other children under local authority functions has been proclaimed as another major impetus for the integration of disabled children, in both law and services. Moreover, if properly resourced, the new law has duties, powers and regulations, and statements of principle which could be used to improve and enhance the quality of life for many children with disabilities and their families (Armstrong *et al.*, 1990).

'Every local authority shall provide services designed: i) to minimise the effect on children within their area of their disabilities; and ii) to give such children the opportunity to lead lives which are as normal as possible' (Schedule 2, paragraph 6). Under the Children Act, local authorities will have a duty to take a more systematic approach to information provision and needs assessment, by maintaining a register of disabled children, publishing information about services available and taking steps to ensure that potential consumers know what is on offer. This is relevant for assessing family needs in partnership (see further, Chapter 7).

Any assessment of need undertaken by the local authority may be part of an assessment made under the 1993 Education Act, the Disabled Persons Act 1986 (which required SSDs to assess young people with disabilities at the time they leave school for a range of welfare services) or the NHS and Community Care Act (1990) (which required assessment of need for services for young people who have a continuing or first-time need for community services at 18 years of age). The Act stipulates increased cooperation between the education, health and social services. Notwithstanding this, attempts to combine assessment of a child's needs under one statute may come up against some complex difficulties in law; the definitions of 'special need' (Education Act 1993) and 'disability' (Children Act) are not apparently compatible and interchangeable. Furthermore, parental powers to intervene in the assessment process are much more clearly delineated under the Education Act 1993 than under the Children Act. No clear powers and responsibilities to participate are enshrined in the latter, although the general right to participate is exhorted.

Much of the strength of the Act will depend on whether local authorities have adequate resources and provision to provide the support and preventative function envisaged. Children with disabilities and their families will be eligible to receive the range of support services listed on p. 263. If implemented, these options should help alleviate some of the enormous stresses on families with disabled children, many of whom receive little support and assistance in their day-to-day care (see p. 107). But where there is a lack of service provision or the local authority adopts a narrow definition of 'children in need' (excluding some families such as those with a child with moderate developmental difficulties), unfortunate consequences may follow. Some families, under great pressure, may start breaking down or resort to treating their child inappropriately or negligently. If the child is viewed as being at unacceptable risk, professionals may have to intervene by law. In this circumstance, professional and parental interests and viewpoints are more likely to deviate and the tendency towards conflict is greatly increased (see Chapter 1).

The Act requires that packages of care from education, social services and health authorities should be developed through inter-agency cooperation (see potential problems on p. 288) and in partnership with the parent wherever possible. But the opportunity for the individual parent to participate in assessment and decision-making with the local authority (as lead agency) or other agencies will depend ultimately on the individual authority or agency's commitment (and the professionals employed by them) to share power and negotiate with the parent and family. The parent could, however, resort to the complaints procedure if they feel their needs and wishes have been inadequately consulted. Local authorities are required to set up a procedure for representations and complaints under the Children Act, with an independent element. Any child in need, or other interested party (such as parents), may use this procedure (such as to challenge a lack of service provision for the particular family), and the local authority must have 'due regard to its findings' (S. 26(7)), but is not bound to implement them.

CHILD PROTECTION

Abuse and child disability

Partnership work with parents is most tested when professionals become worried about a child's wellbeing and safety. It has only recently become recognised that disabled children (and adults) are particularly *vulnerable* to physical, sexual and emotional abuse within a variety of settings (see review by Westcott, 1991, Sinason, 1992). This greater risk of inappropriate care and abuse has been linked to the likelihood of receiving care from multiple caregivers, the increased dependency resulting from a disability, the pressures on families, and the reluctance of parents to voice suspicions or complain for fear of being seen as troublesome or losing a service (Russell, 1995). There has been growing concern about a small, but neglected, minority of children living in residential schools or homes (often at considerable distance from the family home and with little or no family contact), and as a result, new protective regulations have been introduced in the Children Act.

Professionals need much greater vigilance to protect children with disabilities, and it has been argued that assessment for abuse should be placed in the wider context of assessment of the whole child (Marchant *et al.*, 1993). This requires an impetus from professionals from any agency or background to be involved in the initial identification of abuse, but as Phillippa Russell has pointed out in her articles on child abuse and child disability (Russell, 1994, 1995), there is frequently a significant gap between the expertise of disability-specific services and the experience on child protection issues in local authority teams. This can lead to under-reporting of actual or potential abuse and also to inappropriate concerns about abuse (e.g. if the management of a child with challenging behaviour is misunderstood). Closer collaboration is therefore required between disability specialists and child protection teams, and issues around child protection work must become relevant to all professionals working with children with disabilities.

It is beyond the scope of the book to examine this very important subject in depth, but a number of pertinent issues for partnership work are discussed below.

Helping parents protect

Obstacles that get in the way of or undermine parents' ability to protect their disabled child have already been mentioned. The reliance on multiple caregivers to enable the parent to cope reduces the parent's control over the quality of care received by their child. Many parents have anxiety about respite care. Seventy-three per cent of 100 parents in one study were anxious, especially in the early days (Robinson, 1987); a small proportion of these (15 per cent) were actively unhappy about the quality of care. In another study of respite care for young adults with multiple disabilities or challenging behaviour, many parents were found to be desperately anxious about the quality of care available to their son or daughter (Hubert, 1992). Some parents, desperate not to lose a scarce service, may try not to notice inadequate or inappropriate care and abuse. The Children Act has responded to this growing concern of risk by introducing regulations and guidance for voluntary short-term and foster placements, including respite care (DoH, 1991a, Vol. 3), to improve the quality of care and monitoring of standards. A further response for child protection is the introduction of the concept of an *independent visitor* to visit isolated children in residential care with little or no family contact, who can be appointed by local authorities.

Another major strategy for protecting children is *to listen to parents* (Russell, 1995). The negative perceptions applied to disabled people (see Chapter 3) also often get applied to their parents, whose concerns and complaints tend to be viewed as troublesome and are disbelieved. It has previously been mentioned that parents may be afraid to complain or to query a carer's behaviour for fear of losing the service. These factors greatly reduce one of the key means of protecting disabled children: the parent's observation that something is going wrong for their child. Parents' concerns need, therefore, to be listened to seriously, attended to promptly by professionals and channelled through to the appropriate authorities.

Burdened with care pressures and other family stresses, parents too may become unable to give their child adequate care or appropriate handling. Rather than waiting for a crisis to happen (by which time parents may no longer be able to care for their child at home or the child becomes abused), a package of support provision (as envisaged by the Children Act) should be set up with the individual family (see Chapter 7). A crucial preventative function of family support services is to protect the child by ensuring that their carers are sufficiently supported themselves.

Listening to children

In her book on disabled adults, Valerie Sinason (1992) indicated considerable reluctance by professionals to believe that disabled people can be abused or are capable of reporting abuse. Both parents and professionals may make (often inaccurate) assumptions about the inability of children with disabilities to describe and report their feelings and experiences accurately, and both may be reluctant to acknowledge abuse when support services are scarce (Russell, 1995).

It is crucial to *listen to children* directly and carefully, so that they can communicate if they are being abused and are unhappy about something. A number of important studies have shown that children with multiple disabilities or major communication problems, like severe hearing impairment, can indicate abuse if parents, staff and professionals draw on their observations and skills and whatever communication aids or strategies the child uses to assess the occurrence of abuse (Kennedy, 1990, Marchant and Page, 1992). A greater awareness is needed in staff and parents of appropriate communication methods and ways of listening to children with communication problems, learning difficulties and multiple impairments (see articles cited). Vulnerability may be reduced by identifying potentially abusive behaviour early and addressing the situation directly.

A child's relationship with a trusted, familiar professional may also be very beneficial. Under the Children Act, children with disabilities (like other children) have new powers to refuse examination and assessment if they are judged to have sufficient understanding. But many will give consent (and will be able to communicate) if supported by a trusted and familiar professional (Russell, 1995).

It is important to remember that under Article 12 of the United Nations Convention on the Rights of the Child (ratified by the British government in 1991), the child has the right to have their views, wishes and feelings consulted when courts or other official bodies make decisions affecting their lives.

Parent versus child interests

Where parents are willing to talk to a trusted professional and an honest and open working relationship exists, interventions may be possible to help a parent before actual abuse takes place. But once a professional is intervening to protect a child, they may be preoccupied with the child and be unable or unwilling to consider the parents' own interests. The Children Act emphasises that the 'welfare of the child is of paramount consideration under court proceedings' and it follows that in a clash between parent and child interests, the child's interests take precedence.

In the highly sensitive area of familial child abuse (where a family member or someone closely involved with the family is suspected of abusing), encounters between parents and professionals may be extremely emotionally charged and difficult. One or both parents may be unable to communicate honestly with the professional, particularly if they are hiding abuse or protecting the abuser. A parent may stop cooperating, resist professional involvement and withhold access to the child. The professional may find it difficult to share their concerns about the child with the parents, especially if this constitutes a risk to the child's safety. They may view the parents with suspicion and distrust and feel intense emotions about the abusing adult. Fragmentation, suspicion and distrust in the family is often 'mirrored' by difficulties in cooperation and working together in the wider professional network (see p. 69). The professional who suspects or identifies abuse will be required to take up their own authority and intervene without parental consent, whatever their ethical dilemmas of bypassing the parent (this may be particularly difficult for professionals who have built a familiar trusting partnership with the family). Those professionals acting in a custodial statutory function may be forced to use coercive powers (see p. 6) to gain access to and to protect the child. A confrontational conflict can rapidly develop between the parent(s) and the individual professional or the whole professional network.

Notwithstanding this potential conflict, the report of the Cleveland Inquiry (1988) and the subsequent legislation of the Children Act 1989 have striven to find a new balance between adequate child protection and the parents' interests as parents of the child concerned. In the inquiry after the death of Jasmine Beckford, Blom-Cooper (QC) pointed out that *child's needs/interests* do not always correspond with *parents' interests*, and that it was valuable to separate their interests and rights. In the Cleveland Inquiry, the importance of not neglecting parent interests in the pursuit of child interests was highlighted.

The Children Act emphasises that professionals should work cooperatively with parents, wherever possible, and that a *partnership* relationship should be the aim of professional intervention. This is stipulated in the official Guidance documents (Vol. 6: *Children with Disabilities*) accompanying the introduction of the Act, although it is not strictly a legal requirement in terms of regulations. Such guidance acts as a statement of what is to be 'good practice' and local authorities are required to take heed and act in accordance. If a local authority intervenes under its statutory function to protect a child from suspected abuse, parents should still be fully informed of all actions and decisions taken by the local authority. Parents also have the right to challenge decisions made by the local authority and to be represented at court hearings.

Guidance around the Act proposes that, wherever possible, parents should be helped to participate in decision-making, and to have their own interests represented and their opinions consulted. But critics point out that the legislation (particularly Section 47, which deals with child protection) is flawed when it comes to involving parents, because parental participation has been tacked onto a system that was not designed originally to involve parents (Corby, 1994).The real extent of parental (and child) involvement in decision-making remains discretionary. Moreover, the Act has led to Social Service departments and social workers taking up a position of extreme caution, with priorities and budgets tied up with procedural child protection work rather than the wider preventative help and support work envisaged by the Act (BBC Radio 4, *File on 4*, 5.7.1994).

Because of the importance of keeping parent and child interests visible, but separate, the parent may need access to an independent professional or representative (outside the child's professional network) to ensure that they are kept adequately informed and consulted, and that their case is heard. The parent needs to be helped to participate in decision-making (wherever possible) and told about their legal responsibilities and powers under the Children Act. Although not spelt out in the Act, it would appear that an independent professional role may need to be established, similar to the *named worker* role of the Warnock Report 1978, with specific responsibility to support parents in their involvement with local authorities (under statutory intervention with the child). The incumbent of this role would work alongside the child's independent representation by the guardian *ad litem* (under the Act).

Even when parents refuse to cooperate with any professional, a longer-term aim would be to develop a trusting negotiating relationship with them if possible. The Negotiating Model (see Chapter 1) can be applied in child protection cases where the parent and professional are prepared to work cooperatively *within parameters or limits set by the intervening professional or by the Court* (cf. pp. 17–18). The parameters might, for instance, be a set of prescribed family/setting conditions which are viewed as imperative to protect the child's safety. As long as these parameters are adhered to by the parents, then negotiation may be able to proceed within these boundaries in the manner described in Chapters 1 and 4.

This brief introduction to some of the issues of partnership and family work in child protection cases omits several highly complex and difficult issues, such as working with families with distorted family relationships or refusal to admit abuse. Suffice to say here, that those who may wish to take their thinking and practice further will need to consider theory and practice, training and skill development, professional supervision and responsibility (see Marchant *et al.*, 1993).

EMPOWERING PARENTS

Opportunities for parents to use their legal powers may be determined largely by the degree of consultation and empowerment by the professionals involved, as previously demonstrated. In this section, we shall look at some methods of empowering parents (and children), and some of the considerations to be made by professionals when selecting a particular strategy.

'Empowerment' refers to the process whereby people who are disadvantaged are helped to take up a more powerful effectual position in their own lives and in relationship to others. Empowerment by the professional may serve

- to help parents/children be more assertive and have their viewpoint heard,
- to help parents have more power and control over the decision-making process with the professional,
- to help parents exert their legal rights.

Two methods of empowering parents are *enabling* and *advocacy*. Although these terms are often used loosely and interchangeably, it can be useful to distinguish between the two kinds of empowerment, to reach a clearer understanding of the purpose, function and process of each approach. Any professional who attempts to empower a parent needs to know the goal, the breadth and the limit of their intervention.

Enabling

The term 'enabling' refers in this book to a process of assisting the parent to become more confident, assertive and effectual. The professional acknowledges the potential power and capability of the parent, and assists the parent in utilising their own resources. It is a process of authorising or legitimising the parent. The professional uses skills and shares the resources and power to enable the parent to take more control over decisions and actions affecting their own life. Enabling can take many different forms including:

- informing parents, by giving them access to records, reports,
- listening to the parent's viewpoint,
- helping parents reach their own decisions and take action by offering them information, support and counselling,
- helping parents participate with professionals, by allowing them to contribute to review conferences and negotiate decisions,
- helping parents have more control over services, by allowing them to sit on planning/managing committees and seeking their appraisal of services,

- helping parents develop their collective strength, e.g. setting up parents' groups and assisting parent forums,
- training parents in assertiveness skills and other skills in order to be able to deal with professionals.

Advocacy

'Advocacy' refers here to a process whereby the parents' viewpoint and perspective can be heard, and central to the process is the act of *representation* (by another person, under the parent's instruction). The professional may act on behalf of the parent to represent their case to other parties. Advocacy can range from a less formal transmission of the parent's view to another professional (such as at a review conference) to a formal representation pleading on behalf of the parent in a legal dispute case, such as an appeal against a local education authority's decision. Parents may wish to be represented when they feel that their viewpoint has been inadequately consulted or when they wish to take up a formal dispute in law.

Although it can be influential in transmitting the parent's viewpoint, advocacy raises some potential problems for the professional. Negative reactions can be aroused in other professionals because of actively asserting the parent's viewpoint (this was experienced on occasion at the KIDS Family Centre and at the Tower Hamlets Parent Advisory Service, see Buchan *et al.*, 1988). The parent's viewpoint may contradict the consensual view of the professional network or challenge the approach of a service/service provider, and the representing professional (the advocate) could find themselves at odds with colleagues. In a conflict, the advocate may be pulled between diverging interests and pressures of the parent and the employing agency and/or local authority/the State. Therefore, it is advisable to consider relevant issues carefully and be adequately prepared before setting out to represent a parent. (See Appendix 11.1 on guidelines for setting up advocacy.)

What to offer: advocacy or enabling?

If advocacy is distinguished from enabling, the professional wishing to empower a parent will have to decide between either process. Which is more useful to a parent depends on individual circumstances, but the following points are worth noting.

In some cases, *enabling* is preferable because

1. it does not undermine the parent's confidence or make the parent dependent on the particular professional. The parent is facilitated to make decisions and to take action and/or to negotiate with the professional.

2. it is less likely that the professional will be trapped between conflicting pressures from the parent and the professional network system or the professional's employing agency.

In some other circumstances, *advocacy* may be desirable because

1. the parent is unable to communicate for themselves (lack of English, illiterate, disabled/slow learning, unable to be present at case conference). This is also the case for the representation of children (see guardian *ad litem*, as defined in the 1989 Children Act) and disabled people (under the 1986 Disabled Persons Act) (in order to have their interest recognised and viewpoint heard).
2. expert representation is needed to present the parent's case in a legal dispute, e.g. independent professional advice for appeal to S.E.N. Tribunal, a solicitor for a court hearing.
3. the parent has been actively marginalised and disempowered. If other professionals refuse to listen to the parent's viewpoint or to involve the parent, the parent may have no option but to seek representation in order to be heard.

CHILD RIGHTS

There are a number of issues relevant to child rights arising from the legislation discussed previously. Firstly, both the 1989 Children Act and 1993 Education Act place new duties on agencies with regard to involving children in planning for their future. This includes giving them the opportunity to exercise choice, helping and encouraging them to make informed decisions, helping them to communicate, and taking their views seriously if they are unhappy about the arrangements made for them. For this to become a reality for children with special needs, considerable attention will be needed to enhance their communication strategies, using communication aids where necessary, and to increase the communication skills of the adults involved with the child. With parents also being exhorted to participate in decision-making, the possibility of a conflict of interests between the child and parent is self-evident, and in such a circumstance, a professional would need to ensure that the child and parent are separately recognised or represented, whilst striving to reconcile their different needs and viewpoints.

Secondly, although the legislation opens up new opportunities for parental participation and increased scope for partnerships between parents and local authorities, a strong case can still be made for strengthening 'child rights' independently. When access to special needs provision depends on parents assertively appealing against their LEA, then the children with less-assertive parents or those who lose their case may end up more disadvantaged than others. To overcome this potential imbalance, it has been suggested that children need their own legal entitlement to special needs provision, irrespective of parental participation or rights (Wright, 1993).

CONFLICT AND CONFLICT RESOLUTION

Throughout this chapter, the enshrining of parental rights in law has been shown to be double-edged when it comes to parent–professional partnerships. Although new rights in law open the way for greater parental participation in areas which have been traditionally the sole prerogative of the professional, new rights have also given parents powers to challenge and oppose professional decision-making. Thus, legislation can be used to assist and bolster the development of partnerships, or, conversely, to disrupt cooperation and consensus. The right to appeal and challenge gives parents a new *position* power (see p. 6), which puts them potentially on a more equal footing with professionals in certain circumstances. Greater parental power entertains the possibility of greater conflict if the parent views their interests (and those of their child) as differing from the professional's (or authority's). The Local Government Local Ombudsman Annual Reports (1993, 1994, 1995) have shown a significant increase in parental complaints against schools and LEAs leading to 'formal reports' of the Ombudsman.

A conflict position, within the framework of the Negotiating Model (as said before), is one where the parent and professional are unable to resolve their differences cooperatively to reach a shared decision or consensus. If interests, viewpoints, priorities and values become too opposing, the parent and professional may enter into a conflictual relationship and their two positions become antagonistic (see Chapter 1). A parent who formally appeals against a local authority decision has taken up a position of conflict.

Conflict has potential benefits and disadvantages for both parties in the dispute. It can lead to a productive change and resolution in a situation where viewpoints and interests are opposed in an apparently intractable way (see *Options for conflict resolution*, below). For the parent (and child) who is generally in a less powerful position than the professional/authority (see p. 7), legal conflict may be the only means of exerting their interests against a more powerful body. A parent may plead that an authority has breached the law, failed to perform its legal duties, and is liable for causing personal damages. This can be used as a lever to gain greater resources or financial compensation for the individual child. For these reasons, the professional working with the parent needs to accept that conflict may sometimes be in the interest of the parent (and child) and, if possible, to work with it acceptingly.

There are, however, various disadvantages to conflict. It is clearly not in the interests of the local authority (or possibly the professionals representing the authority) to be put on trial in a court or appeal case. During a conflict, the partnership relationship between the two parties of the dispute becomes inoperative, either temporarily or in the longer-term. This prevents future cooperative action and decision-making, and may obstruct the child and parents getting the assistance that they need. It may also hinder the professionals involved from working effectively with the child and family. Conflict is likely to be very stressful for all parties involved, as well as very costly and time-consuming. Even anxiety about possible future conflict could jeopardise or undermine the partnership relationship; professionals who are concerned about being charged for professional liability are likely to work in a cautious manner and avoid risks that entail uncertain outcomes (and this is not necessarily in the best interests of the parent or child).

It may, therefore, be in the interests of all parties to try to avoid a conflict developing in the first place, or to work towards its resolution as constructively as possible (see *Options for conflict resolution*, below). The Negotiating Model aims to assist the professional to actively negotiate and share control over decision-making with the parent so that the likelihood of the parent being cascaded into a conflict position is greatly reduced.

Options for conflict resolution

The following options may be used individually, or in combination, as realistic responses to a conflict situation.

1. A passage of time is allowed to pass before the two dissenting parties try to work together again. Changes occurring within the individuals or in their circumstances during this interim period may permit a constructive resolution of previous conflict.
2. The two parties can no longer work together and separate. This option acknowledges a breakdown of the partnership and therefore negates any further options between the particular professional and parent (at least in the short-term).
3. The parent is given the option of working with another professional/ agency who is not in dispute with the parent. Because each parent– professional relationship is both situationally and interpersonally specific, conflict in one relationship does not preempt a possibility of achieving a partnership(s) with another professional/agency.
4. An independent adjudicator is brought in to try to reconcile the diverging viewpoints and interests, e.g. S.E.N. Tribunal, local authority Ombudsman, third party mediator/arbitrator. This takes the responsibility for resolution away from the constituent members and avoids

the possibility of coercive force being used by the more powerful member. If both parties view the adjudicator as independent of each other, then the final verdict is more likely to be accepted as a 'just' vindication.

5. The judiciary is used as a neutral party to pass judgement on the two cases. The Court is used as an independent adjudicator when professionals and parents come into conflict under childcare statute. The law can be usefully evoked as a 'higher authority' which demands a particular course of action when a professional is required to intervene in statutory functions of childcare. This may defuse some of the parent's antagonism levelled at the professional by reducing the implicated responsibility of the professional for unwelcome interventions, thereby increasing the possibility for cooperation and partnership. The final point made in 4, above, also applies.

To summarise, in this chapter, we have examined the changing parental rights and responsibilities under legislation, and considered some of the implications for professionals (and local authorities) working in partnership with parents and children. Alongside increased rights for participation in local authority decision-making have come increased possibilities for litigation and conflict with the authority. The latter may elicit particular problems for parent–professional partnerships, and also reinforce inequalities between the families who can challenge and appeal and those who are unable to do so. Empowerment by the professional was seen as an important means of assisting the parent to negotiate and share with professional decision-making and to take up their parental powers in law. Empowerment was also seen as crucial for overcoming any disadvantage between families in exerting their rights, but it was concluded that this ultimately could not be a substitute for the child having their own legal entitlement to appropriate educational provision (irrespective of parental rights). The benefits and disadvantages of conflict (and options for its resolution) were discussed.

In the final chapter, we examine organisational issues regarding partnership work with families.

PROFESSIONAL DEVELOPMENT EXERCISE

EXERCISE 11.1 HELPING PARENTS ASSERT THEIR POWERS AND RESPONSIBILITIES IN FORMAL ASSESSMENT

Consider how you assist families through the Formal Assessment procedure (under the 1981 or 1993 Education Acts) and write your responses on a separate sheet of paper. Select the appropriate response to each question, or write 'Don't know'.

1. Do parents you work with receive an oral explanation of the Formal Assessment procedure before receiving the first 'letter'? (Always/Sometimes/Never)

2. Do you use oral interpreters to explain the assessment procedure to families who do not have English as a mother tongue or who are illiterate? (Always/Sometimes/Never)

3. Does anyone inform the parents of their specific rights during the assessment procedure? (Always/Sometimes/Never)

4. Who gives the parents support and information at the beginning and through the assessment procedure, if any one? Name the person, occupation and agency.

   Do parents have access to a *named* worker? (Always/Sometimes/Never)

   Who decides on this person, and who fulfils this role?

   Name their occupation and agency.

5. Do all parents you work with fill in a written parental profile/contribute written evidence for the assessment procedure leading to the draft Statement (consider too parents of ethnic minorities/parents with no literacy skills)? (Always/Sometimes/Never)

   What help is given to parents to write a parental profile/contribute written evidence?

   Are all parents given this help? (Yes/No)

6. Are parents involved in the decision-making around the child's special needs/special provision and school placement? (Always/Sometimes/Never)

To what degree are they involved in decision-making?

What gets negotiated?

7. Are parents given a full explanation of the draft Statement? (Always/Sometimes/Never)

8. Are parents informed about their right to appeal against the LEA's Statement of needs (consider too parents of ethnic minorities)? (Always/Sometimes/Never)

Now look at your responses. A high number of *Always* responses indicates that all parents you are involved with during Formal Assessment of special educational needs are receiving active assistance from you/your agency/some other source to help them exert their legal powers and responsibilities. A high number or a mixture of *Sometimes* responses suggests variation between parents in the degree of assistance they receive. Consider the reasons for this variation and whether you are satisfied that all families are getting sufficient help. A high number of *Never* responses reflects minimum assistance to parents in participating in the procedure. Is this help being offered by another agency? Without help, many families may not be participating in a way that they are entitled to. If your responses are mainly *Don't know*, think through the reasons for and implications of this.

Consider too your responses on parental participation and negotiation in decision-making and how dissent is handled.

Finally, if you are not totally satisfied with your current practice (or that of your agency or local education authority), what kind of changes would you like to see introduced? Write down three immediate changes that you would like to see implemented. Are you in a position to influence change, or who could achieve this?

APPENDICES

APPENDIX 11.1 GUIDELINES FOR SETTING UP ADVOCACY

The following guidelines may be helpful when considering working in advocacy with a parent (they may also be applicable to advocating for a child – in this case, substitute the word 'child' for 'parent').

1. Start by clarifying in your mind why it would be beneficial for you to act as an advocate for the parent. The arguments for and against advocacy help must be clear to you and the parent (see p. 271), and the reasons for this particular intervention accepted by both parties.
2. You and the parent must agree on your understanding of the role and function of being an advocate; it might be advisable to do this in writing.
3. You need to be clear how advocacy fits in with your other responsibilities towards the child and family. For example, if you have a statutory responsibility to assess the child's special educational needs, you may find it difficult to act impartially on behalf of the parent at the same time as providing your own professional opinion on the child.

You need too to ensure that the advocacy does not conflict with your responsibilities to other families or to your employing agency. For example, you may want to represent a family who has been refused admission to an opportunity group. But you know that this child's admission would be at the cost of an existing child in the group (whom you also serve as a professional) receiving less specialist attention.

In some advocacy situations, it is advisable that the professional is *independent*, i.e. not working for the same local authority with which the family is involved, or not part of the network of professionals serving the family, or not part of the statutory sector. This may be critical if the professional is acting as a parental representative in a legal dispute. Some advocacy services provide independent professional advocates from outside the district in which the parent is living (e.g. Children Legal Centre Independent Professional Panel) or employed by voluntary organisations (e.g. Elfrida Rathbone Education Advocacy Service), or they provide trained parents or other lay volunteers (e.g. MENCAP Wales).

4. The nature of your contribution should be planned in advance in negotiation with the parent. It may be advisable to put this in writing, so that the parent is clear about what is going to be transmitted.
5. You need to inform the other professionals involved with the family that you are taking on the role of advocate or 'representing Mr X and Ms Y' (for a particular issue, short-term, or on a regular long-term basis).

6. In advocacy work, it is crucial that the advocate is prepared to represent the parent's view without trying to influence or change it. The advocate needs to act impartially, and be willing to represent the parent, whatever their own viewpoint.
7. The parent's viewpoint may be communicated orally or in writing, depending on the circumstances. The parent may or may not be present during the act of advocacy.
8. During the act of advocacy, you should not go beyond what has been agreed by the parent in advance.
9. The point of terminating the advocacy should be decided upon by you and the parent, and made clear to the other relevant parties.

Chapter 12

Organisational issues

Throughout the book we have explored the wider influences that affect each of the partners and shape the parent–professional's relationship. The professional generally belongs to a team or department or institution which have considerable bearing on what they can do with a family. Even when individual members are trying to work more closely with parents and families, their practical options may be limited by wider organisational issues.

> *A speech therapist, for example, was keen to involve a parent in every stage of the multi-disciplinary assessment of her child, but other colleagues in the assessing team were loath to have the parent present at the assessment review meeting. Unable to proceed without their agreement, the speech therapist was restricted in how she involved the parent.*

How the parent and professional work together may have repercussions throughout the organisation ('systemic' effects). With the speech therapist above, her commitment to working closely with parents led to her colleagues starting to re-examine their practice and gradually begin to involve parents at review meetings.

> *In another multi-disciplinary team, a close cooperative relationship between a parent and a physiotherapist contrasted with a distant and difficult relationship between the parent and the paediatrician. The differences in the quality of their relationships and in their perceptions of the parent led to a tension and disagreement between the two professionals.*

Teams vary considerably in their structure and composition, how they function and their organisational context. Some have progressed far in developing a unified, integrated service for families, and insights from these experiments are examined further in this chapter. Others have many obstacles to cross before they can work cooperatively with parents and families or with each other as professionals, and have yet to achieve a coordinated family-focused approach. This chapter explores some relevant issues of team development and organisational processes for

partnership work. The Negotiating Model will be drawn on to help identify the psychological, interpersonal and wider organisational conditions
for sustaining negotiation at the team level.

THE BACKGROUND TO MULTI-DISCIPLINARY WORK

Historically children with special needs and disabilities received support
through child health services and education services. Social services
involvement was variable (although it has been increasing with the development of respite care services and leisure services and the growth
of multi-disciplinary teams at child development centres). Nowadays,
it is not uncommon for parents of children with disabilities to have at
least five (and sometimes up to ten or more) 'helping' professionals
actively involved with them at any one moment in time (such as the health
visitor, GP, paediatrician, speech therapist, physiotherapist, home teacher,
audiologist, social worker, genetic counsellor, psychologist). The number
is likely to be significantly greater when the child has a severe health or
medical problem (Byrne *et al.*, 1988). Although each will be committed
to helping the child as best they can, the sheer scale of numbers and
different disciplines and agencies involved sets the scene for conflicting
advice, duplication in services, confusing input to the family, as well as
rivalry between colleagues. Contact with suitable support services may be
random and dependent upon the knowledge or goodwill of individual
professionals to make appropriate referrals (Fish Committee Report, 1985,
Brimblecombe and Russell, 1988).

All childcare reports in recent years have emphasised the need for
professionals to cooperate with others, to work together and to have
liaison and joint planning between professionals and agencies (e.g. DHSS
Court Report, 1976, DoH Working Together, 1991b. The concept of a
link or *named* person was proposed in the DES Warnock Report (1978)
to coordinate service input to the family, and it has been a frequent recommendation in recent research studies on families (e.g. Byrne *et al.*, 1988,
Quine and Pahl, 1989, Sloper and Turner, 1993). The Children Act 1989
and accompanying guidance and regulations proposed a common framework of services for *all* children, empowering Social Service Departments
to liaise closely and collaborate with health, education, and the voluntary
sector.

Notwithstanding empowerment, cooperation between multi-disciplinary
professionals and multi-agencies continues to be patchy and haphazard.
Problems have been identified on both the interpersonal level between
multi-disciplinary colleagues (e.g. Cunningham and Davis, 1985, Kraemer,
1994) and on the wider organisational/political level (e.g. Hanvey, 1994).
A striking example of the difficulty in developing coordinated multi-
disciplinary practice is the infrequency and apparent inability of child

development teams to allocate a named/key worker to families of young children with special needs, even though the value of this role has been so repeatedly emphasised (see previously).

In the following sections, we review examples of successful practice, as well as some of the problems impeding cooperation in some instances.

MODELS OF TEAM STRUCTURE

Teams vary widely in their membership and function (DHSS Social Work Inspectorate, 1984); the DHSS Report described a wide range of possible structures and approaches to working successfully with disabled children and their families. This included a district child handicap management team set up by a health authority but chaired by a divisional social services officer, or a community mental handicap team based in a hospital but working extensively outside the hospital with the under-fives and offering a comprehensive assessment service.

Nevertheless, it is useful to classify team structures into *types* which can be compared for their effectiveness in supporting partnership work. One approach has been to divide teams into those which are 'multi-disciplinary' or 'inter-disciplinary' (Cunningham and Davis, 1985). Here, the *manner* in which members relate to each other, rather than the composition of disciplinary backgrounds, is used to distinguish different team structures (see Figure 12.1). Although such classification tends to reduce the complexity and contradictions of a real-life team and present an idealised version (many teams may, for instance, have features of more than one model), it is still useful for comparison and evaluation of what works most effectively for family intervention.

The multi-disciplinary team

In the traditional multi-disciplinary team,

- each child, or family, is treated by several specialists from different backgrounds using different theoretical models,
- each specialist tends to work in a relatively isolated way from colleagues coming from other specialisms.

Cunningham and Davis argue that this model lends itself to various disadvantages in family work. Each specialist may be isolated from others in the team. Each specialist may have a restricted view of a given problem and will contribute strictly limited data – this does not lend itself to a coordinated holistic view which may be important for understanding the overall functioning of the child and the overall functioning of the family. No professional is competent to bring together the various information into a holistic picture. Communication between colleagues may be poor;

each specialist may communicate to the others in specialised jargon, often by written report only. Lack of coordination lends itself to duplication of input to the child and family, and also to conflicting input. The family may be overburdened by too many professional visits and treatment programmes. There may be a professional hierarchy with one or more professionals having overriding authority and power in the decision-making. This model may encourage disciplinary rivalries and competition, and also a lack of understanding of the contribution of different disciplines.

Inter-disciplinary team

The authors (ibid.) emphasise the value of an inter-disciplinary team, where

- specialists work more closely together,
- specialist knowledge is shared across disciplines, and each specialist is able to communicate about their work to the other members of the team,
- each professional takes responsibility for coordinating their information and intervention with that of other members of the team,
- since no single type of specialism is seen as having all the answers, each type is valued and all specialisms have equal status,
- all professionals share core skills, e.g. in counselling, family support work, communication skills, partnership methods.

It may be useful at this stage of the chapter to carry out Exercise 12.1 which allows you to consider your own team and your position in the team, and how members are working together.

We turn now to look at some practical examples of inter-disciplinary team structures, and some of the lessons coming out of these experiments.

Lessons from effective team integration

The Honeylands Family Support Unit

A model *integrated team service* has been set up at the Honeylands Family Support Unit (see full description in Brimblecombe and Russell, 1988), which provides comprehensive family support to families of disabled children in the Exeter area. The Unit has developed within a district general hospital paediatric service. The team includes nursing staff, a nursery teacher, psychologists, speech and occupational therapists, a physiotherapist, a consultant paediatrician, a senior clinical medical officer, and a social worker. In its wider sense, it stretches to include ancillary workers, receptionists, secretaries, volunteer staff, and cleaners. Honeylands'

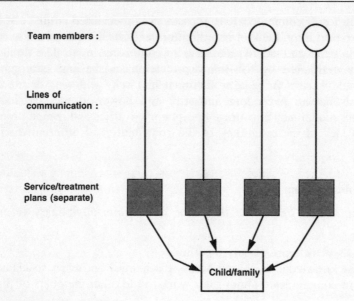

(i) Multi-disciplinary team

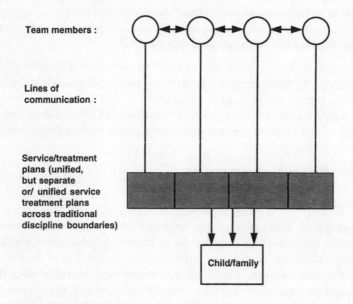

(ii) Inter-disciplinary team

Figure 12.1 Models of team cooperation

core staffing for day-time activities consists of nurses and therapists. The nurses receive additional in-service training, and liaise directly with a wide range of other professionals. The team plans corporately with parents what programme each child will follow, implements and reviews that programme, and modifies the plan as appropriate.

Particular features of the team include:

- an inter-disciplinary team of professionals working with an integrated approach from one location base,
- parents' continuity (with the support of a 'named person' who is attached to each family with a preschool child using Honeylands; the named worker or key worker provides a successful link between the team and individual family),
- mutual support between professional colleagues,
- boundaries between particular disciplines tend to become blurred,
- minimal risk of confusion and fragmentation of services to a particular family.

In a written summary of the project, the authors argued that, in a successful integrated service,

- staff share the same philosophy and aims,
- staff share management decisions for the service provided,
- the team constantly reviews its policy and practice,
- the team works in a complementary, rather than a competitive role, to other services (statutory and voluntary).

The Portage Home Teaching model

Although primarily a home teaching model, the Portage system (see Chapter 8) has important lessons for flexible inter-disciplinary team organisation. It has been run by health authorities, education authorities, social services and voluntary agencies. One of the major features is that professionals in the team, whatever their disciplinary background, receive additional training in teaching skills and thereby gain a unified approach to their work with families and a shared language to communicate with each other and with parents. The additional skills training enables each professional to share their skills and expertise with parents.

Each professional member works autonomously and provides what is essentially an individualised personal service to each family. Nevertheless, the Portage model provides an explicit coordinating structure which links the individual professional to a wider network of professionals. The value of support for professionals engaged in family work is recognised; weekly team meetings bring all members of the team together to support each other. Using social learning principles, the work of each member is received positively, with encouraging attention to individual success in family work (as well as constructive criticism and examination of problems). Each member of the team is valued, whatever their disciplinary background, and guidance to each other is a source of mutual gain. Skills, expertise and ideas are shared across disciplinary backgrounds during team meetings.

The Portage model combines individual autonomy with team accountability; each member reports back to the team the progress of their work with the individual child and their family. Accountability and support are structured in pyramid-shape form. Individual members receive support from and are accountable to the team. In turn, the team (through its representative) receives support and advice from, and is accountable to, a multi-disciplinary advisory committee, made up of senior representatives from health, education, social services and parents. This model has worked with colleagues from a wide range of disciplinary backgrounds, including health visitors, community nurses, home liaison teachers, social workers, psychologists and (in some instances) parents. They learn through using Portage to work together as a team, even if they belong to different employing authorities.

The KIDS Family Centre (see Chapter 10 for a detailed study of the Centre). The staff team here, including a speech therapist, nursery nurse, teacher, social worker and clinical psychologist, worked as an integrated team on an *inter-disciplinary* basis to provide the range of support services for families of children with special needs and disabilities. Each member of staff undertook similar in-service training so that they shared core skills (see p. 227), in addition to their disciplinary qualifications.

The team shared a philosophy and policy of parental involvement and partnership, which was supported by the governing body of the KIDS organisation. Implementation of the policy and philosophy was worked out corporately by the whole team, who met on a weekly basis to discuss such matters. Individual practice was accountable to the whole team, who regularly discussed both individual and group clinical practice and also related administrative matters. Main decisions affecting the Centre were reached through a process of democratic negotiation between all team members. The team was headed by a director, who was the leader responsible for the efficient running of the Centre, its team and services, for the implementation into practice of the partnership policy, and for ensuring quality standards in family intervention. At different periods of the Centre's evolution, supervision of individual staff was provided by the director or by an external supervisor.

Particular features of the team include:

- close mutual support between team members.

  the overall philosophy of KIDS has attracted staff to work at the centre who accept the concept of working in partnership with parents, and who are prepared to work as members of a multidisciplinary team. Whilst the work may be challenging and exciting, it is also demanding and tiring, although the staff acknowledge that the close knit nature of the team provides them with tremendous support.

  (Pugh *et al.*, 1987)

- consensus in philsophy and approach permitting a consistency in practice in working with parents and families, and therefore parents can establish consistent expectations of their role as partners.
- developing a variety of skills and expertises for family work in each team member, which draw from and build on their initial disciplinary training and experiences.
- negotiation as the main process of decision-making between team members; the team process mirrors and upholds negotiation as the main process of decision-making between the individual staff members and parents. The team becomes a 'learning ground' for exploring and combining different perspectives, negotiating, handling dissent, and provides an endorsement and supportive framework for similar processes between the parent and professional.

  This corresponds to the observation made by Cunningham and Davis (1985) that inter-disciplinary cooperation depends on

  team members to respect each other and to establish good relationships in order to negotiate mutually acceptable goals and actions. ... In principle such partnerships should be the same as with parents. A prerequisite is that each member of the team brings his/her own expertise and complementary skills and has equal status.

  (Cunningham and Davis, 1985, p. 158)

- a strong corporate identity as the KIDS team, rather than a set of separate professionals. Parents refer frequently to 'KIDS' as a Centre or team, even though they highly appraise the support they receive from their named worker (Dale, 1992). They are prepared to turn to other team members for support, and this appears to increase their sense of the availability of support. Moreover, experiencing the KIDS team as an important source of support seems to facilitate a smooth transition from one named worker to another for the family, if one departs.

Both the Honeylands Unit and the KIDS Family Centre found value in having a single location or 'base' for providing services for families with children with special needs (see too Fish Committee Report, 1985). A team base can make for a coordinated assessment and service input to families, avoiding the risk of fragmentation and confusion in service delivery. It may simplify the process of allocating a key/named worker to each family. It can also act as a focal point, providing a seamless link between health, social services and education provision. The exchange of information between different specialists may be easier when information is centralised under one roof. The base needs to be attractive, comfortable and accessible for staff and parent and child users. It is ideal if the home base 'belongs' to the team so that the sense of belonging can be extended to the parent and child users.

The commonality of features across these examples is very striking, suggesting that we are on the way to some consensus about what makes for effective team structures and process for partnership work (although we lack controlled comparisons with other team models). All of them put an emphasis on participatory team decision-making and shared responsibility for the management of individual and team practice. This suggests that negotiation is a key transaction between colleagues for partnership work (as for professionals with parents).

Dissent within the team and the inter-agency network

If negotiation is so important for team work, what is it that gets in the way of negotiation, or why is there such difficulty in cooperation between multi-disciplinary and multi-agency staff (see previously)? Cunningham and Davis (1985) have identified a variety of disadvantages in the traditional multi-disciplinary team structure that prohibits negotiation (see p. 282). But, additionally, the Negotiating Model (with its emphasis on the links between the personal, interpersonal and organisational levels) may also be applied to thinking about the difficulties.

Differing perspectives

The premise of shared understandings and consensus implicit in the rhetoric on inter-professional cooperation may be inappropriate or illusory in some circumstances (as has been argued in this book for the parent–professional relationship). Professionals from different disciplines and agencies enter collaboration with different viewpoints and ways of construing the child with special needs because of their different disciplinary knowledges and also different role functions and constraints. When working with a very vulnerable family, a social worker with statutory responsibility for the protection of child welfare may begin collaboration from a very different starting position to a family adviser attached to a non-statutory family centre; the former may be primarily concerned with the child, whereas the latter may have a strong relationship with the mother which they wish to preserve. Because of these differences, there is a real possibility of disagreement and dissent within the team or network, which is, however, rarely acknowledged (Kraemer, 1994). Dissent within teams is often concealed and pushed below the surface. The costs of this to the team or network is discussed on p. 291.

Differing interests

External conditions affecting any inter-professional collaboration include the way in which the organisation operates, how public services are arranged across local authority agencies, and governmental policies affecting public service delivery and budgeting. Agencies differ in their responsibilities or 'primary tasks'. Divided responsibilities across health, social services, education and the voluntary sector has tended to lead to confusing variations in local management and many conspicuous gaps in services. Managing disability has often been managing crisis (Russell, 1995), and services have tended to be apportioned to segmented, rather than the holistic, needs of the child. Even with goodwill between professionals and a commitment to joint cooperation, conflicting employer interests and budgets for childcare divided between different agencies mitigate against productive cooperation between agencies (Hanvey, 1994). In multi-agency Area Child Protection Committees set up since the implementation of the Children Act 1989 to reduce the risks of local child protection committees remaining uncoordinated, there are few signs of little willingness to share power and little experimentation in moving money between health, education or social service agencies to best serve the complex needs of abused children (ibid.). 'The agendas of the various agencies are too disparate to believe cooperation will assist in producing more than a bland planning document'(ibid.), and they appear driven by a mixture of motivations (political imperatives, financial constraints and empire building).

Agency constraints will affect the possibilities for cooperation between multi-agency professionals. One social worker, when deciding on a child's school placement, was advised by his agency not to assess the child as needing a boarding school on social grounds because the Social Services would have to pay for the placement. The educational psychologist, in contrast, was very keen for the child's problems to be seen as social because otherwise it was unlikely that she would get a much-needed place at a boarding school. His employers (the LEA) were reluctant to place this child in a boarding school for educational reasons, since they would end up footing the bill. Neither professional could reach a mutually acceptable decision because their disagreement was of a 'zero-sum' nature (see p. 2) (one agency would lose financially at the other's gain). Limited financial resources and rivalry between the two agencies on the funding level was echoed by rivalry, and lack of collaboration, between the two professionals.

To sum up, when professionals come together to collaborate, they are likely to be bringing differing perspectives and role responsibilities, and if working cross-agency they may be representing or constrained by differing agency interests. As with the parent–professional relationship, a realistic partnership approach must establish some of the conditions that are necessary to permit negotiation with these differences (or to establish the bounds beyond which partnership and cooperation between professionals become impossible).

Psychological conditions for negotiation

At different points in the book, attention has been made to the high levels of stress and distress in professionals working with families of children with special needs which can intrude on their work. This can lead to reduced sensitivity and ability when delivering a diagnosis or first assessment; it may cause unhelpful 'mirroring' of the family (see p. 69 and p. 144); and it may show itself in a variety of 'defence' strategies or coping methods to minimise distress. These include detachment, avoidance, selective attention, inappropriate cheerfulness or false reassurance. Although humour and laughter are signs of enjoying the work and team work, they can signify a defence against mental pain and distress. Any of these defence strategies may be employed when working with a family or they may enter into the way the team functions together. In a classic study of nursing, Menzies-Lyth (1960) described how the nursing staff and institution adopted a 'social defense system' to cope with the intense emotions and anxiety which could overcome nurses who were having to deal with death, dying and invasive procedures on a daily basis. She identified a range of coping methods including ritualised tasks aimed at detachment, and the use of the primitive defences of 'splitting' and 'projection'.

As in the nursing team described previously, the multi-disciplinary team may adopt a variety of social rituals and mechanisms to defend themselves from stress and anxiety. The team may 'mirror' family reactions, and show problems with open communication and handling dissent openly and constructively. W.R. Bion (1961), in his pioneering study of group behaviour, showed how divisions and splitting between members and the projection of unresolved feelings and conflicts onto others could get in the way of mutual trust, honesty and openness. The organisational context may add further pressures and stresses that intensify competitive and antagonistic relations between staff members (see p. 91).

A number of measures may be helpful to enable the team to cope effectively with stress and distress, which could enhance its ability to work cooperatively and negotiate together and with families (Mercer, 1994). These include holding a psychosocial meeting for the staff team, to encourage open communication and for consultation on individual family work, and a network meeting with professionals that is more psychologically directed to help professionals discuss their feelings of despair, anger and uncertainty, which they may have projected onto the family and one of its members. Other measures include having training and education on psychological issues and research findings to help develop the psychological awareness of the staff group. Training in stress management techniques can help members cope with conflicts and stresses. Support and guidance to meet the psychological needs of staff can take the form of supervision, formal induction for new members, peer consultation groups, and consultancy assistance to team managers and senior staff.

These support structures may play a crucial role in enabling professionals to negotiate with each other. Drawing on the work of W.R. Bion on group behaviour (1961), each member of a working group has to have some authority of their own to be able to hold an opinion, while at the same time being prepared to change it. This requires the capacity in each member to manage their own rivalrous feelings and other more profound anxieties. (This capacity, and how easy it is to 'contain' the feelings one is experiencing, are going to be affected by how secure and respected one feels within the team and wider organisation.) Without this psychological capacity, team members cannot negotiate and cope with dissent in the team.

Team conditions for negotiation

Although dissent is a real possibility between professionals because of their differing role perspectives and responsibilities, disagreement is often concealed in everyday teamwork or wider network relations. But there are various costs incurred in not permitting its expression. Kraemer (1994) suggests that in teams where dissent is forbidden, certain problems cannot be experienced or thought about or talked about. But these problems do not evaporate, and the team may become unstable so that some members have to leave, or the team may become inert and dead (appearing to discuss, but not allowing any meaningful collaboration or debate). Apart from inadequate communication, this may lead to patchy or minimal joint decision-making.

Active collaboration between partners with differing perspectives, as suggested by the Negotiating Model, requires a dynamic process of resolution between consensus and disagreement. This is a very different interpersonal positioning from that of 'competing', 'avoiding' or 'accommodating' (see Thomas' conflict model on p. 91), where differences of

opinion are not openly addressed or resolved. To move towards collaboration, colleagues would need to start from a position of mutual respect
and commitment to working together. But this must be accompanied by
a willingness to acknowledge and work with any differences of opinion
and to develop a method of negotiation that can bring together the various
viewpoints.

This depends primarily on an acceptance of dissent as a useful and an
inevitable part of team collaboration.

> A good team is not, as one might suppose, one in which everyone
> agrees. There would be no point in having one if that were the case
> ... the problems of mental health are so complex that different points
> of view are necessary to get a full picture. Therefore conflict is part of
> the design.
>
> (Kraemer, 1994)

We have already discussed some of the difficulties of handling dissent in
Chapter 4 and previously. To move towards coping with it, members
would need to be acquainted with constructive strategies for resolving
disagreement (e.g. p. 93). In addition, the internal organisation of the
team or the relationship between colleagues (as with the parent–
professional relationship) would have to be such that it 'tolerates, or
actually encourages, conflicts of opinion without fear of disaster' (ibid.).
In the same way that we have started to explore the limits of collaboration and partnership work in the parent–professional relationship (i.e. the
conflict phase), so the limits of collaboration and partnership must be
established for inter-professional work.

Apart from these personal and interpersonal capacities, however,
certain *organisational and socio-political conditions* are needed to foster
this kind of negotiating collaboration between professional colleagues.
These are discussed further in the following sections.

ORGANISATIONAL AND SOCIO-POLITICAL CONDITIONS FOR NEGOTIATION

Team management and leadership

A well-functioning team depends on effective organisation and regulation.
Some of the issues requiring organisation and regulation include allocation of resources, corporate policy decisions, admission/referral policies,
staff allocations, involvement of parents in services, delivery of services,
relationships between team members and external bodies, the extent of
autonomous functioning of the team in relation to senior managers and
employers, overseeing changes in policy and practice. The arrangement
of who decides on, or has final responsibility and authority over, any of

the above issues will affect the whole team. Whether members of the team are satisfied with the management arrangements or not will affect their willingness and ability to cooperate together, how they work with parents, and also with senior managers and employers.

For example, in one team a consultant psychiatrist had overriding authority for clinical decisions in the team. Two members of the team disagreed with this authority, and reacted by withholding information on families as a means of maintaining their own autonomy. The resulting lack of transmission of information between the members and the psychiatrist hindered effective joint decision-making and planning on behalf of their families. Their family work was severely compromised by the lack of cooperation between team members.

Teams vary in their structure of management. In some *consultant-led* teams, the overriding authority and management of practice issues is restricted to one key professional, such as a consultant psychiatrist or paediatrician. The rest of the team are accountable to the consultant or senior member with practice responsibility. In some *whole-team* models, management is spread across all members of the team, who carry equal responsibility for organising and regulating the practice of the team. Members are accountable to the whole team. The issue of supervision of less experienced staff is separated from the issue of team accountability, which is the same irrespective of status or experience. In other teams, management issues are split between an administrative manager, responsible for administrative organisation of the team, and a professional manager, responsible for organising the professional work of the team.

Even in the most democratically functioning of teams, leadership is still necessary for efficient organisation. The team might be led by a competent chairperson and deputy, who may be elected or appointed on some kind of rotational system. At a Child Development Centre which has actively adopted a policy of working in partnership with parents, it was found that a post was needed to ensure that the work was done according to policy and for overseeing the processes of change (Appleton, 1987). The author reports that the postholder, the Centre Manager, was responsible to a Centre Management Committee, and that their tasks included helping to develop the details of the preliminary home visit before the family attended the Child Development Centre, overseeing the key workers responsible for family work, sitting in on case reviews with the specific role of ensuring parents had a central voice in the reviews, and monitoring links with other agencies. Each member of staff had a dual responsibility – to his or her line manager, and also to the Centre Manager who represented team policy.

It is perhaps premature, in this early period of development of partnership practice, to make categorical statements about which form of leadership works most effectively. Many of the early experiments in partnership work in the late 1970s and 1980s were to be found in self-managing, relatively autonomous units/services in voluntary organisations and statutory sectors (with senior managers giving team leaders and staff members considerable autonomy to pursue their own ideas). The projects were often headed by founders or leaders who provided a strong leadership. They had a strong sense of mission about partnership work which defined the culture of the unit and inspired staff members and families. They tended to attract creative, innovative, non-conformist staff, who shared their philosophy and wanted to challenge and alter the power structures of mainstream services for the benefit of families and their children. The teams were often closely-knit, mutually supportive, with interchangeable roles, and infused with a 'pioneering' spirit. (See models on pp. 283–7 and case studies described in Pugh et al., 1987.) The culture and structure of these teams and services often bore the features of an organisation in its early 'pioneer phase' (Lievegoed, 1973) before it develops into a larger, more differentiated organisation. This raises many, as yet unanswered, questions of how successfully the partnership method can be sustained in a larger, looser, more differentiated team, where there is greater role specification, specialisation and staff turn-over. The importance of a strong personal conviction in the justice and possibilities of partnership work and a determination to overcome the many obstacles to partnership work (see Pugh et al., 1987) is probably just as crucial in the present day as in previous years.

What can be said at this stage is that a certain form of leadership style has been found to be particularly effective in some of the early experiments on partnership work. It has many of the elements of the leadership style described as the 'open manager' in Makin et al., 1989, in their book on managing people at work. This refers to someone who provides a strong leadership role in their designated position of leader/manager and takes their management responsibilities seriously. What defines their management is their style, which is highly participative. They hold a firm belief in the value of participation and getting everyone involved. They will resort to position and resource power (see p. 6) only as and if required. This means that they are likely to hold regular meetings to review progress and decide on future actions, and all staff (whatever their level in the unit or service) are encouraged to engage in democratic decision-making and to share the responsibility for the service delivery (see whole-model team described previously). They will be supportive of the staff and engender high commitment and affiliation from individual members. The leader sets high standards of performance and expects similar standards to be demonstrated by staff members. This leadership style provides a role model for and encourages mutual respect, support and negotiated decision-making between team members, and thereby provides a facilitating framework for the negotiating partnerships between the staff and the families.

Makin *et al.* distinguished this leadership style from that of the 'bureau-crat', the 'autocrat', the 'wheeler dealer', the 'laissez-faire' or the 'reluctant manager' (see Makin *et al.*, 1989, for further descriptions).

It is essential too that the leader demonstrates a principled, anti-discrim-inatory approach to all parents, children and staff, whatever their gender, ethnic or class background. They will expect and assist staff to work in an anti-discriminatory approach and to take responsibility for challenging any forms of discrimination.

This *consultative model of leadership* has usually been extended to consultative engagement with the service users and carer groups, as well as with external professionals from other agencies. Many centres/services developing partnership work have had a structure of a centre or service management committee, which the team is accountable to, and which is composed of professional representatives and parent representatives (Appleton, 1987, and see Chapter 10: KIDS Family Centre). This allows a direct route for parents through to policy-making and developments in day-to-day patterns of working. As McConachie (1994) has pointed out, parents on management committees are likely to be essential in keeping a focus on family needs (especially when the emphasis of the broader management structures may be on budgets). These services and centres have also tended to hold regular meetings with all service users to review and inform them of existing policies and practices, and to seek their opinion before introducing any major changes. Their desires and wishes for new service developments have also been sought.

Experiments in consultative work have also been attempted at the inter-agency level. Cameron and Sturge-Moore (1990) describe a successfully functioning special interest group or action forum, the Special Needs Under 5s Group (SNUG) in Riverside Health Authority, London, which was set up to improve inter-agency relations and coordinate policy formation at a local district health level. The catalyst for developing the group and then supporting its growth administratively came from two development officers employed by the voluntary organisation MENCAP. Membership and participation was strengthened by acquiring institutional commitment from the involved institutions and agencies and representa-tive membership from a wide variety of experiences. For statutory cooperation to be effective, feedback was needed between fieldworkers and policy-makers. SNUG adopted a cooperative model, whereby each person could contribute fully as a partner, whatever their status. Listening to parents was put at the forefront of the group's operation. Successful outcomes included identifying an urgent unmet need for a family respite care scheme, campaigning to set up this service, organising a training seminar for local fieldworkers and a conference for policy-makers, helping to set up a project steering committee (which then collaborated with a voluntary organisation to set up an integration programme in local parent-toddler groups and playgroups).

The organisational and socio-political context

Throughout the book, specific examples have highlighted how elements of the employing agency, the organisational setting, the legal framework for services, and the wider socio-political context can restrict or open up the individual professional's options for negotiation and the parent's willingness or capacity to negotiate and be involved with the professional. Mention has been made of the budgetary or political interest of the employing authority, its competing interests with other authorities and services, directives from upper management and from central government, and legal imperatives. Some differing implications for the parent–professional relationship of working for the non-statutory or statutory sector were discussed in Chapter 10. Although these issues have received only brief coverage and deserve much greater study, it has been shown repeatedly that the viability and possibilities of negotiation at the *interpersonal* level are intimately bound up with issues of the wider *organisational and socio-political/cultural* context.

We know very little yet about the kind of socio-political context and organisational setting and employing agency that can support and maintain the kind of team which has been shown to be effective for partnership work (see previously) or can enable the individual professional to negotiate successfully with the parent. Many of the early experiments in partnership work in local authorities and the voluntary sector had their roots in the community developments of the late 1960s and 1970s, which were allied to a broad civil rights movement to increase the rights of disadvantaged groups in society. This movement became co-opted to and strengthened by a political movement of radicalisation of local authorities in the late 1970s and early 1980s. Labour-controlled local authorities, such as the Greater London Council and Inner London Education Authority, were pursuing policies of increased democratic local control, decentralisation and equal opportunities for disadvantaged individuals. The emphasis of these authorities was strongly on positive discrimination for disadvantaged groups, including parents, in order to enable them to work in partnership with professionals and public service providers. Political priorities led to substantial resourcing of partnership experiments in local authorities and the voluntary sector.

The context of political priorities has changed drastically in the 1980s and 1990s. The Conservative central government has directed a major programme of reorganisation in the public sector of local government, social services, health and education. Power has been shifted away from local authorities, local politicians and professionals to central government or to local self-regulating units. The management of services has been emphasised, with personnel and principles drawn in from private sector management practices. In education, the power of local education authorities and of local politicians has been decreased; some schools have become self-managing and in control of their budgets, with increased power to school governors, including parent governors. The power of local politicians has decreased in the health sector, with their removal from health authorities. Health services are being run by self-managing hospital and health trusts. Local authorities are required to compete with the private sector in supplying services through competitive tendering, to contract for services rather than provide them directly, and to enable private and voluntary organisations to be service providers. The public health service has been transformed into an internal market, with a purchaser/provider split and sectors within the service competing with other health sectors and the private sector for securing contracts for service delivery.

Consumer participation, customer choice, decentralisation of services and the devolution of management are all being emphasised. The 'consumer' or parent has gained some limited powers, such as the right to select one's child's school, though grant-maintained schools also have the right to select pupils. Under the Citizen's Charter, the 'consumer' or 'customer' is encouraged to expect and monitor the standards of public services and to complain if quality and efficiency are poor. At the same time, local government and health authorities have been operating in a climate of funding constraints and increased controls on expenditure by central government. Professionals may find themselves trapped between rising expectations and demands on the consumer/user's side and financial constraints and managerial restrictions on the employing side. At the same time, services have been expected to achieve high performance standards as well as value for money. Evidence of this dilemma is shown in the internal debate among public authority managers about who is the 'client' and where the professional's loyalty should lie; examples have been given of some NHS Trust managers emphasising that employees should be loyal first to their organisation (e.g. *The Independent*, 15.11.94).

In a report of a short-life project (the Birmingham Action on Child Care) set up to review the whole range of services for children and families in Birmingham, UK, and to lead the implementation of the Children Act 1989 for Birmingham City Council Social Services, the impact of the organisational/political context on the possibilities for change in child-care services was discussed (Coffin, 1993). The author, Gill Coffin, noted that although some of the new requirements on local authorities opened up new challenges and opportunities, others appeared difficult to reconcile with each other. Any local authority has to grapple with competing or conflicting interests, such as those of the multiple 'customers' (e.g. the child, the parents, other carers, the family, society in general) and with the difficulty of fitting demand-led services into fixed budgets and budget forecasts because of the unpredictability of demand. The author saw the main challenge for the public sector of being required to 'provide quality services with limited resources, to satisfy the demands of a number of interest groups, and still motivate staff to work hard and adapt to change and new legislative requirements' (ibid., p. 32).

The 1990s are witnessing major changes in the relationship and power distribution of the local politician and the electorate to public services, of the professional to the parent, of local government to central government, and of the citizen to the State. Within this rapid change and reorganisation, the need to pursue the question of which organisational settings work best for partnership practice (and what socio-political conditions can sustain this form of organisation) takes on a particular urgency.

In the final section of this chapter, we consider a number of issues for furthering partnership practice and managing the changes involved in this.

FURTHERING PARTNERSHIP WORK

Developing a direction

Through an extensive overview of parental involvement in a range of preschool centres and facilities across the UK, Pugh and De'Ath (1989) concluded that successful partnership with families depended on the team/centre/agency having

1. a policy statement on parental involvement. This needed to be at two levels:
   - the employing/managing body – local authority, hospital managing board, school governing body, voluntary organisation, etc.
   - the individual team/department/unit.

   The authors noted that local authorities who devised coherent policies on their provision for children under 5 were now including parent involvement and the need to consult parents in planning services as a central theme in their manifesto. They found that many of the most innovative centres visited were in local authorities that had stated their commitment to developing work with parents and were prepared to make some additional funds and support available to enable this to happen.
2. practice guidelines on how the policy statement is to be implemented.

An individual centre/unit/team needs

● a clear statement of the role of parents in the aims of the centre/team,
● parents and staff to be clear about what they expect of themselves and of each other.

Pugh and De'Ath (1989) noted that a common difficulty found in implementing partnership work in preschool centres was a confusion of what was expected of parents, of what role they should play, and of what the staff should either ask or expect them to do. Each centre or service needed an explicit set of objectives for working with parents and families, and an ability to translate these into individual 'contracts' of roles and expectations with each parent and family (see Chapter 2, p. 42).

Examples of centre or service objectives for working with parents might include 'to help parents extend their parenting skills' or 'to build on their self-confidence and coping skills'. Specific partnership objectives might be stated as 'to confirm parents in their role as contributors to or consumers of services' (from the Moorland Children's Centre, Pugh *et al.*, 1987), or 'to include parents as negotiating partners in all decisions and services related to their child/family' or 'to share in the formulation of policy'.

The management of change

In the BACC project mentioned previously (p. 297), it was found that, although leadership was required from the top, service improvements and a change in culture could not be achieved within limited resources through imposition from above (a 'top-down' approach). They required the commitment of staff at all levels to make them happen (Coffin, 1993). This was found too by Pugh and De'Ath (1989) in their review of partnership services across the UK.

It is very interesting to note that many of the features that were found important for effecting positive change in services by the BACC project were similar to those found to be important in effective teamwork for partnership practice (see previously). These included:

1. a mandate for service improvement and changes from the top managerial level,
2. a strong leadership for change, in this case provided by the BACC Project Team, which modelled high standards of performance and expected high standards at all levels,
3. a participatory process of change, which involved staff at all levels of the organisation and drew on a wide cross-section of knowledge, skills, levels and types of responsibility from within and without the agency. This was achieved through the forum of Topic Study Groups, which

brought participants together to work on a particular topic for a time-limited period. The Group cut across traditional lines of hierarchy and departmental sections. All participated on a basis of equality, and participants were able to develop and promote ideas for good practice through a process of negotiated decision-making (thus 'owning' both the problems and the solutions),

4. the Project Team bringing in a challenging attitude to preconceptions and assumed constraints, thus freeing thinking and creativity,

5. communication being facilitated between different sections and Topic Study Groups. An emphasis was on understanding and using the whole system, rather than allowing changes in one section to create unintended consequences for other parts of the service. This helped reinforce commitment to the whole organisation and build cooperation between elements within it.

Negotiating and participatory decision-making across different levels and sections of an agency were effective in leading to a large variety of important changes and improvements (see further details in Coffin, 1993). This suggests that the method of decision-making of the Negotiating Model can be usefully applied for creating change within an organisation.

We can place these observations within the context of changing towards or furthering partnership practice. The participatory approach to change within an organisation that has been described previously differs from the present trend towards 'performance management' in the public sector. In performance management, targets are set at the top of the organisation, and aims, objectives, goals and requirements are then sent downwards. Although this management approach has the advantage of setting clear 'performance standards' for managers and staff to achieve, there are a number of problems (see Coffin, 1993, and following). Firstly, there may be an inability to manage the ongoing transitions for change required by partnership practice, whereby managers will need feedback from staff at all levels concerning whether the policy and practice guidelines are working on the grassroots level and what some of the constraints are against implementation. Secondly, lack of consultation and participatory decision-making undermines the negotiating framework that is needed at all levels of an organisation to support negotiation *within* the team and between the professionals and families. Most importantly of all perhaps, this method of management intensifies low morale and a sense of disempowerment and disillusionment in professional staff (Coffin, 1993). But only staff with a high morale, a vision and a sense of empowerment have the mandate, the energy and the commitment to engage in the kinds of partnership work described throughout this book. Respecting others starts from being respected.

This final chapter has related the partnership work with families to partnership relationships between professionals. A critical element identified for partnership work was the participatory style of decision-making and negotiation between the team members and a participatory style of team leadership and management, which complemented the negotiation between the professionals and the families. Some necessary conditions at the personal, interpersonal and organisational level were proposed for permitting professionals to negotiate and handle dissent with each other.

PROFESSIONAL DEVELOPMENT EXERCISE

EXERCISE 12.1 MAPPING YOUR ORGANISATION

1. On a large sheet of plain paper, draw a map of your organisation *as you see it*. This may not necessarily be as the managers view the organisation.

   Use the following questions to guide your mapping:

   - Who is in the system/organisation, and what is your role in it?
   - What are the lines of accountability, and to whom are you accountable?
   - Who has control?
   - Who has power through their formal role?
       delegated power?
       personal authority?
     Are they the same people?
   - How coordinated is your team? Who works cooperatively with whom?
   - Who engages in shared decision-making and negotiates with whom?

2. Then use your map to answer the following questions:

   - What is your primary task/mission of the team?
   - What needs to change for you to work in a more partnership way?

3. Who would benefit most/least if you shifted further to a partnership way of working?

4. Are you in a position in the organisation to assist implementing changes in partnership ways of working?
   If not, how might you make your views known?

APPENDIX 12.1

GUIDELINES FOR EFFECTIVE TEAM WORK WITH FAMILIES

The following recommendations are derived from the experiences of the projects described on pp. 283–8.

1. The staff team shares the same philosophy and aims. This includes valuing working with children, parents and families in partnership.
2. The team follows a policy statement outlining the main aims and objectives of the team's work/its primary task or 'mission'.
3. Equal opportunity and anti-discriminatory policies are endorsed and pursued at all levels of team practice including staff recruitment. Issues of multi-ethnicity are kept to the forefront of team functioning.
4. The team is organised along inter-disciplinary lines.
5. Participatory decision-making requires team members to 'own' both their problems and their solutions. Agreed goals and practices are reached through a process of negotiation and democratic decision-making, so that the interactive decision-making process within the team complements and supports that of the parent and professional.
6. Written policies and procedural guidelines are available on parental involvement and partnership, disclosure of diagnosis, record-keeping, confidentiality, etc.
7. The roles and functions of each team member are clarified, so that each team member has a clear idea of their responsibilities and what they can expect from other members.
8. Roles need to be defined with clear reference to accountability (DHSS Social Services Inspectorate Report, 1984), whatever the structure of the team.
9. Some core services may cross disciplinary boundaries; members of different disciplines may combine together to provide the same service.
10. Core skills cross disciplinary boundaries. Shared skills assist communication, understanding and complementary approaches across disciplines.
11. Training of all staff in basic core skills and knowledge of parents' and families' needs and procedures.
12. Regular team meetings bring members together for joint decision-making, information exchange, mutual accountability and support, group identity and cohesion.
13. Organised support and guidance are provided for all members of the team, whatever their seniority or experience.
14. A suitable location and sufficient time are allowed for informal exchange of ideas in working with parents and families and mutual support and for developing a sense of the team as a corporate group with a unique identity and culture.

15. A leader is appointed to act as the named, delegated person responsible for assisting team development, managing the team, and helping the team implement its policies into practice.
16. Procedures for regular review of policy and practice of the team are built in through policy meetings, review documents, internal workshops, etc.
17. The team engages in quality assurance of services by setting standards of good quality practice and monitoring and evaluating quality. Measures include audit, surveys, consumer interviews, and research projects. Consumer feedback may provide an important feedback loop on outcomes to shape future service delivery.
18. Relationships between the team and management must permit sufficient control and 'ownership' by the team of its own practice, whilst being accountable at the same time to management.

Looking back, looking forwards

This book has argued for a particular conceptual framework to help shape professional practice with families of children with special needs. This framework takes into account differences of perspective and dissent between the professional and the parent, as well as issues of common interest and consensus. To support this model, examples have been given of what may go wrong if negotiation is missing within professional–parent encounters. My analysis has also highlighted the positive outcomes when negotiation is completed and dissent is satisfactorily resolved. It has only been possible to explain the opposing tendencies to dissent and agreement in various circumstances and encounters by adopting a multi-level approach (see Social Constructionism, p. 29). This has necessitated exploration of the interconnections between the personal and interpersonal, the familial and the organisational and the wider societal levels of functioning (including governmental policy and legislation).

What has been challenged in this book is the notion that cooperation between parents and professionals is always or easily achievable. A negotiating partnership may not necessarily be reached or a relationship may disintegrate, if destructive and irreconcilable pressures are imposed on either side. By incorporating dissent in the conceptual framework, I have suggested that the parent–professional relationship has an *inherent* possibility of becoming fractured and prone to conflict. I have shown that competition for scarce resources, higher demands and expectations of parents, coupled with their increased legal power, a shortfall between parental aspirations and professional delivery and greater divisions and competition between and within professional agencies may increase the likelihood of conflict and mistrust. Unresolved distress in the parent, antagonism in the family, lack of empathy and poor communication skills in the professional as well as a refusal to share power could also hinder cooperation.

It has been important to give a detailed account of some present-day contexts to demonstrate their impact on practice and relationships. A picture has been drawn of a shifting set of roles and relationships within changing contexts that have differing opportunities and constraints. In the light of this complexity, it is not surprising that no simple prescription for partnership practice has been given in this book and no easy remedy for dissent. What may be possible when working in one setting may be less easily attained when working in another setting. Various theories of parental and family adaptation, such as stage theory, personal construct theory, symbolic interactionist theory, stress/coping models, and other conceptual frameworks for partnership practice, such as the consumer model and empowerment model, have been drawn on to develop practical ideas and guidelines for partnership practice that may work within present-day contexts. But this is not to exclude the possibility of other forms of partnership practice in the future, as parents and professionals' roles continue to change and the whole nature of the relationship between citizens and public agencies and agents under-goes further development in ways that are perhaps inconceivable at present.

Looking back over twenty years of ideological and professional commitment to partnership practice in the United Kingdom, it has been possible to start mapping the conditions which have been found so far to be necessary or important for working together. Exciting projects such as the KIDS Family Centre (see Chapter 10), the Honeylands Family Support Unit and the Parent Advisory Service, Tower Hamlets as well as many Portage services, have all shown that successful partnership practice is a real possibility when the optimum conditions are in place.

Negotiation and what it entails has been subjected to detailed scrutiny in the book. Features that have emerged as important include an authority and scope to experiment, explore and take risks; a balance of power that permits each partner to have a leading role in decision-making and in achieving ends; and finally, time to familiarise, to consult, to discuss and to adapt. Without options and choices and the possibility of diverse routes and outcomes, negotiation is a stifled process that cannot bring together and reconcile two or more sets of perspectives and interests. These elements pose many demands and challenges for the professional and parent or family, and for the organisation and agency.

I hope that I have offered many constructive ideas and directions for moving partnership practice forwards. Many of these ideas and practices are already apparent in the practice of increasing numbers of professionals, as the concept of partnership becomes more accepted. But it fits within the tenor of this book to qualify this optimism with a note of caution. As the demand for welfare services grows and as public spending becomes more over-stretched or restricted, a prime question for public welfare services of the future must be, 'Can we afford the kind of negotiating described and promoted in this book?' What makes it so hard to evaluate is that the real cost can only be assessed through establishing the cost of its absence: of families who are frustrated and dissatisfied and who fail to be helped by the services on offer and therefore perceive themselves as unsupported. Partnership practice has a price – but can we as a society afford or justify the alternative?

Bibliography

ACE (1988) *Annual Report of ACE Special Education Advice Service for the Bangladeshi Community*, London: Advisory Centre for Education

Affleck, G., McGrade, B.J., McQueeney, M. and Allen, D. (1982) 'Promise of relationship-focused early intervention in developmental disabilities', *Journal of Special Education*, 16, 413–430

Alderson, P. (1990) *Choosing for Children: Parents' Consent to Surgery*, Oxford: Oxford University Press

Ali Choudury, P. (pers. comm.) Senior Bangladeshi Parent Adviser, Parent Advisory Service, Tower Hamlets, London

Appleton, P.L. (1987) 'Working together for young children: parent partnership and multidisciplinary teams', unpublished paper given at the Third Annual Conference of the Clwyd Association for the Development of Young Children, Mold, Wales

Appleton, P.L. and Minchom, P.E. (1991) 'Models of parent partnership and child development centres', *Child: Care, Health and Development*, 17, 27–38

Armstrong, H., Elfer, P., Gardner, R., Hodgson, D., Hollows, A., Smith, P. (1990) *Working with the Children Act 1989: An introduction for practitioners in education, health and social services*, London: National Children's Bureau

Association of Community Health Councils for England and Wales (1994) *Annual Report 1993/4*, London: Association of Community Health Councils

Ayer, S. and Alaszewski, A. (1984) *Community Care and the Mentally Handicapped: Services for mothers and their mentally handicapped children*, London: Croom Helm

Ballard, R. (1979) 'Face to face with the unthinkable' in G. Lonsdale, P. Elfer and R. Ballard (eds) *Children, Grief and Social Work*, Oxford: Blackwell

Banion, J.R., Miles, M.S. and Carter, M.C. (1983) 'Problems of mothers in management of children with diabetes', *Diabetes Care*, 6, 548–551

Bardsley, J. and Perkins, E. (1985) 'Portage with Asian families in Central Birmingham' in B. Daly, J. Addington, S. Kerfoot and A. Sigston (eds) *Portage: The Importance of Parents*, Windsor: NFER-Nelson

Barna, S., Bidder, R.T., Gray, O.P., Clements, J. and Gardner, S. (1980) 'The progress of developmentally delayed pre-school children in a home training scheme', *Child: Care, Health and Development*, 6, 157–164

Barnett, B. (1985) 'The concept of "informed consent" and its use in the practice of psychology', *Journal of Educational and Child Psychology*, 2 (2), 34–39

Bayley, M. (1973) *Mental Handicap and Community Care*, London: Routledge and Kegan Paul

Beck, A.T. (1976) *Cognitive Therapy and Emotional Disorder*, New York: International Universities Press

Beckman, P.J. (1983) 'Influence of selected child characteristics on stress in families of handicapped infants', *American Journal of Mental Deficiency*, 88, 150–156

Bennett, W.S. and Hokenstad, M.C. (1973) 'Full-time people workers and conceptions of the professional' in P. Halmos (ed.) *Professionalism and Social Change*, Keele: University of Keele Press

Bentovim, A., Gorell Barnes, G. and Cooklin, A. (eds) (1987) *Family Therapy: Complementary Frameworks of Theory and Practice*, London, Academic Press

Beresford, B.A. (1994) 'Resources and strategies: how parents cope with the care of a disabled child', *Journal of Child Psychology and Psychiatry*, 35(1), 171–209

Berg, J.M., Gilderdale, S. and Way, J. (1969) 'On telling the parents of a diagnosis of mongolism', *British Journal of Psychiatry*, 115, 1195–1196

Berger, M. and Foster, M. (1986) 'Applications of family therapy theory to research and interventions with families with mentally retarded children', in J.J. Gallagher and P.M. Vietze (eds) *Families of Handicapped Persons: Research, programs and policy issues*, Baltimore: Paul H. Brookes

Betz, M. and O'Connell, L. (1983) 'Changing doctor–patient relationships and the rise in concern for accountability', *Social Problems*, 31, 84–95

Bidder, R.T., Hewitt, K.E. and Gray, O.P. (1982) 'Evaluation of teaching method in a home-based training scheme for developmentally delayed pre-school children', *Child: Care, Health and Development*, 9, 1–12

Bion, W.R. (1961) *Experiences in Groups*, London: Tavistock Publications

Blacher, J. (1984a) 'Sequential stages of parental adjustment to the birth of a child with handicaps: fact or artifact?', *Mental Retardation*, 22, 55–68

—— (1984b) *Severely Handicapped Young Children and their Families: Research in Review*, Orlando, Fl: Academic

Black, D. (1980) *Inequalities in Health*. Report of a research working group. London: DHSS

Black, Dora (1987) 'Handicap and family therapy' in A. Bentovim, G. Gorell Barnes and A. Cooklin (eds) *Family Therapy: Complementary Frameworks of Theory and Practice*, London: Academic Press

Boyle, C.M. (1970) 'Differences between patients' and doctors' interpretations of common medical terms', *British Medical Journal*, 2, 286–289

Bradshaw, J. (1990) *Child Poverty and Deprivation in the UK*, London: National Children's Bureau

Bradshaw, J. and Lawton, D. (1978) *Tracing the Causes of Stress in Families with Handicapped Children*, York: University of York

Brewin, C.R. (1992) 'Measuring individual needs for care and services' in B.J.B. Kat, *On Advising Purchasers: Part II*, Leicester: the British Psychological Society

Bricker, D., Bailey, E. and Bruder, M.B. (1984) 'The efficacy of early intervention and the handicapped infant: a wise or wasted resource', *Advances in Developmental and Behavioural Paediatrics*, 5, 374–423

Brimblecombe, F. and Russell, P. (1988) *Honeylands: Developing a Service for Families with Handicapped Children*, London: National Children's Bureau

Bristol, M.M. (1984) 'Family resources and successful adaptation to autistic children' in E. Schopler and G.B. Mesibov (eds) *The Effects of Autism on the Family*, New York: Plenum Press

British Medical Society (1990) *Guidelines on the Access to Health Records Act 1990: Guidance Note Ethics No. 1 (Nov.)* (Professional Division), London: BMA

British Psychological Society (1991) *Code of Conduct, Ethical Principles and Guidelines*, Leicester: BPS

—— (1992) *Access to Health Records Act 1990: Briefing paper* (Division of Clinical Psychology Special Interest Group for Children and Young People), Leicester: BPS

Bromwich, R. (1976) *Working with Parents and Infants: an Interactional Approach*, Baltimore: University Park Press

Broome, A.K. (ed.) (1989) *Health Psychology: Processes and Applications*, London: Chapman and Hall

Brown, G. and Harris, T. (1978) *Social Origins of Depression*, London: Tavistock Press

Bruner, J.S. (1983) *Child's Talk*, New York: Norton

Buchan, L., Clemerson, J. and Davis, H. (1988) 'Working with families of children with special needs: the Parent Adviser Scheme', *Child: Care, Health and Development*, 14(2), 81–91

Burden, R.L. (1980) 'Measuring the effects of stress on mothers of handicapped infants: must depression always follow?', *Child: Care, Health and Development*, 6, 111–123

Butler, N., Mill, R., Pomeroy, D. and Fartrell, J. (1978) *Handicapped Children – their Homes and Life-Styles*, Bristol: University of Bristol

Butler, R.E. and Nicholls, D.E. (1993) 'The Access to Health Records Act: What difference does it make?', *Psychiatric Bulletin*, 17, 204–206

Button, E. (ed.) (1985) *Personal Construct Theory and Mental Health*, London: Croom Helm

Byrne, E.A. and Cunningham, C.C. (1985) 'The effects of mentally handicapped children on families – a conceptual review', *Journal of Child Psychology and Psychiatry*, 26, 847–864

Byrne, E.A., Cunningham, C.C. and Sloper, P. (1988) *Families and Their Children with Down's Syndrome: One Feature in Common*, London: Routledge

Cameron, J. and Sturge-Moore, L. (1990) *Ordinary Everyday Families...a Human Rights Issue. Action for Families and Their Young Children with Special Needs, Disabilities and Learning Difficulties*, London: MENCAP

Cameron, R.J. (1985) 'A problem-centred approach to family problems' in B. Daly, J.Addington, S. Kerfoot and A. Sigston (eds) *Portage: The Importance of Parents*, Windsor: NFER-Nelson

—— (1986) 'Research and evaluation: how effective is Portage?' in R.J. Cameron (ed.) *Portage: Pre-schoolers, Parents and Professionals, Ten Years of Achievements in the UK*, Windsor: NFER-Nelson

Caplan, G. (1964) *Principles of Preventative Psychiatry*, London: Tavistock

Card, H. (1983) 'What will happen when we've gone?', *Community Care*, 28 July

Carey, G.E. (1982) 'Community care – care by whom? Mentally handicapped children living at home', *Public Health, London*, 96, 269–278

Carr, J. (1970) 'Mongolism: telling the parents', *Developmental Medicine and Child Neurology*, 12, 213–221

—— (1975) *Young Children with Down's Syndrome*, IRMMH Monograph No. 4, Sevenoaks: Butterworth

Cartright, D. (ed.) *Studies in Social Power*, Ann Arbor, Institute for Social Research: University of Michigan

Choudhury, P.A. (personal communication) Senior Bangladeshi Parent Adviser, Parent Advisory Service, Tower Hamlets, London.

Clegg, J. (1993) 'Putting people first: A social constructionist approach to learning disability', *British Journal of Clinical Psychology*, 32, 389–406

Clements, J. (1985) 'Update; training parents of mentally handicapped children', *Association of Child Psychology and Psychiatry Newsletter*, 7(4), 2–9

Coffin, G. (1993) *Changing Child Care: The Children Act 1989 and the Management of Change*, London: National Children's Bureau

Corby, B. (1994) Broadcast interview on BBC Radio 4 *File on 4*, 5.7.1994

Cottrell, D.J. and Summers, K. (1990) 'Communicating an evolutionary diagnosis of disability to parents', *Child: Care, Health and Development*, 16, 211–218

Craft, M. (ed.) (1979) *Tredgold's Mental Retardation*, 12th ed., London: Bailliere Tindall

Cranwell, D. and Miller, A. (1987) 'Do parents understand professionals' terminology in statements of special educational need?', *Educational Psychology in Practice*, 3(2), 27–32

Crichton, P., Douzenis, A., Leggatt, C., Hughes, T. and Lewis, S. (1992) 'Are psychiatric case notes offensive?', *Psychiatric Bulletin*, 16, 675–677

Crnic, K.A., Friedrich, W.N. and Greenberg, M.T. (1983) 'Adaptation of families with mentally retarded children: a model of stress, coping and family ecology', *American Journal of Mental Deficiency*, 28, 125–138

Crowe, B. (1979) *Group Therapy for Parents of Mentally Handicapped Children in Southend-on-Sea*, Essex, Mimeo

Cummings, S. (1976) 'The impact of the child's deficiency on the father: A study of fathers of mentally retarded and of chronically ill children', *American Journal of Orthopsychiatry*, 46, 246–255

Cunningham C.C. (1979) 'Parent counselling' in M. Craft (ed.) *Tredgold's Mental Retardation*, 12th ed., London: Bailliere Tindall

—— (1983) 'Early support and intervention: the HARC Infant Project' in P. Mittler and H. McConachie (eds) *Parents, Professionals and Mentally Handicapped People: Approaches to Partnership*, Beckenham: Croom Helm

—— (1984) 'Down's Syndrome: disclosure and early family needs', *Down's Syndrome: Papers and Abstracts for Professionals*, 7, 1–3

—— (1985) 'Training and education approaches for parents of children with special needs', *British Journal of Medical Psychology*, 58, 285–305

Cunningham, C.C. and Davis, H. (1985) *Working with Parents: Frameworks for Collaboration*, Milton Keynes: Open University Press

Cunningham, C.C. and Sloper, P. (1977a) 'Parents of Down's syndrome babies: their early needs', *Child: Care, Health and Development*, 3, 325–347

—— (1977b) 'Down's syndrome: a positive approach to parent and professional collaboration', *Health Visitor*, 50, 32–37

Cunningham, C.C., Morgan, P.A. and McGucken, R.B. (1984) 'Down's syndrome: is dissatisfaction with disclosure of diagnosis inevitable?', *Developmental Medicine and Child Neurology*, 26, 33–39

Dale, N. (1983) 'Early Pretend Play in the Family', unpublished doctoral thesis, University of Cambridge

Dale, N.J. (1986) 'Parents as partners: what does this mean to parents of children with special needs?', *Educational and Child Psychology*, 3(3), 191–199

—— (1992) 'Parental involvement in the KIDS Family Centre: who does it work for?', *Child: Care, Health and Development*, 18, 301–319

Dale, N. and Woollett, C. (1989) *Parent Support Link Service Training Manual: Training Manual to Prepare Parent Befrienders to Support Other Parents of Children with Special Needs*, London: KIDS

Daly, B., Addington, J., Kerfoot, S. and Sigston, A. (eds) (1985) *Portage: The Importance of Parents*, Windsor: NFER-Nelson

Darling, R.B. (1979) *Families against Society: A Study of Reactions to Children with Birth Defects*, Beverley Hills: Sage

—— (1983) 'Parent-professional interaction: the roots of misunderstanding' in M. Seligman (ed.) *The Family with Handicapped Child. Understanding and Treatment*, Orlando, Fl.: Grune and Stratton Inc.

Davis, H. (1985) 'Developing the role of parent adviser in the child health service' in E. De'Ath and G. Pugh (eds) *Partnership Paper 3*, London: National Children's Bureau

—— (1993) *Counselling Parents of Children with Chronic Illness or Disability*, Leicester: British Psychological Society

Davis, H. and Cunningham, C. (1985) 'Mental handicap' in E. Button (ed.) *Personal Construct Theory and Mental Health*, London: Croom Helm

Davis, H. and Rushton, R. (1991) 'Counselling and supporting parents of children with development delay: a research evaluation', *Journal of Mental Deficiency Research*, 35, 89–112

Davis, H., Buchan, L. and Choudhury, P. Ali (1994) 'Supporting families of children with chronic illness or disability: multi-cultural issues' in P. Mittler and H. Mittler (eds) *Innovations in Family Support for People with Learning Disabilities*, Lancashire: Brothers of Charity, Lisieux Hall

Daws, D. (1984) 'Consent in psychotherapy: the conflicts for child, patients, parents and professionals', symposium, British Psychological Society Conference, Warwick, April 1984

De'Ath, E. and Pugh, G (eds) (1985) *Partnership Paper 3*, London: National Children's Bureau

De Maso, D.R., Campis, L.K., Wypij, D., Bertram, S., Lipshitz, M. and Freed, M. (1991) 'The impact of maternal perceptions and medical severity on the adjustment of children with congenital heart disease', *Journal of Pediatric Psychology*, 16(2), 137–150

Department for Education (1994) *Education Act 1993: Code of Practice on the Identification and Assessment of Special Educational Needs*, London: HMSO

Department of Education and Science (1967) *Children and their Primary Schools: a Report of the Central Advisory Council for Education, Vol. 1 (Chair: Lady B. Plowden)*, London: HMSO

Department of Education and Science (1978) *Special Educational Needs: The Report of the Committee of Enquiry into the Education of Handicapped Children and Young People (Chair: M. Warnock)*, London: HMSO

Department of Education and Science (1983) *Assessments and Statements of Special Educational Needs. Circular 1/83*, London: HMSO

Department of Education and Science (1989) *Assessments and Statements of Special Educational Needs: Procedures within the Education, Health and Social Services, Circular 22/89*, London: HMSO

Department of Health (1990) *Access to Health Records Act 1990*, London: HMSO

Department of Health (1991a) *The Children Act 1989 Guidance and Regulations Vols 1– 9*, London: HMSO

Department of Health (1991b) *Working Together: A Guide to Arrangements for Inter-agency Cooperation for the Protection of Children from Abuse*, 2nd ed., London: HMSO

Department of Health and Social Security (1976) *Fit for the Future: the Report of the Committee on Child Health Services, Vol. 1 (Chair: Prof. D. Court)*, London: HMSO

Department of Health and Social Security (1984) *Data Protection Act 1984*, London: HMSO

Department of Health and Social Security Social Work Inspectorate (1984) *Local Authority Social Services for Handicapped Children in England*, London: HMSO

Department of Health and Social Security (1988) *The Access to Medical Reports Act 1988*, London: HMSO

Dessent, T. (ed.) (1984) *What is Important about Portage?*, Windsor: NFER-Nelson

Dimmock, B. and Dungworth, D. (1985) 'Beyond the family – using network meetings in statutory child care cases', *Journal of Family Therapy*, 7, 45–68

Doise, W. (1986) *Levels of Explanation in Social Psychology*, Cambridge: Cambridge University Press

Dowling, E. (1985) 'Theoretical framework – a joint systems approach to educational problems with children' in E. Dowling and E. Osborne (eds) *The Family and the School: a Joint Systems Approach to Problems with Children*, London: Routledge and Kegan Paul

Dowling, E. and Osborne, E. (eds) (1985) *The Family and the School: a Joint Systems Approach to Problems with Children*, London: Routledge and Kegan Paul

Drillien, C.H. and Wilkinson, E.M. (1964) 'Mongolism: when should parents be told?', *British Medical Journal*, 2, 1306–1307

Drotar, D., Baskiewicz, A., Irvin, A., Kennell, J. and Klaus, M. (1975) 'The adaptation of parents to the birth of an infant with a congenital malformation: A hypothetical model', *Pediatrics*, 56, 710–717

Dumas, J.E. and Wahler, R.G. (1983) 'Predictions of treatment outcome in parent training: mother insularity and socioeconomic disadvantage', *Behavioural Assessment*, 5, 301–313

Dunn, J. and Kendrick, C. (1982) *Siblings: Love, Envy and Understanding*, London: Grant McIntyre

Dunnette, M. (ed.) (1975) *Handbook of Industrial and Organizational Psychology*, Chicago: Rand McNally

Dunst, C.J. and Leet, H.E. (1987) 'Measuring the adequacy of resources in households with young children', *Child: Care, Health and Development*, 13(2), 111–125

Dunst, C.J., Jenkins, V. and Trivette, C.M. (1984) 'The Family Support Scale: reliability and validity', *Journal of Individual, Family and Community Wellness*, 1(4), 45–52

Dunst, C.J., Trivette, C.M. and Cross, A.H. (1986) 'Roles and support networks of mothers of handicapped children' in R.R. Fewell and P.F. Vadasy (eds) *Families of Handicapped Children: Needs and Supports across the Life-span*, Austin, Texas: Pro-Ed

Eisenthal, S. and Lazare, A. (1979) 'Adherence and the negotiated approach to patienthood', *Archives of General Psychiatry*, 36, 393–398

Eiser, C. (1990) 'Psychological effects of chronic disease', *Journal of Child Psychology and Psychiatry*, 31, 85–98

—— (1993) *Growing Up with a Chronic Disease: the Impact on Children and Their Families*, London: Jessica Kingsley

—— (1994) 'Making sense of chronic disease', The Eleventh Jack Tizard Memorial Lecture, *Journal of Child Psychology and Psychiatry*, 35(8), 1373–1391

Elfrida Rathbone Education Advocacy Service Guidelines, unpublished, London: Elfrida Rathbone

Emde, R. and Brown, C. (1978) 'Adaptation to the birth of a Down's syndrome infant: grieving and maternal attachment', *Journal of the American Academy of Child Psychiatry*, 17, 299–323

Evans, K. and Carter, C.O. (1954) 'Care and disposal of mongolian defectives', *Lancet*, ii, 960–963

Evans, L., Forder, A., Ward, L. and Clarke, I. (1986) *Working with Parents of Handicapped Children. A guide to Self-help Groups and Casework with Families*, London: Bedford Square Press/NCVO

Farber, B. (1959) 'Effects of a severely mentally retarded child on family integration', *Monographs of the Society for Research in Child Development*, 24(2, Serial no. 71)

—— (1960) 'Family organisation and crisis: Maintenance of integration in families with a severely mentally retarded child', *Monographs of the Society for Research in Child Development*, 25 (whole no. 75)

Featherstone, H. (1980) *A Difference in the Family*, New York: Basic Books

Ferraro, G. and Tucker, J. (1993) 'Group work with siblings of children with special needs: a pilot study', *Group work*, 6(1), 43–50

Fewell, R.F. and Vadasy, P.F. (eds) (1986) *Families of Handicapped Children: Needs and Supports Across the Life-span*, Austin, Texas: Pro-Ed

Filkin, E. (ed.) (1984) *Women and Children First: Home-Link – a Neighbourhood Education*, Michigan: High Scope

Fost, N. (1981) 'Counselling families who have a child with a severe congenital anomaly', *Paediatrics*, 67, 321–325

Fraiberg, S. (1971) 'Intervention in infancy: A program for blind infants', *Journal of the American Academy of Child Psychiatry*, 10, 381–405

French, J.R.P. and Raven, B. (1959) 'The bases of social power' in D. Cartwright (ed.) *Studies in Social Power*, Ann Arbor, Institute for Social Research: University of Michigan

Frey, K.S., Greenberg, M.T. and Fewell, R.R, (1989) 'Stress and coping among parents of handicapped children: A multidimensional approach', *American Journal on Mental Retardation*, 94, 240–249

Friedrich, W.N. and Friedrich, W.L. (1981) 'Psychological assets of parents of handicapped and non-handicapped children', *American Journal of Mental Deficiency*, 85, 551–553

Friedrich, W.N., Greenberg, M.T. and Crnic, K. (1983) 'A short-form of the Questionnaire on Resources and Stress', *American Journal of Mental Deficiency*, 88, 41–48

Gallagher, J.J. and Vietze, P.M. (eds) (1986) *Families of Handicapped Persons: Research, Programs and Policy Issues*, Baltimore: Paul H. Brookes

Gardner, S. (1984) 'What the . . . does the psychologist do?', *Division of Clinical Psychology Newsletter*, 43, 45–48

Garralda, M.E., Jameson, R.A., Reynolds, J.M. and Postlethwaite, J.R. (1988) 'Psychiatric adjustment in children with chronic renal failure', *Journal of Child Psychology and Psychiatry*, 29, 79–90

Gath, A. (1973) 'The school age siblings of mongol children', *British Journal of Psychiatry*, 123, 161–167

—— (1974) 'Siblings' reactions to mental handicap: a comparison of the brothers and sisters of mongol children', *Journal of Child Psychology and Psychiatry*, 15, 187–198

—— (1977) 'The impact of an abnormal child upon the parents', *British Journal of Psychiatry*, 130, 405–410

—— (1978) *Down's Syndrome and the Family: The Early Years*, London: Academic Press

Geiger, W.L., Brownsmith, K. and Forgnone, C. (1978) 'Differential importance of skills for TMR students as perceived by teachers', *Education and Training of the Mentally Retarded*, 14, 259–264

Gill, M.W. and Scott, D.L. (1986) 'Can patients benefit from reading copies of their doctors' letters about them?', *British Medical Journal*, 293, 1278–1279

Glendenning, C. (1983) *Parents and Their Disabled Children*, London: Routledge and Kegan Paul

Goldberg, S., Marcovitch, S., MacGregor, D. and Lojkasek, M. (1986) 'Family responses to developmentally delayed preschoolers: Etiology and the father's role', *American Journal of Mental Deficiency*, 90(6), 610–17

Gough, D., Li, L. and Wroblewska, A. (1993) *Services for Children with a Motor Impairment and their Families in Scotland*, Reference report to the Scottish Office Education and Home and Health Departments, University of Glasgow: Public Health Research Unit

Gray, S. and Wandersman, I. (1980) 'The methodology of home-based intervention studies: problems and promising strategies', *Child Development*, 51, 993–1009

Greenwood, E. (1966) 'The elements of professionalisation' in H.M. Vollmer and D.C. Mills (eds) *Professionalisation*, Prentice-Hall

Grossman, F.K. (1972) *Brothers and Sisters of Retarded Children: an Exploratory Study*, Syracuse, NY: Syracuse University Press

Halmos, P. (ed.) (1973) *Professionalism and Social Change*, Keele: University of Keele Press

Handy, C.B. (1985) *Understanding Organisations*, Harmondsworth: Penguin

Hannam, C. (1975) *Parents and Mentally Handicapped Children*, Harmondsworth: Penguin

Hanvey, C. (1994) Director of Thomas Coram Foundation for Children, *The Guardian* 27 April 1994

Hare, E.H., Laurence, K., Payne, H. and Rawnsley, K. (1966) 'Spina bifida cystica and family stress', *British Medical Journal*, 2, 757–760

Hargis, K. and Blechman, E.A. (1979) 'Social class and training parents as behaviour change agents', *Child Behaviour Therapy*, 1, 69–74

Harris, V.S. and McHale, S.M. (1989) 'Family life problems, daily caregiving activities and the psychological well-being of mothers of mentally retarded children', *American Journal on Mental Retardation*, 94, 231–239

Hatch, S. and Hinton, T. (1986) *Self-Help in Practice: A Study of Contact a Family, Community Work and Family Support*, Social Work Monographs, Joint Unit for Social Work Support

Hedderly, R. and Jennings, K. (eds) (1987) *Extending and Developing Portage*, Windsor: NFER-Nelson

Hewett, S. (1970) *The Family and the Handicapped Child*, London: Allen and Unwin

—— (1972) *The Need for Long-term Care*, London: Butterworth

Hirst, M. (1982) *Young Adults with Disabilities and their Families*, York: Department of Social Administration and Social Work Social Policy Research Unit, University of York, Working Papers DHSS 112. 7/82 MH

HMSO (1994) *Social Trends*, 24th ed., London: HMSO

Hogg, J. and Raynes, N.V. (eds) (1987) *Assessment in Mental Handicap: A Guide to Assessment Practices, Tests and Checklists*, London: Chapman and Hall

Holland, F.L.U. and Noaks, J.C. (1982) 'Portage in Mid-Glamorgan: description and comment on this pre-school home intervention scheme', *Journal of the Association of Educational Psychologists*, 5(9), 32–37

Holmes, N., Hemsley, R., Rickett, J. and Likierman, H. (1982) 'Parents as cotherapists: their perception of a home based behavioural treatment for autistic children', *Journal of Autism and Developmental Disorders*, 12, 331–342

Holt, K.S. (1958) 'The home care of the severely mentally retarded', *Paediatrics*, 22, 744–755

Hornby, G. and Singh, N.N. (1982) 'Group training for parents of mentally retarded children: A review and methodological analysis of behavioral studies', *Child: Care, Health and Development*, 9, 199–213

Hornby, G., Murray, R. and Cunningham, C.C. (1987) *Parent to Parent Leaders Training Manual*, unpublished manuscript, Manchester: Hester Adrian Research Centre

House of Commons Education, Science and Arts Committee (1987) *Report of Enquiry into the Implementation of the 1981 Education Act*, London: HMSO

Hubert, J. (1992) *Administering Drugs to Young People with Severe Learning Difficulties. Social Care Research Finding Number 18*, Joseph Rowntree Foundation

Illich, I. (1975) *Medical Nemesis: The Expropriation of Health*, London: Calder and Boyars

Independent Development Council for People with Mental Handicap (1982) *Elements of a Comprehensive Local Service for People with Mental Handicap*, IDCPMH

Ineichen, B. (1986) 'A job for life? The service needs of mentally handicapped people living in the community and their families', *British Journal of Social Work*, 16, 311–323

Inner London Education Authority (1985) *Educational Opportunities for All. Report of the committee reviewing provision to meet special educational need. (Chair: J. Fish)*, London: ILEA

Jolly, H. (1984) 'Have parents the right to see their children's medical reports?', *Archives of Disease in Childhood*, 59, 601–602

Kat, B.J.B. (1992) *On Advising Purchasers*, Leicester: BPS (The British Psychological Society)

Katz, L. (1984) Paper given at seminar organised by National Children's Bureau, London, May 1984

Kazak, A.E. (1986) 'Families with physically handicapped children: Social ecology and family systems', *Family Process*, 25, 265–281

Kazak, A.E. and Marvin, R.S. (1984) 'Differences, difficulties and adaptations. Stress and social networks in families with a handicapped child', *Family Relations*, 33, 67–77

Kazdin, A.E. (1977) 'Assessing the clinical or applied importance of behaviour change through social validation', *Behaviour Modification*, 1, 427–452

Kelly, G.A. (1955) *The Psychology of Personal Constructs*, New York: Norton

Kennedy, J.F. (1970) 'Maternal reactions to the birth of a defective baby', *Social Casework*, 51, 411–416

Kennedy, L. (1994) Unpublished training material, London: Tavistock Clinic

Kennedy, L. (pers. comm) Lecturer in Educational Psychology, London: Tavistock Clinic

Kennedy, M. (1990) 'The deaf child who is sexually abused – is there a need for a dual specialist?', *Child Abuse Review*, 4(2), 3–6

KIDS agency (1987) *Annual Report*, unpublished, London: KIDS

KIDS Family Centre (1987) *Policy Document: Named Worker Service*, Unpublished, London: KIDS

KIDS Family Centre (1988) *Policy Document: Confidentiality*, unpublished, London: KIDS

Kiernan, C. (1987) 'Criterion-referenced tests' in J. Hogg and N.V. Raynes (eds) *Assessment in Mental Handicap: A Guide to Assessment Practices, Tests and Checklists*, London: Chapman and Hall

Klein, S. and Simmons, R. (1979) 'Chronic disease and childhood development: kidney disease and transplantation' in R. Simmons (ed.) *Research in Community and Mental Health. Vol. 1*, Greenwich, CT: JAI Press

Korsch, B., Gozzi, E. and Francis, V. (1968) 'Gaps in doctor–patient communication. I: Doctor–patient interaction and patient satisfaction', *Pediatrics*, 42, 855–871

Kraemer, S. (1994) 'On working together in a changing world: dilemmas for the trainer', *Association of Child Psychology and Psychiatry Review Newsletter*, 16(3), 120–130

Lane, D. (1988) article in *What Now? Conference Report*, unpublished, PIP/CASE/Lambeth Education Authority/MENCAP

Lazarus, R.S. and Folkman, S. (1984) *Stress, Appraisal and Coping*, New York: Springer

Levy, A. (ed.) (1995) *Re-Focus on Child Abuse*, Hawksmere Press

Ley, P. (1979) 'Memory for medical information', *British Journal of Social and Clinical Psychology*, 18, 245–256

—— (1989) 'Improving patients' understanding, recall, satisfaction and compliance' in A.K. Broome (ed.) *Health Psychology: Processes and Applications*, London: Chapman and Hall

Ley, P. and Morris, L.A. (1984) 'Psychological aspects of written information for patients' in S. Rachmann (ed.) *Contributions to Medical Psychology 3*, Oxford: Pergamon Press

Ley, P., Whitworth, M.A., Skilbeck, C.E. *et al.* (1976) 'Improving doctor–patient communication in general practice', *Journal of Royal Collage of General Practitioners*, 26, 720–724

Lievegoed, B.C.J. (1973) *The Developing Organization*, London: Methuen

Lillie, D.L. (1975) *Early Childhood Education*, Chicago: Science Research

Linder, R. (1970) 'Mothers of disabled children: the value of weekly group meetings', *Developmental Medicine and Child Neurology*, 12, 202–206

Lloyd-Bostock, S. (1976) 'Parents' experiences of official help and guidance in caring for a mentally handicapped child', *Child: Care, Health and Development*, 2, 325–338

Local Government Ombudsman Annual Reports (1993, 1994, 1995) London: Local Government Ombudsman

Lonsdale, G. (1978) 'Family life with a handicapped child: the parents speak', *Child: Care, Health and Development*, 4, 99–120

Lonsdale, G., Elfer, P. and Ballard, R. (eds) (1979) *Children, Grief and Social Work*, Oxford: Blackwell

McConachie, H. (1986) *Parents and Young Mentally Handicapped Children: A Review of Research Issues*, London: Croom Helm

—— (1991a) 'Breaking the news to family and friends: some ideas to help parents', *Mental Handicap*, 19, 48–50

—— (1991b) 'Families and professionals: prospects for partnership' in S. Segal and V. Varma (eds) *Prospects for People with Learning Difficulties*, London: David Fulton

—— (1994) 'Implications of a model of stress and coping for services to families of young disabled children', *Child: Care, Health and Development*, 20, 37–46

McConachie, H. and Domb, H. (1981) 'An interview study of the siblings of mentally handicapped children', *Mental Handicap*, 11, 64–66

McConachie, H., Lingham, S., Stiff, B. and Holt, K. (1988) 'Giving assessment reports to parents', *Archives of Disease in Childhood*, 63, 209–210

McConkey, R. (1986) *Working with Parents; A Practical Guide for Teachers and Therapists*, London: Croom Helm

MacKeith, R. (1973) 'The feelings and behaviour of parents of handicapped children', *Developmental Medicine and Child Neurology*, 15, 24–27

McKinney, B. and Peterson, R.A. (1987) 'Predictors of stress in parents of developmentally disabled children', *Journal of Pediatric Psychology*, 12(1), 133–150

McNamee, S. and Gergen, K. (1992) *Therapy as Social Construction*, London: Sage

Makin, P.J., Cooper, C.L. and Cox, C.J. (1989) *Managing People at Work*, Leicester: BPS Books (The British Psychological Society)

Marchant, R. and Page, M. (1992) 'Bridging the gap: Investigating the abuse of children with multiple disabilities', *Child Abuse Review*, 1(3)

Marchant, R., Page, M. and Crane, S. (1993) *Child Protection Work with Children with Multiple Disabilities*, London: NSPCC

Marks, D. (1992) 'Decision-making in case conferences: an example from education', *Clinical Psychology Forum (The British Psychological Society)*, 45, 14–17

Marteau, T.M. (1989) 'Health beliefs and attributions' in A.K. Broome (ed.) *Health Psychology: Processes and Applications*, London: Chapman and Hall

Marteau, T.M., Johnston, M., Baum, J.D. and Bloch, S. (1987) 'Goals of treatment in diabetes: A comparison of doctors and parents of children with diabetes', *Journal of Behavioural Medicine*, 10, 33–48

Martin, H., McConkey, R. and Martin, S. (1984) 'From acquisition theories to intervention strategies: an experiment with mentally handicapped children', *British Journal of Disorders of Communication*, 19, 3–14

Mead, G.H. (1934) *Mind, Self and Society: From the Standpoint of a Social Behaviourist*, Chicago: University of Chicago

Meltzer, B.N., Petras, J.W. and Reynolds, L.T. (1975) *Symbolic Interactionism: Genesis, Varieties and Criticism*, Boston and London: Routledge and Kegan Paul

Menzies-Lyth, I. (1960) 'A case study in the functioning of social systems as a defence against anxiety', *Human Relations*, 13, 95–121

Mercer, A. (1994) 'Psychological approaches to children with life-threatening conditions and their families', *Association of Child Psychology and Psychiatry Newsletter*, 16(2), 56–63

Miller, S.G. (1974) 'An exploratory study of sibling relationships in families with retarded children', *DISS Abstracts International*, 35, 2994B–2995B

Minuchin, S. (1974) *Families and Family Therapy*, London: Tavistock

Mittler, H. (1986) 'A report shared', *Community Care*, 7 August

Mittler, P. and McConachie, H. (eds) (1983) *Parents, Professionals and Mentally Handicapped People: Approaches to Partnership*, Beckenham: Croom Helm

Mittler, P. and Mittler, H. (1983) 'Partnership with parents: an overview' in P. Mittler and H. McConachie (eds) *Parents, Professionals and Mentally Handicapped People: Approaches to Partnership*, Beckenham: Croom Helm

—— (eds) (1994) *Innovations in Family Support for People with Learning Disabilities*, Lancashire: Brothers of Charity, Lisieux Hall

Nagy, S. and Ungerer, J. (1990) 'The adaptation of mothers and fathers to children with cystic fibrosis: a comparison', *Children's Health Care*, 19, 147–154

Nazarian, L.F., Mechaber, R.N., Charmey, E. and Coulter, M.P. (1974) 'Effect of a mailed appointment reminder on appointment keeping', *Pediatrics*, 53, 349–352

Neimeyer, R.A. (1985) 'Problems and prospects in personal construct theory' in D. Bannister (ed.) *Issues and Approaches in Personal Construct Theory*, London: Academic Press

Nelson-Jones, R. (1983) *Practical Counselling Skills*, London: Holt, Rinehart and Winston

New, C. and David, M. (1985) *For the Children's Sake: Making Childcare More Than Women's Business*, Harmondsworth, Penguin

Newmann, F. and Holzman, L. (1993) *Lev Vygotsky: Revolutionary Scientist*, London: Routledge

Newson, E. (1976) 'Parents as a resource in diagnosis and assessment' in T. Oppe and P. Woodford (eds) *The Early Management of Handicapping Disorders*, Elsevier, N. Holland: IRMMH

Newson, E. and Davies, J. (1994) 'Supporting the siblings of children with autism and related developmental disorders' in P. Mittler and H. Mittler (eds) *Innovations in Family Support for People with Learning Disabilities*, Lancashire: Brothers of Charity, Lisieux Hall

Newson, E. and Hipgrave, T. (1982) *Getting Through to Your Handicapped Child: A Handbook for Parents, Foster-parents, Teachers and Anyone Caring for Handicapped Children*, Cambridge: Cambridge University Press

Newson, J. and Newson, E. (1976) *Seven Year Olds in the Home Environment*, London: Allen and Unwin

Nihira, K., Meyers, C.E. and Mink, I.T. (1980) 'Home environment, family adjustment and the development of mentally retarded children', *Applied Research in Mental Retardation*, 1, 5–24

Nolan, T., Desmond, K., Herlich, R. and Hardy, S. (1986) 'Knowledge of cystic fibrosis in patients and their parents', *Pediatrics*, 77, 229–235

O'Dell, S. (1974) 'Training parents in behaviour modification: a review', *Psychological Bulletin*, 81, 418–433

Office of Population and Census Surveys (1989) *Surveys of Disability in the UK. Report 3: The Prevalence of Disability; Report 5: Financial Circumstances of Families; Report 6: Disabled Children, Services, Transport and Education*, London: HMSO

Olshansky, S. (1962) 'Chronic sorrow: A response to having a mentally defective child', *Social Casework*, 43, 190–193

Overholser, J.C. and Fritz, G.K. (1991) 'The impact of childhood cancer on the family', *Journal of Psychosocial Oncology*, 8 (4)

Pahl, J. and Quine, L. (1984) *Families with Mentally Handicapped Children: A Study of Stress and of Services Response*, Canterbury: Health Services Research Unit, University of Kent

Palazzoli, M.S., Boscolo, L., Cecchin, G. and Prata, G. (1978) *Paradox and Counterparadox: A New Model in the Therapy of the Family in Schizophrenic Transaction*, London and New York: Jason Aronson

Partridge, J.W. (1984) 'Putting it in writing: written assessment reports for parents', *Archives of Disease in Childhood*, 59, 678–681

Paul, J.L. (ed.) (1981) *Understanding and Working with Parents of Children with Special Needs*, New York: Holt, Rinehart and Winston

Piaget, J. (1950) *Psychology of Intelligence*, London: Routledge and Kegan Paul

Pryzwansky, W.B. and Bersoff, D.N. (1978) 'Parental consent for psychological evaluations: legal, ethical and practical considerations', *Journal of School Psychology*, 16(3), 274–281

Pugh, G. (1981) *Parents as Partners: Intervention Schemes and Group Work with Parents of Handicapped Children*, London: National Children's Bureau

— (1987) 'Portage in perspective: parental involvement in pre-school programmes', in R. Hedderly and K. Jennings (eds) *Extending and Developing Portage*, Windsor: NFER-Nelson

Pugh, G. and De'Ath, E. (1989) *Working towards Partnership in Early Years*, London: National Children's Bureau

Pugh, G. and Russell, P. (1977) *Shared Care: Support Services for Families with Handicapped Children*, London: National Children's Bureau

Pugh, G., Aplin, G., De'Ath, E. and Moxon, M. (1987) *Partnership in Action: Working with Parents in Preschool Centres. Vol. 2*, London: National Children's Bureau

Quine, L. and Pahl, J. (1985) 'Examining the causes of stress in families with severely mentally handicapped children', *British Journal of Social Work*, 15, 501–517

— (1986) 'First diagnosis of severe mental handicap: characteristics of unsatisfactory encounters between doctors and parents', *Social Science Medicine*, 22, 53–62

— (1987) 'First diagnosis of severe mental handicaps: a study of parental reactions', *Developmental Medicine and Child Neurology*, 29, 232–242

— (1989) *Stress and Coping in Families Caring for a Child with Severe Mental Handicap: A Longitudinal Study. Final Report*, Canterbury: University of Kent

Quine, L. and Rutter, D.R. (1994) 'First diagnosis of severe mental and physical disability: a study of doctor–patient communication', *Journal of Child Psychology and Psychiatry*, 35(7), 1273–1287

Rachman, S. (ed.) (1977) *Contributions to Medical Psychology, Vol. 1*, Oxford: Pergamon Press

Raven, J. (1980) *Parents, Teachers and Children: A Study of an Educational Home Visiting Scheme*, Sevenoaks: Hodder and Stoughton

Rayner, H. (1978) 'The Exeter home-visiting project: the psychologist as one of several therapists', *Child: Care, Health and Development*, 4, 1–7

Reid, K. (1983) 'The concept of interface related to services for handicapped families', *Child: Care, Health and Development*, 9, 109–118

Rennie, E. (1987) 'Evaluation – the parental perspective' in R. Hedderly and K. Jennings (eds) *Extending and Developing Portage*, Windsor: NFER-Nelson

Report of the Inquiry into Child Abuse in Cleveland 1987 (Butler-Sloss Report) (1988), London: HMSO

Revill, S. and Blunden, R. (1979) 'A home training service for preschool developmentally handicapped children', *Behaviour Research and Therapy*, 17(3), 207–214

Richards, H. (1994) 'Should patients see the letters sent to GPs by consultants?', *Association of Child Psychology and Psychiatry Review Newsletter*, 16(1), 9–12

Rickel, A.V., Dudley, G. and Berman, S. (1980) 'An evaluation of parent training', *Evaluation Revue*, 4, 389–403

Riley, D. (1983) *War in the Nursery: Theories of the Child and Mother*, London: Virago

Robinson, B. (1987) 'Key issues for social workers placing children for family based respite care', *British Journal of Social Worker*, 17, 257–284

Robinson, E.J. (1989) 'Patients' contributions to the consultation' in A.K. Broome (ed.) *Health Psychology: Processes and Applications*, London: Chapman and Hall

Royal College of Psychiatrists (1992) 'Access to Health Record Act 1990. College Guidance', *Psychiatric Bulletin*, 16, 114–116

Russell, P. (1983) 'The parents' perspective of family needs and how to meet them' in P. Mittler and H. McConachie (eds) *Parents, Professionals and Mentally Handicapped People: Approaches to Partnership*, Beckenham: Croom Helm

—— (1994) 'Children with disabilities and special needs: Current issues regarding child protection', in A. Levy (ed.) *Re-focus on Child Abuse: Medical, Legal and Social Work Perspectives*, Hawkesmere Press

—— (1995) 'Children with disabilities and special needs: Current issues and concerns for child protection procedures', unpublished, London: National Children's Bureau

Ryan, J. and Thomas, F. (1981) 'Mental handicap: the historical background', in W. Swann (ed.) *The Practice of Special Education*, Oxford: Blackwell/The Open University Press

Sampson, N. (1984) '*Parents, preschoolers and Portage: An investigation of parents' views of Portage and a comparison of attitudes of parents with "handicapped" and "normal" children'*, unpublished MSc dissertation, London: Institute of Education

Sandow, S. (1984) 'The Portage project: ten years on' in T. Dessent (ed.) *What is Important about Portage?*, Windsor: NFER-Nelson

Sandow, S.A. and Clarke, A.D.B. (1978) 'Home intervention with parents of severely sub-normal pre-school children: a final report', *Child: Care, Health and Development*, 7, 135–144

Sandow, S., Stafford, D. and Stafford, P. (1987) *An Agreed Understanding? Parent–professional Communication and the 1981 Education Act*, Windsor: NFER-Nelson

Schilling, R.F., Gilchrist, L.D. and Schinke, S.P. (1984) 'Coping and social support in families of developmentally disabled children', *Family Relations*, 33, 47–54

Schopler, E. and Mesibov, G.B. (eds) (1984) *The Effects of Autism on the Family*, New York: Plenum Press

Schwartz, A.L. and Lees, J. (1994) 'Children and young people: an area of need', *Clinical Psychology Forum (Division of Clinical Psychology), The British Psychological Society*, No. 71, Sept. 1994, 30–36

Seed, P. (1988) *Children with Profound Handicaps: Parents' Views and Integration*, London: Falmer

Segal, S. and Varma, V. (eds) (1994) *Prospects for People with Learning Difficulties*, London: David Fulton

Seligman, M. (ed.) (1983) *The Family with Handicapped Child: Understanding and Treatment*, Orlando, Flo: Grune and Stratton Inc.

Seligman, M. and Darling, R.B. (1989) *Ordinary Families, Special Children: A System Approach to Childhood Disability*, New York: Guilford Press

Shah, R. (1992) *The Silent Minority: Children with Disabilities in Asian Families*, London: National Children's Bureau

Shearer, M.S. and Shearer, D.E. (1972) 'The Portage Project: a model for early childhood education', *Exceptional Children*, 39(3), 210–217

Sheehan, R. (1988) 'Involvement of parents in early childhood assessment' in T.D. Wachs and R. Sheehan (eds) *Assessment of Young Developmentally Disabled Children*, New York: Plenum Press

Sheehan, R. and Sites, J. (1989) 'Implications of PL 99–457 for assessment', *Topics in Early Childhood Special Education*, 8(4), 103–115

Sherif, M., Harvey, O.J., White, B.J., Hood, W.R. and Sherif, C.W. (1961) *Intergroup Conflict and Cooperation: The Robbers Cave Experiment*, Oklahoma: University of Oklahoma Book Exchange

Shotter, J. and Gergen, K. (1989) *Texts of Identity*, London: Sage

Simmons, R. (ed.) (1979) *Research in Community and Mental Health, Vol. 1*, Greenwich, CT: JAI Press

Sinason, V. (1992) *Mental Handicap and the Human Condition*, Free Association Books

Sloper, P. and Knussen, C. (1991) 'Risk and resistance factors for family stress', Unpublished paper presented at the Annual Meeting of the European Academy of Childhood Disability, 5–7 Sept. 1991

Sloper, P. and Turner, S. (1992) 'Service needs of families of children with severe physical disability', *Child: Care, Health and Development*, 18, 259–282

—— (1993) 'Risk and resistance factors in the adaptation of parents of children with severe physical disability', *Journal of Child Psychology and Psychiatry*, 34, 167–188

Sloper, P., Cunningham, C.C., Knussen, C. and Turner, S. (1988) *A Study of the Process of Adaptation in a Cohort of Children with Down's Syndrome and their Families*, Final report to the Department of Health and Social Security (unpublished), Manchester: Manchester University, Hester Adrian Research Centre

Sloper, P., Knussen, C., Turner, S. and Cunningham, C.C. (1991) 'Factors related to stress and satisfaction with life in families of children with Down's Syndrome', *Journal of Child Psychology and Psychiatry*, 32, 655–676

Smith, J., Kushlick, A. and Glossop, C. (1977) *Wessex Portage Project: A home teaching service for families with a pre-school mentally handicapped child. Research Report No. 125*, University of Southampton: Wessex Health Care and Evaluation Research Team

Smith, T. (1980) *Parents and Pre-school*, London: Grant McIntyre

Sourkes, B.M. (1987) 'Siblings of the child with a life-threatening illness', *Journal of Children in Contemporary Society*, 19, 159–184

Sperlinger, A. (1990) *Making a Move: A Resource Pack for Training Staff who Support People with Learning Disabilities*, Berkshire: NFER-Nelson

Sroufe, L.A. (1983) 'Infant-caregiver attachment and patterns of adaptation in preschool: the roots of maladaptation and competence', *Minnesota Symposium on Child Development*, 16, Hillsdale, NJ: Erlbaum

Stallard, P. and Hudson, J. (1994) 'The Access to Health Records Act 1990: a survey of practice and implications for professionals', *Clinical Psychology Forum (Division of Clinical Psychology, The British Psychological Society*, 73 (Nov.), 22–27

Stobbs, P. (1993) 'The Education Act 1993 and Special Educational Needs', *Highlight No. 123*, unpublished, London: National Children's Bureau

Sturmey, P. (1987) 'The implications of research for the future development of Portage' in R. Hedderly and K. Jennings (eds) *Extending and Developing Portage*, Windsor: NFER-Nelson

Sturmey, P. and Crisp, A.G. (1986) 'Portage Guide to Early Education: a review of research', *Educational Psychology*, 6(2), 139–157

Suelzle, M. and Keenan, V. (1981) 'Changes in family support networks over the life cycle of mentally retarded persons', *Journal of Mental Deficiency*, 86, 267–274

Svarstad, B. and Lipton, H.L. (1977) 'Informing parents about mental retardation: a study of professional communication and parent acceptance', *Social Science and Medicine*, 11, 645–671

Swann, W. (ed.) (1981) *The Practice of Special Education*, Oxford: Blackwell/The Open University Press

Tew, B. and Laurence, K.M. (1975) 'Some sources of stress found in mothers of spina bifida children', *British Journal of Preventive and Social Medicine*, 29, 27–30

Thomas, K. (1975) 'Conflict and conflict management' in M. Dunnette (ed.) *Handbook of Industrial and Organisational Psychology*, Chicago: Rand McNally

Tizard, B., Mortimore, J. and Burchell, B. (1981) *Involving Parents in Nursery and Infant Schools*, London: Grant McIntyre

Tritt, S.G. and Esses, L. M. (1988) 'Psychosocial adaptation of siblings of children with chronic medical illness', *American Journal of Orthopsychiatry*, 58, 211–220

Tuckett, D., Boulton, M., Olson, C. and Williams, A. (1982) *Final Report on the Patient Project*, London: Health Education Council

—— (1985) *Meetings between Experts*, London: Tavistock

Turnbull, A.P. (1988) 'The challenge of providing comprehensive support to families', *Education and Training in Mental Retardation*, 23, 261–272

Turnbull, A.P. and Strickland, B. (1981) 'Parents and the educational system' in J.L. Paul (ed.) *Understanding and Working with Parents of Children with Special Needs*, New York: Holt, Rinehart and Winston

Turnbull, A.P. and Turnbull, H.R. (1982) 'Parent involvement in the education of handicapped children: a critique', *Mental Retardation*, 20, 115–122

Vadasy, P.F. (1986) 'Single mothers: A social phenomenon and population in need' in R.R. Fewell and P.F. Vadasy (eds) *Families of Handicapped Children*, Austin, Texas: Pro-Ed

Vadasy, P.F., Fewell, R.R. and Meyer, D.J. (1986a) 'Grandparents of children with special needs: insights into their experiences and concerns', *Journal of the Division for Early Childhood*, 10, 36–44

Vadasy, P.F., Fewell, R.R., Greenberg, M.T., Desmond, N.L. and Meyer, D.J. (1986b) 'Follow-up evaluation of the effects of involvement in the fathers' program', *Topics* in *Early Childhood Education*, 6, 16–31

Van der Eyken, W. (1982) *Home-Start: A Four Year Evaluation*, Leicester: Home-Start Consultancy

Vollmer, H.M. and Mills, D.C. (eds) (1966) *Professionalisation*, Prentice-Hall

Waechter, E.H. (1977) 'Bonding problems of infants with congenital anomalies', *Nursing Forum*, 16, 299–318

Waisbren, S.E. (1980) 'Parents' reactions after the birth of a developmentally disabled child', *American Journal of Mental Deficiency*, 84, 345–351

Wasserman, G.A. and Allen, R. (1985) 'Maternal withdrawal from handicapped toddlers', *Journal of Child Psychology and Psychiatry*, 26(3), 381–387

Watzlawick, P. (1974) *Change: Principles of Problem Formation and Problem Resolution*, London and New York: W.W. Norton and Co.

Wedell, K., Welton, J., Evans, J. and Goacher, B. (1987) 'Policy and provision under the 1981 Act', *British Journal of Special Education*, 14(2), 50–52

Wells, C.G. (1981) *Learning through Interaction: The Study of Language Development*, Cambridge: Cambridge University Press

Wertsch, J.V. (1985) *Vygotsky and the Social Formation of Mind*, Cambridge, Mass.: Harvard University Press

Westcott, H.L. (1991) 'The abuse of disabled children – a review of the literature', *Child: Care, Health and Development*, 17(4), 243–258

White Paper (1990) *Caring for People: Community Care in the Next Decade and Beyond. Chapter 3, Care Management and Assessment*, London: HMSO

Wikler, L. (1986) 'Periodic stresses in families of children with mental retardation', *American Journal of Mental Deficiency*, 90, 703–706

Wikler, L., Wasow, M. and Hatfield, E. (1981) 'Chronic sorrow revisited: parent vs. professional depiction of the adjustment of parents of mentally retarded children', *American Journal of Orthopsychiatry*, 51, 63–70

Wilkin, D. (1979) *Caring for the Mentally Handicapped Child*, London: Croom Helm

Wishart, M.C., Bidder, R.T. and Gray, O.P. (1981) 'Parents' reports of family life with a developmentally delayed child', *Child: Care, Health and Development*, 7, 267–269

Wolfendale, S. (1983) *Parental Participation in Children's Development and Education*, London: Gordon and Breach Science Publishers

—— (1985) 'Involving parents in assessment' in E. De'Ath and G. Pugh (eds) *Partnership Paper 3: Working Together with Children with Special Needs: Implications for Preschool Services*, London: National Children's Bureau

—— (1989) (ed.) *Parental Involvement: Developing Networks Between School and Community*, London: Cassell

—— (1990) *All About Me*, Nottingham: NES Arnold

Wolfensberger, W. (1972) *The Principle of Normalization in Human Services*, Toronto: National Institute on Mental Retardation

—— (1975) *The Origin and Nature of our Institutional Models*, Syracuse, NY: Human Policy Press

Woodley, A. (pers. comm) Centre Director, KIDS Family Centre, Camden, London

Wright, J. (1993) 'Pistols at dawn', *Special Children*, Nov/Dec. 1993, 9–10

Younghusband, E., Birchall, D., Davie, R. and Pringle, M.L.K. (eds) (1970) *Living with Handicap*, London: National Children's Bureau

Yule, W. (1975) 'Teaching psychological principles to non-psychologists: training parents in child management', *Journal of the Association of Educational Psychologists*, 10, 5–16

Yule, W. and Carr, J. (1980) (eds) *Behaviour Modification for the Mentally Handicapped*, London: Croom Helm

Name index

Subject index